A PRIVILEGE OF INTELLECT

CONSCIENCE AND WISDOM

IN NEWMAN'S NARRATIVE

TO TEACHERS, STUDENTS, CLIENTS.

TO THOSE FROM WHOM I LEARNED AND

WHO LEARNED FROM ME;

TO THOSE WHO LISTENED AND WERE LISTENED TO.

A PRIVILEGE OF INTELLECT

CONSCIENCE AND WISDOM

IN NEWMAN'S NARRATIVE

Dr. D. A. Drennen

University of Scranton Press

Library of Congress Cataloging-in-Publication Data
Drennen, D. A.
A Privilege of intellect : conscience and wisdom in New-
man's narrative / D.A. Drennen
   p. cm.
  Includes bibliographical references (p.   ) and index.
ISBN 978-1-58966-210-0 (pbk.)
1. Newman, John Henry, 1801-1890. 2. Intellectual life--
Religious aspects--Christianity--History--19th century.
I. Title.
  BX4705.N5D74 2010
  282.092--dc22

                              2010044693

le genti dolorose
c'hanno perduto il ben de
l'intelletto.

Inferno, 3, 17–18

mai non si sazia
nostro intelletto, de 'l ver
non lo illustra
di fuor dal qual nessun vero
si spazia.

Paradiso, 4, 124–26

CONTENTS

The ideals of devotion and learning typified Newman's
life and mind, and were rooted in a sacramental presupposition which views mankind as imago Dei, gifted
with a privilege of intellect. His thought and personality are binomially balanced, expressing far-ranging
powers of character and a distinctive voice.

The University emerges in medieval Europe, being unfurled by a new cultural consciousness. To Newman,
University is not only "a seat of universal learning,"
but is also the "perfecter" of intellect, and an imperium
of intellect. While America holds uncertain views of
the University, Newman's idea of it is, like his personality, binomial, balanced, and connective.

Intellect, having many linguistic cognates, expresses a
duality which Dante dramatically unveils as either perfective or corruptive. This separation bespeaks a tragic
Fall, which Newman admits, but whose necessity he
denies. His desideratum is that intellect be religious,
and that devotion be intellectual.

Church and University constitute the axis on which
Newman's life and thought turned. At Anglican Oxford, he set upon a religious and intellectual career, but
spiritual doubt led him to convert to Catholicism,
where he replicated dedication to Church and University. Dublin's Discourse V and Appendix implicitly

contrasts a True University / True Church with its alternatives.

Fusing the disposition of an artist and the rigor of a
saint, he transformed ordinary life in holiness and in
perfecting action. In the period 1829–50, he developed
from a Protestant to a Catholic Englishman. Attacks on
him reveal something about English national psychology, which is behavioral/attitudinal, and enshrines
ethics and modes of conduct.

A person of enlargement and development, Newman
drew on Johannine-Pauline-Patristic pleromaic views,
and an imago-exemplaristic-theophanic theology.
Stretching the heart and enlarging the mind became for
him a condition of thought, viewing religion and education as transformative processes. As he enlarged his
mind and views, his critics minimized both.

Philosophy has inspired the interconnective aims of education, and undergirds the ideals of "Liberal Education" which re-shapes and perfects the intellect.
Development is a Christian religious idea which, applied to education, reveals a spiritual enlargement in
learning. Education begins in motivation, advances to
guidance, and concludes in governance.

Newman's "gentleman" symbolizes integrative ideals
of classical balance of mind-body. The "popular" version of Newman's gentleman contains an implicit dual-
portrait, as is borne out by contrasting Discourse VIII
with other sources. The semantic ambiguity of intellect
disports an English morality of aesthetics. Yet, religious
faith is compatible with intellectual excellence.

Gospel parables of enlargement parallel intellectual ascent, which is directly related to the fact that intellect
is imago Dei. Theology's "loving inquiry" is an ascentive kind of knowing which serves the cause of Newman's civilization of intellect. It culturally fuses the
insights of Athens and Jerusalem, and shapes the relation between Christianity and culture.

ACKNOWLEDGMENTS

I take sincerest, but saddened, pleasure in expressing my gratitude for the cordial support and perfect kindness of the late Rev. Dr. Vincent Ferrer Blehl, S.J. At his death, Father Blehl was Visiting Professor at Freiburg's Albert Ludwigs University, and Postulator of Newman's Cause for Canonization. His passing impoverishes not just Newman Studies the world over, but all those who were gifted to know him, however slightly or however well.

With no less gratitude for generous and conscientious cooperation, I thankfully express my appreciation to Caroline A. Wertz, Head Librarian of Florida State University's Strozier Library, as well as to the Reference and Circulation Librarians of Leroy Collins Library— both of Tallahassee.

Dr. D. A. Drennen

INTRODUCTION:
THE NEWMAN NARRATIVE

> "Grace is lodged in the heart, it purifies the thoughts and motives, it raises the soul to God, it sanctifies the body, it corrects and exalts human nature."
> "A well-trained mind will act . . . with propriety. It will . . . conduct itself exactly as it should do."

This is a narrative written by an admirer for other admirers—present and yet-to-be—of Venerable ** John Henry Cardinal Newman. Although he was the pivotal spiritual genius of the nineteenth century, he maintains an influence, and retains a voice, which still resonates in the twenty-first century. Newman's own life revolved around two loving and intellectual ideals—devotion and learning—which reflected the Anglican tradition of Caroline Divines to seek "true devotion with sound learning." Those ideals penetrated Newman's innermost being, and taught him how to listen, and how to see. They ordained his vision of Church, and his expectations of University, illumined his image of religion and education, and enkindled his moral and intellectual fervor. They became, in short, his conscience and his wisdom.

Through devotion and learning, in spiritual equilibrium, Newman creatively investigated the depths of Christian experience. With bipolar balance, he fused devotion and learning, just as he united his own moral and intellectual powers—traditionally distinguished as being separate—into coalescing thought and spiritual action. Through devotion and learning, Newman forged a new and factual synthesis of Christian faith and understanding. Doing so, he revealed the larger dimensions of these sanctifying mysteries, and their greater relevance to ordinary intellectual life.

PRIVILEGE OF INTELLECT

With such dimensions in mind, this book specifically seeks to explore Newman's mature concept of intellect, which is implicitly grounded in a sacramental presupposition about the meaning of mankind. Simply put, that presupposition states, "Mankind is what is created in, and as, the image of God."[1] (Such a presupposition seems to shape Newman's view of the human person as being—first and foremost, intrinsically and substantially—an intellectual enfleshment of the image of God, *imago Dei*. This concept of intellect dwells implicitly in Newman's prayers and orations, is rooted in his vision of faith, adorns his epistemology, sets off his theology of experience, and ratifies his notion of an illative sense. Put another way, Newman's mature grasp of the meaning of intellect can be more explicitly formulated in the proposition: To be *imago Dei* is, for mankind, a privilege of intellect.

This formulation, *a privilege of intellect*, also implies that Newman understood the human intellect as empowered—in the words of St. Thomas—to "acquire universal and perfect goodness" because it can "acquire beatitude" (*Sum. Theol.*, 1, q. 77). The formulation likewise assumes that, with St. Bonaventura, Newman discerned that the human intellect is *capax Dei*—"capable of God" (Comm. in II Libr. Sent., 19, 1). Finally, the formulation suggests that, in the spirit of St. Benedict's Regula, Newman construed the human intellect as endowed with the power to be aware of the "presence of God." Upon such formulated foundation, this book will attempt to explain the emphatic stress which Newman placed upon the need—through University training and liberal studies— to "perfect" the intellect.

Elucidating the implications of this view, then, is the central purpose and task of this book. If such efforts serve to guide us towards a new appreciation of Newman's life, thought, and narrative, or to direct us towards a new sensibility about his mind-set and attitudes, or to help us understand Newman's intellectual accomplishments, they will have met my aspirations.

NEWMAN'S COMPLEXITY

Discerning the inner workings of Newman's subtle mind and sweeping personality inevitably presents a serious challenge to any inquiry. This is largely because Newman's widely ranging interests continued to enlarge his complex and manifold spirit, and that enlargement clearly illustrates the developmental nature of his consciousness. In approaching Newman from the viewpoint of intellectual development and enlargement, it may be useful to recall Alfred North Whitehead's ontological theory that the manner in which an entity becomes constitutes its being.

In almost any study of Newman, of course, the idea of intellectual development deserves an eminent place, if only because Newman, in his own life and thought, replicated the very essence of intellectual development. Developmentally speaking, then, Newman invariably appears as a "work in progress." Attempts to narrow interpretation of his views and accomplishments—thereby restricting his intentions, and delimiting the patterns of his mind and personality— may simply slur over the creative processes of his spiritual (and spirited) life. Developmental complexity seems, then, to characterize Newman's mental habits. It may also explain why (with modest exception) his writings appear to be both creative—in a spiritual, not fictional, sense—and devotional. Such creative writing seems to have been inspired by his developmental commitment to the central sacramental themes of Christianity.

DISTINCTIVE VOICE

There may be some who, however unwisely, imagine that Newman speaks to his audience—specifically, to us—with a single voice. The exact opposite is true. In surprisingly textured discourse of widely ranging forms of literary expression, Newman possessed a charm and brilliance of complex narrative repertoire. He ranged from chatty, loquacious informality, as in his mountainous letters, to measured, bold sonority, as in his lectures and treatises. With equal force, he could move from intimate meditation to declarative sermon, from ceremonial lecture to intricate theological discourse. Whether addressing ministers of the state, or titled nobility, or talking to the publicly forgotten and politically powerless, Newman spoke with the same reassuring voice, ease of diction, gentleness of spirit, and equitableness of mind. He conversed as calmly, and as naturally, with a prince or bishop of the Church, as if he were speaking to an ordinary parishioner, an undergraduate, or his own companions.

Newman was perfectly skilled in the subtle arts of speech, which require mastery of different colorations, contrasting tints, and discriminative shades of meaning. He could be diplomatic and adroit, shrewd and subtle. Equally so, he was open and artless. If warranted, he was bluntly frank, or sharply candid. With clarifying ease, he could be plain and even elusively delicate. Yet whatever his tone, he was always veraciously fair, blazingly truthful, and outrageously honest.

With a distinctive voice—we recognize it anywhere—Newman possessed polyphonic resonance, and the deepest secrets of verbal art. Uniquely, he spoke in swift, inflective cadence, and with unmistakable rhythms. Like Santa Teresa of Avila, he could lift his voice with ardor appassionata. Or, like St. Francis of Assisi, he could incline it in sibylline silence of murmuring prayer. Ranging in mood and sensibility, he could be serious or jocular, tactile or impalpable, solemn or playful, publicly transparent, but always privately reserved.

Indisputably, Newman was a rhetorical genius, and master of his mother tongue. With music in his voice, he was more eloquent than Cicero, more cheerful than Shakespeare, more serious than Dante—and surely more concerned with God than was Sir Thomas Browne, and with man than was Montaigne. As structural as Euclid, as clear-eyed as Pascal, he was as prophetic as Sophocles, and more consoling than Seneca. He matched Aristotle in argument, Dean Swift in ironic controversy, and Voltaire in intelligent colloquy.

Poised and lively, then, Newman's style is the poetic imitation of Renaissance sculpture, which shifts—with *contrapposto* realism—the hip-weight to one side of the statuesque body, bends a knee, and brings forward a shoulder in organic simulation. Newman's prose—surprising as a fanfare of trumpets, interwoven like sennets and tuckets in Elizabethan drama—simulates life. In discriminating prose, he can be as elevating as Beethoven's Chorale, or, like a Mozart string quartet, he can ascend to meditative peace and quietude—and prayer.

MEANING OF CHARACTER

In his literary creations, Newman is unquestionably alive—a fact which reflects the vitality of his character. Now, that imponderable reality we call character is determined (as is often said) by a multiplicity of variables. So, for any person, the greater the positive traits and the richer their spiritual correlatives, the more substantial will be the emerging dignity of such a person's character. Similarly, an author, a painter, a composer—through some inner creative unity—attains an artistically personal character, which will issue in specific artistic characteristics, inherent in his or her own creative work. Such characteristics make an artist immediately familiar. So, we cannot fail to recognize a melodic line by Bach, a halo by Fra Angelico, a feminine eye by Botticelli, the grain of a Dürer woodcut, a brush stroke of van Gogh, the sound of a sonnet by Shakespeare, or a paragraph by Henry James.

As such creative powers come alive, they likewise contain clues to an artist's personal traits and perspectives. Like a psychological mirror, these powers artistically reflect a living artistic creator. In his achievements (this book will suggest), Newman seems similarly and clearly to have revealed his characteristic imago-Dei perspective, which, exemplaristically, can be called a human privilege of intellect. Still, there may be some who view such interpretation as controversial—or others who instinctively, reactively, reflexively object to such a view, or frown upon any intellectual focus in Newman. They might say, "See here. Wasn't Newman always really suspicious of the intellect?" Or protest, "Doesn't Newman observe that intellectual liberal studies can also corrupt the human mind? At least be ambiguous enough to make Basil a saint, but Julian an emperor?"

Admittedly, Newman was not always a champion of intellect. Indeed, young and evangelical Mr. Newman seems to have shared an Anglo-Saxon doubt, and a Roundhead misgiving, about the nature of the human intellect itself. In such mood, young Scholar Newman of Trinity, or Fellowship Newman at Oriel, rightly discovered no Hebrew word for intellect, no biblical bias towards philosophical speculation, no Judean doctrine of ontology. Youthfully comforted (as he was) by Calvinistic caution, young Mr. Newman seems to have preferred certain diaphragmatic symbols of the spirit, and thus often invoked petitions from out of a ventricular heart. Yet, all the while, what young Mr. Newman may implicitly have been appealing to was the sacramental process of mind—which is to say, to the process and privilege of loyal intellect.

Frowning views of young Mr. Newman's idea of intellect are, of course, historically accurate. But, when describing the mature Dr. Newman, such views are certainly inaccurate. The mature Newman—especially after his Catholic conversion of 1845—can hardly be thought of as an anti-intellectual. He was, of course, always sensitive to the ambiguities of human nature. Clearly and unequivocally, he understood that intellect is capable of love, as well as of rebellion—and can be brought to the brink of sin, but also to the promise of redemptive resurrection. In maturity, Newman unquestionably perceived that intellect is not naturally corrupt, and knew that intellect does not remain untouched by grace. He asserted the former knowledge with Aristotle and the latter with Thomas Aquinas, Richard Hooker, and Lancelot Andrewes. The simple reason for such a claim is that Newman understood that God had not created a corrupt universe. Just as surely, he accepted the fact that mankind may freely create sin—but just as freely create love. Otherwise, he could never have been committed to the meaning of beatitude, a reference which inspired—as its spirit also breathes within—the life of Newman's mind.

Living Presence

For this reason, and others, this book suggests that Newman's writings are replete with a living authority which precisely simulates his "living presence." How often, for example, does he seem to be at the reader's elbow? How frequently does he appear to be addressing us personally? In *The Idea of a University*, he is not only speaking with us. He even seems to know us, as well as we know him—so close, so intimate, is his verbal presence. Rhetorically ambulatory, Newman is ever alive. In narration, he companionately walks with us. He accompanies us. He leads us. By overmastering our doubts, he exactingly renews our hopes, and exactly redeems our intuitions.

Stylistically, such powers lie beneath Newman's startlingly magnificent and trenchantly precise prose. These powers are properly suggestive of the facility with which, on the target range, the crack shot always hits the bull's-eye. Newman's prose invariably hits the right word, with the right emphasis, at the right time, for the right reason, and in the right mood. It is as if he were constantly illustrating the power of Aristotle's genius for urging right action. So, perhaps the ultimate explanation of why Newman's prose appears so alive is that he actually "lives" within it. This, in turn, may also explain why there are very few readers who will come away from his *Apologia pro vita sua*, and not already have become an admiring friend.

Yet, we are also faced with a strange, perhaps even paradoxical characteristic of Newman's style. On the one hand, although he appears straightforwardly before us in his prose, he can also sometimes and somehow—especially in his letters and diaries—appear occluded. This means that he is never so transparent as to be known completely. For he consistently retains a personal mystery, if only because—despite that multitude of diaries and letters—he retains an Englishman's civil liberty of personal privacy. Those who have tried to storm that privacy usually succeed only in inventing an amorphous and speculative version of John

Henry Newman.

Newman's Silence

Perhaps it is a paradox that, even as Newman stylistically reveals himself, there always remains so much about him of which he is personally unindulging. For instance, he delighted in listening to gossip, to the "latest tidings" or rumors of his friends. Yet he was never a tattler, a telltale, a newsmonger, or a hawker. One can only intuit that, in his letters, and especially in his private diary entries, he guarded with restraint so much more than he was willing to disclose. In such writings, he seems to have had so much more to say than he did say. It is as though he were constantly resisting the temptation to say it all, to uncover too much. It is quite likely—perhaps even highly probable, then—that no one will ever really know the real Newman. No one will ever completely unlock Newman's heart and mind. No one will ever strip away the sacred camouflage of his soul. To imagine such invasive tactics to be successful, or to achieve their illicit purpose, may only betray the psychological delusion with which such tactics are undertaken in the first place.

Still, the obverse side of this probability is also undoubtedly clear. For, while Newman's personal depths may be hidden, his authorial person is not. This paradox is because any work of articulate creation entails some indirect, oblique, and allusive form of autobiography. Therefore, as a "living" author, Newman can never fully disguise his literary presence. And this is so because he continues, evocatively, to speak out in the explicitly living artistry of his work.

In many ways, for example, *The Idea of a University* discloses in its second half (we shall later suggest) certain autobiographical vignettes suggestive of a young (as well as of an older) Newman. More importantly, however, it is that work's central, first-half lectures which autobiographically display Newman's ascentive and intellectually uncompromising spirit. This is because the *Idea* expresses a narrative portrait of Newman's mind—and becomes, in short, an intellectual bildungsroman.

Newman Narratives

There are many narrative stories of Newman written in this book—stories of Newman as a religious genius, an educative force, a political and controversial magnet, and a model for human spirituality. There are stories of his life, his mind, his experience, his gentle self, and stories of how he was understood and misunderstood, of how he was both praised and blamed. But, through it all, there is that central story of how Newman managed the intellectual and spiritual mastery of himself—and of his environments.

This book also tries to take the Newman narrative into our own millennium. For in some unexpected but perhaps providential way, Newman now addresses our contemporary world. This is so, only because stories of our own times also shed significant and symbolic light upon Newman's life and times. We, in our time, have created special stories about the powers of psychological and spiritual identity, about the meaning and relevance of gender, about the flowering of historical self-consciousness, and about the personalizing force of history, as it molds itself into human personality. We have created stories about the destructive potential of an overweening national pride that arouses nations to wage wars indiscriminately. To our personal stories, we can add Newman's own prophetic personal narratives. This is especially true of how, in his own times, Newman understood what it means to be human, to be gendered, to be intellectual, to be moral, and to be mortal.

Newman narratives dominate this book. Just as the story of his own career began with intellectual life at University—in his case, Oxford—so too, this book begins with a historical idea of the intellective University. At Oxford, Newman began the enlargement, development, and maturation of his own intellect. He progressed from scholar and undergraduate at Oxford's Trinity College, to fellow and tutor at Oxford's Oriel College, to pastoral vicar at Oxford's St. Mary's Church, and then became the leader of Oxford's Trinitarian Movement.

WHERE THE NARRATIVE BEGINS

It is in the University that John Henry Newman undertook to forge his conceptual model of perfection of the intellect. For Newman, University is the singular place wherein intellect can become perfected. This is another reason why this book begins its narrative with the University. From such beginnings, we then proceed to explore the idea of intellect which requires perfecting. For we need to see what intellect is, what it portends, and why, later, intellect appears—in company with Church and University—to loom so revealingly large upon Newman's mental horizon.

In following such a narrative, we ought constantly, and at the sharpened edges of our attention, to retain a heightened sense of these two institutions—Church and University. We can then pursue the narrative of their influence on Newman, throughout his life, as they help him burnish his version and vision of the meanings of Christian experience. As Newman heightens his religious awareness, he also lengthens his sense of the educative reach of that experience.

In the narrative, Newman thinks about and lives through the spiritual reality of what for him, analogically, were bicameral institutions. Through developing and enlarging intuitions, as well as through enhancing and integrating insights, Newman came to the point where he could ultimately perceive these institutions and learn from them. He could perceive how religion and education truly enlarge, develop, enhance, and integrate the human intellect. He could learn how Church and University deepen and extend the idea of religion and education. For religion goes beyond the Church, as education must go beyond the University, but both can penetrate deeply into the interior meanings of creative Christian experience.

Renewing, elevating, and raising higher the religious and educative significance—as well as the significations—of Christian experience, Newman more readily, properly, and realistically came to understand that experience. He saw how it is semantically unfurled in intellect's "ascentive" powers. Eventually, he came to acknowledge and to apprehend that special spiritual upward reach—or "ascentive journey"—towards which religion and education invite the human species.

By synthesizing Christian experience, Newman interiorized—as he helps us interiorize—basic themes of Christian life, including faith and understanding, grace and nature, reason and revelation. To these, Newman could append his own themes of devotion and learning, Church and University, religion and education, conscience and wisdom. Upon such inspiring themes, Newman lovingly dwelt. Upon them—as being ever renewable and always renewing inspirations—he also invites us to dwell.

CONNECTEDNESS

From this vantage point, the present book seeks—in modest reflection upon Newman's polymathic personality—to stretch the reader's attention across what, at first, might appear diverse topics. To Newman, however, diverse topics are not disparate. Rather, they are instantiations of a fundamental principle of connectedness, and one which is inherent in a singularly created reality. Once recognized, such a principle reveals Newman's concept of enlargement—which is to say perfection—of intellect. As expressed in his *The Idea of a University*, that principle deserves to be quoted in context:

> That only is true enlargement of mind which is the power of viewing many things at once, as one whole, of referring them severally to their true place in the universal system, of understanding their respective values, and determining their natural dependence. Thus is that form of Universal Knowledge ... set up in the individual intellect, and constitutes its perfection. Possessed of this real illumination, the mind never views any part of the extended subject-matter of Knowledge without recollecting that it is but a part, or without the associations which spring from this recollection. It makes every thing in some sort lead to every thing else; it would communicate the image of the whole to every separate portion, till that whole becomes in imagination like a spirit, every where pervading and penetrating its component parts, and giving them one definite meaning.[2]

This passage, in which Newman so breathtakingly articulates his creationally based principle of connectedness, also formulates his view of "illuminative reason"—or synoptic intellect—which he would later identify with Aristotle's concept of Nous ($\nu o \tilde{u} \varsigma$). In matters of knowing and of being, this connective principle (and the maxim by which he expresses it) uncovers Newman's sense of the relational integrity of the universe—in all its variations and with all its variability. This is because Newman's maxim—that makes every thing in some sort lead to everything else—likewise articulates the relationality of God's singular creation of the universe. It must be declared, then, that only that fact, and that fact alone, can explain the ontological interrelationship of reality by which everything leads to everything else.

BROAD SPECTRUM

Another aspect of Newman's sense of universal diversity intimately affects his own mind and experience. That relation is encased in a now commonplace truism that every person (even every entity) inhabits his, or her, or its own special environment. No person (we can surely agree) and no other entity can adequately be described or understood apart from his or her or its differential contextual references.

Because Newman lived—and thought—along an unusually broad spectrum of spiritual, intellectual, religious, literary, institutional, and intricately political events, his was, environmentally, a polymorphic experience. This experience constituted for him a multitudinous life. For instance, Newman enjoyed many warm and ardent friendships. But he also had to endure many candent and arduous enmities. Such enmities might be either rhetorical, or personal, or both. So, it should not seem unusual that Newman, a superb controversialist in his own right, would himself become so controversial.

Particularly after 1839, but especially after his conversion in 1845, Newman encountered scorn and attack—vocally and graphically, in person and in print. His enemies insultingly questioned his gender,[3] publicly disputed his heritage, impugned his sincerity, challenged his integrity, scorned his beliefs, scoffed at his religious faith, and cast doubt on his national loyalty.

Yet, in his own spiritual decisions and public actions—ranging from Oxford eminence to post-Oxford personal humility—Newman's personal life was publicly transduced into controversial life. To this day—despite his veneration; despite what he nobly was, what he generously thought, and what, in saintly manner, he actually did; and despite his undeniable devotion and learning—Newman continues to be criticized. It should come as no shock that Thomas Hobbes, who saw man as a wolf to fellow man, describes this kind of competition as one of the major "causes of quarrel."[4] It seems legitimate, then, to ask—as this book does ask—why this should be so.

DEVELOPMENTAL NEWMAN

Looked at from several differentiating angles, Newman is not in the least diminished. For he is always perceptually identifiable and recognizably understood. And Newman's many dimensions cannot disguise that salutary and restorative person who is balanced and balancing—whose identity, however complex, remains sturdy, stalwart, stable, and undoubtable. In a contemporary sense, his plurifaric personality is very much a part of his abounding, multitudinous life.

On the other hand, no single, specific, solitary, or exclusive image of Newman is capable of—or gratuitously entitled to—having the last word. No single interpretation of his life and work completely satisfies the complexities of his life and mind. Developmentally, then, there seem to be "many" Newmans—so various and variant is his title and his personality. Yet, all such aspects notwithstanding, Newman is somehow perceptually accessible, and integrally available to us, even though some facets of his personality will appear contrary, even paradoxical.

Being sensitive to the need for personal renewal, Newman fortuitously lived in an age that was attracted to the reforming idea of history, whether written or experienced. He lived in a century when a more complex sense of history attained new popularity. One might almost say that, in nineteenth-century European speculation, history became a new, evolutionary ontology—much as language has become a new ontology for our own age.

Newman appears personally, then, to have evolved in an evolutionary age. Transforming himself, he is also transformed by events and intuitions. His mind matures, his insight stretches, his thoughts ascend, his wisdom mounts higher, his spirit surges upward. So, in an utterly personal and evolutionary sense, Newman becomes more truly himself. He changes, but only in order to appropriate, more perfectly, his own identity—that is, to become, more perfectly, who he really is. As Newman wisely put it, in a work that all but announced his Catholic conversion: "In a higher world it is otherwise, but here below to live is to change; and to be perfect is to have changed often."[5]

Over the course of a long life, Newman personally acceded to more realistic forms of his own identity. Despite the gender chauvinism of his country, and of his age, he developed new forms of gentleness and saintliness, together with original forms of moral integrity, intellectual ardor, and conscionable wisdom. In this sense, Newman added new dimensions—new possibilities—to human personality. While, admittedly, his "child" was father to the man, Newman eventually attained a level of spiritually heroic identity which far outstripped the mannerisms and temperament of his early years. By thought and action, he transcended the heroism of his own times, in order, perhaps providentially, to become a perfect hero for our own.

NEWMAN AS GUIDE

In our contemporary world, where the virtues of a well-formed and spiritually abundant mind are hardly commonplace, John Henry Cardinal Newman remains for this time—for any time—the perfect model of what he called the "cultivation" and "perfection" of the intellect. As such, because he urges us towards higher levels of discernment, Newman becomes for us a prophetic guide. He motivates us to undertake serious consideration of the nature of University education, serious reflection upon the scope of human experience, and serious contemplation of the idea of intellectual attainment.

In a world such as ours, the very meaning of education is challenged. Its costs, funding, and availability are discredited, and national pride becomes an issue—as German education dips downward, as America's remains suspect. Even educational epistemology is now questioned.[6] Under such circumstances, Newman speaks out forthrightly to us. He especially does so in his composite masterpiece of educational vision, *The Idea of a University*, where he reveals the fundamental process of all attempts to perfect the intellect. As a bedrock educational tract, that work survives for at least two good reasons. It embodies, with unrivaled inspirational power, a many-layered educational vision, and it expresses that many-layered vision in a language that is unrivaled in literary eminence. Indeed, *The Idea of a University*, one observer suggests, is "the finest extended example of non-fictional prose in the English language."[7]

RECOGNITION OF NEWMAN

Fortunately, Newman's genius and sanctification have repeatedly been celebrated in recent years. The centenary of his death was observed in 1990, while the following year he was declared venerable. The bicentennial of his birth was commemorated in 2001, while the following year marked the sesquicentennial of his Dublin lectures on University education. February 2003 marked the book-publishing anniversary of those lectures as *Discourses on the Scope and Nature of University Education.* That work, revised and expanded—and memorably retitled *The Idea of a University*—will have its own sesquicentennial celebration in 2023.

In similar celebratory spirit, this book suggests that Newman was endowed with a fearless genius for enlarging, developing, and integrating disparate parts of mankind's spiritual and practical experience. Keenly aware, as he was, of the contradictions, antinomies, disparities, and separations in human life, he was also equally keen in discerning, in a patristic sense, that all things ought, intelligently, to be gathered together in Christ. Just such a sacramentalizing activity is what Newman meant by the concept: perfection of the intellect.

PLAN OF THE BOOK

This book follows some of the roads along which, as it were, Newman's privileged intellect traveled. To follow the narrative of intellect, in its many guises, is also to explore Newman's own intellect—as a central theme of his work, a leitmotiv of his life and mind, an armamentarium of his controversies. Thus, Chapter 1 briefly considers the University—technically a medieval institution—as the special environment in which, as Newman insists, the human intellect can be perfected. Chapter 2 attempts to clarify the identity and similitudes of intellect, by proposing that intellect opens more gates than it closes, and is more comprehensive a term than *cold-blooded reason*. Chapters 3 and 4 trace the course of Newman's spiritual and intellectual life, as it coincides with the ideals of Church and University—institutions which played palmary roles in his own personal and public life. Chapter 5 argues that Newman's public—but very personal—life was somehow crystallized in his metaphorically enlarging heart and mind. Chapter 6 examines Newman's idea of liberal education as a process which enlarges, develops, and enhances human intellect. Chapter 7 explores how Newman configured and creatively personified the circle of the intellect's liberal studies. Chapter 8 suggests that the ideal of liberal education, in its widest and symbolic sense—and as Newman appears to have envisioned it—is a personal intellectual ascent.

RELIGIOUS PERSONALITY

Newman's single most important aspect—that is, that he was essentially a religious personality—requires special attention. Whether as educator, literary artist, philosopher, or theologian, he was, to the very roots of his being, dedicated to God. In an ever present tense, and with piercing clarity, Newman seems always to have understood the divine implications of human experience. He thereby discerned that any prehension of God is complexly—occludedly, even secretly—intertwined in the simplest of integrative intellectual and moral ventures. Like Augustine, Anselm, and other Doctors of the Church, John Henry Newman also perceived that, as we go more deeply and spiritually into ourselves, becoming more intensely aware of our unique identity, we "find" God.

In this, Newman inspiringly reflects the insights of St. Augustine and especially those of St. Anselm. For it is Anselm who—directively, in prophetic lineage and fellowship-of-spirit with Newman—notably obtrudes upon the explorations of this book. Prototypically, Anselm provides a spiritual presupposition, which centers Newman's view of intellect and gives it ancestral documentation. Just so, Anselm lends expressive, precursor language to Newman's prehension of God. For example, with Newman's sensibility, Anselm can say, "I thankfully confess, Lord, that you have made me in your image, so that I can be mindful of you, think of you, and love you" (*Proslogion 1*).

Newman and Anselm also share a sense of a spiritual presence which lies beneath the commonalities of human experience. Both shaped a new kind of theology, which focused on the implications of mankind as *imago Dei*. Both were inspired—in viewpoint and expression—liturgically, literarily, philosophically, and theologically. Their dedication to sacred devotion, as well as their concern with the literature of devotion, is unquestionable. Newman's psychology of prayer is also comparable to Anselm's. With spiritual identity of purpose, their mind-set approaches identity of motive.

Both dwelt in the spirit and governance of the Church, and their political experience in Church administration is mutually suggestive. In their processive search for God, Newman and Anselm discovered, each in his own way, that the finality of human knowledge extends deeper than speculation. Hence, both understood that—like the link between faith and understanding—the purpose of knowledge is love. Each was committed to a Pauline view that love outlasts both faith and hope. If consciousness, as Pierre Teilhard de Chardin proposed, is an "addition" to being, then love itself—Newman and Anselm would doubtless agree—becomes an enhancing form of consciousness, and endows the world with new life.

In this sense (in the words of Jean Guitton), "Newman, like Augustine, offers to the days to come a tool of the spirit with which to found a new City of God."[8] This same spirit may likewise explain why many today venerate John Henry Cardinal Newman, and continue ceaselessly to pray for his elevation to that glorious company of perfected saintly Doctors of the Church, whom Dante in his Paradiso mimetically envisions gathered together in the everlasting fullness of actual life in the presence of God.[9] The spirit of such prayer has been the inspiration of this book.

** In July 2009, Pope Benedict XVI approved Cardinal Newman's beatification. (Editor's note)

CHAPTER 1:
UNIVERSITY

> "A University seems to be in its essence, a place for the communication and circulation of thought, by means of personal intercourse . . . [and] does but contemplate a necessity of our nature."

> "Greatness and unity go together, excellence implies a centre. And such . . . is a University . . . a seat of wisdom, a light of the world, a minister of the faith, an Alma Mater."

Three prominent European institutions emerged in the Middle Ages— Parliament, Cathedral, and University. Although all three typified the inspiration of intellect, only the University made itself intellect's special residence. As a unique creation of medieval Europe, the University is clearly distinguishable, therefore, from all earlier kinds of school, including the ancient "schools" of higher learning, such as Athens, Alexandria, or Rome.

Parliament, of course, represented, as it still does, what is wholly secular and political. In contrast, Cathedral and University revealed special congruous aspects of intellect. Indeed, both institutions were once linked in spirit and jurisdiction, and, by fostering religious education in Christendom, apparently engaged in parallel, if not often congruent, tasks. Despite their historical coincidence of purpose, however, only relatively recently has the spiritual nexus between University and Church been disengaged.

RELIGION AND EDUCATION

Clearly, every religion establishes, in different ways, its own representative institutions of learning, and customarily extends its jurisdiction into everyday practice and concerns. Such custom and practice have certainly been emblematic of Judaism, Christianity, and Islam.

In Islam, for example, *the madrasa*—the generic term for any school—incorporates within its instructional setting the spirit of the *masdjid*, the mosque. In this special setting, Muslim students learn both their religion and their cultural heritage. So too, from the Middle Ages on well into modern Europe, Christian students learned about their religion and its Christian culture, and did so in a setting of monastic and cathedral school, *schola, collegium, studium generale*, and later yet, University. The practice of Christian school and its Church, therefore, might seem to parallel the Islamic custom of unifying the needs of school and mosque.

Such apparent parallelism is interpreted by some Muslim scholars to support a claim that the University was actually the creation of Islam, and they point to al-Azhar as the exemplar of the original University. Founded after the Fatimid conquest of Egypt in 972, with construction of its *Masjid-i-jami al-Azhar* (Great Mosque) at its capital, *al-Qahirah* (Cairo, "victory city"), Al-Azhar—being an institute of higher learning—would predate, by at least two centuries, comparable European universities, including medical Salerno, legal Bologna, and theological Paris. As Al-Azhar taught Muslim law, Muslim theology, and Arabic, before the universities of Salerno, Bologna, and Paris taught Christian law, Christian theology, and Latin, the argument insists that these European institutions were simply imitating the educational practice at Al-Azhar.

LINGUISTIC ARGUMENT

Another similarity between Islamic and European institutions of higher learning, so the argument goes, is their shared use of a term, which is as ambiguous in Arabic as it is in Latin and Greek. Meaning knowledge as well as science, that term is *scientia* in Latin, *episteme* ($\acute{\varepsilon}\pi\iota\sigma\tau\acute{\eta}\mu\eta$), in Greek, and *'ilm* (علم) in Arabic,—three references to the same semantic heritage.

Thus, "knowledge in general" and "scientific " were commonly taught in both Islamic and European institutions. In Islam, there was a "teaching center of knowledge," or *dar al 'ilm*—"abode of knowledge" (دار العلم). For scientific knowledge, there were "abodes" of wisdom— *diyar al hikma* (ديار الحكم). In medieval Europe, by contrast, here was the *schola* (place of learned instruction in knowledge) and the collegium (legal connection of learned associates in knowledge). Later still, there would be developed a new corporate union for knowledge and science, which would be called universitas.

With that Latin name, *universitas*, and a corporate idea embedded in that name, any claim that Al-Azhar was the original University faces an insurmountable hurdle. True, Al-Azhar was an early institute of higher Islamic learning. True, too, Al-Azhar did predate comparable institutions in Europe. Still, the very word for, and the very idea of *universitas*, are explicitly, and exclusively the cultural linguistic and ideological property of medieval Europe.

The word University derives from classical Latin, but its strictly medieval intonation, accompanied by a distinctively medieval idea, makes all the difference. Furthermore, this novel idea, as newly named, emerged only in twelfth-century Europe. By such measure, Al-Azhar was not, is not—could not be—a University.

While Islamic Al-Azhar, then, is not precisely the same sort of place as a University, there is, nonetheless, one important cultural and historical link connecting European and Islamic educational establishments of higher learning, and it is one which ought not be glossed over. The historical connection between Al-Azhar and (for example) the University of Paris is rooted in the fact that what was taught at the former was also taught at the latter. And this common teaching, as mediated by Islam, was derived from a common source.

Such a relationship deserves a proprietary backward glance.

CAROLINGIAN RENAISSANCE

Before the emergence of University, European educational agencies—especially during the Carolingian ninth-century Renaissance—were undergoing fundamental change. The most important of these changes was initiated by well-born Yorkshire Englishman, Alcuin Albinus Flaccus (732–804), whose own teachers had been taught by the preeminent Bede the Venerable.[1]

An educator, Anglo-Latin poet, grammarian, logician, and liturgist, Alcuin was a deacon-cleric, and headed York's Cathedral School. In 781, he met Frankish King Charlemagne, later Holy Roman Emperor, and was promptly invited to direct the Palatine school at Aachen. Since Charlemagne boldly advocated the maxim, "Let those who can, teach," he gathered leading scholars at Aachen, with Alcuin chief among them. Soon, Alcuin would be called "Schoolmaster of the Empire." Considered by Charlemagne biographer Eginhard, "the most learned man of his time," and by Charlemagne himself as his "Master," Alcuin introduced at Aachen—and, eventually, at other European schools—the tradition of Anglo-Saxon humanism. Almost at one stroke, he improved European standards of scholarship, raised the level of intellectual discourse at Charlemagne's court and school, and sparked the European study of the seven liberal arts.[2] He therefore inspired what has come to be known as the Carolingian Renaissance.

Alcuin's influence was especially felt in matters of liturgy, theology, and general culture. "Writing books," he is reported to have said, "is better than planting vines," because "he who writes a book serves his soul." Above all a born teacher, he elevated the ideal of using the best Latin style and its literature, and he particularly urged the view that the True Faith, and all other true teaching, ought to be expressed seriously and eloquently. His recorded dialogues were deemed both instructional and lively.[3] Exalting the practice of penmanship in service to Christian learning, Alcuin devised lowercase letters, known as [Carolingian] minuscule, the precursor of the modern roman typeface. In 789, Charlemagne appointed Alcuin Abbot of St. Martin at Tours on the Loire. Thus, as one writer puts it, Alcuin became "the moving spirit in the revival of education at the court of Charlemagne and the monastic school of Tours."[4]

UNEXPECTED INFUSION

Still, something unexpectedly new, which would go far beyond Alcuin's contributions, was about to burst upon medieval Europe. That unexpected event would renovate, revise, and expand the medieval mind, and, in doing so, create unique cultural and educational prosperity for Europe's twelfth century. All this would be due to a singular civilizing influence by Islam. In this sense, the intellectual prosperity of Christendom's Middle Ages would depend, almost exclusively, on the cultural vitality and vigor of Islam's Early Ages, in a process which would be called the Islamization of the West.[5] What do we mean by *Islamization*? Or by *Islam*?

Arising from humble desert beginnings in seventh-century Arabia, *Islam* was established by the inspired words and actions of Muhammad (570–632)—Apostle (*Rasul*) and Prophet (*Nabs*) of God (*Allah*). *Islam* is Arabic for "covenant" or "act of agreement." The teachings of Muhammad the Prophet began rapidly to spread throughout the Middle East. Upon Muhammad's death, Islam was supreme in military, political, religious, legal, economic, and cultural force. Geographically, it circumfused the Near East, North Africa, the Iberian Peninsula, Malta, Sicily, the Balkans, Western Asia, India, and eventually spread from the eastern Atlantic Ocean to the western Pacific Ocean.

ARABIC INNOVATION

In relatively short order, Islam became the world's leading power, and its expansion was accompanied by cultural maturation. From translations from Greek into Syriac or Aramaic, and then into Arabic, Islam became sole heir to the fullness of ancient Greek civilization. Yet almost from the beginning of the European Middle Ages, this amalgam of Greek-Arabic culture began to trickle—later to flood—into newly forming Europe. Infusions of new ideas, techniques, insights neatly encased in Arabic texts began to stream westward across the Maghreb of North Africa, and along the Mediterranean Sea. As the possessions of war-uprooted émigré scholars, these texts were destined to arrive in economically and culturally rich Islamic Spain, whence they spread upward, and outward, to the rest of Europe.

This *hijra*, or migration, of Islam to Europe, soon yielded a capital abundance of learning, and previously unimaginable intellectual prosperity. This was brought about, not so much by Christian Crusaders, or by the Norman invasion of Arabic Sicily in the eleventh century, as by the establishment of a translation network—indeed an industry—partly in Sicily, but largely in Spanish Toledo. That city, recaptured from the Muslims in 1085 by Alfonso VI of Castile and Leon, soon became the center of translation activity. What had once been translated from Greek into Arabic, was now being retranslated, after the late tenth century, from Arabic into Spanish, and then into medieval Latin.

ARABIC-GREEK INFUSION

In newly available translation were Greek-Arabic sciences—medicine, mathematics, theology, philosophy, astrology-astronomy—and massive chunks of Greek culture. Such cultural riches—each a kind of miracle drug—were being injected into the intellectual bloodstream of the newly gathering Europe. What, hitherto, had been culturally inconceivable, was now being articulated in a new vocabulary of terms—*alchemy, alcohol, alembic, algebra, algorithm, alkali, almanac, cipher, magazine, nadir, syrup, zenith*. With these and other new words, there also came Arabic—actually Indian—numerals, which rapidly replaced the cumbersome Roman numerals (based on Latin letters) in commercial arithmetic. Equally so, Arabic numerals inspired innovative methods of mathematical computation and invention.

Also in translation came life-giving medical secrets of Hippocrates and Galen, geometrical and celestial mysteries of Euclid and Ptolemy, sublime truths of Plato and Aristotle. Prior to this, medieval learning had possessed (mostly by way of Boethius) a mere fifty-three chapters of Plato's *Timaeus*, and but snippets—*Categoriae* and *De Interpretatione*—of Aristotle's work. Until now, Aristotle's other works—*Metaphysica, Physica, Ethica Nicomachia*, and *De Anima*—were unknown. But these inspiring works were also embedded in "heady" commentaries by Muslim philosophers and theologians, which caused psychological and conceptual repercussions in unprepared, nascent Europe. Such text-bound ideas likewise confected radical shifts in thought, and profound theoretic realignments. No less unexpectedly, these translated treasuries of ideas also stirred European creative genius into retributive life. From the High Middle Ages to the Early Modern Age, a newly manifested genius flourished with surprising achievements. Paradoxically, these imports from Muslim sources, as refined in Europe, represented, in fact, the West's own ancient Greek heritage, which had been "diverted" by, but recovered from, Islam.

RENAISSANCE EFFECT

Europe's High Middle Ages emerged, then, as a direct result of the Islam-mediated cultural influx. Like celebratory fireworks, they announced cultural rebirths, or renaissances, such as Italy's rinascimenti of the fourteenth to sixteenth centuries. Other rebirths followed, moving geographically westward, in clockwise fashion, from Italy to France to England, and later still, to the Germanies. Together, these created Early Modern Europe.[6]

Schoolchildren are taught about these cultural achievements, which prepared the way for Early Modern Europe. But they are rarely told about the linking processes by which modern Europe embodied the culmination—rather than the rejection—of the Middle Ages. In place of this fact, schoolchildren passively accept politically correct notions that Europe's Renaissance arrived one day from nowhere—just "popped up." Europeans looked around and suddenly discovered, to their surprise, that they had become "modern."

BEGINNINGS OF UNIVERSITY

But the foregoing complicated cultural transference, says one historian, precisely emerged in the twelfth century, which "begins with the cathedral and monastic schools and ends with the earliest universities."[7]

During periods of Islamic-European cultural interchange, Europe's *studia* and *scholae* had slowly been reforming into new communities of higher learning, including the *collegium* and the (generalist) *studium generale*. Out of that educational milieu, there emerged a newly titled institution, whose name derives (as already suggested) from classical Latin usage. The term *universitas* had for example, been used by Marcus Tullius Cicero (106–43 BC) to describe "the universe," or "the whole world," or "everybody in the world." Adverbially, *universatim* meant "together," or "entirely." Yet, in twelfth-century Europe, and for the first time, the term was used technically to signify a "corporation," or "institutional corporate union."

As initially adapted to medieval Latin, *universitas* indiscriminately applied to any group. A Pope might address members of a diocese, a monastic community, or a guild of craftsmen with the phrase *universitas vestra*, which simply meant "all of you." Gradually, the term came to denote "a universitas of something," and evolved as guild shorthand to represent *universitas magistrorum*, the corporate guild of professors, who claimed the right—*ius ubique docendi*—to teach anywhere. Equally, the term represented the corporate guild of scholars, *universitas scholarium*. Thus, a papal document of 1205, addressed to the University of Paris, reads simply, "To the corporate masters and scholars at Paris," *Universis magistris et scholaribus Parisiensis*.[8] The term universitas came then to denote a higher "universe" of teaching and learning.

A reordered perception of Europe's then recently acquired cultural riches soon came to occupy the *Universitas*, so as to accommodate such riches to traditional Christian ways of understanding. *Universitas*—that corporate union of teaching and learning—was then thrust into the business of absorbing, discussing, debating, reviewing, challenging, classing, clarifying, cross-examining, renovating, systematizing, illuminating, codifying, and glossing most, if not all, of its cultural heritage.

Such an enormous task was also undertaken in the spirit by which early Christian apologist, Flavius Justinus—St. Justin Martyr (c.100–c.165)—had argued was the prerogative of any Christian thinker. Having access to all truth, however, or wherever, it is found was Justin's sense of what it means to be a Christian. "Whatever things were rightly said among all men," Justin said, "are the property of us Christians" (*Second Apology*, 10). Similarly, St. Augustine (354–430) heralded such a Christian right of intellectual acquisition, which he compared to the ancient Jewish right of "spoliation of the Egyptians."

CONSECRATION OF LEARNING

The University thus became the most important medieval institution which devoted itself to a Christian spiritual transformation of all available knowledge and learning into Christian knowledge and learning. Hastings Rashdall put it this way: "The great work of the universities was the consecration of learning, and it is not easy to exaggerate the importance of that work upon the moral, intellectual, and religious progress of Europe."[9]

The historical development of the University, in Western as well as in Eastern Europe, describes a complex story. By the nineteenth century, Europe sensed its world dominance in University education, which seemed to support its alleged dominance in world politics. A united Germany introduced a concerted (even conceited) redefinition of the University, and of its political self, as the world's center of scientific advancement through research. In contrast, England envisioned the task of the University as that of teaching—"handing on"—the tradition of Judeo-Christian and Greco- Roman culture. By the close of the nineteenth century the American University had clearly chosen to follow the German model. In recent times, however, a traditional view of University has not gone unchallenged in Europe, in England, or in America.

MODERN UNIVERSITY

The University, John Henry Newman once suggested in a well-turned phrase, constitutes "an imperial intellect." Yet, well-turned or not, well-known or not, that phrase does not seem, as it were, to ring a bell in contemporary America. Americans are not fond of empires (although they have one), nor are they attached to things imperial (although often enough they do them). Americans seem even less enamored of intellect—although they have that, too. So far as the University is concerned, they may, or may not, approve of it. Perhaps they are unsure of what it is, what it does, and what it is supposed to do, or what purpose, other than to mind the young, it ultimately serves. Plausibly, it may not be radical enough to assume that America's University has no idea of itself. It may not feel it needs one.[10]

Is the purpose of a University to generate "school spirit," or to commandeer funds? Both ideas may explain why the American University expends such effort in athletic ventures, and in persuading alumni and alumnae to attend these. America's University may also reflect the nation's traditionally ambivalent views of education. While Europe's University is largely state-endowed and strictly supervised by state policy, America's has, at different times, served different purposes, and for different audiences. Its higher learning is accustomed to being its own experimental subject or, more likely, the object of social experimentation by others.

This fact may only reflect tensions in what is poetically called the "American Mind," which reveres the law, but despises lawyers; esteems business, but disdains CEOs; venerates education, but distrusts teachers. Does this also explain why Newman's views on education are often mentioned, but largely ignored there? Or why *The Idea of a University* is praised as a classic, but rarely read? Perhaps this is because "a classic" is cynically defined as a book esteemed by many, but read by few.

ACADEMIC CRITICISM

American and British academics have also suggested that, had Newman spent twenty years heading up a modern university, he would have had more sense than to write about it—least of all, as an Idea, and especially not with a straight face. Although Yale church-scholar Jaroslav

Pelikan has expressed admiration for Newman's Idea, he despaired of its contemporary relevance. Recently deceased Roy Lord Jenkins of Hillhead, Chancellor of Oxford, found it impossible to imagine Newman as "patron saint of a university as a republic of ideas, as unfettered as it was broadbased." Lately Warden of Oxford's Merton College, J. M. Roberts, argued that Newman's *Idea* is "narrow and sterile," does not possess many new ideas, and those it does have are "ultimately cramping" and merely evidence a "sometimes useful mythology."[11]

Newman's *Idea* is, of course, biographical, but in wonderfully revealing ways that quite distinguish it from his *histoire de l'ame—Apologia pro vita sua*. Still, Newman's *Idea* contains more than biography. *The Idea of a University* is least like a mirror—in the Renaissance sense—of the University, because it does not conclude, but initiates, thinking about the University and University education. It opens up implications. In other words, it has not yet had its last say.

Nonetheless, executives of Academe assert that Newman's *Idea* does nothing for us. In today's complex educational environment, it does not help us make decisions, does not tell us what to do or how to do it. It does not promote managerial solutions to educational chaos, or tell us who is to be educated, how this is to be done, how it will be paid for, and who is to do the paying? Of what use then, they seem to ask, is Newman's *The Idea of a University*?

Utilitarian Problem

Of what use, Michael Faraday once asked, is a child? If such comparison with Faraday's concept of utility appears an evasion, or disclaimer, of the *Idea*'s "real" problems, or if such a comparison is deemed a simple-minded cop-out (which is quite understandable), perhaps this is because ghostly utilitarianism, so hauntingly intrusive in Newman's life, has so insistently obtruded in our own. "Use," after all, is not the final criterion it is often assumed to be. Though the idea of utility is important, it is only sequentially so. Essentially, this explains why a University implies more than a quadrangle of bricks, and why "the lilies of the field" are more than flowers.

Barely a generation ago, America was thriving in "The Age of Knowledge." Today it exists, perhaps more realistically, in "The Information Age." One may imagine that this is because information is more easily dealt with than knowledge. But what are we to do with wisdom?

John Henry Newman knew how to respond to such a question. For one thing, he knew that wisdom has a direct relation to conduct and to human life. He has, indeed, much to say to our contemporary world about education, and about much else. While his Idea is clearly not a predictive mirror of the University, it is surely a telescope which refracts the celestial possibilities of the human mind and spirit. In another sense, it is also a spiritual glass, through which we discern multidimensional images of what an educated person looks like, or is capable of becoming. Newman's Idea can thus encourage everyone—students, teachers, and the rest of us—to search out our unique intellectual identity, to determine who, intellectually and individually, we really are, and thereby to take ourselves seriously—for education is a serious business. Newman's Idea suggests that one important task of the University is to exhort—and in such exhortation to help discipline—students to expand, enhance, enlarge, perfect, and thereby to fulfill their intellectual, personal, and spiritual identity. To Newman, this kind of perfecting self-knowledge is the key to personal realization.

NEWMAN'S VIEW

For this reason, Newman understands the University as "a seat of universal learning, considered as a place of education" which is designed to help the student to apprehend "the great outlines of knowledge, the principles on which it rests, the scale of its parts, its lights and its shades, its great points and its little, as he otherwise cannot apprehend them. Hence it is that his education is called 'Liberal.' A habit of mind is formed which lasts through life, of which the attributes are freedom, equitableness, moderation, and wisdom; or what . . . I have ventured to call a philosophical habit."[12]

That philosophical habit, which is a self-searching for wisdom, implies that the goal of the University is likewise the goal of liberal education. This goal is no less than the perfection of the intellect. Newman says that only such an intellectually perfecting and liberating education

> gives a man a clear conscious view of his own opinions and judgments, a truth in developing them, an eloquence in expressing them, and a force in urging them. It teaches him to see things as they are, to go right to the point, to disentangle a skein of thought, to detect what is sophistical, and to discard what is irrelevant. It prepares him to fill any post with

credit, and to master any subject with facility. It shows him how to accommodate himself to others, how to throw himself into their state of mind, how to bring them before his own, how to influence them, how to come to an understanding with them, how to bear with them. . . . He has the repose of a mind which lives in itself, while it lives in the world, and which has resources for its happiness at home when it cannot go abroad. . . . The art which tends to make a man all of this, is, in the object which it pursues, as useful as the art of wealth or the art of health.[13]

INTELLECTUAL MATURITY

Such a passage reveals certain important characteristics of Newman's vision of liberating University education, which involves the intellect in the process of perfection. When intellect developmentally becomes what it is divinely created to be, then intellect is brought to the fruition of its inherent powers. Such powers of intellect, as Newman describes them, also express a wide range of ancillary intellective accomplishments, which implicitly include psychological, emotive, and moral powers. These powers include all of the following:

☐ Enveloping insight (clear, calm, accurate vision)
☐ Percipience (clear, conscious view)
☐ Sagacity (truth in developing)
☐ Language competence (eloquence in expressing)
☐ Persuasive power (force in urging)
☐ Discernment (seeing things as they are)
☐ Acumen (going right to the point)
☐ Inferential power (disentangling a skein of thought)
☐ Trenchancy (detecting the sophistical)
☐ Judgment (discarding the irrelevant)
☐ Career competence (filling any post)
☐ Mental range (mastering any subject)
☐ Sensitivity (adjusting to others)
☐ Empathy (feeling the other person's state of mind)
☐ Understanding (comprehending the other person's point of view)
☐ Suasion (influencing others)
☐ Interiorization (coming to an understanding with others)

☐ Sympathy (bearing with others)
☐ Wisdom (repose of mind)
☐ Spiritual independence (living in oneself while living in the world)
☐ Spiritual contentment (having resources for happiness)
☐ Spiritual relevance (as useful as the art of wealth or health)

Exercised together, such characteristics constitute intellectual maturity, which Newman premises can be attained—(perhaps only?)—through University education. This is because the University provides a unique environment, which precisely begets enlargement, encourages development, and stimulates enhancement of mind. These verbal acts, which issue in maturation of the mind, are the means by which intellect is perfected.

ENCOURAGING MATURITY

Looked at from a different angle, the passage above, from *The Idea of a University*, also suggests that the art of perfecting the intellect implicitly adopts those conceptual patterns of the liberal arts which, in medieval tradition, constituted the Trivium,[14] consisting of the arts of grammar, rhetoric, and logic. The title Trivium refers to three ways (tri viae) or roads on the journey towards liberating the mind from smallness and ignorance. The term also described common crossroads, thus giving rise to the words trivial and trivia.

Recast from this same passage, and in Newman's own words, grammar would provide "a truth in developing [that] clear, conscious view . . . of opinions and judgments"; rhetoric, "an eloquence in expressing them, and a force in urging them"; logic, the power "to go right to the point, to disentangle a skein of thought, to detect what is sophistical, and to discard what is irrelevant."

As *The Idea of a University* makes plain, the primary and essential task of the University is to inaugurate perfection of the intellect. This idea provokes sharp contrast with the modem American assumptions that the University's task—apart from athletics and fund-raising—is to prepare students to "get a good job." Ironically, Newman asserted that, by perfecting their own intellect, students would already have been prepared to "fill any post with credit." In regrettable contrast, an American University degree may have been reinvented as a ticket to an uncertain job market. A one-time general assumption was that a student, by means of University training, and before getting a job, was self-reflectively learning about his or her own identity.

Altered Objectives

In America, the University has become the principal agent of higher education. But, the kind and quality of that education becomes, conversely, the yardstick by which the University itself can be judged. Stuffing students with information, inflating them with clever sayings to "pass the finals," and then stamping them out as graduates, in order that they may "land a good job"—such actions, for Newman, do not constitute the true business of a University.

Job skills are usually what a prospective employer prefers to work out "on the job." What cannot be worked out on the job is an employer's expectation that a college graduate will be intellectually self-propelled, psychologically self-motivated, emotionally stable, morally mature, and possessed of implied mental skills and intellectual vision. A prospective employer is thus bound to ask, "Does this graduate have a well-formed mind? Does he or she know how to think, how to make sound judgments? Does she or he have structured mental skills of historical discernment, mathematical precision, humanistic balance? Skills of reading perceptively, writing coherently, accurately, and persuasively? Can she or he contribute personal achievements of psychological maturity to meet our organization's challenges?" A prospective employer needs to be satisfied that the University has effectively accomplished its task of educating, and has not left general remedial work for the employer to sort out.

But should career success be what a prospective student (or a prospecting parent) might seek in a University education? Or should both student and parent envision the University as simply a place that passes on techniques for making money? If so, then both student and parent are bound to be disgruntled at outcomes.

Of course, lifetime earnings of University graduates tend to exceed those of nongraduates. That excess is now projected to rise as high as $2,000,000—higher yet for professional and doctoral degrees. The central, but more difficult, question is this: Which is more important as a motive for going to a University—the prospect of making money, or (however vague the phrase) the prospect of becoming intellectually mature, so that one can pursue almost any career?

There are many ways to make money. But, there are very few ways to learn how to use one's mind expansively and effectively. Judging by the world's "success stories," one need not attend a University to acquire skills in inflating corporate profits, sequestering corporate expenses in fraudulent earnings reports, unobtrusively defrauding a bank, secretly leveraging corporate buyouts, or deftly perpetrating quiet larceny on Medicare. These are skills of shrewdness. But the University cannot teach native shrewdness, since that, by definition, is unteachable, and because—being a given—it is unlearnable.

DISTRACTION OF MIND

Neither ought the University be designed as a distraction for the mind (a practice now almost commonplace) by offering a warehouse collection of polychromatic subjects. The University, as Newman warns, ought not be organized around

> the error of distracting and enfeebling the mind by an unmeaning profusion of subjects; of implying that a smattering in a dozen branches of Study is not shallowness, which it really is, but enlargement, which it is not. . . . All things are to be learned at once, not first one thing, and then another. Learning is to be without exertion, without attention, without toil; without grounding, without advance, without finishing. . . . [Such] ill-used persons . . . are forced to load their minds with a score of subjects against an examination . . . have too much on their hands to indulge themselves in thinking or investigation . . . devour premise and conclusions together with indiscriminate greediness . . . hold whole sciences on faith, and commit demonstrations to memory, and who too often, as might be expected, when their period of education is passed, throw up all they have learned in disgust, having gained nothing really by their anxious labours. . . . [And then] they leave their place of education simply dissipated and relaxed by the multiplicity of subjects, which they never really mastered, and so shallow as not even to know their shallowness.[15]

LATEST TRENDS

Still, there are also those who complain that Newman does not know "the latest trends in education." In making such a claim, such critics nicely miss the point of what Newman is actually saying. To him, the single most important criterion for estimating the educative success of a University is in how well that University intellectually engages students in realizing—in both senses of the term, namely, "comprehending" and "making real"—their competence, their perceptual endowment, their understanding.

Other theorists of educational trends argue that the University now requires "contextual definers," because "European culture" is, allegedly, a trap of sexist, racist, and class-centered passé ideas. For such reasons, these theorists maintain that the liberal arts curriculum must be replaced by a "multicultural" curriculum. Similar attempts to reformulate the University insist that computer and TV instruction is better (incidentally, cheaper) than live teaching. But, as Newman believed, a genuine University is precisely the place where live professors can wear their learning (as Alfred North Whitehead was wont to say) with imagination, and where teachers are dedicated (pity the cliché, but not its truth) to making a difference in the lives of their students.

USE AND WORTH

These competitive views prompt us to ask this: What in reality is the use, and what truly is the worth, of a University education? Newman poses such questions in *The Idea of a University*, just as he posed them in 1852 in his *Dublin Lectures on Education*. The use and worth afforded by the University is not wealth, not power, not convenience, not comfort of life. Rather, he said, it is "an object, in its own nature, so really and undeniably good, as to be the compensation of a great deal of thought in the compassing, and a great deal of trouble in the attaining."[16]

In this so finite mortal time at our disposal, the University's worth and its use should turn us toward acquisition of a global comprehension of human experience. But we first achieve such comprehension by personally understanding our spiritual and intellectual identity. In doing this, says Newman, "We are satisfying a direct need of our nature in its very acquisition."[17]

Despite inaccurately being charged with doing so, however,

Newman does not legislate narrow or dogmatic definitions of the University endeavor. Neither does he assume a dictatorial tone, nor issue imperious prescriptions. He does not proclaim, for example, "Here, now, is what your University ought to look like." Nor does he muse, with quizzical, affably academic indecision, "Well now, what do you think we ought to do about this sort of thing?" His central message is more descriptive and less prescriptive, because he maintains a tone of appreciative interest, as if he were describing a perfectly shaped tree, a delicately designed flower, or an artistically perfect statue. It is as if he were saying,

> Here are some characteristics of the well-endowed, well-shaped, decisively disciplined, vision-taught, and skill-taught mind. How can you achieve this result?
>
> This is what transfigured understanding is capable of. This is what the human mind can be helped to achieve and sustain. Here is the principle. Can you find the best way to concretize it?
>
> This is what University graduates should be intellectually, even morally, capable of. How can you achieve this result?
>
> Knowing what the ultimate goal of higher education is, how can you construct the best means of attaining it?

By such imaginative interrogation, and with dedication to a view of human possibilities, Newman descriptively portrayed the genuine University. He perceived the University as that special residence of intellect, that unique educative venue, which fosters "the culture of the intellect." University is a supportive nurturer, "an Alma Mater, knowing her children one by one,"[18] and a provider of a nutritive abundance of knowledge. It is also a place of spiritual restoration, of intellectual guidance and nurturance. Having commanding jurisdiction over the full range of intellectual subject matters, the University is also an imperial intellect.

INTELLECTUAL RESIDENCE

University, as Newman understood it, is "not a foundry or a mint, or a treadmill."[19] Rather, it is an intellectual home, a spiritual dwelling place of interpersonal contact. Its essential prerogative is as "a place of concourse, whither students come from every quarter for every kind of knowledge," and "a place for the communication and circulation of thought, by means of personal intercourse." This view assumes that the University is an environment in which teaching of the highest order takes place through "the personal influence of a master."[20]

If, as Newman states, we want to "cultivate" and "perfect" the intellect, we cannot simply resort—even while admitting their importance—to books. On the contrary,

> if we wish to become exact and fully furnished in any branch of knowledge which is diversified and complicated, we must consult the living man and listen to his living voice. . . . No book can convey the special spirit and delicate peculiarities of its subject with that rapidity and certainty which attend on the sympathy of mind with mind, through the eyes, the look, the accent and the manner, in casual expressions thrown off at the moment, and the unstudied turns of familiar conversation. . . . The general principles of any study you may learn by books at home; but the detail, the colour, the tone, the air, the life which makes it live in us, you must catch all these from those in whom it lives already.[21]

A living intellect requires the living teacher, who is endowed with a living voice. This condition also requires presence of a living community, which has been shaped by a living tradition, and with a lively sense of living intellect to guide it. If we seek fresh water, we go to its wellspring, and if we seek wisdom, we must go to that wellspring of teachers of wisdom.

LIVING COMMUNICATION

Instinctively, we know that it is only from the vivifying voice of the vitalizing teacher that we can begin the process of understanding. We sense that it is only from the living voice of the living teacher that we can attain the spiritual sustenance we need. We learn effectively, and learn deeply, only when we live in the precincts of those who themselves live out the wisdom we pursue. Learning through living contact means learning through conscious mimesis. The idea and ideal of living a cultivated intellectual life is what brought Newman to imagine its personification in a figure whom he designated the gentleman. By himself embodying that ideal of cultivation of intellect, Newman was, in a quite realistic sense, drawing a self-portrait.

Undertaking cultivation of the intellect is a task so developmentally difficult, and so entrancingly personalized, Newman argued, that it can be realized only in an environment of mental growth. That environment Newman precisely signified by the term *University*, where, mimetically, the gentleman is formed: "All that goes to constitute a gentleman,—the carriage, gait, address, voice; the ease, the self-possession, the courtesy, the power of conversing, the talent of not offending; the lofty principle, the delicacy of thought, the happiness of expression, the taste and propriety, the generosity and forbearance, the candour and consideration, the openness of hand;—these qualities . . . the full assemblage of them, bound up in the unity of an individual character, do we expect they can be learned from books?"[22]

GENTLEMAN AS EXEMPLAR

The educational intention of Newman's gentleman should not, however, be confused with some model of nineteenth-century British deportment. His gentleman (we shall later suggest) is not so much historical as symbolic. It is more important, then, to understand the significance of what Newman was suggesting by means of that figure, than to be mesmerized or even confused by the figure itself. Change the century, change the setting, change the wardrobe, change the name, Newman's intention to portray educated mental and personal conduct still persists. Once we accept this, our own symbols of Newman's intention will become realistically relevant to our own day, as Newman's was to his.

To be sure, some of Newman's gentlemanly traits are old-fashioned. But not all are. Qualities still relevant to our day include those of self-possession, courtesy, ease of stance, brightness of conversation, effectiveness of thought and expression, forbearance, propriety, candor, generosity, openness, and consideration of others. Such characteristics are appropriate to any civilized life. Consequently (not to put too fine a point on it), it is not Newman's precise social context of a "gentlemanly portrait" which matters. What do matter are the educative idea and the psychological intention which lie behind that portrait. This is to say that the best thoughts and the most cultivated actions are always imitative. Only a society's best minds can stimulate other best minds.

IMITATIVE BEHAVIOR

Just as the worst behaviors tend to arise in the worst environments, so too, the best behaviors tend to blossom in the best environments. This is because all behavior is learned behavior. Behavior that is acquired in a University ought to then, first and foremost, be mental, intellectual behavior. Social amenities consonant with the deportment of the best minds will also tend to be available where the best minds congregate. This is why Newman laid down the principle that the University provides the mind its best environment. To learn to converse well, to speak effectively, to communicate thoughtfully, to think precisely, to imagine creatively—all these imply cultivation of intellect. Such cultivation requires a particular residence, a special setting, in which good conversation, serious speech, a "bodily communication of knowledge," precision of thought, and intensity of mind will already have become habits of the place. Such habits will, in turn, fare well, and fruitfully, when they become habits of mind for those who dwell in that place. Only in such a place, Newman contends, can enlargement of mind—intellectual and moral—take place.

We have said that the University's environment depends upon the presence there of living models of teaching. In the same way, Newman, suggests, the environment of the Church—also a teaching institution—depends upon the presence of living teachers, because the Church

> concurs in the principle of a University so far as this, that its great instrument, or rather organ, has ever been that which nature prescribes in all education, the personal presence of a teacher, or, in theological language, Oral Tradition. It is the living voice, the breathing form, the expressive countenance, which preaches, which catechizes. Truth, a subtle, invisible, manifold spirit, is poured into the mind of the scholar by his eyes and ears, through his affections, imagination, and reason; it is poured into his mind and is sealed up there in perpetuity, by propounding and repeating it, by questioning and requestioning, by correcting and explaining, by progressing and then recurring to first principles.[23]

LEARNING ENVIRONMENT

Primarily a learning-teaching place, the University literally incorporates an intellectual environment as the genius of its place. The University's essential characteristic, therefore, is excellence—of mind and imagination, aspiration and duty—in short, excellence of intellect. As Newman observes,

> In the nature of things, greatness and unity go together; excellence implies a centre. And such . . . is a University. . . . It is the place to which a thousand schools make contributions; in which the intellect may safely range and speculate, sure to find its equal in some antagonist activity, and its judge in the tribunal of truth. It is a place where inquiry is pushed forward, and discoveries verified and perfected, and rashness rendered innocuous, and error exposed, by the collision of mind with mind, and knowledge with knowledge. It is the place where the professor becomes eloquent, and is a missionary and a preacher, displaying his science in its most complete and most winning form, pouring it forth with the zeal of enthusiasm, and lighting up his own love of it in the breasts of his hearers. It is the place where the catechist makes good his ground as he goes, treading in the truth day by day into the ready memory, and wedging and tightening it into the expanding reason. It is a place which wins the admiration of the young by its celebrity, kindles the affections of the middle-aged by its beauty, and rivets the fidelity of the old by its associations. It is a seat of wisdom, a light of the world, a minister of the faith, an Alma Mater of the rising generation.[24]

For the University, "cultivation" of intellect creates a "thematic essence" and an "existential center" which constitute the University's raison d'être. The genius loci of the University likewise create that special place which provides for "the force, the steadiness, the comprehensiveness and the versatility of the intellect."

For this reason, Newman insists that the business of the University is to make "intellectual culture its direct scope, or to employ itself in the education of the intellect." Whatever else the University does, it dare not renounce its fundamental responsibility to challenge intellect "to reason well in all matters, to reach out towards truth, and to grasp it."[25]

Whenever Newman describes the well disciplined, well shaped, and perfectly formed mind, he does so very much in the spirit of Aristotle, and also uses a language similar to that of Aristotle—who was, Dante said, "the master of those who know" *(il maestro di color che sanno)*. Like Aristotle, Newman also considers education a process that is not about factual information, but rather about knowing the meaning—therefore the connectedness and implications—of factual information, which means knowing what information can lead to. Of itself, information is simply raw material, not a finished product. Any form of education, then, which merely provides information cannot, ultimately, be educative.

But suppose we assume the contrary case. Suppose information were to be confused with education. Then—so rapid is the velocity with which information now ranges into our experience—the mind would automatically become a servant of obsolescence, or a pensioner of memory loss. If the mind were merely used as a storage depot for information, it would simply become one more parcel of electromagnetic real estate—like the computer's RAM (random access memory) or a hard drive of so many gigabytes.

NEWMAN AS MODEL

But let us shift from the *Idea* as a portrait of the University in order to engage a wider scope, which encompasses Newman himself. Quintessentially, *The Idea of a University* reveals Newman as one who has perfected his own intellect. Equally, the *Idea* is also typical of Newman's other works, because its metaphoric fabric contains threads characteristic of them. Some passages in the Idea, for example, are suggestive of his *Parochial and Plain Sermons* and *Sermons Preached on Various Occasions*. Other passages structurally reflect arguments similar to those which Newman used in *A Grammar of Assent*, or in *An Essay on the Development of Christian Doctrine*. Certain others simulate the linguistic intimacy, even humor, of his *The Present Position of Catholics in England*. All these tracts appear as if they were plucked (a favorite Newman word)—although they were not—from the *Idea*, or as if the *Idea* were plucked from them. Similarly, parts of the *Idea* might easily be imagined—so intensely spiritual is this work—as having originated in prayer, meditation, or sermon.

CONVERGENT ASCENTS

Yet there are actual instances in which portions of the *Idea* were borrowed from another Newman work. For example, Discourse VI of the *Idea* contains a passage originally appearing as Sermon XIV of Newman's *University Sermons* ("Wisdom, as Contrasted with Faith and with Bigotry").[26] Such conceptual "contagion" seems to suggest how Newman could intuit how religion and education—although absolutely different—can nonetheless share in certain spiritual references. Thus, in the worship of God, religion clearly exhorts us to aspire to illuminative and ascentive enlargement of soul, heart, and mind. Similarly, true education encourages us to ascend towards clarity of mind and spirit.

Similarly, intellective ascent reaffirms the complementary nature of spiritually centered themes, such as those of faith and understanding, grace and nature, revelation and reason. To these, we add, Newman's themes of devotion and learning, religion and education, Church and University, conscience and wisdom. These themes have implicit place and express standing in *The Idea of a University*. For one thing, Newman viewed such themes as integrative, complementary, collaborative, and perfective of one another, rather than as conflictive, or contradictory.

SPECIFIC INSTANCE

University Sermon XIV, "Wisdom, as Contrasted with Faith and with Bigotry," contains linking expressions, assimilative figures of speech, and doctrinal formulations which link it to the *Idea*. Together, these formulations represent the interests of both religion and education. For example, in this sermon, Newman defines wisdom as "the clear, calm, accurate vision, and comprehension of the whole course, the whole work of God; and though there is none who has it in its fullness but He who 'searcheth all things, yea, even the deep things of' the Creator, yet 'by that Spirit' they are, in a measure, 'revealed unto us.'"[27]

Smoothly, almost effortlessly, Newman reflects this modular text in *The Idea of a University*, when he defines the goal of education as "perfection of the intellect" which is "the clear, calm, accurate vision and comprehension of all things, as far as the finite mind can embrace them, each in its place, and with its own characteristics on it."

Newman adds to this educative endorsement a religious sub-strate and conviction which marks such perfection of the intellect as "almost prophetic from its knowledge of history; it is almost heart-searching from its knowledge of human nature; it is almost supernatu-ral charity from its freedom from littleness and prejudice; it is almost the repose of faith, because nothing can startle it; it has almost the beauty and harmony of heavenly contemplation, so intimate is it with the eter-nal order of things and the music of the spheres."[28]

INTELLECTUAL PERFECTION

Perfecting the intellect, then, means no less than wisdom in the making, a conclusion which implicitly affirms affinity between perfected intel-lect and achievable wisdom. Such affinity (we shall notice)[29] is not merely conceptual, but linguistic as well. Thus, a metaphoric line can be drawn, which links this passage about wisdom with that about perfected intellect. Therefore, complementarity unites Newman's University "ser-mon" with his University "lecture." Hence, what Newman religiously addressed to the soul can be identified with what he intellectually ad-dressed to the mind. The difference, customarily made between soul and mind, in other words, is labeled as a formal (rather than real) dis-tinction. Spiritual complementarity between soul and mind thereby reprises that stereopticon connection between what is considered moral, and what is accounted intellectual.

Going a step further, may we not likewise infer Newman's un-derlying sense of complementarity between what he believes to be re-ligious and what he views as educative? Are we not, once again, confronted with Newman's binomial sensitivity to what is both distinct but related? If this is so, can we not also forge another link—*religare*—not only between religion and education, but also between the tasks of their related institutions, Church and University? If such inference can legitimately be drawn, we may then also be justified in comprehending such complementarity not only as attributes of subject matters, but, more importantly, as attributes of Newman's mind.

BINARY IMPLICATIONS

The binary characteristics already attributed to Newman (see Introduc-tion) seem to be central to his thinking and writing, as well as to his life and mind. His binary genius, which implies polar balance, also uniquely reflects the Newmanesque "principle of interconnectivity." This is the principle which "makes every thing in some sort lead to every thing else."[30] And this principle, with its accompanying principle of complementarity, is suffused throughout The Idea of a University, only because both represent central aspects of Newman's mind.

To advance the point further, we need merely recall that, to Newman, an author's literary style is an affirmation of that author's literary mind. While M. le comte de Buffon is credited with expressing a similar point in his way—Le style, c 'est I 'homme meme, "Style is the intrinsic man"—Newman can be credited with articulating the point even more precisely by saying that "the style of original writers is stamped with the peculiarities of their minds."[31]

BINARY PATTERN

The Idea of a University appears to present prima facie evidence of Newman's binary patterns, in a manner similar to how Gustav Mahler's Second Symphony, "Resurrection," evidences his own illuminative emotional commitments. Thus Newman's lectures and Mahler's music embrace, like an exaltation, the essence of each creator's reality. In exemplaristic vocabulary, the complementary genius of Newman's *Idea* presciently unites his educative vision of religion with his religious vision of education.

Although Newman preserves an absolute distinction between religion and education, he also provides for their conceptual coherence—perhaps, in some way, even their spiritual convergence. He seems to comprehend religion and education as they were grasped by a spirit of theological congruence similar to that by which Nikolaus Cusanus [Kues] (1401–64) once perceived the richness of divine life as coincidentia oppositorum.[32] Perhaps, more importantly, Newman's binary patterns of perception appear to be simultaneously noetic and psychological. That is to say, they seem to represent a synthesis of epistemological process and personality process.

By reinforcing intellectual power with the force of his personal psychology, Newman appears to lend a new kind of strength and dimension to his thought. Such synthesizing proclivity could easily be imagined as uniting faith and understanding as two forms of perception, or interpreting revelation and reason as two sources of knowing, or construing conscience and wisdom as two modes of virtue—moral virtue (conscience) and intellectual virtue (wisdom).

Newman's binary powers likewise suggest a psychological polar balance which combines dialectical and intuitive powers, and thus also suggest a mirrored neuroanatomical polar balance of left-brain / right-brain co-dominance. Such psychological and neuroanatomical powers might then cast new light on Newman's so-called contrarieties, which view him as both tough and sensitive, both forceful and gentle, or as simultaneously cautious and brave, meticulous and assertive, militant and serene. Newman's balancing polarities appear to combine temperamental and ideological strengths, thereby explaining Newman's emotive and intellectual acuity as being conservative and innovative, traditional and progressive. Existentially, Newman also lived, intellectually and psychologically, in both the present and the past, and so he could fuse imaginative insight with hard-edged fact.

BINARY PRECEDENTS

These arguments, emphasizing Newman's binary energies, have also been remarked by other authors. For example, Wilfrid Ward, as Newman's first biographer,[33] drew attention to the fact that "in Newman apparent contradictions form a part of the consistent whole," and so, in him, "nothing is more remarkable than the consistency of view underlying variations of feelings and the recognition of opposite aspects of the same situation." Other writers advance similar views.[34] Ian Ker, for one, unequivocally identifies Newman's power to hold, in fruitful tension, obverse sides of experience, and draws "particular attention to that preoccupation with the 'real' and the 'unreal' which pervades his [Newman's] writings." Newman's mind, he says, "is characterized not by contradictions but by complementary strengths, so that he may be called, without inconsistency, both conservative and liberal, progressive and traditional, cautious and radical, dogmatic yet pragmatic, idealistic but realistic."[35]

One special aspect of Newman's "many-layered" complementary and binary powers is that they illuminate and enhance his insistence on the human need for spiritual growth, enlargement, and development. Such binary-complementary patterns thus empower Newman's conceptual and spiritual need to unify what may, at first sight, appear to be contrary elements. Perhaps from this perspective, we can explain why Newman envisions the University as a ruling and imperial institution of "bipolar balance." It possesses power to unify disparate subject matters within its jurisdiction, and in this way, institutionally reflects the interconnected nature of the universe.

As an imperial intellect, the University retains authority over various, and apparently conflicting, subject matters. The University—as if replicating Roman, British, Austro-Hungarian, or Ottoman empires, which ruled a contrariety of peoples—possesses intellectively complementary powers, which can reorder, reaffirm, and reunite disparate but related realities. This view also elucidates how Newman understands the distinct but complementary natures of moral and intellectual authority, as representing integrative powers of the human person and personality.

Spiritual union of moral and intellectual aspects of mankind, Newman tells us, was originally intended by God's creative purpose. Yet Newman reminds us that such union was rent asunder by humankind's disruptive aptitude, which subverted the original divine purpose. Still, Newman argues that disruption of unity, and de-linking of integral human traits, is not based on necessity, as he himself said it in a well-known sermon: "I grant that there is a separation, though I deny its necessity."[36]

NEWMAN MISUNDERSTOOD

There are critics who dismiss the notion that Newman possessed binary patterns and unifying prospects of thought and personality. They apparently prefer to interpret Newman's views simply as inconsistencies and contradictions. The roster of those who charge Newman with such inconsistencies, is rather extensive,[37] even though one sympathetic observer[38] reasons that, because of his copious writings describing his religious development, Newman gave ammunition to his foes, since he had moved with agonizing steps, each precisely marked, from one church to another, each stage in effect canceling what was said before, so that his words could be pitted against each other in apparent contradiction.

Yet Newman stood firmly in an outer real world, while still being deeply rooted in an inner, spiritual world. He lived, simultaneously, in two environmental dimensions of reality, but, consciously and concretely, he united such environments, as is illustrated in a story of how he responded to a question posed to him. One day, the story goes, Newman's sister, Jemima, brought her grandson to visit the famous great-uncle Cardinal, and the boy asked, "Which is greater, a cardinal or a saint?" Posed in real time, the question was promptly answered in existential time. "Cardinals," Newman said, "belong to this world, and Saints to heaven."[39]

BRAIN COMPLEMENTARITY

Gentle and gentle-minded, Newman was also steel-minded and iron-willed.[40] Equally resilient, flexible, sensitive, interpersonal, unquestionably nonconfrontational, he was also widely focused. In neuroanatomical terms, he was both right-brained and left-brained. Such bipolar balance sharply revealed his powers of creative language as well as his capacity for critical analysis. Because of his manifold linguistic and analytic gifts, it might be useful, but briefly for now, to introduce the issue of hemispheric dominance.

Although language usage is assigned to localized functions of the left brain,[41] Newman's linguistic genius involved more than left-brain competence. Indeed, it rather suggests unusually high right-brain function. While the right brain has no known local area of language usage, it nonetheless, and in some as-yet-unspecified fashion, determines language genius. Thus, "higher" language competence is more apparent among (right-hemisphere) females than among (left-hemisphere) males, whereas higher spatio-mathematical competence is more prevalent among males than among females. The language genius of Shakespeare, Dante, Cicero, St. Augustine, and Newman reflects just such linguistic prowess of the right-brained. This feat may also illuminate what have been designated as Newman's so-called feminine traits.[42]

Newman's bipolar balance may reflect what he clearly demonstrated conceptually and behaviorally which is that he possessed imaginative, intuitive, and poetic (right-brain) powers, and, at the same time, mathematical, structural, and dialectical (left-brain) acuity. It is not surprising that, as an undergraduate, he chose to pursue a double-honors degree in (right-hemisphere) classical literature and in (left-hemisphere) mathematics, which together clearly suggest binary powers of mind. This is not to imply that brain function is the same as intellect (which it is not). But intellect does itself provide complementary binary capacity for intuitive and dialectical powers.

Binary Restatement

Indeed, *The Idea of a University* seems superbly to illustrate the neuroanatomic themes of right-brain / left-brain, as well as the intuitive-dialectical complementarity of intellect. More importantly, the *Idea* also appears semantically poised in moral-intellectual balance. Would it not follow that such a work is also a repository of binomial balance? Indeed, such balance is likewise characteristic of Christianity's redeeming, paradoxical mysteries—for example, faith and understanding. Coming to grips with the *Idea*'s intuitive and dialectic mysteries—even though they are of a different order—seems at least analogous to the attempt to come to grips with the mystery of the confluence of faith and understanding. Faith, like understanding, Newman carefully points out, is essentially an intellectual activity: "Faith, being an act of the intellect, opens a way for inquiry, comparison and inference."[43]

Much as did St. Anselm, John Henry Newman attended, in both private thought and public assertion, to the meaning and relevance of faith. To Anselm, faith necessarily implied faithfulness—whose opposite was denominated felony. Anselm also understood faith (fides) as identifiable with—because always referent to—"God's mind," or "God's reason," or "God's knowing." By contrast, understanding (intellectus) referred to mankind's responding mind. Through faith, mankind could know—and thus try to understand—what, otherwise, only God alone could know.

Such a formulation appears fully congenial to Newman's thought. Although he clearly asserted the distinctiveness of faith and understanding, he also recognized their interconnection. For Newman, there was a human need to accentuate a twinned response—intercommunication, as well as an intercommunion—between faith and understanding.[44]

Knowledge and Virtue

Distinctions, of course, still have to be made, and made not just between faith and understanding, but also between, say, conscience and wisdom. Always sensitive to such distinctions, Newman also made them quite fortuitously. For instance, there is his renowned formula: "Knowledge is one thing, virtue is another, good sense is not conscience; refinement is not humility; nor is largeness and justness of view faith."[45]

Because the *Idea* considers University education integral to the needs and nature of the human person, that work implies that, underlying the contrast of knowledge and virtue, or of goodness and usefulness, there resides a more sublime, "twinning," geminated truth. University education, Newman contends, is primarily dedicated to the cultivation of intellect, which means that it is dedicated to the good of the intellect. Both the action prompted by that dedication, and the object of that action, refer to what is good. The process through which cultivation is achieved, University, and the object of that cultivating process, intellect, are also demonstratively useful. Newman argued his point this way:

> Let us take "useful" to mean not what is simply good, but what tends to be good, or is the instrument of good; and in this sense also . . . a liberal education is truly and fully a useful . . . education. "Good" indeed means one thing, and "useful" means another; but I lay it down as a principle . . . that, though the useful is not always good, the good is always useful. Good is not only good, but reproductive of good; this is one of its attributes; nothing is excellent, beautiful, perfect, desirable for its own sake, but it overflows, and spreads the likeness of itself all around it.
>
> Good is prolific. A great good will impart great good. If then the intellect is so excellent a portion of us, and its cultivation so excellent, it is not only beautiful, perfect, admirable, and noble in itself, but in a true and high sense it must be useful to the possessor and to all around him; not useful in any low, mechanical, mercantile sense, but as diffusing a good, or as a blessing, or a gift, or a power, or a treasure, first to the owner, then through him to the world. I say then, if a liberal education be good, it must necessarily be useful too.[46]

Newman's insight into the reciprocating relation between what is good (bonum honestum) and what it useful (bonum utile) may have been inspired by the reciprocating nature of health, which, being a good, is also a useful good. A healthy mind and a healthy body—Roman poet Juvenal phrased it mens sana in corpore sano—thus incorporate both what is good and what is useful. Taking care to lay out the implications of healthfulness, Newman asserts, "Health is good in itself, though nothing came of it, and is especially worth seeking and cherishing."[47] But health is applicable not only to the good of the body, but equally implies the adequate use (the usefulness) of the body. So it is with the mind.

Characteristics of the healthy body which Newman delineates include "strength, energy, agility, graceful carriage and action, manual dexterity, and endurance of fatigue."[48] Can we not, by shifting the context, say that bodily characteristics of healthfulness prefigure—and thus, spiritually, parallel—mental traits of constancy, competency, grace, agility, energy, and strength. Sanitas of a healthy body is thematically congruent to sanitas of a healthy mind, because both are good and usefully good. Similarly, Newman envisions liberal education as a confluence of what is good with what is useful. Liberal education, being dedicated to "real cultivation of mind," brings with it "the force, the steadiness, the comprehensiveness, and the versatility of the intellect, the command over our own powers, the instinctive just estimates of things as they pass before us. [And this] makes itself felt in the good sense, sobriety of thought, reasonableness, candour, self-command, and steadiness of view which characterize it."[49]

Here we have what portends to be the ultimate usefulness of University liberal education—as being a good which confers "cultivation" and "perfection" upon the mind. Such a perfected mind possesses the power to produce concrete and evident effects. Thus, anyone

> who has learned to think and to reason and to compare and to discriminate and to analyze, who has refined his taste, and formed his judgment, and sharpened his mental vision, will not indeed at once be a lawyer, or a pleader, or an orator, or a statesman, or a physician, or a good landlord, or a man of business, or a soldier, or an engineer, or a chemist, or a geologist, or an antiquarian, but he will be placed in that state of intellect in which he can take up any one of the sciences or callings I have referred to, or any other for which he has a taste or special talent, with an ease, a grace, a versatility, and a success, to which another is a stranger. In this sense then . . . mental culture is emphatically useful.[50]

INTELLECTUAL USEFULNESS

For the person who undertakes it, cultivation of the intellect becomes both a good in itself and a good in use. In this way, an implicit good can become an explicit good, which also extends the intellectual cultivation of the person beyond that person and into society. Hence, perfection of the intellect—"which is the proper function of a University"—is functionally transposed into a good for society. By enabling the person of cultivated intellect to discharge his duties to society, that personal perfection of intellect, says Newman, thereby transmutes itself into a social good.

This process of reasoning leads Newman to his well-known conclusion regarding the practical end of University training:

> If then a practical end must be assigned to a University course, I say that it is that of training good members of society. Its art is the art of social life, and its end is fitness for the world. It neither confines its views to particular professions on the one hand, nor creates heroes or inspires genius on the other. . . . But a University training is the great ordinary means to a great but ordinary end; it aims at raising the intellectual tone of society, at cultivating the public mind, at purifying the national taste, at supplying true principles to popular enthusiasm and fixed aims to popular aspiration, at giving enlargement and sobriety to the ideas of the age, at facilitating the exercise of political power, and refining the intercourse of private life. . . . For why do we educate, except to prepare for the world? Why do we cultivate the intellect of the many beyond the first elements of knowledge, except for this world? If then a University is a direct preparation for this world, let it be what it professes. It is not a convent, it is not a seminary; it is a place to fit men of the world for the world. We cannot possibly keep them from plunging into the world, with all its ways and principles and maxims, when their time comes; but we can prepare them against what is inevitable; and it is not the way to learn to swim in troubled waters, never to have gone into them.[51]

UNIFIED ACTIONS

From theoretic seeds, which Newman planted, certain harvestable ideas can be derived. One of these is that moral and intellectual actions enhance one another. Plausibly, electing both forms of action, as Newman does, may suggest that moral action is the existential complement of intellectual action, and, conversely, intellectual action fosters the essential, intentional integrity of moral action. Perhaps this relationship may explain why both kinds of action are complicitly conjoined in the pursuit and performance of religion and education. Therefore, moral and intellectual actions will not be seen as dichotomous in—or disjunctive of— the tasks of Church and University. Such actions may, indeed, under certain circumstances become congruent.[52]

It remains for us to suggest later on that Newman's vision of the tasks of Church and University is one of complementarity, not of competition. That vision, it can be argued, appears grounded in Newman's binomial powers of mind, as well as in his principle of the interconnectivity of realities. Perhaps this will explain why Newman can understand religious and educative institutions as being Almae Matres—nourishing mothers. For one thing, their common endowment is intellect, and their connecting link resides in those fostering ideals of conscience and wisdom.[53]

CHAPTER 2:
INTELLECT

> "Intellectual culture is its own end; for what has its end in itself has its use in itself also."

> "Cultivation of the intellect . . . is an object in its own nature so really and undeniably good, as to be the compensation of a great deal of thought in the compassing, and a great deal of trouble in the attaining."

> "Faith, being an act of the intellect, opens a way for inquiry."

> "No one can deny to the intellect its own excellence, nor deprive it of its due honours."

How obvious, yet how intriguingly true it is, that whatever else we human beings share with other animals of our planet, one thing we do not share is the semantic incandescence of intellect. This is so obvious that it needs to be said.

Another way of looking at the issue is that only men and women are *eligible*, or *selected* for, or (by similar *logic*) *elected* to the *dialectical elegance* of intellect. Human beings have a *predilection* for intellect, which means that women and men really are the world's *loyal elite*. We need not *apologize* for that, even though we often *diligently neglect* the *privilege* of intellect. We possess intellect, or perhaps it could be said that we are represented by intellect.[1]

INTELLECT'S DISGUISES

It is at least instructive that each of the italicized words in the paragraph above is but another "disguise" for the term *intellect*. That is, these italicized words are some of intellect's language cognates, or semantic kinfolk. Even the word *privilege* is intellect's linguistic cousin.[2] That having been said, we have obviously, and so far, encountered two innocent truisms about intellect: Here below, only human beings have intellect, and because of its linguistic "disguises," intellect extends its reach to other experiences—in other words. Intellect has a talent for "hiding" in other words.

Still, there are even more substantive forms of innocent truism about intellect to be discovered. For example, in his large-scale, moral-poetic epic, *Commedia* (to which title Boccaccio cleverly added the modifier *Divina*), Dante Alighieri eloquently dramatized several. For our purposes, two such truisms, resident in two special scenes from that work, particularly invite attention.

First, there is the innocent truism which appears in *Inferno*'s Canto 3, and occurs just after the reader is confronted by that startling proclamation which, like a serpentine, sinuous banner, unfurls before the gates of Hell. Imperatively, that banner decrees that all those who enter within these gates must forsake (*lasciate*) every hope. The meaning could not be clearer—no hope can ever enter Hell, because Hell is hopeless. Not the scantiest, sliver-thinnest wedge, not a microscopic speck of hope can slip undetected through the gates of Hell. Each and every hope—*ogne speranza*—must be forsaken. No exceptions.

Such a metallically bitter message is the verbal ambassador of Hell's relentless, repetitive, everlasting suffocation of the lost, whom Gerard Manley Hopkins once imagined thus: "The lost are like this, and their scourge to be/ . . . their sweating selves; but worse." Moreover, those who penetrate Hell must not only forsake hope—they have already been forsaken by it. Through their admissive betrayals, they have stripped themselves of every hope.

INTELLECTUAL TRUISMS

The first of Dante's innocent truisms about intellect, then, appears just after this opening, as Florentine poet Dante is escorted by Roman poet Virgil toward hidden, desperate inversions of the place. It is then that Dante begins to understand why the wicked gnash their teeth and melt away, and just why Hell is Hell. It is because Hell is that never ceasing orb of all those hopelessly wretched, wailful, keening people—*le genti dolorose*—"who have lost the good of the intellect."³ Grieving and dirgeful, these dolorous figures have already plundered themselves of the privilege of loyal intellect, and thus denudated their humanity. Without the good of the intellect, not even what was once human life could—corruptively, in perdition, or elsewhere, or otherwise—be worth the living. This is Dante's first innocent truism about intellect.

The second truistic scene takes place in *Paradiso*'s Canto 4. There, on a contrastingly pure-air, life-inspiring, and gloriously widening esplanade of Heaven, Dante discovers the veracious semantics of intellect. It is that "never can we satisfy our intellect unless it is illumined by the Truth, beyond which there is no other truth."⁴ Intellect, Dante is telling us, is truly itself only when it grasps, or is grasped by, Truth. For Truth is precisely the "light"⁵ by which intellect "envisions," and by which intellect humanly "lives." Truth is the ontological lens by which intellect "sees" outwardly, as well as the ontological mirror in which it "recognizes" itself. Acknowledging its own powers, intellect then perceives what it truly means to be a human self. This is Dante's second innocent truism about intellect.

NATURE OF INTELLECT

Dante's truisms may help us to disentangle two (not always obvious) facts about the nature of intellect. The first fact about intellect is that it can be corrupted. If it is corrupted, then intellect loses its "good," which is its true power, and only by which power it can properly achieve its identity. The second fact—and, realistically, the more important—is that intellect can be perfected. When intellect is so perfected, or is in the process of being perfected, it truly becomes, as St. Anselm might say, what truly it is—that is, what it ought to be, and what, existentially and providentially, it is meant to be.

The fact that intellect is affirmed in, and by, Truth is a truth which Dante deems eminently worth dwelling on. That same truth about intellect, John Henry Newman likewise deems eminently worth pondering. In *The Idea of a University*, Newman specifically portrays intellect as acting in, and for, and as the true self—wearing no disguise, suffering no interruption, submitting to no betrayal. He portrays intellect as standing forthrightly forward, and being staunchly loyal to its own prerogatives and obligations. Acting as its true self, intellect has "a special claim upon our consideration and gratitude."⁶

Indeed, intellect is what Christian tradition has called the "image of God"—*imago Dei*.[7] Because intellect is created in (and as) the image of God, its real business ought clearly to be with God's images—which is to say, with Truth itself, and with replicas of Truth itself. For Dante—as for St. Augustine, St. Anselm, St. Bonaventura, and John Henry Newman—this process of being "en-truthed" is how intellect properly becomes itself, and properly functions as itself. In this process, intellect is, through transfusive communion, transfigured by its spiritual companion, Truth. Intellect, as the power of human knowing (as opposed to neurological knowing),[8] thus possesses the exclusive, and therefore exclusionary, power to know. Intellect is paradoxically, however, equally capable of trafficking with error and with evil. The difference between truth and error may or may not be plain to some, but Newman instructively observed that "Truth is bold and unsuspicious; want of self-reliance is the mark of falsehood." He also made quite plain that "errors in reasoning are lessons and warnings, not to give up reasoning, but to reason with greater caution. It is absurd to break up the whole structure of our knowledge which is the glory of the human intellect, because the intellect is not infallible in its conclusions."[9]

The truistic power of intellect then, is that it is capable of choosing perfection or corruption. This implies that intellect is intrinsically subject to the moral order, although in early sermons, and in the *Idea*, Newman, by distinguishing between the virtue of intellect and moral virtue, seems (unintentionally, but not for long) to slight this implication.

DUAL POWERS

Christian tradition, therefore, consistently maintains that intellect is empowered freely to accept, or freely to disdain, not merely its own perfection, but (because of that) its own identity—which consequently means its own ultimate destiny. Intellect is free, through Truth, to develop, to enhance, to enlarge its powers. Equally, it is free, through Evil, to deny, to disdain, to reject its own identity, and thus its own Truth. This duality is possible, not because intellect is, of itself—in some corruptive Calvinist sense—a truly corrupted nature. Rather, intellect is agent of the person who incarnates it. Exclusively, it is the person, not the abstract intellect, who is empowered to elect glory or damnation. This is so obvious that it requires constant repetition.

Furthermore, although we sometimes speak of intellect in the abstract, it is never disembodied, and can never appear abstractly. As Newman might say, here below, intellect is always—and can only be—incarnate. Existentially, intellect is always the intellect of a particular human person. Hence, we cannot hold intellect, of itself, or of its nature, accountable for its use or misuse. As its glory arises from its proper engagement, so too, its self-contamination derives from its improper engagement, or mismanagement. Whom we finally hold accountable for the provident—or improvident—use of intellect is the person who incarnates it.

This notion bears iteration, largely because there are those who decry intellect as a deceptive agent, as something contaminated by evil, as something to be held under close watch, under strict guard, under lock and key, like automatic weapons or gelignite. Intellect, allege opponent turnkeys, can never be trusted alone, because "it goes its own way." Such opponents apparently prefer—or at least appeal to—a good heart, not to a good intellect. Do they mean that a heart is more trustworthy, more easily grasped, more symbolically accessible or socially acceptable, perhaps more "clubbable"? Or is it because, in this world, there appear to be more good hearts than good minds? But, all along, such reference is implicitly and factually to what the mind does. The heart, after all, does not think;[10] only intellect does.

Hence, predisposition to provide disjunction between heart and mind may, of course, bespeak some sense of tragic flaw—a Fall—which separates one set of our mental functions from another. There is some sense that some division occurs between our intellectual and our moral actions, in private as well as in public life, in society as also in culture.

DISJUNCTION

John Henry Newman addressed this very issue in a sermon preached at Dublin's Catholic University Church, on 4 May 1856, Feast of St. Monica, mother of St. Augustine.

In that sermon, "Intellect, the Instrument of Religious Training," Newman said that the human mind is perceivable as both intellectual and moral. Intellectually, the mind apprehends truth, where the perfection of intellect is "ability and talent"; morally, the mind apprehends duty, where "perfection of our moral nature is virtue." Even as he puts it this way, there already seems to be division, because Newman makes this telling point:

> And it is our great misfortune here, and our trial, that, as
> things are found in the world, the two are separated, and in-
> dependent of each other, that where power of intellect is,
> there need not be virtue; and that where right, and goodness,
> and moral greatness are, there need not be talent. It was not
> so in the beginning; not that our nature is essentially differ-
> ent . . . but that the Creator, upon its creation, raised it above
> itself by a supernatural grace, which blended together all its
> faculties, and made them conspire into one whole, and act
> in common towards one end; so that, had the race continued
> in that blessed state of privilege, there would never have
> been distance, rivalry, hostility between one faculty and an-
> other. It is otherwise now; so much the worse for us—the
> grace is gone; the soul cannot hold together; it falls to pieces;
> its elements strive with each other."[11]

In Newman's words, we can hear the echoes of John Donne's "Anniversary," "'Tis all in pieces, all coherence gone"—or a premoni- tion of Yeats's "Second Coming," "Things fall apart; the centre cannot hold." Newman was clearly confronting here, and doing so head-on, that primordial Fall from grace, which Augustine had denominated "original sin." Moreover, Newman's was a phenomenological assess- ment of how human beings actually can, and do, act—not always in their best interests, not always with a sense of their promise, not always with the promise of their potential end. Regrettably, they act with "dis- tance, rivalry, hostility" toward themselves, and toward others. Sigmund Freud never put it so succinctly. Then, Newman continues, "You find in one man, or one set of men . . . the acknowledged reign of passion or ap- petite; among others, the avowed reign of brute strength and material re- sources; among others, the reign of intellect; and among others . . . the more excellent reign of virtue."[12]

OPPOSITIONS

In this sermon, Newman is addressing students of the Catholic Univer- sity, and is speaking not only as Rector of the University but also as pastor of its population. He is counseling the young person who comes to "years of discretion, and begins to think," and, in thinking, realizes that there is intense factional warfare being waged "in his own breast."

There, lie opposing emotions and mental forces—"appetite, passion, secular ambition, intellect, and conscience"—all attempting, and at the same time, to seize the soul of the unsuspecting. Newman knew that it is difficult for a young person to be faced with such internecine warfare in his or her own soul, especially because there is no easy solution to the difficulty. A solution requires courage, commitment, and determination. Newman then advances the telling point: "It comes to be taken for granted that they [the opposing mental-emotional forces] cannot be united, and it is commonly thought, because some men follow duty, others pleasure, others glory, and others intellect, therefore that one of these things excludes the other; that duty cannot be pleasant, that virtue cannot be intellectual, that goodness cannot be great, that conscientiousness cannot be heroic; and the fact is often so, I grant, that there is a separation, though I deny its necessity."[13]

Uncovering this simple truth, Newman also reveals that there is, indeed, no intrinsic necessity to exclude moral from intellectual experience. Surely, each time we speak of intellectual honesty, do we do not include in that phrase the expectation that moral activity is the condition of intellectual activity? And do we not also implicitly admit that intellectual honesty is as important as honest intellection? Do we recognize thereby that it is moral action which elevates intellectual activity, and conversely, that it is intellectual exertion which ennobles moral performance?

Of course, Newman understands that, while there may be conflict between, there may also be confluence of, intellectual and moral needs. And this, he says, is because young men, "are not only moral, they are intellectual beings; but, ever since the fall of man, religion is here, and philosophy is there; each has its own centre of influence, separate from the other; intellectual men desiderate something in the homes of religion, and religious men desiderate something in the schools of science."[14]

REUNITING AND INTEGRATING

For just such reason, Newman argues, the Catholic Church and the Holy See, in setting up the Catholic University of Ireland, determined "to re-unite things which were in the beginning joined together by God, and have been put asunder by man." Thus, intellect and religion should enjoy equal prestige of action, equal power of access, equal opportunity to converge in human experience. He then asserts:

> I wish the intellect to range with the utmost freedom, and religion to enjoy equal freedom: but what I am stipulating for is that they should be found in one and the same place, and exemplified in the same person. . . . The same individuals to be at once oracles of philosophy and shrines of devotion. It will not satisfy me, what satisfies so many, to have two independent systems, intellectual and religious, going at once side by side. . . . It will not satisfy me if religion is here, and science there, and young men converse with science all day, and lodge with religion in the evening. . . . I want the same roof to contain both the intellectual and moral discipline. Devotion is not a sort of finish given to the sciences; nor is science a sort of feather in the cap . . . an ornament and set-off to devotion. I want the intellectual layman to be religious, and the devout ecclesiastic to be intellectual.[15]

By this declaration, Newman states that sanctity and intellect have an observant relation to life—sanctity more "in the long run," he says, and intellect more "at the moment." He exhorts that we "may excell in intellect as we excell in virtue," because of the principle that intellect should be religious, and devotion should be intellectual.

LINKED BY LOVE

Are we justified, then, in linking Dante's "innocent truisms" with the "innocent observations" of Newman? Yes, because that link, indeed, may lie in the centrality which both ascribe to love. Explicitly stated in Dante, implicitly certain in Newman, love becomes the key to human life as well as the secret of Divine Life. Because love is an intellectual act, its convergence with intellect, however enigmatically achieved, is also a convergence of the powers of intellect. Movement from intellect to love is only just so much a "Christian truism" as St. John makes it in his Gospel and First Letter. God Who is the Word, Who enlightens every human being, is also God Who is Love.[16] This synonymy of *logos* and *agapē* essentially identifies divine intellect as divine love.

In contrast to the divine eminence of love, those dark, dolorous figures in Dante's *Inferno*, who lack intellect, also lack love, because without the power of intellect there can be no power of love. This also explains why the "lost" are submerged helplessly in hopeless, repetitive misery. Having lost the good of the intellect, they have simultaneously lost the power of love. And, similarly, because they have lost the power of love, they have also lost the good of the intellect.

The protagonist in Georges Bernanos's *Diary of a Country Priest* said it this way: "Hell is not to love any more, Madame. Not to love any more! . . . To understand is still a way of loving. But suppose this faculty which seems so inseparably ours, of our very essence, should disappear! Oh, prodigy! To stop loving, to stop understanding—and yet to live."

For Dante, the relationship between intellect and love seems straightforward enough. No intellect, no love. Conversely, no love, no true intellect. This relation thus implies that intellect cannot rightly and properly act—as intellect—without a valuative moral companion, of which love is the triumphant instance. Because intellect is itself a valuative reality, it is, so to speak, nourished by other valuative realities, as by valuation itself. Thus intellect, although its powers are borrowed by the dialectical and logical force of reason, is never "cold-blooded" and is not as narrowed as reason.[17]

IMAGO INTELLECT

To Newman, as to St. Anselm, intellect, as *imago Dei*, is truly itself only when it does what it ought to do, and is what it ought to be.[18] As *imago Dei*, intellect ought to be in attendance upon love, and mindfully in the service of love, which is intellect's appreciative power. This is the power to respond to valuation—that is to say, to the good. In an early sermon, John Henry Newman puts it this way: "Love, then is the seed of holiness, and grows into all excellences, not indeed destroying their peculiarities, but making them what they are."[19] Newman, then, was aware—as were Augustine and Anselm—that the true meaning of intellect arises from its transformation in love. In love, intellect truly represents itself as *imago Dei*.

We have previously alluded to the allegation—especially popular in times of authoritarian ascendance and anti-intellectual sentiment—that intellect requires a special keeper and strict supervision. Such a view stipulates that intellect must be "reined in" by a heart, a will, a conscience, or, perhaps, a policeman. Truly, the human intellect is a powerful instrument, and no one could sanely deny that. Truly, too, intellect can be used wisely or foolishly—can be enhanced or debased; perfected or corrupted. But, as Dante well knew, evil is not the "good of the intellect." Only the good (however redundant it appears to say it this way) is the "good of the intellect." Thus, intellect cannot afford to confuse good and evil. Indeed, intellect is precisely equipped, by its semantic sovereignty, to recognize the cognitive difference between good and evil. Confusing good and non-good is an intellective as well as a moral cause for woe, as Isaiah (5:20) reminds us: "Woe to those who call evil good, and good evil, who substitute darkness for light."

FINITE IS NOT DEFECTIVE

Once again, we need to say that human intellect is not properly self-subsistent, because it is never "on its own." Its power (we repeatedly emphasize) is that of someone upon whom we ought more realistically to concentrate any censure. As a power and instrument of what is more than itself, human intellect can not, by definition, be its own agent. Rather, it is the agent of the human person, for whom it "speaks." The human person is not so much *other than*, as it is *more than* intellect. As agent of a person, intellect may, regrettably, be engaged unlovingly, but this is through no intellective defect of its own. The point is, intellect is not—of itself or of its nature—defective. While human intellect is finite, finite does not mean defective. If or when intellect is brought to act defectively, or to connive in its own defection, it does not do so necessarily, or by its nature. In the same way, we have said, neither is intellect, of itself cold-blooded or uncaring, neutral or improvident or irreligious—although it may be made to act in any or in all these ways.

Yet, in a clinical sense, and not just through sinful defection, intellect may become pathological. That is, intellect may be subject to distortive conditions of perception or interpretation, or to semantic disconnection with reality.[20] Although there are those who interpret sinful defection as equivalent to clinical deficit, such a judgment is inexact. Sinful defection requires choice and election, for when these are absent, there can be no sin.

Suppose, for example, you are required to seek professional psychiatric intervention. You would not seek such intervention for your intellect, but for yourself. Similarly, suppose my knee develops a sarcoma. I do not say, "My knee has a sarcoma." I say "I have a sarcoma," because the tumor involves all of me, and—though at the moment it may be confined to my knee—it is potentially systemic. The tumor does not just threaten my knee, it threatens my life. It threatens me.

"I" of the Beholder

In comparable language, my intellect is always referable to me. And I, therefore, am the principal who is responsible for my intellectual power. My intellect bespeaks me. In another sense, I may even be said to be responsible to it. Intellect, after all, is a privileged gift; and I am also responsible to that gift, as well as responsible for the integrity of that gift. In keeping with the fact that it is a valuative gift in itself, intellect ought then to be valuatively employed, and employed according to its own (best) nature.

Newman was, of course, keenly aware of how intellect could be dislocated, that is to say, put in the wrong place. He consequently deemed disjunction between intellectual values and moral values a moral disaster. And, the separation of "that union of intellectual and moral influence," he called "the evil of the age."[21]

Newman also understood the instrumentality of intellect and recognized it in all its remarkable power. This is why he cautioned that use of the intellect cannot be regarded as self-sufficiently private, because intellect has relations to other spiritual faculties. No other faculty can perform the tasks for which intellect alone is appropriate. Even conscience—which is clearly, in his words, "a moral sense"—is also, as he says in the same passage, "an intellectual sentiment." Being also "a sense of admiration and disgust," conscience is something more than a moral sense, it is always . . . emotional. . . . This implies that there is One . . . before Whom we are ashamed, whose claims on us we fear."[22]

Verbs of Intellect

Powers of intellect are frequently described in *The Idea of a University*. In one passage, for instance, Newman describes intellect in action-verbs of a clearly executive nature:

> The intellect of man . . . energizes as well as his eye or ear, and perceives in sights and sounds something beyond them. It seizes and unites what the senses present to it; it grasps and forms what need not have been seen or heard except in its constituent parts. It discerns in lines and colours, or in tones, what is beautiful and gives them a meaning. . . . It has a keen sensibility towards angles and curves. . . . It distinguishes between rule and exception . . . assigns phenomena

to a general law, qualities to a subject, acts to a principle, and effects to a cause. In a word, it philosophizes.[23]

If we strip away from this passage everything but the action-verbs, we can explore intellect as that power which

- ☐ energizes
- ☐ seizes
- ☐ unites
- ☐ grasps
- ☐ forms
- ☐ discerns
- ☐ has keen sensibility
- ☐ distinguishes
- ☐ assigns
- ☐ philosophizes

In choosing such verbs to characterize what intellect does, Newman interestingly begins with the verb, energize. To energize is a life-verb, because, strictly speaking, only life-forms have energy to expend.[24] In the somatic order, this is analogous to the way in which electrical current of the sinoatrial node of the human heart—a life form—can energize the human body.[25] Thus describing intellect as an energizer, Newman considers intellect as the initiator of mental activity. It is in this sense that we might compare it to the sinoatrial node which initiates cardiac activity in the body.

From another angle, Newman's action-verbs also include those of seizing-grasping. Curiously, these latter are verbally suggestive of intellect's linguistic root of collecting-gathering (see note 2 in this chapter). To the verbal complex, *seizing-grasping*, Newman also adds other pairs of action-verbs, namely, *uniting-forming*, and *discerning-distinguishing*. Intellect's keen sensibility may, additionally, remind us of how often intellect has been described as an instrument, whose keen-edged sharpness is like that of a scalpel that can dissect cognitive "tissue." Finally, there is that triumphant intellect-verb, *philosophizing*. In many respects, this verb sums up intellect's powers of uniting-forming-distinguishing-discerning-seizing-grasping. But, beneath all of these verbs, there is that verbal descriptor of intellect as the power to energize while, above all of these verbs, there is intellect's cultivated habit of mind to philosophize.[26] For Newman, philosophy seems to be what intellect tends to do best.

INTELLECT AS PHILOSOPHIZER

Consider a complementary passage in which Newman describes how this "philosophical power" reveals "the highest state to which nature can aspire, in the way of intellect," and how intellect can be "disciplined to the perfection of its powers." In this passage, Newman employs terms which are implicitly intellective, but explicitly moral-ethical—and, thus, adjacently intellective—functions. Here he argues,

> the intellect, which has been disciplined to the perfection of
> its powers, which knows, and thinks while it knows, which
> has learned to leaven the dense mass of facts and events with
> the elastic force of reason, such an intellect cannot be partial,
> cannot be exclusive, cannot be impetuous, cannot be at a
> loss, cannot but be patient, collected, and majestically calm,
> because it discerns the end in every beginning, the origin in
> every end, the law in every interruption, the limit in each
> delay; because it ever knows where it stands, and how its
> path lies from one point to another.[27]

It is noteworthy that Newman here uses characterizing-words which, prima facie, appear as not merely intellective verbs and adjectives, but also appear to be associated with emotive-ethical-moral functions. Such, especially is his central affirmative adjective—*patient*.

Patience is of particular interest in this case, if only because St. Augustine characterized it as "the companion of wisdom," and because patience also denotes one of the Fruits of the Holy Spirit.[28] Of the seven adjectives Newman uses in this passage, four are used in a restrictive sense (*partial, exclusive, impetuous*, and *at a loss*) and three in an affirmatively relevant sense (*patient, collected*, and *calm*). In its noun form, patience resonates with apostolic and patristic usage. By far, *patience* is the single term which enhances Newman's rhetorical glossary, and makes evident the specifically Christian association of his intellective terms.

These terms also share emotive and ethical denotations. In addition, thematic pairing of the negative *impetuous*, with the affirmative *calm* provides a polarity plexus, which is suggestive of a network of emotive and ethical significance, and which can be used separately, or together. Another pairing is that of the affirming *collected-calm*, which furnishes an emotive, and not just an ethical context. By contrast, the thematically negative *exclusive-partial* might suggest a methodological failure, as well as an emotive-dysethical deficit, which might herald bigotry or bias. Furthermore, the classification, *at a loss*, seems to have a similar mixture of methodological and emotive force, which might be characteristic, perhaps, of being at the end of one's logical tether.

Practically, then, Newman seems to employ these terms as descriptive powers of intellect. If so, then any assumption that Newman regards intellect as "cold-blooded"—in need of a keeper, apt to "go off on its own"—appears groundless. True, Newman sometimes appears to come down hard on intellect. But he does so mostly before 1845. Finally, we need to notice that Newman is speaking here about the perfection of powers of intellect—that is, about intellect when it is "disciplined to the perfection of its powers." He also meditates on the "influences, which intellectual culture exerts upon our moral nature." Despite essential differences between moral and intellectual acts—on which Newman repeatedly insists—he also sees "how striking is the action of our intellectual upon our moral nature, where the moral material is rich and the intellectual cast is perfect."[29]

LOVE AND INTELLECT

Although in just such a passage as the foregoing Newman appears more explicit than Dante, he nonetheless shares with Dante certain perspectives on intellect. Having made comparably explicit his estimate of the dark side of his own modern world, Newman would doubtlessly join Dante in deploring our modem world and the manner in which it borrows and adopts false assumptions about love and intellect.

If our modem world seems to have little, if any, confidence in intellect, it may only be because it has no patience with love. Rarely does our modem world speak of intellect, unless in skeptical scorn, but it is always talking about "love." Yet its road to "love"—usually more, rather than less, traveled—is not that arduous, rewarding, royal, and heavenly highway that Dante and Newman contemplated. Nor would it be the same itinerary that St. Bonaventura described.

Yet why, one may ask, is Dante's and Newman's view of love and intellect so different, in so many ways, from so many contemporary views? For one thing, Dante was a medieval personality, and, for another thing, Newman was a religious personality. As such, both were likely to have been more familiar with a profounder way than ours of regarding human experience. Although some may protest that Dante's perspective was cruder than ours, or that Newman's was more innocent than ours, both views are true. But it is also true that, in other ways, Dante's and Newman's view of love and intellect are much more refined and more civilized than are our own. We should remind ourselves that, in his *Paradiso* cantos, Dante is in the inspiring company of medieval, or proto-medieval, Church personalities—Augustine, Benedict, Anselm, Thomas, Bonaventura, Bernard of Clairvaux—all of whom gave close, and reverent, attention to the meaning of love and intellect. Remind ourselves, too, that in the generality of his work, Newman had the same Church personalities at both the center and the edge of his mind. Despite minor differences of interpretation, Newman, Dante, and all of these churchly personalities were quite clear about the implications which they all drew from the *imago* text of Genesis-Bereshith (1:26–27). For that text, read in the light of Gospel tidings, signifies a reciprocal relation between divine love and divine intellect. The textual language insistently invites repetition—"Then God said, 'Let us make humankind in the image and likeness of us.'"

GOD AS MODEL

For a medieval personality, such as Dante, and a religious personality, such as Newman, these textual words impose (in several senses of the term) a powerful portrait. To put it with radical simplicity, the biblical portrait implies that God is the model of as well as for, humankind. That Infinite Power Who creates, and Who centers the world, does, at the same time, lovingly "image" Himself in finite humanity. Love and intellect are, therefore, no less than reminders of that Divine Image. In another sense, our sense of love and intellect are images of that Divine Image. Furthermore, love and intellect, being forms of knowing, as well as of self-knowing, reveal how we can create an interpretive and interiorizing knowledge, which is bent on making connections that link the person of self-knowing to more than appearances. Such a life, so interiorized, becomes fully real when it unites itself to what is more than—and transcendent of—self-life. This may partially explain why Newman is able to say that self-knowledge "is at the root of all religious knowledge." And he implies by that statement that genuine self-knowledge is implicitly theological knowledge.

To Newman, God speaks to us "primarily in our hearts," or in our conscience. Yet clearly, without intellect, there can be no conscience. Similarly, without intellect there can be no wisdom. This is to say, conscience and wisdom in the human experience would be impossible without intellect, because human experience would be impossible. Intellect might be considered, as it were, the escutcheon of humanity. But it is more than that, since it is not merely the symbol, it is the reality of the human person. Without intellect, there would be no human soul, since the soul is an intellectual soul. And without the human soul, there could be no humanity.

PROPHET AND APOSTLE

Conscience, indeed, appears as the moral prophet of intellect, as, in like fashion, wisdom appears as the noetic apostle of the intellect. Although intellectual, conscience is clearly not the intellect, but rather its moral power. And wisdom is also not the intellect, but rather the intellect's potential destiny. Conscience and wisdom reflect moral and noetic powers, or functions, of intellect. But they are not reducible to intellect after the fashion of a "nothing but" reduction.

We can say this another way, by means of an analogy of physical functions. For example, sports buffs pretty well know how the human arm works while playing tennis, or while throwing a javelin. Of the deep and superficial elements involved in active working of the arm, three muscle groups signify the dynamics involved—first, at the top, the shoulder-girdling deltoid muscle, and below that, the biceps and triceps of the upper arm. These muscles, in different ways, extend, contract, and flex the arm. They are musculature powers, or functions, of the arm. But they are not reducible to the arm, nor is the arm reducible to them. We cannot say, for example, that the triceps or biceps, or even the deltoid, is "nothing but" the arm, or that the arm is "nothing but" each, or any, of them. None of these muscles can take the place of one another, nor can they take the place of the arm. These are definitely not abstract muscles, but real muscles, and they work together. Without the arm, they could not function, because without the arm, they could not exist.

CONDITIO SINE QUA NON

In roughly similar fashion, we can say that conscience and wisdom could not exist without intellect. Conscience and wisdom are not (we have said) "nothing but" intellect. Rather, conscience and wisdom extend the powers and reach of intellect, which itself is the condition— necessary and sufficient, *conditio sine qua non*—of, in the first place, their actually being conscience and wisdom. Thus, we can say, "No intellect, no conscience," as we might say, "No arm, no muscles." We should add, "No intellect, no wisdom." And this is so because, in human terms, "no intellect" means for us "no human being."

Now conscience, in order to be itself, does not require great intellectual attainment. But it does require intellect, if only because to be human requires intellect. In contrast, wisdom does, in fact, require great intellectual attainment, because such is the definition of wisdom. To acquire wisdom, it is first necessary that one have an intellect. But for wisdom, just having an intellect is not sufficient. Wisdom involves a transformation—a perfection—of intellect. The intellect that has been transformed by and in wisdom must also imply that *something* had to have occurred in and to intellect—whether by grace, or by effort, or by effort in conjunction with grace. Otherwise, there could be no attainment of that height of spiritual-noetic experience that we call wisdom.

Also, without conscience in full flower, there can be no attainment of wisdom. For who can be wise without conscience? And conscience also has it owns forms of growth. But, conversely, we need to add that, like intellect, conscience is subject to possible corruption. Wisdom, however, does not, by definition, suffer corruption, because if it were to become corrupted, it would no longer count as wisdom.

PRIVILEGES OF INTELLECT

Conscience and wisdom are clearly among the privileges of intellect, which is to say, the privilege of being *imago Dei*. Without intellect, there could be neither conscience nor wisdom, in or out of the University. All the more so, without intellect, there could be no University. Newman would be quite sensitive to this claim, because he repeatedly sets it down that the central business of the University is "cultivation of the intellect." And for a similar reason, he quite explicitly defines University as an "imperial intellect"—an empire of intellect.

What, then, it may be asked, is attractive about intellect? And why does it attract us? Similarly, there is the complementary question: What is attractive about love, and why does it attract us?

It may be helpful, once again, to remind ourselves that St. Bonaventura defined humankind as being *capax Dei*, "capable of God," or having a capacity for God. Thus, if we pose questions about the attractive nature of intellect and of love, the answer, in Bonaventura's language, is already within our grasp. In human experience, intellect and love are revelations of the Divine Reality—better, of the Divine Presence, somehow within us—who are *imagines Dei*.

Naturally, there are those who might be tempted to argue that, in saying this, we are just raising intellect up to too high a status, perilously close to summoning before us the tempting sin of human pride—or, conversely, that this might seduce us, complacently, into ignoring the fact of our finitude. Paradoxically, just the opposite would be true. To recognize that we are human embodiments of intellect is, simultaneously, to recognize that we are referents—or images—of God's intellect. We cannot account for ourselves, and thus we cannot, of ourselves, account for our intellect. What would be so disastrously prideful in proclaiming that? And how could we ignore our finitude by expressly glorying in the feat of its capacity to attain God? Or, as St. Thomas would say, its "capacity for beatitude" (see note 1 for this chapter).

Because we do not, cannot, stand on our own (which is our finitude), and because we are enfleshed imitators of love and intellect, our pride would be merely reflective pride in being *imagines Dei*. True, we do know how to sin. But we also know how to love. Perhaps we, as finite, imperfect human beings, would not know how to do the one, unless we also knew how to do the other. The power to know how to sin and how to love illustrates how ambiguous it is to be human. The more important action, however, is to know how to love, since, this, ultimately, is what intellect is all about. Just as St. Paul tells us, "We will never be finished with love" (1 Cor. 13:8). So, we may add that, in learning to love, we will never be finished with intellect.

CHAPTER 3:
CHURCH AND UNIVERSITY

> "The Catholic Church has ever, in the plenitude of her divine illumination, made use of whatever truth and wisdom she has found."

> "To maintain in life and vigour a real University is . . . one of the greatest works, great in their difficulty and their importance, on which are deservedly expended the rarest intellects."

> "University . . . [is] the representative of the intellect, as the Church is the representative of the religious principle."

> "University is an intellectual power, as such, just as the Church is a religious power."

Two institutions loom graphically large in the life, work, and spiritual experience of John Henry Newman. Indeed, they tower at the spiritual center of everything we know about him, whether as Mister Newman, Father Newman, Doctor Newman, or Cardinal Newman.

Newman thought long and diligently about these institutions, insistently meditated on them, consistently spoke of them, and persistently wrote of them. Intermittently, he even dreamed of them. They are Church and University—the one a symbol of conscience, the other, of wisdom. As the central institutions of his life, separately or together, Church and University encouraged Newman's belief in the deeper realities for which they are ambassadors. From his earliest years, they remained with him, being almost at his cradle, and certainly at his grave. They inspired him, uplifted his mind; they made his language sing and his spirit soar. More than institutions, always meaning more than they seemed to mean, they were, for Newman, splendorous reminders of truth.

Yet there were times, before but especially after his conversion to Catholicism, when Church dignitaries and University governors—out of spite, jealousy, envy, bias, or misconstruction—betrayed or deceived him. They doubted his motives, scorned his best efforts, and frustrated his serious plans. And an English papal chamberlain in Rome once called him "the most dangerous man in England."[1] Still, Newman endured such intrusions, obeyed authorities of record, but uncalculatingly girded about himself a simple saintly courage, by which he related not just to political authorities, but to the spiritual realities which those authorities represented.[2]

HOW IT BEGAN

Into a thoroughly English family, attending a thoroughly English church, Newman was born, baptized, and comfortably reared to be, above all, a thoroughly English gentleman.[3] Eldest and brightest of six children of a middle-class banker's family, Newman's English mind and memory were symmetrically patterned upon the glorious language of the English Bible. "I was brought up from a child," he said, "to take great delight in reading the Bible," because English Christianity had become a "Bible religion." Reading the Bible "in Church, in the family, and in private," and learning "portions of the Scripture by heart," imbued "the mind with good and holy thoughts," as "a resource in solitude, on a journey, and in a sleepless night."[4]

ENGLISH BIBLE

Newly sculpted by William Tyndale in 1534, and conflated with the Authorized Version of 1611, the English Bible was Newman's earliest schoolroom. From childhood—he read perfectly at five[5]—to old age, Newman could recite from memory vast stretches of that English Bible, and, throughout his life, he drew upon its treasury of spiritual and linguistic riches. Crafted in Tyndale's "linen words" of "grave majestic English,"[6] the English Bible molded young Newman's precocious vocabulary, just as its biblical scenes, resonant with hovering rhythms, entered into his memory and mind's eye.[7] In that biblical scenery, he saw Matthew's laborers, who "have born the burden and heat of the day," and Luke's "shepherds abiding in the fields"; he attested with Mark that "the spirit is willing, but the flesh is weak," and overheard the rich farmer advise his soul, "Take thine ease, eat, drink, and be merry." He listened as St. Paul warned against the "wages of sin," whose "enticing words" could make the proud "wise in your own conceits," and witnessed the words of St. Paul to doubters that "in him we live and move and have our being," or to the faithful to make "melody to the Lord in your hearts." He persevered with St. Peter "until the day dawn, and the daystar arise in your hearts." How could he forget the riveting simplicity of Tyndale's Twenty-Third Psalm?—"The Lord is my Shepherd, I shall not want." In such magnificent English scriptural prose, etched, as it were, upon eternal copper plate, Newman was inspired by biblical sentiment fused into lively biblical image. Indeed, both sentiment and image had already become the mark of the English Protestant Church.

Newman, age fourteen, was tempted to fancy Paine's antibiblical tracts, and inquisitively to indulge in skeptical bitterness with Hume's anti-Church essays. Abruptly, however, in March 1816, such temptations were shattered by the shocking news that his father's bank, Ramsbottom, Newman, Ramsbottom—squeezed in the post-Napoleonic financial slump—had been forced to close its doors forever. At that dark news, young Newman's treasured sense of family security vanished, like uncertain assets, and he fled into an oppressive and startling wilderness of the soul. Other members of the family, however, took the news in stride, only scurrying in search of less expensive quarters.[8]

COLLEGE AND CRISIS

Family crisis, with its intense emotional stress, had punctured the protective dome of Newman's young life. Yet it may, at the same time, explain why, in the autumn of 1816, young Newman experienced such a deeply felt conversion to the zealously Evangelical-Calvinist wing of the English Church.[9] Coming, as he had come, from a comfortably modest, and modestly uncomplicated Anglican family, such an Evangelical turn seemed a radical change.[10] That same year, young Newman was also introduced to what would become for him the ideal university. On Saturday, December 14, together with his father and the Rev. John Mullens of Piccadilly, Newman traveled to prestigious Oxford, daughter of the more prestigious University of Paris. Accepted there by Trinity College's President, Dr. Thomas Lee, "a courteous and gentlemanlike man" who was also University Vice-Chancellor, Newman "was matriculated as a commoner of that society," and of its "most gentlemanlike college."[11] Trinity, immodestly short of lodging at the time, forced young Newman to postpone formal matriculation until June, 1817.

Young as he was, Newman was clear-headedly ahead of older peers. With a grasp of Euclid well beyond expectation, and a flair for English, Latin, and Greek, he was soon recognized as being academically talented and of unusual promise for further achievement. Within a year, his tutor, Thomas Short, prompted him to enter Trinity's Blount Exhibition, which would guarantee a nine-year scholarship, paying £60 per annum. He won it, of course, and thus became young Scholar of Trinity. Thus enhanced in his standing among students and his popularity among tutors, he was also flattered in his hopes of a public career. His feat likewise encouraged the rising academic expectations of his own College, and he was advanced to a Foundation Scholarship. Young Mr. Newman had nicely settled in to Oxford life.

OXFORD LIFE

He would later write to his youngest brother, Frank, "Here at Oxford I am most comfortable. The quiet and stillness of everything around me tends to calm and lull those emotions which the near prospect of my grand examination, and a heart too solicitous about fame and too fearful of failure, are continually striving to excite. I read very much, certainly, but God enables me to praise Him with joyful lips when I rise, and when I lie down, and when I wake in the night."[12]

Poetic sights and sounds and sentiments of Oxford University thoroughly captivated young Newman, as he walked, or rode, through nearby verdant countryside, or set his stride to the patiently pealing bells of royal Oxford. With close companion, John William Bowden, he rowed, or punted, on the Cherwell and the Isis—nominal disguises worn by the Thames River—from Iffley Lasher to Godstow. Though bent on a secular career, Newman was, by 1817, writing sermons, and apparently also bent towards theology, which "filled his mind and never relaxed its hold." But, simultaneously, and with mysterious apprehension, he felt an implausible invasion of his Oxford tranquility: "Sunday evening bells pealing," he wrote in his journal. "The pleasure of hearing them. It leads the mind to a longing after something, I know not what . . . a longing after something dear to us."[13]

Protracted grinding days of study—eight to ten hours daily—exacerbated Newman's longstanding axial myopia, or nearsightedness, and forced him to wear corrective lenses. Still, despite optical stress and bouts of dental pain, he unhesitatingly knew that he "went to the University with an active mind, and with no thought but that of hard reading." Read he surely did, even when interrupted by recurring toothache, headache, or nagging worry about the financial well-being of his family, for whom, as Trinity Scholar, he was now the financial mainstay. Yet, if he were to fulfill his father's dutiful high hopes of one day commanding a prestigious legal or ministerial post, young Mr. Newman would have to magnify his Oxford career. In his chosen fields of mathematics and classics, he would need to achieve a Double-First Honours Degree. So he stretched himself, and his study hours longer, farther, harder—up to fourteen hours a day.

Two academic years in advance of his age, young Newman was suddenly aware of actually how young he was, and how fast his final exam was approaching. His youth had actually been working against him. "My age was such a stumbling block," he would later say, as he now bitterly detected "the disadvantage of going too soon to Oxford." But he had overreached himself by venturing into geology, mineralogy, chemistry, anthropology, linguistics, the Church Fathers, Edward Gibbon, Walter Scott, and John Locke—topics quite unrelated to his major field of concentration. He had to confess, "My mind is a labyrinth."

Even with such a wide array of annotated reading behind him, a gathering fearful sense of inadequacy began to disturb his days and dreams. He also carried the burden of others' expectations—they would settle for nothing short of a brilliant academic success. Abruptly, unexpectedly, however, he was summoned before his time to the final exam. Psychologically off stride, he felt he could not be at his best. Stress had at last achieved that disaster which had haunted him, and which he had tried his best to avoid.

Under the Line

Much later, in an abstract, distancing, third-person narrative, Newman quixotically recorded the convoluted feelings of a sensitive nineteen-year-old, who, unwittingly, had asked far too much of himself: "At his final examination in November 1820, at which alone honours were given, he stood for the highest, in both classics and mathematics, and suffered an utter breakdown, and a seeming extinction of his prospects of a University career. . . . When the class list came out, his name did not appear at all on the Mathematical side of the Paper, and in Classics it was found in the lower division of the second class of honours, which at the time went by the contemptuous title . . . 'Under-the-line.'"[14]

Despite discomposure, Newman's university career was by no means at an end. He still held his Trinity exhibition scholarship, and he was prepping private pupils. He was supporting himself and his family—including his youngest brother, Frank, just then coming up to fee-laden Oxford. But, with a sense of promise and his usual naive buoyancy, and in spite of his under-the-line exam, he had a clear faith in his own powers. We can test this assumption by measuring the exuberant tone with which he wrote his sisters, just three weeks and two days after his unsuccessful exam: "I have brought home for my amusement the original Greek of Aeschylus, and have begun learning his choruses by heart. I have some thoughts of setting one or two of them to music, then I have to compose a concerto, then to finish the treatise on Astronomy, part of which I took up for my examinations, then to peruse a treatise on Hydrostatics, then Optics, Euripides, Plato, Aristophanes, Hume, Cicero, Hebrew, Anatomy, Chemistry, Geology, Persian, and Arabic Law. I could mention many other things. I do not know what to say more, indeed my last sentence was so pithy that it is sufficient to make up for a short letter."[15]

This letter reveals more than it appears to say, and provides a sympathetic peruser much to think about. It also shows how easily a gifted person—but one with a weaker mind than Newman's—might easily have thinly spread his attention, like butter on bread, over such a wide array of "viewy" topics. Yet it mattered not that Newman had done poorly on his final exam, nor that he had thereby forfeited a chance at a Trinity Fellowship. He still nursed a deep ambition to attain some sort of Fellowship at an Oxford college. Like his mirror image, Charles Reding in his later novel, *Loss and Gain*, Newman, doubtless often, and from an Oxford height, looked "down into the deep, gas-lit dark-shadowed quadrangles," and wondered "if he should ever be a Fellow of this or that College, which he singled out from the mass of academical buildings."[16]

In November 1821 (so much happens in November in Newman's life, just as in Descartes'), "he conceived [he later wrote] the audacious idea of standing for a fellowship at Oriel." This was a time when

Oriel College had become "the object of ambition of all rising men in Oxford," and "the acknowledged centre of Oxford intellectualism."[17] Although it got its common name from its upper-storey oriel, or gold-encrusted, corbeled bay window, Oriel's official title was impressive— "The House of the Blessed Mary the Virgin in Oxford," given at its founding in 1324 by Adam de Brome, Rector of St. Mary the Virgin Church, Clerk of the Chancery, and Edward II's Almoner.[18]

No matter how dimly he may have been aware of it, Newman grasped the clear fact that he possessed precisely the kind of intellectual force of mind and brilliance of talent which Oriel was seeking. With interests far beyond those of the typical school-successful candidate, and gifted with intellectual élan, his mind was alive. He knew how to think for himself, and he fused wide and scrupulously annotated reading with an urge to inquire. He had a sense of exactitude, a resplendent imagination, a prowess of attainment, and a genius for language and rhetorical expression. He possessed, in short, a perfection of intellect. Sensing what the future might bring, he wrote to his father on 15 March 1822, "I think (since I am forced to speak boastfully) few have attained the facility of comprehension which I have arrived at from the regularity and constancy of my reading, and the laborious and nerve-bracing and fancy-repressing study of Mathematics, which has been my principal subject."[19]

Readers of *The Idea of a University* will immediately catch those words—*comprehension, regularity, constancy, laborious*—which are words of method, as well as of attitude. Projected geometrically against a disciplinary background, they convey an Englishman's endorsement of nerve-bracing and fancy-repressing study, and an Englishman's appreciation of an ethnic moral and empirical imperative. Three days after the letter to his father, he confided, in a secret memorandum what appears to be unconditional conviction: I think I have a great chance of succeeding. . . . When I was going up for my degree examination every day made my hopes fainter, so now they seem to swell and ripen as the time approaches."[20]

FELLOWSHIP

A five-day examination to determine the recipient of the Oriel Fellowship began on Holy Saturday, 6 April 1822, and concluded on Thursday, April 11. Astride a hard wooden bench, during eight- and nine-hour days, which were illumined only by sunlight and a sandwich lunch, Newman, with ten other equally ambitious candidates in the room, wrote doggedly, but brilliantly. The exam confronted candidates with challenging English essays to be spirited into felicitous Latin, and with dense Latin to be resurrected in masterly English prose. There were sight-translations of nine refractory Greek and Latin authors, two dozen prickly essay topics in philosophy, and demonstrations in logic and mathematics. Emotionally uncertain or mentally querulous, with a back inflamed by pain, Newman probably rose several times from that hard, rebellious bench, just to walk and stretch. Yet, he was also "much comforted" in this University exercise by a welcoming verbal reminder of the Church, as etched upon a nearby Oriel window. The words and sentiment were simple—*Pie repone te*—something like, "Reserve yourself devoutly in the confidence of the Lord."

TURNING POINT

Results of the examination were published (but privately conveyed to Newman) on Friday, April 12, the "turning point of his life," which would live long in Newman's memory, and would be celebrated every subsequent year. That day, Newman joyfully inscribed in his diary, "I have this morning been elected Fellow of Oriel." To his father, he giddily confided, "I am just made Fellow of Oriel. Thank God!" The news spread rapidly, causing Trinitarians to tremble in merriment. "The bells were set ringing from three towers (I had to pay for them)," he recalled. One Trinity Tutor, reckless with delight, wrote the Newmans to detail the jolly news: "In point of emolument it is great; in point of character it is immortality."[21] Newman had just turned twenty-one years old.

Now lifetime Fellow of Adam de Brome's Oriel, Newman would be carefully nurtured in University and Church endeavor. Richard Whately, lately (before his marriage) resident Tutor at Oriel, and later Archbishop of Dublin, would take Newman in hand, and stiffen him with Logic. Dr. Whately, Newman later wrote, "emphatically, opened my mind, and taught me to think and use my reason . . . taught me to see with my own eyes and to walk with my own feet." There was also Edward Hawkins, later Provost of Oriel, who challenged Newman's rhetorical skills. As Newman later said, Dr. Hawkins, "was the first who taught me to weigh my words, and to be cautious in my statements. He led me to that mode of limiting and clearing my sense in discussion and in controversy, and of distinguishing between cognate ideas, and of obviating mistakes by anticipation. I gained from Dr. Hawkins . . . the doctrine of Tradition."[22]

TWO INSTITUTIONS

From the time of his teenage conversion, holiness had come to claim a central place in Newman's life, so it is not surprising that he would make the Church a spiritual preoccupation. On Trinity Sunday, 13 June 1824, he was ordained Deacon, and the following year, 29 May 1825, he was ordained Priest in the Anglican communion. Simultaneously, he was entering on a solid academic career, and he would continue to grow in both vocations. In University experience, he was made Dean and Bursar, and Vice-Principal at St. Alban's Hall, Oriel Tutor at age 25, and Oxford University Examiner at age 26. He wrote and published scholarly articles. He preached at the tiny church of Over Worten, and then was named Curate of St. Clement's, where he often gave sermons twice weekly. Later, he preached at Adam de Brome's University Church of St. Mary the Virgin, of which he soon became Vicar. Also, in the decade from 1833, Newman was the acknowledged intellectual leader of Oxford's Tractarian Movement, which itself was a force for change in the English Church, and most especially at Oxford, the Anglican University. Already "in his blood," Church and University had now combined to be his sacred and singular vocation.

That binary vocation certainly developed and enlarged Newman's mind and spirit, as he developed from teenage "carelessness" to Calvinist Christianity, then from Evangelicalism to Anglican Christianity in his twenties, and as he advanced, once again, in his thirties toward the Anglo-Catholic and Sarum heritages of the English Church. He was arriving at a productive and happy stage of his life, both publicly and privately. He was consulted widely, and became a figure of consequence in English life.

Still, just beneath the satisfying surface of a satisfying life, there grew slowly, steadily, a dark and mute uneasiness. Serious student of Patristic writings, Newman had been sorting through the controversies of the early Church. One day, suddenly, looking through the Christian glass of schismatic disputes, Newman was jolted as he "saw my face in that mirror." Stretched before him was an open vista of sacred history, whose meaning he immediately knew, whose import he rapidly sensed. It would mean a wrenching away, a painful parting of friends, a loss of place in the English Church and at Anglican Oxford, "to which I was bound by so many strong and tender ties."

THE ROAD AHEAD

Newman had often mused on the springtime resurrection of Oxford snapdragons, as they grew "on the walls opposite my freshman's rooms." So many years he had taken them "as the emblem of my own perpetual residence even unto death in my University," and had even put the sentiment to verse: "Then well might I / In college cloister live and die." Of himself he wrote, "He never wished anything better or higher than . . . 'to live and die a fellow of Oriel.'" Often enough, the night air had carried the joyful-plaintive pealing and tripling of Oxford's chanticleer bells, leading his mind "to a longing after something, I know not what." Equally often, the silences of Oxford reminded him of its ancient delights. Yet that once-bright historical dome of academic happiness was turning darker, as "the stars of this lower heaven were one by one going out."[23]

Gathering clairvoyance about the dubious identity of the English Church was also a clarifying, oracular insight into the darkened edges of his soul. Long bent towards a sacramentally one, truly holy, and apostolically catholic Church of Christendom, Newman was, all that doubtful while—subliminally but inevitably—advancing on the eternal road towards Rome. He implored the help which God had bestowed on Joseph (Gen.-Ber. 41:51), and sought, with the Psalmist, "to forget his people and his father's house" (Ps. 45:10).[24] The final breach with his Anglican past came on the rainy evening of 9 October 1845. Anglican Rev. Mr. Newman became Catholic Mr. Newman.[25] At loss were his academic comfort at the university of his dreams and an ambiguous eminence in the Anglican Church. At gain were the True Faith and an equally ambiguous status in the historical Church of Catholic Christianity.

NEW LIFE

Although Newman's conversion was the beginning of a new life, that life would be curiously analogous to the old. He would, of course, deepen his understanding of the Church, and broaden his intuitions about the University. Within six years of his conversion to Roman Catholicism—he was now ordained Catholic priest, and elected Superior of the English Oratorians at Birmingham—Newman accepted an unexpected appointment as Rector of Dublin's about-to-be established Catholic University. With the precision which marked the seven days of creation, however, he precisely restricted his tenure there to seven years, 12 November 1851 to 12 November 1858.

The first important task of the new Rector, The Very Reverend Doctor John Henry Newman, D. D. (he had been awarded Doctor of Divinity at Rome), was to honor a request made by Roman-trained, soon-to-be Irish Primate, Archbishop Paul Cullen, to "give us a few lectures on education."

To Archbishop Cullen,[26] the idea of "lectures" might finesse a plan to encourage the Irish faithful to attend the new Catholic University, by his simply discouraging attendance of the faithful at the local Queen's Colleges, which had been inaugurated in 1845 by the British government. Dr. Cullen's expected triumph in such a matter would, at a single stroke, eliminate the dreaded "irreligious mixed education" of Catholics and Protestants, and thus thwart the discomforting stratagem of Her Majesty's "duplicitous" government. To other Irish bishops, however, the idea of "lectures" might also serve a covert objective of inaugurating an Irish institution, thus denying the hated Brits a further assault on their Irish nation, which, since Henry II in 1171, had been occupied by English overlordship. Also (the bishops might muse), would there really be any need, aside from the name, for a University? Better, a lay seminary, or, why not just a religious college?—enough to check inflated ambitions of the Irish middle class. Such camouflage sadly betrayed the Irish episcopate's dreaded fear of unintentionally developing an enlightened Irish laity.

A FEW LECTURES

Yet to Newman, lectures would mean something quite different. Here was an opportunity for him to state, eloquently and prophetically, just what a University really is. This might be especially helpful, since in Ireland there were apparently few who had any notion of what University meant. His sensitive knowledge of Oxford both personal and historical, could also serve a wider and a wiser purpose to articulate the significance, intent, objectives, and integrity of a University. Simultaneously, he could oppose any narrow-minded clerical subterfuge. More importantly, he could clearly demonstrate the claim that a University enlarges the power and privilege and promise of the human mind.

To Newman, showing how a University conducts its professional and spiritual affairs, how it organizes its curriculum, and what exactly that curriculum should be, seemed a significant goal. Defining those special, higher purposes of human destiny, towards which University students could be inspired, would round out what Newman had already expressed in his anti-Utilitarian "Tamworth" articles in the London Times. But in lectures, there would also be a chance to say more. By proposing just how, with enlightened governance, a University can inspire its faculty—in order, more fundamentally, to inspire its students—appeared to Newman a task worth the effort of undertaking. Effort, indeed, these lectures would surely cost him, as he made known to his friends, both then and later. These lectures would be the hardest thing that he had ever done.[27]

UNIVERSITY INTELLECT

Reflected in the mirror of the University, Newman discerned the pledge to shape and cultivate the human intellect, and according to a promise for which, all along, the intellect had been destined. In that same mirror, Newman also perceived the nature of the University as an institution possessed of imperial powers of intellect, which could extend its range and rule of mind to all who were touched by it.

Such a vision of the University, Newman rhetorically unveiled at the Exhibition and Concert Rooms of Dublin's Rotunda, on five successive Mondays, from 10 May until 7 June 1852. The delivered lectures consisted of half his ten planned discourses on education, first appearing in periodic pamphlets, and then in book form on 3 February 1853, reprinted in 1859, as *Discourses on the Scope and Nature of University Education*. But in 1873, Newman republished these *Discourses*, now become nine, together with ten chapters of his *Essays and Lectures on University Subjects*, in a two-part single volume, with the momentously memorable title, *The Idea of a University*. That title went through nine editions, with subsequent appearances simply labeled "new edition."

Of all the myriad educational tracts the world has ever known, wherever or whenever written, however or whenever published, Newman's *The Idea of a University* stands forth, preeminently, as the most eloquent, incisive, brightest illustration of the educative possibilities of human beings. As if from some great cascading cataract of eloquence, Newman's vision of intellect flows through that work, revealing, in its course, what no other educational tract has ever before, or ever since, attempted to portray. What it portrays is an image of how the human mind and spirit—intellect—can ideally be transformed to that state which has ever been its destiny to fulfill. This work suggests major questions about the University, such as these:

> What, beyond circumstantial pomp of raiment and ritual, is a University?
>
> What, beyond professorial ranks, academic inventories, investment trusts, and clerical haste, is the real business of a University?
>
> What can be (what *should* be) the University's ultimate effect upon its "people"—students, faculty, staff, graduates, administrators, overseers? And upon its "environment"—society and the world?

As *The Idea of a University* unfolds, it becomes clear that, through liberal education, the University can inspire, in a heretofore unimagined manner, all those who enter into its work. Newman's image of the University—particularly by reason of its enormous power to reshape human minds—sheds new light upon the spiritual implications of that institution. But one other question is also implied. It is this: How, if at all, would the transformative powers of the True University relate to the transformative prerogatives of the True Church?

IMPLICIT LINKAGE

To explore these questions, we need to reach back, beyond the text of the 1873 *Idea*, and mentally enter into the environment of the 1852 *Discourses*, just as Newman gave, and first published them. We particularly need to dwell on the original Discourse V in its historical and ideological setting. It may then become possible to discern something which, over the intervening years, seems to have gone largely unremarked—something which bears exactly upon the spiritual connection between Church and University.

The original Discourse V—which Newman delivered in Dublin's Rotunda on that last Monday session, 7 June 1852—was for various reasons excluded from later editions.[28] Entitled "General Knowledge Viewed as One Philosophy,"[29] the original Discourse V, as it first appeared in the 1853 *Discourses on the Scope and Nature of University Education*, differentiates the seriousness of the True University from the geniality of its utilitarian counterpart. And this is done in the context of an accompanying appendix, which, almost symmetrically, differentiates the True Church from its feel-good alternative. The True University, Newman declares here, is known for the seriousness and universality of its curriculum. For, unless all serious academic subjects are accorded their rightful place in the University curriculum, "not to be at peace is to be at war." War occurs whenever a University fails to bring together, within its intellectual circle, all sciences, including theology. As Newman expresses it, "Take away one of them, and that one so important in the catalogue as Theology, and disorder and ruin at once ensue. There is no middle state between an equilibrium and chaotic confusion; one science is ever pressing upon another, unless kept in check; and the only guarantee of Truth is the cultivation of them all. And such is the office of a University."[30]

The True University, furthermore, is not a monadic but a poladic institution—that is, in it, there are many different and self-supportive intellectual fibers woven into both its design and its jurisdiction. It is just such jurisdiction, Newman will later say, which constitutes the University as an imperium, with extended rule and responsibility. The True University has, although in a caring, considerate manner, command over all sciences. Thus it "is the home, it is the mansion-house, of the goodly family of the Sciences, sisters all, and sisterly in their mutual dispositions."

But, there is always a danger in determining just how, and by what rule, to integrate University studies. The specific identity of this rule consequently poses a danger of disconnection. For there are those who forget that "ideas are the life of institutions," or that the human mind "is ever seeking to systematize its knowledge," or "to find a science comprehensive of all sciences." And there are those who, amid such competing ideas, wish to avoid complexity, simply by adopting "the completeness and precision of bigotry."[31]

CONSULTING NATURE

Because of his admiration of John Locke, it should not be surprising that Newman approaches the issue of University education in a somewhat Lockean manner, and thus initiates his analysis by "inquiring of Nature," or by "soliciting" Nature's response. Just as Locke might also do, Newman seeks to determine how the University fits the demands or requirements of human nature. In a different context, Newman will argue that "a University does but contemplate a necessity of our nature . . . [which is] the order and gravity of earnest intellectual education."[32] In the original Discourse V, with a revealing twist, Newman says that he will "adopt a method founded in man's nature and the necessity of things, exemplified in all great moral works." By having recourse to the nature and necessity of education, Newman delineates the coherence of the True University:

> We start with an idea, we educate upon a type; we make use, as nature prompts us, of the faculty, which I have called an intellectual grasp of things, or an inward sense, and which I shall hereafter show is really meant by the word "Philosophy." Science itself is a specimen of its exercise, for its very essence is this mental formation. A science is not mere knowledge, it is knowledge which has undergone a process of intellectual digestion. It is the grasp of many things brought together in one, and hence is its power. . . . Imagine a science of sciences, and you have attained the true notion of the scope of a University. . . . There is an order and precedence and harmony in the branches of knowledge one with another, as well as one by one, and . . . to destroy that structure is as unphilosophical in a course of education, as it is unscientific.[33]

In the nineteenth century, Nature was viewed, emotionally and technically, as a central category of appeal, to which both artists and scientists could dedicate energies and careers. In everyday consensus, Nature's exclusive portraitist and—because of his *Principia*—the foremost architect of the Science of Nature (who always had the last word) was Sir Isaac Newton (1643–1727). But Newton's theory of celestial mechanics you will recall, was also a specialty of Newman's under-graduate reading at Oxford, and he had studied it in detail. Newman could knowledgeably concur with his contemporaries in recognizing that Newton had attributed to the Universe a new and commanding sense of coherence. In Newton, then, Newman had at his disposal an indisputable model on which to draw. Just as Newton attributed coherence to the Universe, so too, Newman could metaphorically attribute coherence to the University curriculum.[34]

CIRCLE OF LEARNING

To the coherence of a scientific curricular structure, Newman would add the appeal of a classical tradition of the harmonic circle of knowledge. This traditional encyclopedia, "circle of learning," or "circle of the sciences," provided him an additional metaphoric force to his argument for coherence in the University, wherein "we form and fix the Sciences in a circle and a system, and give them a centre, and a name."[35]

In the utilitarian University, in contrast, sciences "wander up and down" in "helpless confusion," because in such an environment they have no center and no aim. But, since all sciences together represent the unity of physical reality, only when these sciences are together can they achieve a replicating reality of balance and coherence. Delete one such science, and "disorder and ruin ensue." The "truth" of the sciences is therefore in their coherence, one with another.

With this thought, Newman portrays the University curriculum as a fusion of classical harmony and scientific structure. In a single flourish, he unites the University in a binomial image of harmonic structure and structural harmony. Here, noetic harmony among curricular subjects reflects the ontological structure of the universe. As the University borrows its intellectual coherence from the "circle of sciences," so also the University's choice to include in its curriculum all knowledge reveals fidelity to that same coherence.

UNIVERSITY AS UNIVERSE

In Newton's celestial system, the Universe attained an unsurpassed mathematical coherence.

By metaphorically borrowing such coherence, Newman might also ascribe to the True University a rule of order, consistency, uniformity of purpose, and simplicity. Like the macrocosmic planetary system of the Newtonian Universe, everything in Newman's microcosmic University can explain—or be explained by—everything else. The True University thus becomes as self-assuring as is the Universe. In the True University, every curricular element has its intellectual place, and there is place in the curriculum for every intellectual element.

This Newman-Newton comparison can be carried further. Just as in the Newtonian Universe, every mass attracts, or is attracted by, another mass, so also, in the True University, every intellectual element attracts, or is attracted by, every other intellectual element. The True University is "a circle and system" which has "a centre, and an aim."[36] Moreover, in Newton's Universe, every mass attracts, or is attracted by, another mass, with a force varying directly as the product of their masses, and inversely as the square of the distance between them. Newton's gravitational constant, G, is such that, the greater—more "important"—a mass, the greater the attraction. Analogically, in Newman's True University, the more important an intellectual element, the more it "attracts" or "governs" other sciences. By the University's curricular balance and harmony, as in Newton's third law, for every intellectual force there is an intellectual counterforce, which thereby maintains balance.[37]

In respect of such curricular balance and harmony, Newman's University is thereby fundamentally different from the utilitarian counterfeit university. Whereas the utilitarian institute may be a workshop for "picking up a trade," or "feeling good," or "being entertained," the True University is a place for the "perfection" of intellect. The utilitarian counterfeit should, therefore, not be mistaken for its better. As Newman put it, "Do not say, the people must be educated, when, after all, you only mean, amused, refreshed, soothed, put into good spirits and good humour, or kept from vicious excesses."[38]

ORGANIC PRINCIPLE

Unlike the utilitarian institution, the True University is a serious institution, whose work can never be painless. For true learning, as Aristotle says, always involves pain—a point dramatically underscored by a Greek chorus, which warns that understanding comes only by way of suffering—($\pi\acute{a}\theta\epsilon\iota$ $\mu\acute{a}\theta o\varsigma$). Also, unlike the utilitarian institution, the True University is based on a principle of universal public judgment, as opposed to "excesses of private judgment," as in Protestantism and political Liberalism.[39] Such "private judgment" makes itself known through discordant actions "of committees and boards, composed of men, each of whom has his own interests and views." Further, in contrast to the True University, the utilitarian institution "is an accumulation from without, not the growth of a principle from within." It is "a sort of bazaar or hotel, where everything is showy, and self-sufficient, and changeable." It is thus not a vitally organic institution. Its committees and boards, having lost, as Newman says, "philosophical comprehensiveness," have thereby "lost the idea of unity, because they have cut off the head of a living thing, and think it is perfect."[40]

Perhaps instinctively, Newman understood that true learning does not bloom unbidden, nor can it be copied from a textbook. He certainly knew that wisdom cannot be created by, or in, committee. Long before his Tamworth Reading Room letters,[41] Newman was familiar with the educational plans of the Utilitarians. Their attacks on Oxford, which Newman outlines in the early pages of the *Idea*, had been concerted by northern wizards of the *Edinburgh Review*, who argued that the purpose of the University should be to prepare students to be "practical," "acquire a skill," and "fill a job." Such wizardly reasoning was naturally political, and had, therefore, acquired for the Utilitarians the popularity of English political theater.

TWO VERSIONS

Educational business, as promised and premised in Utilitarian theory, would in the first place be as easy as setting up a fruit stand. By contrast, the educational business of the True University is to enable students to enlarge, develop, and enlighten their minds, and thus humanity. Although mankind is what used to be an animal—and, in part, retains a patch of that heritage[42]—the task of satisfying human intellectual needs is quite distinct from that of satisfying a primate's utilitarian needs.

Neither expedience, nor simple experience, should be mistaken for education. Quite the contrary, for as Newman points out, education[43] "is a higher word; it implies an action upon our mental nature and the formation of a character; it is something individual and permanent, and is commonly spoken of in connexion with religion and virtue." Were it is assumed that the University is merely an academic music hall for the amusement of the human animal, or a tool employed politically to blunt the sharp edges of social discontent, or merely a vocational resource, then the University would already have betrayed its traditional historical purpose and obligation. Moreover, there could be any number of other, less costly amusements, which need not themselves incur the expense of academic pretension.

Here, then, Newman points up the fundamental issue: Is the University established in order to placate and amuse? Or, contrariwise, is it founded in order to raise up the level of human intellectual achievement? If we mean truly to undertake University education, Newman argues, we must gird our expectations in serious effort, and prepare for the achievement of knowledge, not just the acquisition of information. Without knowledge, there can be no approach to the highest levels of human understanding. Because it is alive, the mind is not a storage trunk, or a filamentous fungus which increases by "an accumulation from without." Because it is alive, the mind will grow and enlarge by "metabolizing" its special nutrients—knowledge and truth.

THEMATIC CODE

Newman's 1852 Discourse V was focused on University education. By adding an illustrative appendix—although apologizing for its inadequacy—Newman also appears to refocus his argument: "I am very sensible of the meagreness of the following illustrations of the main principles laid down in the foregoing Discourses; but, as I am so situated that I cannot give the time or labour necessary for satisfying my own sense of what they ought to be, I avail myself of such as happen to be at hand or on my memory."[44] If we view this 1852 appendix, as it originally appeared with the original Discourses, including its previously published sermon, we may intuit a special and revised emphasis, one that implicitly reshapes Newman's argument. Like the original Discourse V itself, this appendix was subsequently discarded, because no longer needed. Hence this (intuited) emphasis may no longer seem obvious. But here it may be worth pausing to review the publishing history of the *Discourses*.

ESTABLISHING PRIORITY

In the two decades which separate the February 1853 publication of the *Discourses on the Scope and Nature of University Education* from the appearance in 1873 of *The Idea of a University*, something of note seems to have occurred. At first glance, *The Idea of a University* appears as no more than a mere re-titling of a set of previously published lectures, since in the book trade, re-titling is often devised to stimulate wider sales and a new readership. But here, there seems to be not so much a re-titling as a reconceptualization, which might ultimately involve a substantive reinterpretation of the lectures themselves. As clearly stated in the original title, *Discourses on the Scope and Nature of University Education*, Newman's original concern seems to have been with University education and not with the University. But, as an expert on development, Newman might well appreciate that ideas, when they are alive, always grow, since growth is the inevitable sign of life. It may (or it may not) be mere speculation to suggest that, during the two decades which separate the original *Discourses* on education from the final discourses on the University, a new accent is discernible. It is an accent which, developmentally, shifts the description of a process, which is what education is, to delineation of an organism or agency—the University—by which that process of higher education is created. Thus, educatively, in 1873 the University suddenly seems to be the focus (as, institutionally, it is the locus) of the process of higher education.[45]

NEW ACCENT

Perhaps only an idea of a University can properly explain the meaning of the educative process. Only the University represents an organic agency of higher education, and by which education can be "existentialized." That is, only an idea of a University can configure the idea of higher education, which does not—because it cannot—exist in the abstract. Education requires a local habitation and a name. Thus the conceptual development of the idea of education, as encompassed in the idea of a University—and as here proposed—may also bespeak a psychological development. If so, attention can now be focused on framing the idea of education as a University-idea. Whatever higher education means, it can only take place in a special—therefore specialized and conditionalizing—setting. This condition suggests an interrogative complex, which prompts contextual questions: What is that setting? What happens in that setting? Why does it happen in that setting?

REFOCUSING

By means of conceptual and psychological refocusing, as embodied in the contrasts of the 1852 appendix, Newman appears to have refined—and thus to have redefined—higher education from four institutional perspectives. This redefinition (1) ratifies the True University as the agency and the symbol of higher education, (2) represents the University's companion institution as the True Church, (3) depicts the utilitarian university as symbol of impostrous education, and (4) characterizes a spurious religion—"the religion of the day"—as allied with an impostrous church and university.

The original Discourse V states its view of University education[46] in a series of theses:

1. Knowledge is the direct end of University education.
2. All branches of knowledge are the subject matter of University education.
3. Mere acquirement is not real knowledge.
4. The branches of knowledge form one whole and are complements of each other.
6. Knowledge under this aspect is philosophy or liberal knowledge.
7. Liberal knowledge acts partly on the side of Christianity, partly against it.

BINARY MATCHING

It is more important, however, to notice that the original Discourse V, taken together with the appendix of 1852, bespeaks a more direct association of Church and University. Re-imaging these institutions must necessarily reimage the meaning of religion and education. Then, taken in conjuction with Discourse V, the 1852 appendix may provide an implicit binary contrast between, on the one hand, True Church and True University, and on the other, their competitors—utilitarian feel-good church and feel-good university. Entangled in such a contrast, there may be an implicating knot which binds together the parallel spiritual tasks of True Church and True University. One remaining question requires response: Do these institutions—True Church and True University—express concordance of spirit? Or are they irreconcilable adversaries—

the one rootedly moral, the other radically intellectual? If irreconcilable, would this also imply that moral and intellectual concerns must, as Sir Thomas Browne might say, be "dispos'd to live in divided and distinguished worlds"?

But, indeed, there is some indirect affirmation of concordance between True Church and True University, and it may be discernible in the way in which Newman opposes, on one side, the utilitarian university's English pleasantries of "good cheer" and "take your ease," and on the other, the True University's serious endeavor. Such comparison is also indirectly mirrored in the cheery affability of the feel-good church, as against the sacred seriousness of the True Church. The True Church is a sacred society, not a social club, just as the True University is a serious commonwealth of learning, engaged in perfection of the intellect, and not a practical diversionary amusement.

RELIGION OF THE DAY

Affirming the seriousness of the True University, the 1852 appendix has already provided a mirror image of institutional seriousness in the True Church, at least based upon the fact that this appendix includes generous portions of an earlier Newman sermon, "The Religion of the Day." Are we not then justified in concluding that the 1852 appendix, in comparing a false church, which caricatures religion, and the True Church, which incorporately expresses religion, will also simultaneously parallel the comparison between a utilitarian false university which mimics education and the True University which incorporates education?

Newman's sermon, "The Religion of the Day,"[47] portions of which are included in the 1852 appendix, illustratively supplements his "University Discourses." In that sermon, there is a looking-glass parallel between an impostrous religion and an impostrous church, which comparison suggests the consequences of altering Christianity to suit the passing fancies of the moment. Echoically, the parallel of impostrous education and its impostrous cupbearer, the utilitarian university, subsumes—as it subtends—the concept of what happens when we alter Christian education to suit the conveniences of the times.

The religion of the day, says Newman, as if in a protocol of Discourse VIII of the *Idea*, cultivates "only one precept of the Gospel to the exclusion of the rest" (which, of course, heresies always do), and so "in reality attends to no part at all," because it has taken the brighter side of the Gospel—its tidings of comfort, its precepts of love; all darker, deeper views of man's condition and prospects being comparatively forgotten. . . . That beauty and delicacy of thought, which is so attractive in books, then extends to the conduct of life. . . . Our manners are courteous; we avoid giving pain or offense; our words become correct; our relative duties are carefully performed. Our sense of propriety shows itself . . . also in our religious profession. Vice now becomes unseemly and hideous to the imagination, or, as it is sometimes familiarly said, "out of taste." Thus elegance is gradually made the test and standard of virtue. Conscience is no longer recognized as an independent arbiter of actions, its authority is explained away.[48]

SENSE OF SENSIBILITY

Here, the reference, "we avoid giving pain or offense," summons up an image of Newman's Discourse VIII gentleman as one "who never inflicts pain." Had Newman already cached this image of such a gentleman as resident of such a "refinement-of-sensibility-community"? If so, this might confirm how (doubly) erroneous (and perhaps ironical) is that misconception which assumes that this sort of gentleman did, in fact, represent Newman's idealized educated person.

While such a "gentlemanly" image would possess the procedural traits, refinements, and courtesies of a disciplined mind, it would lack the substantive traits of a disciplined soul. While reflective of liberal education, such a figure would be barren of spiritual achievement, and of the fusion of intellectual and moral virtue. Newman suggests[49] that such a figure might as easily be Constantine's nephew-emperor, Julianus Apostata, as he would be the Cappadocian Basilus, saint and Doctor of the Church.

Where the spirit of mere "refinement" dominates, however, the spirit of conscience, and of "those fearful images of Divine wrath with which the Scriptures abound," can simply be explained away, because in "the religion of the day,"

> everything is bright and cheerful. Religion is pleasant and easy; benevolence is the chief virtue; intolerance, bigotry, excess of zeal, are the first of sins. Austerity is an absurdity.
> . . . On the other hand, all open profligacy is discounte-

nanced; drunkenness is accounted a disgrace. . . . To a cultivated mind . . . religion will commonly seem to be dull, from
want of novelty. Hence excitements are eagerly sought out
and rewarded. New objects in religion, new systems and
plans, new doctrines, new preachers, are necessary to satisfy
that craving. Mere refinement of mind is . . . more or less all
that is called religion at this day . . . as the counterfeit of the
Truth. . . . To be benevolent, courteous, candid, correct in
conduct, delicate . . . includes no true fear of God, no fervent zeal for His honour, no deep hatred of sin . . . no loyalty
to the Holy Apostolic Church . . . no seriousness. . . . we have
not acted from love of Truth, but from the influence of the
Age.[50]

RELIGIOSITY

In this case, Newman—much like Friedrich Nietzsche, but in a different context—is drawing attention to a moral disease of nineteenth-century life.[51] Newman points to "benevolency," which substitutes for
religiosity, "refinement of mind," and "social affability" for religion.
Church-goers, as if setting off for the races, trot to social centers, and
find there, not God, but refined sociabilities. Indeed, refinement of
mind, rarefaction, and sense and sensibility bespeak little of mind and
much of sensation, and thus are the complete opposite of cultivation of
the intellect. Indeed, refinement of mind, far from being religion, is
rather a religiosity of etiquette—literally, a "ticket" or "stub" of social
status. Hence, this unseriousness of a spurious church opposes any cultivation of the intellect and therefore, substitutively opposes the serious
task of the True University.

  Might Newman be implying that the very utilitarians, who med-
dled with the English University, had all along, through churchly co-
horts, been meddling with the English Church? As he once said, "The
same spirit which destroyed the legal incorporation of the religious principle, was the jealous enemy also of the incorporation of the intellectual;
and the civil power could as little bear a University as it bore a
Church."[52] Newman may then implicitly be drawing attention to a plausible symmetry between a feel-good religion and a feel-good church,
which also (implicitly) extends to a symmetry between a feel-good
church and a feel-good university—and, in turn, to a feel-good education.

But graver causative questions arise. How, in the first place, one might ask, had such a basic religious and moral shift occurred in the English Church? Was it an effect of untrammeled English ethnicity? Had the historical Christian Church in England become, with the 1534 Act of Henrician Supremacy, merely an ethnic Church of England?— thereupon ceasing to be a spiritually Christian Church?[53] Had the English—Protestant—Church, confronted by what Emanuel Mounier once called Christianity's tragic optimism, simply disregarded the tragic, and embraced the optimism of the religion of the day?[54] Had salting away optimism, and the brighter side of the Gospel—along with English "good cheer" and Tyndale's "take thine ease"—turned the historic English Church into the church of the day? Had it thereby formulated a counter-religion in Christianity, and a counter-Church in Christendom? And would this not comport, in fact, with what Newman means when he says, in the 1852 Discourse V, that "Catholics and Protestants . . . hold nothing in common in religion"?[55]

SYMBOLS OF TRUTH

In the 1852 Discourse V, two additional terms are also binomially presented—namely, Catholic Creed and philosophy—which, symbolically, seem to understudy the terms, *True Church* and *True University*. This is how Newman phrases the contrast: "The Catholic Creed is one whole, and Philosophy again is one whole; each may be compared to an individual, to which nothing can be added, from which nothing can be taken away. They may be professed, they may not be professed, but there is no middle ground between professing and not professing. A University, so-called, which refuses to profess the Catholic Creed, is, from the nature of the case, hostile both to the Church and to Philosophy."[56] This appears to be a full-blown contrast between, on the one hand, True Church/True University, and on the other, false church/false university. This contrast also suggests symmetry between both instances of true institutions and both instances of falsifying institutions. True Church and True University seem thematically related—by reason of their seriousness and truthfulness. Despite obvious distinctions between Church and University, they may be symbolically identical—that is, "separate, but indistinguishable"—by reason of corporate loyalty to truth.[57]

Consider now, how philosophy symbolizes—and is identified with the work of—the University, because philosophy, as Newman sees it, is the University's essential theme. Consider, too, how the Catholic

Creed symbolizes—and is identical with—the Church. Because philosophy and the Catholic Creed are concordant in their search for truth, so, and quite naturally, can their institutionalizations be concordantly perceived.

Almost like an institution of learning and instruction, the Church of Catholic Christendom, Newman observes, "is a vast assemblage of human beings with wilful intellects and wild passions, brought together into one by the beauty and Majesty of a Superhuman Power, into what may be called a large . . . training-school . . . [or] brought together as if into some moral factory, for the melting, refining, and moulding, by an incessant, noisy process, of the raw material of human nature, so excellent, so dangerous, so capable of divine purposes."[58]

SERIOUS TASKS

The teaching-renovating task of the Church is "to rescue human nature from its misery" and, analogously, with almost University-intent, to "lift . . . it to a higher level." With "the first springs of thought," the Church's task is "to teach that each individual man must be in his own person one whole and perfect temple of God." As the University seeks to encounter and master human ignorance, so, analogously, the Church is "sent upon earth to encounter and master a giant evil."[59]

Church and University are, of course, institutions which are absolutely different in kind—the one being temporal-eternal, the other temporal only. But, in some ways they share in much more (particularly in renovation of spiritual behavior) as they diverge in much less (especially seriousness of spiritual intent). So then, Church and University appear to be symmetrical in type. Their task is transcendent, with consequences that reach beyond immediate experience. Both are concerned with fulfillment of human potentialities. Their purpose is spiritual because they are dedicated to truth. They can therefore be of "one mind and one spirit"—by "stepping out," in the words of Josef Pieper, from the "workaday world."[60]

Church and University—we sense how much, and how often, they captured Newman's extraordinary mind. Nourishing his life and spirit, the Church, "imperial . . . One and Catholic," was the means of spiritual grace and sacred sustenance, and it was at one with conscience. The University, on the other hand, meant intellectual renewal and comprehension of wisdom. Who could doubt that there is also wisdom in the

Church, as there could be conscience in the University? (See SCHEMA "A.")

ENRICHING EXPERIENCE

As radiant disciple of the Church and inspired spokesman for the University, Newman can be said to have enlarged and enriched the meaning and legacy of both institutions. He seemed almost expressly bred to them, for his desire to serve them was unreserved, his readiness to focus on them was boundless, and in their behalf he expended the largess of his energetic genius. They, in turn, centered his spiritual life and nourished his intellect. Together, these institutions described and defined the interests of his life and the devotion of his spirit.

SCHEMA "A"

CHURCH		UNIVERSITY
	CONCERN	
RELIGION		EDUCATION
	FUNCTION	
SALVATION		ENLIGHTENMENT
	PURPOSE	
ENLARGEMENT OF SOUL		ENLARGEMENT OF MIND
	METIER	
SACREMENTAL LIFE		INTELLECTUAL LIFE
	TYPE	
COMMUNITY OF WORSHIP		COMMONWEALTH OF LEARNING
	CONCEPT	
EMPIRE OF FAITH		EMPIRE OF INTELLECT

IMAGES OF CHURCH AND UNIVERSITY. Comparison of these institutions in John Henry Newman's explicit (and implicit) vocabulary reveals a symmetry and parallelism that might not otherwise be recognized.

> Whatever we know about Newman—his young life and his mature experience, his loyalty to family and friends, his vocation and diffidence toward what (for some) was his fame and (for others) his notoriety—all seem to be linked to these two institutions, Church and University. They were the pivot, as well as the circumference, of his life.

Each institution, Church and University, has historically been a caregiver—being caring, caring for, caring about, and taking care of—those for whom each was responsible. Both institutions share an ideal and a parent-gendered identity—being "Mothers." Both share a generous and unstinting resemblance—being guiding, nourishing, and bountiful. That is, they are both *Almae Matres*. While their magisterial orders are distinct—the one of the Holy Spirit, the other of the human intellect—they nonetheless share a special spiritual concern for human beings. The distinction between them is both formal and real. For Newman, the Church is a kind of spiritual university, engaged in the sacramental education of humanity. For instance, Newman once referred to revelation as a kind of spiritual syllabus, a new kind of curriculum for human beings, because the "object of Revelation was to enlighten and enlarge the mind, to make us act by reason, and to expand and strengthen our powers." In contrast, the University seems to be a sort of "secular church" for the enlightenment and mental enlargement of its members, and of society. Indeed, Newman often speaks of one institution as if it were the other.[61]

In some of Newman's writings for or about the Church, there seems to be a similar educative-religious binomialism. As author of one-third of the Oxford Movement's *Tracts for the Times*, Newman initiated the series, in August 1833, with an educative Tract I, just as he issued the last, pro-Catholic educative Tract XC (90) in February 1841. He wanted not so much to inform as to educate members of the Anglican community—also to raise their spiritual consciousness, and to shape, through the nascent Oxford Movement, their understanding and perception of Church issues. He was often criticized for doing so. "I have heard so much criticism of my tracts," he wrote John Keble in November 1833, "that it is comfortable to have heard one or two things of a more pleasant kind."[62] Unfortunately, the *Tracts*, being more Christian than was politically correct or acceptable, evoked strong resentments among many Oxford and Anglican authorities. In the same way that Newman sought to make them educative and not merely instructional, he exercised a similar prerogative in his *Grammar of Assent* (1870), whose passages seek not simply to provide information about belief and real assent. They are intent on educating, enlarging, and developing the minds of readers.

BINOMIAL INSTITUTIONS

Educative-religious binomialism also extends, in some of his sermons—both Anglican and Catholic—to Newman's treatment of University themes. For example, in his Anglican *Parochial and Plain Sermons* (1829–43), as in his *Oxford University Sermons* (1826–43), Newman drew parallels between matters bearing on the Church and those bearing on the University. And, as we have already seen from one of the Oxford Sermons, Newman extracted almost verbatim a portion of the *Idea*'s Discourse VI. In his Catholic *Sermons Preached on Various Occasions* (1857), he reveals binary interest in the themes of conscience and wisdom, which he also treats in a political setting—for example, in his *Letter to the Duke of Norfolk* (1875), as a response to former Prime Minister W. E. Gladstone's criticism of papal infallibility. He treated the same themes, conscience and wisdom, in an epistemological setting (as in *Grammar of Assent* in 1870), as well as in an educational setting (as in *The Idea of a University* in 1873).

But most of all, what Newman's Church and University shared so thoroughly in common was Newman himself. And he further fused Church and University by being pastoral in both. For whatever else Newman appears to be, his primary identity is that of pastor. As Charles Stephen Dessain has said, "It can hardly be sufficiently emphasized that Newman was first and foremost a pastor."[63] As pastor, Newman understood how learning is associated with devotion and sanctification, just as sanctification can imbue learning with devotion, and thus extend its reach.

PASTORAL IMPERATIVE

Because Newman had considered his role as Oriel Tutor a pastoral role, Newman came into conflict with Oriel's Provost Hawkins, and was subsequently forced to abandon that tutorial post. There was no doubt in Newman's mind that teaching (an obligation of both Church and University) extended far beyond the simple task of instruction and supervision of students. The clear fact was that teaching is a pastoral—caring, nourishing, and guiding—activity. Newman always "maintained, even fiercely, that my employment was distinctly pastoral [and] . . . of a religious nature. I considered a College Tutor to have the care of souls. To this principle I have been faithful through my life."[64]

Newman's gift for pastoring may also tell us something. Because he was a pastor, he intuited that teaching is, first and foremost, a spiritual, and therefore a religious activity, if only because it is concerned with making connections (*religare*). Teaching is also, by nature, a caring, "curative-curating," and shepherding activity. From this we may derive the view that, for Newman, the University also has spiritual obligations, which are complementary to those of the Church.

SPIRITUAL COMMUNITIES

John Henry Newman understood Church and University primarily as communities, having special spiritual empowerment, dominion, leadership, rule, and imperium. This is why Newman also spoke of Church and University as empires. The Church he called "an Empire of Faith," and the University, "an imperial intellect"—or "an Empire of Intellect," perhaps an "Empire of Understanding.[65] Newman's idea of the University as empire reveals that, of all the objects of purely human enterprise,

> none higher or nobler can be named than that which is contemplated in the erection of a University. To set on foot and to maintain in life and vigour a real University, is confessedly, as soon as the word "University" is understood, one of the greatest works, great in their difficulty and their importance, on which are deservedly expended the rarest intellects and the most varied endowments. . . . Nothing is too vast, nothing too subtle, nothing too distant, nothing too minute, nothing too discursive, nothing too exact, to engage its attention.[66]

Newman conceptualized the University as a "sovereignty," because, in the realm of knowledge, it is a sovereign. It is not, he said, "that it occupies the whole territory of knowledge merely, but that it is

the very realm." The prerogative of the University is like the prerogative of a political empire, because it assigns the scope and task and jurisdiction of each of its constituent parts. Hence, the University

> professes to assign to each study . . . its own proper place
> and its just boundaries; to define the rights, to establish the
> mutual relations, and to effect the intercommunion of one
> and all; to keep in check the ambitious and encroaching, and
> to succor and maintain those which from time to time are
> succumbing under the more popular or the more fortunately
> circumstanced; to keep the peace between them all, and to
> convert their mutual differences and contrarieties into the
> common good. . . . It learns to do it, not by rules reducible
> to writing, but by sagacity, wisdom, and forbearance.[67]

IMPERIAL VIRTUES

Sagacity, wisdom, and forbearance—these, according to Newman, are
the means by which a University endows its governance. These are not
managerial techniques, as academic deans and presidents might prefer,
nor are they political expediencies, as chancellors and governors are
wont to seek. Rather, they are intellectual and moral virtues—sagacity
and wisdom being intellectual virtues, and forbearance being a moral
virtue. As virtues, they are, of course, mutually and complementarily
enhancing, because (in binary fashion) intellectual virtue is enhanced by
its moral structure, just as the richness of moral virtue is revealed in its
intellectual integrity. Here, Newman appears to be suggesting that the
very governance of the University requires the complementary presence of moral truth and intellectual truth. Although categorized in different theoretic, epistemological, and psychological orders, moral and
intellectual truths coexist in the same ontology, because, as Newman
said, truth is truth, and is coherent and harmonious with itself.

In view of how often Newman refers, not just to the differences,
but to the connections between intellectual and moral actions, this
should not appear unusual. In retrospect, we can cite several instances
of how Newman proclaims such interconnectedness: [68]

> his sense of the union between the pastoral and the educative
> influence of the Tutor, the separation of which, like the dis-
> junction of moral-intellectual ideals "is the evil of the age";

his belief that his Dublin University Church showed "the indissoluble union of philosophy and religion";

his assertion that liberal education forms a life-long habit "of which the attributes are freedom, equitableness, calmness, moderation, and wisdom";

his declaration that discipline of mind should rely "on the slow silent, penetrating, overpowering effects of patience, steadiness, routine, and perserverance";

his view that "a really cultivated mind" will act "with grace and propriety . . . with calmness and as it ought to do";

and his conviction that "intellectual culture exerts upon our moral nature . . . [influences] manifesting themselves in veracity, probity, equity, fairness, gentleness, benevolence, amiableness."

REFLECTION

Because the University is "an imperial minister," it also has relations with the Church. This is so, as Newman phrases it, because the University

is ancillary certainly, and of necessity, to the Catholic Church. . . . It is ministrative to the Catholic Church, first, because truth of any kind can but minister to truth; and next, still more, because Nature ever will pay homage to Grace, and Reason cannot but illustrate and defend Revelation; and thirdly, because the Church has a sovereign authority, and, when she speaks *ex cathedra*, must be obeyed. [The University's] . . . immediate end . . . is to secure the due disposition, according to one sovereign order, and the cultivation in that order, of all the provinces and methods of thought which the human intellect has created. . . . Its true representative defines, rather than analyzes. He aims at . . . following out, as far as man can, what in its fulness is mysterious and unfathomable.[69]

With self-reflective realism, Newman can also describe how the University's "true representative" acts. Like Newman, that representative "takes things as they are."[70]

COMPLEMENTAL THEMES

Newman's interpretation of Church and University as religious and educative institutions implies their complemental representations in Christian civilization. Church—defined, in Vatican II's *Lumen Gentium*, as the whole body of the faithful, engaged in furthering the coming of the Kingdom of God—is concerned with the sacred and spiritual development and enlargement of humanity, the redemption and salvation of human souls. In another order, but similarly, University is concerned with the secular and intellectual enlargement and development of its members, the renovation and inspiration of human minds. Between enlargement of spirit and expansion of mind, there can be no unbridgeable opposition. "Religion has its own enlargement," said Newman, polysemantically, in *The Idea of a University*. So then, enlargement of mind and perfection of spirit can become truly religious acts. If growth—familiarly recognized as a Newman signature—is the sign of life, then, whatever helps us truly to grow in spirit and intellect, serves, in some way, the coming of the Kingdom of God. And because, in Newman's vocabulary, self-knowledge "is at the root of all religious knowledge," any institution that encourages self-knowledge, whether in a sacred or secular context, serves, in some way, a kingdom beyond itself.

UNITY OF TRUTH

Although Newman appreciated the spiritual advantages of bringing together truths of one kind with truths of another, he encountered much misunderstanding in trying to do so.[71] Bringing together Church and University—by making them of one harmoniously spiritual mind, and without compromising the integrity of either—initiates, indeed, a religious action. Attempting to unify spiritual experience, and to bring all things together in Christ, is also a sacred act. Truth, Newman was fond of saying, cannot contradict truth. He was fond, too, of recalling St. Augustine's assertion that God is found in truth—"for wherever I found truth, there I found my God who is truth itself"—*ubi enim invent veritatem, ibi inveni deum meum, ipsam veritatem* (Conf., X, 24).

And God is found in truth, Newman would add, of whatever variety, including the truth of life's ordinary events. For if we live and move and have our being in God, then in the truth of ordinary events, even in "the remains of the day," we find a way of "seeing all things in God." William James appropriately summed up that point in his Gifford Lectures: "When we see all things in God, and refer all things to him, we read in common matters superior expressions of meaning. The deadness with which custom invests the familiar vanishes, and existence as a whole appears transfigured."[72]

Just such an act of vision seems very close to what Newman had in mind when he remarked that the Christian is one who can "see Christ revealed in his soul amid the ordinary actions of the day, as by a sort of sacrament."[73] With William James, Newman would surely agree that religion is of an existential nature, whose practice is not merely verbal or theoretic, but, at root, actionate. In the words of William James, "If religion be a function by which either God's cause or man's cause is to be really advanced, then he who lives the life of it, however narrowly, is a better servant than he who knows about it, however much."[74]

UNIQUE VOCATION

The essential characteristic of Newman's intellectual and moral genius is to be found in how he tried to "bring all things to God." This was possible, Maisie Ward once remarked, because "Newman's genius found its scope in a unique vocation—at once spiritual and intellectual—of drawing the world near to God not by prayer but by thought."[75] In attempting to express such a synthesis of Newman's gifts, J. Lewis May once said, "Besides being a genius, Newman was a saint, and besides being a saint, he was a gentleman."[76]

CHAPTER 4:
GENIUS AND GENTLEMAN

"I wish to go by reason, not by feeling."

"I am a very ordinary person."

"My smile is bright, my glance is free, my voice is calm and clear."

"I have been so little used to praise in my own life."

"Those sad long years have stamped themselves upon my face."

"I have not lost either my intimate sense of the Divine Presence in every place, nor the good conscience and peace of mind that flows therefrom."

Newman expressed his genius in ministry to Church, and in service to University. Whether priest of Canterbury or Rome, he pursued holiness rather than peace. As Oxford Tutor or Dublin administrator-teacher, he cultivated intellect, rather than repose. To Church and University, therefore, Newman dedicated his devotion, his learning, and his genius.

And real genius it was, embodying talent, enterprise, competence, and solicitude—all concentrated (better yet, consecrated) in one person, with a genius as variegated as it was various.[1] At any one time, it was as if Newman were thirty-seven different people: priest, pastor, preacher, and devotional writer; patristic scholar, theologian (the most seminal of the nineteenth century, says Avery Cardinal Dulles), ecclesiologist, apologist, ecumenist, spiritual guide, confessor, scriptural scholar, and divine; founder and superior of the English Oratorians, and first-class religious thinker. He was also poet, critic, translator, philosopher, musician, violinist, composer, historian, satirist, novelist, rhetorician, controversialist, epistolary giant, and diarist. He was teacher, speaker, educator, University Tutor, University Rector, educational theorist, and not least, public figure.

Any single such talent might be enough for an ordinary person. But being so extraordinarily ordinary, Newman achieved them all. For example, although his fame was not in music, he played violin quartets of Haydn, Beethoven, and Mozart, and also composed original music. Underwebbing such talent, he complementarily fused the disposition of an artist and the fierce inflexible rigor of a saint. But even this does not say it all. In uniquely expressing what he perceived, Newman necessarily became a great author and attained unusual literary eminence as a master of the English language.[2] As he once said (while unconsciously including himself), a great author is one who has mastered the double *logos* of distinct thought and inseparable word, because a great author not only has something to say, but knows precisely how to say it well.[3] Expressly describing Cicero's art, he implicitly described his own when he said that such art, "whether engaged in statement, argument, or raillery, never ceases till it has exhausted the subject; going round about it and placing it in every different light, yet without repetition to offend or weary the reader."[4] Also unaware of self-portraiture, Newman defined the poetical mind as "full of the eternal forms of beauty and perfection," as "imaginative or creative, from the originality and independence of its modes of thinking," and as one which "feels a natural sympathy with everything great and splendid in the physical and moral world."[5] Perhaps, as Sean O'Faòlain once suggested, "The great attraction of the adult Newman is this blending of intellect and poetry, of brains and imagination."[6]

HOLINESS THE END

Dedicated to personal holiness, Newman transformed his everyday life by unifying whatever he thought, or whatever he did, through the practice of religious truth. Preaching from the pulpit, he once said that the life of the Spirit helps the Christian "to labour diligently in his calling," so that Christ's revelation comes by "a sort of sacrament."[7] "Holiness is the great end" of preaching, he said,[8] and it consists in doing what we ought daily to do, by doing well whatever we are doing. Such an admonition, Newman once enveloped in a short, innocently moving, but realistic meditation:

> If we wish to be perfect we have nothing more to do than to perform the ordinary duties of the day well. . . . Perfection . . . does not mean any extraordinary service . . . but it means what the word perfection ordinarily means. . . . That which has no flaw in it, that which is complete, that which is consistent, that which is sound—we mean the opposite to imperfect. . . . He, then, is perfect who does the work of the day perfectly, and we need not go beyond this to seek for perfection. You need not go out of the round of the day.[9]

Ordinary everyday action, like ordinary biblical action, is exactly what constitutes "ordinary experience," which is lived with ordinary hope and in ordinary time. This kind of ordinariness was implicit in every act that Newman performed, because he especially believed that his own life was quite ordinary. "I am," he wrote a friend, "a very ordinary person." Once he described the University as "the great ordinary means to a great but ordinary end." And of his "Illative Sense," his biographer Charles Stephen Dessain said that it was "a solemn word for an ordinary thing." Through ordinary means, however, he could nonetheless create extraordinary effects, perhaps because, as he himself said, "God does great things by plain methods."[10]

Newman's formula for being ordinary was quite simple. It meant "nothing short of perfection," as that exhortation is expressed in the Gospel summons: "Be perfect, therefore, as your heavenly Father is perfect" (Mt. 5: 48); or in the invitation: "If you wish to be perfect, then come, follow me" (Mt. 19: 21). Being perfect, in Newman's sense, is God's exquisitely ordinary invitation which, through ordinary means, can make perfect our everyday experience.

CHURCHLY GENIUS

It was in precisely such ordinary ways that Newman could devote his extraordinary mind to the Church of England, and later, to the Church of Rome, and left upon them both lasting and salutary impressions. Even in an otherwise negative assessment, Dean Inge of St. Paul's, London, made plain that Newman had "left an indelible mark on two great religious bodies. He has stirred movements which still agitate the Church of England and the Church of Rome."[11] But, contrastingly, Richard Holt Hutton believed that Newman had a distinctly liberating effect upon the Church of England. Hutton, well-known editor of the Spectator and Newman biographer, had followed his subject's public career almost from its beginnings, and perceived that he was "penetrated by a fervent love of God, a fervent gratitude for the Christian revelation, and a steadfast resolve to devote the whole force of a singularly powerful and even intense character to the endeavor to promote the conversion of his fellow-countrymen from the tepid and unreal profession of Christianity to a new and profound faith in it. . . . A man so genuine in character, so ingenuous in judging himself, has hardly ever made himself known to the world."[12]

In the Catholic Church, Christopher Hollis envisioned Newman's role as being that of "forerunner of things to come." As Hollis said, Newman's was "a spirit which more than any other was to direct the future of the [Catholic] Church."[13] Yet, it was in service to the Anglican Church that Newman engendered even in his lifetime, the sort of testimonial that rarely, if ever, was accorded him after he became a Catholic.

For example, Principal J. C. Shairp, a Presbyterian, spoke warmly of this "most transparent of men," who had so profoundly influenced Oxford and, consequently, English life and society.

> Where was the centre and soul from which so mighty a power emanated? It lay, and had for some years lain, mainly in one man, a man in many ways the most remarkable that England had seen during this century, perhaps the most remarkable the English Church has possessed in any century— John Henry Newman. . . . [It was] as though some Ambrose or Augustine of older ages had reappeared. . . . His power showed itself chiefly in the new and unlooked-for way in which he touched into life old truths, moral or spiritual, which all Christians acknowledge, but most have ceased to feel.[14]

PARALLEL GENIUS

Richard William Church, Newman's former student and friend, then Dean of St. Paul's, London, also extolled Newman as being "the founder, we may almost say, of the Church of England as we know it."

Curiously, Dean Church published another descriptive passage, so evocative of Newman, about one

> who joined the largeness and daring of a powerful and in-
> quiring intellect, with the graces and sweetness and un-
> selfishness of the most lovable of friends, and with the
> fortitude and clearsightedness and dauntless firmness of a
> hero . . . [who] impressed permanently on the tradition of
> Christendom higher conceptions of Christian saintliness,
> Christian philosophy, and the obligations of a Christian
> teacher. . . . [He was,] as a thinker, a Christian leader . . . one
> of the most remarkable and most attractive characters . . . of
> the whole Christian history.[15]

This was descriptive of Newman, surely. But Dean Church was writing, not about his friend, John Henry Newman, but about the thirty-sixth Archbishop of Canterbury, and Doctor of the Church, St. Anselm (1033–1109).[16] Giant of Christian spirituality, and seminal thinker of Christendom, St. Anselm seems now as if he were Newman's prophetic antecedent.

Like Newman, St. Anselm—whose name means "God's hel-met" or "God's headband"—rejuvenated devotional and homiletic literature in a violent, Norman-dominated England. As if an ancestral mirror of Newman, Anselm acted with radiant intellectual acuity that lent to his religious expression a tender generosity of mind and spirit, which would later be called "true piety with sound learning." Anselm's prayers and meditations, much like Newman's, established a new voicing, a new consciousness, a new form of intimacy in religious meditation. Everything Anselm did (again, like Newman), he did with a simple, compelling charm, and personal attractiveness, which bespoke resplendent saintliness.

ANSELM AS MATRIX

Intermediary between Anselm and Newman, there is the astonishing figure of Lancelot Andrewes, Caroline Bishop of Winchester, a quietly influential member of the KJV translation team—and master of English expression. The Anselmian imprint on Bishop Andrewes was also carbon-copied on Newman, as attested by the fact that Newman translated Andrewes's *Preces privatae*, or Personal Devotions.[17] Thus, even indirectly, Anselm set a mark upon Newman.

In his *University Sketches*, Newman hails "the great St. Anselm and the school of Bec as the proper source of scholasticism." Another clear Anselmian influence can be found in a passage from Newman's *Lectures on the Difficulties of Anglicans*, wherein he weighs the damaging enormity of sin against the enormous damage of cosmic disaster—a comparison first proposed by Anselm in his *Cur Deus Homo*.[18]

Anselmian influence also reveals its mark on Newman's theology, but not by reason of what is dubbed Anselm's ontological argument—which declares the necessity of God's existence in "existential logic."[19] Rather, that influence is felt in Newman's admiration for how Anselm boldly sculpts human thought at the noetic edges of faith, which is always in quest of understanding—*fides quaerens intellectum*. Anselm endowed that search with the affirmative response: *Credo ut intelligam*—I believe in order that I may understand the content of what I do believe.

Newman was similarly drawn, in his own theology of conscience, towards Anselm's *imago*-theology (Gen-Ber. 1: 26–27). To Anselm, God speaks to us through His image in us. To Newman, God emphatically speaks to us—is within us—through our conscience.[20]

GOD'S GRANDEUR

Newman's theological power derives, much like Anselm's, from recognition that experience is soaked in the ambiguity of a deeper existential truth about the "grandeur of God." Also like Anselm, Newman proposes that, in the act of really thinking, we somehow recognize the presence of God, and are thus impelled, with the Psalmist, to seek His face.[21] For Newman, really thinking, like really praying, is consequently a covenantal act in a thoughtful quest for God. In such a quest, prayer becomes thoughtful, just as thought is bidden to devotion. The quest for God is thus not for the purpose of "dialectical satisfaction." On the contrary, the prayerful-thoughtful quest for God is an act of intellectual reverence, which issues in the spiritual joy of worship.

Because mankind is made in the image of God, then, for Newman, self-knowledge implicitly becomes theological knowledge. Self-knowledge draws the mind more deeply into the noumenal presence of God. Upon just such foundation, Newman can say,

> Self-knowledge is at the root of all religious knowledge. . .
> For it is in proportion as we search our hearts and understand
> our own nature, that we understand what is meant by an In-
> finite Governor and Judge.... God speaks to us primarily in
> our hearts. Self-knowledge is the key to the precepts and
> doctrines of Scripture. The very utmost any outward notices
> of religion can do, is to startle us and make us turn inward
> and search our hearts; and then, when we have experienced
> what it is to read ourselves, we shall profit by the doctrines
> of the Church and the Bible. [22]

In thought, in prayer, and in devotion, Newman was himself "so upright, so firm, so wonderfully well-balanced."[23] If we forget that Newman's "child is father of the man," we need only turn to the fictional portrait, drawn by his sister Harriet, of "a very philosophical young gentleman, always full of thought, and never at a loss for an answer." Having learned to read by age five, Newman's brightness was acknowledged, but his first letter from his father cautioned, "You must learn something new everyday, or you will no longer be called a clever boy."[24]

BRIGHTER THAN THE REST

Newman began serious writing of prose and verse at age 11, and was marked out as different. He was brighter, taller, and kinder than his peers, and "of a studious turn, and of quick apprehension."[25] He was also ringleader of a secret club, editor of several school-age papers, and went through his Great Ealing prep years, said headmaster Dr. George Nicholas, in record advance. His grey-blue eyes, even as a youth, might flair at some unexpected obstacle, which his strong will might encounter. Sean O'Faólain speculates that he had "a tongue that could clip a hedge."[26] He also inherited, says Meriol Trevor, "his father's irascibility, a quick-come, quick-gone impatience at what crossed his will, which he himself called 'impetuousness.'"

Yet this did not hide his affectionate nature. Ms. Trevor adds, "It was unusual that anyone with such high intellectual gifts should also possess such an affectionate heart." Later, when people were told of his "impetuousness," they disbelieved it, because he was so gentle. Possessed of imaginative and intellectual talent, and endowed with extraordinarily sound mentality in a reasonably sound body, he early on displayed "a mind capable of the clearest abstract reasoning, logical and mathematical." He was a youth of enormous sensitivity, and had the "power to be a poet or a philosopher." Newman's mature, unmistakable voice, especially from the pulpit, had, as one listener reported, "Angel eloquence." You "felt your heart turn towards him," because his words possessed "a religious music—subtle, sweet, mournful."

Even in old age, Newman's voice would be approvingly noticed.[27] Richard Holt Hutton said of it, "Never did a voice seem better adapted to persuade without irritating. Singularly sweet, perfectly free from any dictatorial note, and yet rich in all the cadences proper to the expression of pathos, of wonder, and of ridicule, there was still nothing in it that any one could properly describe as insinuating, for its simplicity . . . was as remarkable as its sweetness, its freshness, and its gentle distinctness."[28] Like others of high intellectual acumen, Newman had a lively sense of humor, which had great effect upon his companions. "As usual," wrote one colleague, "he is the life of the whole party, and keeps all cheerful and in good humour." Said another, "He shed cheerfulness as a sunbeam sheds light, even while many difficulties were pressing."[29]

At a deeper level, Newman reveals, in a self-correcting verse, that he recognizes what others see in him—his smiles, his brightness, his cheerful manner. Yet he also sees what no one else can detect—his inadequacies of what he should do and does not, of what he should not do but does. So, just before his Mediterranean journey in 1832, he versified his confession of inadequacy.[30] The words of James Anthony Froude describe him during his Oxford years:

> His appearance was striking. He was above the middle height, slight and spare. His head was large, his face remarkably like that of Julius Caesar. The forehead, the shape of the ears and nose, were almost the same. The lines of the mouth were very peculiar, and I should say exactly the same. I . . . believe that [the resemblance] extended to the temperament. . . . There was original force of character . . . clearness of intellectual perception, a disdain for conventionalities, a temper imperious and wilful, but along with it, a most attaching gentleness, sweetness, singleness of heart and purpose. . . . His natural temperament was bright and light, and his senses, even the commonest, were exceptionally delicate. . . . For hundreds of young men, *Credo in*

Newmannum was the genuine symbol of faith.[31]

Newman's body language was as striking as his personality. He walked with a rapid stride, with an always-leaning-forward gait, as if pushing against a gale. He looked, said his brother-in-law, Tom Mozley, like someone "on serious business bent, and not on a promenade." With a companion, he was "always talking while he was walking." John Augustus O'Shea, repeating that striking motif, recalled Newman during the Dublin years: "He was a striking figure as he walked with short, rapid steps . . . tenuous and angular, his head bent forward, his ascetic features shrouded in meditation, and his keen eyes looking neither to the right nor to the left, but introspectively, as it were, with contemplativeness far removed from things of the thoroughfare. He was invariably dressed in a clerical frock coat and knee britches, and usually carried an umbrella."[32]

SERIOUSNESS OF PURPOSE

Despite his biblically merry heart, Newman was also serious. Just as he walked fast, so too, he worked fast, and tried quickly to get to the bottom of every difficulty. He disapproved of remaining idle—"To be doing absolutely nothing is injurious," he wrote a young Frederic Rogers, as he himself prepared for his Mediterranean journey. For Tom Mozley, "It never was possible to be even a quarter of an hour in his company without a man feeling himself incited to take an onward step, sufficient to tax his energies or his faith."[33]

Portraits of Newman, whether those of his youth or of old age, reveal an intensely present, deeply aware, and (pity the term, unless properly understood) soulful person. The implicit spirituality of these portraits shows, indeed, remarkable likeness to certain young-and-old pictures of Pierre Teilhard de Chardin. Portraiture of the bespectacled young Newman at Oriel, with its implicit spirituality, shows a remarkable likeness to certain pictures of eighteen-year-old Pierre Teilhard de Chardin, Jesuit seminarian at Aix in 1899. There is also a striking spiritual resemblance between the 1874–76 paintings of Newman by Lady Coleridge and the photograph, taken by Philippe Halsman, of Pierre Teilhard de Chardin, at relatively the same stage of his life. Mature portraits of both men have much to say, and what one observer wrote of Teilhard's eyes surely applies also to Newman's: "When they met your eyes [they] revealed the man's soul: his reassuring sympathy restored your confidence in yourself. Just to speak to him made you feel better. His own faith was in the invincible power of love."[34]

Both Newman and Teilhard possessed a similar spiritual depth, and a special kind of sadness. Even a dozen years before the 1874 Coleridge portrait, Newman was acutely aware of how "those sad long years of anxiety have stamped themselves upon my face." Yet, when he shut his eyes, and thought about it, he confessed, "I can't believe I am more than 25 years old, and smile to think how differently strangers must think of me from my own internal feelings."[35] Such feelings were, however, hidden at least from James Russell Lowell—poet, critic, editor, and America's holdover ambassador to the Court of St. James—when he saw Newman publicly in 1884. Lowell later wrote of the occasion: "[A] more gracious senescence I never saw. . . . [A] serene decay, like that of a ruined abbey. . . . [H]is benignity as well as his lineaments remind me of the old age of Emerson."[36]

As his friends aptly knew, Newman was of an unusually calm temperament, eminently rational, and persevering. "I wish to go by reason," he wrote Dr. Charles Russell of Maynooth on 5 May 1841, "not by feeling."[37] But, especially after his conversion in 1845, his enemies considered him quite the opposite. Then, he was caricatured, lampooned, scorned, belittled, and condemned, all the while in quite scathing language. These were Newman's painful days and nights of the long knives, which suggest that his aggressors must have felt that large scores were still to be settled.

SETTLING SCORES

Favorite targets of Newman's critics were his intelligence and honesty. Among others, for example, there was Congregationalist Principal A. M. Fairbairn, who denounced Newman as a "sceptic," supporting his thesis by passages from Newman's *Apologia pro vita sua* and *Grammar of Assent*. The latter Fairbairn considered "pervaded by the intensest scepticism." Fairbairn also charged, "He has a deep distrust of the intellect, he does not trust his own, for he does not know where it might lead him, and he will not trust any other man's."[38]

Although Newman twice controverted this attack, his response remained unacknowledged, even ignored. Still, Newman declared his unalterable commitment, not to scepticism, but to its contradictory—

intellect. Thus, he could write:[39]

> "The independent faculty which is . . . the ultimate warrant
> of the reasoning act . . . has . . . a larger name than moral
> sense, as including intuitions, and this is what Aristotle calls
> ($\nu o\hat{v}\varsigma$)."

Rather than acknowledge Newman's honesty and intelligence, his critics alleged that he was cunning and insincere. For example, E. A. Abbott, in his *Philomuthus* ("Lover of Tall Tales") described Newman's *The Idea of a University* as concealing "contempt for readers," "contempt for facts," and a wish to betray Irish bishops and students of the Catholic University. Although Richard Holt Hutton, after Newman's death, exposed Abbott's bigotry in this attack,[40] Hutton's defense had little effect. In similar vein, a later critic deplored Newman's alleged "distrust" of the human mind: "He was of a childlike nature, wanting to be led. . . . He knew everything about the Fathers, except what made them what they were. . . . He failed to see . . . the way truth is always coming into the world, how there is nothing else here than an appeal to the reason he so much distrusted."[41]

UNJUSTIFIED CRITICISM

Criticism of Newman became a kind of public lottery—in which anyone might hazard at gambling. Thus, Thomas Carlyle suggested that Newman had "the brain of a moderate size rabbit," while classicist Benjamin Jowett, who had once sat angelically at Newman's feet, accused Newman of speculative untruthfulness, and of being "not much better in practice. His conscience had been taken out and the Church put in its place." Sir Leslie Stephen, Virginia Woolf's free-thinking, plain-speaking father, charged that "Newman was simply a sceptic who backed out of it." Social theologian Frederick Denison Maurice (whose acolyte, Charles Kingsley, would later unsuccessfully tangle with Newman) said that Newman was "governed by an infinite Scepticism, counteracted by an infinite devoutness." Thomas Henry Huxley (bluffly threatening, but never attempting, to mine Newman's works for direct evidence) asserted, "That man is the slipperiest sophist I have ever met with. Kingsley was entirely right about him."[42]

Newman's rejoinder was appropriate, but was inappropriately

scorned when he said this: "Scepticism is the refusal to be satisfied with reasons which ought to satisfy." Or this: "To be sceptical is to be unreasonable." Newman, who wished "to go by reason," could not be (it seems fair to say), by definition, a sceptic.[43] Knowing that "no one can be too suspicious about himself," however, Newman—had he been a sceptic—would certainly have admitted it. But as Meriol Trevor once put it, "Conservative minds were unable to see the difference between understanding a sceptic's argument and being a sceptic oneself."[44] Had Newman decided (*tenter l'impossible*) that he was a sceptic, he would have told the whole world about it. But of course he wasn't, and therefore he didn't.

REMAINS OF THE DAY

Bitter criticism, however, did not cease with Newman's death—and this suggests how very much alive he and his ideas still remain. For example, one recent critic says, with some self-satisfaction, that Newman "didn't have what it takes to be an Anglican"; and, on the claim that Newman "loved the English Church," another replies sarcastically, "If he loved it, then why did he leave it?" An Anglican bishop, not long ago, charged that Newman was "a ruthless and unscrupulous controversialist."[45] Such animus seems as alive today as it was more than a century ago. The question still arises: Why?

Still, not every Englishman was insensitive to the hostility shown to Newman. For example, Algernon Cecil, Barrister of the Inner Temple, was confused that Newman could simultaneously be accused of both unbelief and credulity. Arthur Quiller-Couch—that gentle Cornishman who neighbored Daphne Du Maurier—was quickly struck by "how just this man can be to his great enemies," especially when those enemies considered Newman's works "beneath the notice of their stern and masculine minds."[46]

DISTURBING THE ESTABLISHMENT

Newman's conversion to Catholicism, following upon years of his own anti-Roman rhetoric, disturbed the Establishment's political-psychological sensitivities and balance: One of ours joined them—a sentiment which, by definition, is always returnable in retributive kind. Some may have interpreted Newman's life and work, after 1845, as being detrimental to the English nation, or to its Protestant citizen-psyches. It was sometimes even charged that Newman "abandoned" the English (which he did not do).

The great English flaw, Newman once said, was "the habit of measuring everything by the standard of success."[47] Did the Establishment, then, consider Newman a failed Englishman? In his *Apologia*, he said, "I think, indeed, Englishmen the most suspicious and touchy of mankind. I think them unreasonable and unjust in their seasons of excitement; but I had rather be an Englishman (as in fact I am), than belong to any other race under heaven. They are as generous, as they are hasty and burly; and their repentance for their injustice is greater than their sin."[48]

Newman, as Fr. Henry Tristram pointed out, "claimed to be an Englishman *tout court* and without qualification."[49] But, apparently, Newman's Englishness was seen differently by his opponents. This awareness once prompted him to ask rhetorically, "Why was I to be dishonest and they immaculate?"[50] Still, his opponents were not all Protestants and secularists, since there were also anti-Newman English Catholics—some of them old-line Catholics, while others were converts from Anglicanism, many of whom were now Catholic prelates. Thus, Msgr. George Talbot (papal chamberlain in Rome and a convert), in a letter to Cardinal Manning, exuded his own brand of ethnic venom: "To be a Roman [he said], is to an Englishman an effort. Dr. Newman is more English than the English. His spirit must be crushed."[51]

Unrelenting attacks on Newman—whether Protestant, secular, or Catholic—pivot around issues of politics and ethnicity, religion and theology, as well as Victorian versions of gender. Pivot, that is to say, around a psychology of identity. Consider, then, the background.

IDENTITY PROBLEM

During the course of three decades, the 1820s to the 1850s, Newman developed from a Protestant Englishman to a Catholic Englishman. Before 27 February 1841 and the publication of his *Tract XC* (90)—which interpreted the Thirty-Nine Articles of Anglican Supremacy as a "catholic" document, devoid of Reformation bias—there had been little criticism of Newman. Prior to that date, Newman had apparently not been saying or doing anything which was considered publicly suspect. But from the year of his conversion in 1845 until the present day, he has been unsparingly criticized. Why?

One might easily say, "Well, it's because he became a Catholic, and the English haven't liked Catholics since Elizabeth I." This response, however, does not move the issue forward, or spread it wider, or sink it deeper into causative explanation. Start, then, if you will, with the fact of Newman's development. It is a development which suggests that Newman changed in some ways, but did not change in other ways.

Over the years some things about Newman did change. He matured marvelously, he became less insular, he widened his awareness of Christian civilization, and he deepened his understanding of spiritual experience. He became, in a word, more human. In 1833, for example, English-Protestant Rev. Mr. Newman found Rome mostly—and Naples completely—intolerable. After 1846, English-Catholic Father Newman found both cities wonderful.[52] The decades from Oxford to Dublin— the 1820s to the 1850s—simply signify a period of the most obvious changes. By 1851, with his *Lectures on the Present Position of Catholics*, English traits which Newman had hitherto taken for granted, now became unacceptable to him. Prior to 1843, Newman's sermons refer to intellect in ways that differ from his vocabulary of 1852–73— that is, in the *Discourses on the Scope and Nature of University Education* and *The Idea of a University*. Those differences reveal a change in cultural perspective.

On the other hand, there were some things about Newman that never changed. In the first place, he was always an Englishman, living in an England that still looked, in the nineteenth century, very much as it had in the eighteenth century. As an Englishman, he necessarily shared with other Englishmen a specific cultural psychology. What, then, distinguishes Newman's later "Englishness" from his earlier "Englishness," or from the "Englishness" of his opponents? Had he become, betweentimes, less insular, less ethnically English? To try to answer such questions, it may be useful briefly to consider the ways of national psychologies.

NATIONAL PSYCHOLOGY

Not everyone does see, hear, or experience the world in exactly the same way. In language, for example, English-speaking students, just learning French, often imagine that certain words or expressions that look so English, cannot really be too much different from English meanings.

Such words and expressions are called *les faux amis*—phony friends. Thus, some English-speaking students of French may translate *sensiblement* as "sensibly," instead of "approximately," or *actuellement* as "actually," instead of "at the moment." Perhaps *les faux amis* denote, not so much a language barrier, as a psychological barrier. Like words, there are also feelings, gestures, and perceptions which, the world over, are not experienced in exactly the same way, but are experienced uniquely, because they are expressed in a unique language. A particular spoken language will shape expectations, and, therefore, the experiences of those who speak it, and who identify with it. Thus, there is a great and clear difference between English-speaking characters, doing English things in an English novel by Englishman Dickens, say, and French-speaking, French-acting characters in a French novel by Frenchman Honoré de Balzac. This is because different languages mean different experiences, which provide different mind-sets, or distinct national "moods."

PSYCHOLOGICAL REFLECTION

John Henry Newman was very close to this kind of distinction when, in his *Lectures on the Present Position of Catholics*, he dealt with the cultural and psychological differences between English Protestants and English Catholics. How is it, he asked, that in the same nation, England, there exist two different kinds of Englishman, each experiencing a different set of values, each with different loyalties, each despising the other? His initial remarks in the *Lectures*, state not only his intention to describe this phenomenon, but also imply his experience of the phenomenon.

> I am going to inquire why it is that, in this intelligent nation, and in this rational nineteenth century, we Catholics are so despised and hated by our own countrymen, with whom we have lived all our lives, that they are prompt to believe any story, however extravagant, that is told to our disadvantage; as if beyond a doubt we were, every one of us, either brutishly deluded or preternaturally hypocritical, and they themselves, on the contrary, were in comparison of us absolute specimens of sagacity, wisdom, uprightness, manly virtue, and enlightened Christianity. I am not inquiring why they are not Catholics themselves, but why they are so angry with those who are. Protestants differ among themselves,

without calling each other fools and knaves. . . . I do but pro-
pose to investigate how Catholics come to be so trodden
under foot, and spurned by a people which is endowed by
nature with many great qualities, moral and intellectual. . . .
[F]acts, and logic, and justice, and good sense, and right, and
virtue, are all supposed to lie in the opposite scale. . . . Such
a state of things is not only a trial to flesh and blood, but a
discomfort to the reason and imagination: it is a riddle which
frets the mind from the difficulty of solving it.[53]

To unfret this riddle, Newman tells the fable of a lion who is invited by an affluent man to his expansively expensive home. The host
shows his lion guest through room after room of representations of lions
snagged, lions trapped, lions defeated, and lions killed. When the host
asks the guest lion what he thought of all these works, the lion replied,
"Lions would have fared better, had lions been the artists." Thus, in
dominantly Protestant England, Establishment Protestants were empowered to set the rules, and to "draw the pictures" of reality, while the
minority Catholics played the role of the visiting lion. For Newman,
these two different kinds of Englishman—Protestant and Catholic—
represented two different psychologies, and spoke two different psychological languages. Hence, for Newman, the real issue was the utter
inequity of such a relationship, and especially in a country which prided
itself on being equitous, on respecting fair play, honesty, and openness—all of which traits can be assumed to apply to every Englishman.
Except Catholics.

Technically termed *Great Britain* by the Acts of Union of 1707
and 1801, Newman's England was also the world's dominant power—
its wealth and dominion being buttressed by the seemingly invincible
pound sterling, invulnerable Royal Navy, and far-flung army, upon all
of which "the sun never set." But Newman, unlike Rudyard Kipling,
began (especially after 1845) to think, to act, and to respond differen-
tially from the Establishment model of English bias and bigotry. The
difference between Newman's "Englishness" and that of others began
perhaps as a psychological distinction, but it rapidly developed into a
moral and intellectual distinction. Such a distinction is manifest, for example, in the way Newman understood English virtues—candor, honesty, openness—as being apolitical, but essentially moral. The Victorian
Establishment, however, interpreted those same English virtues as being
political, and essentially amoral. Perhaps the differences were not rooted

merely in personal psychology, but in cultural psychology.

Newman, in his 1851 *Present Position* lectures, expressed humorously, even ironically, his own uneasiness with Establishment-English traits. Established State, Established Church, Established University, he said, were not as truly English as they could, or should, have been. Of course, it was not that Newman—by his Catholic conversion—ceased to be English. Rather, he had ceased to be Establishment English. His attacking enemies, then, were foremost and variously anti-Catholic, power-centered, Establishment English, or, Secular-Liberal-Dis-believing English, or in lesser numbers, Old-Catholic, psychologically assimilated, and Establishment-connected (even Ultra-montane) English. The foremost, being dominant, and of greater number, would sadly include members of Newman's own family.[54]

Normally, of course, diversity of attack—religious, theological, social, political, personal—on a single target, is suggestive, not of a diversity of views, but of a commonality of view, wherein diversities turn into convergence. Hence, to understand the import of violent, unforgiving anti-Newman sentiment, in the nineteenth century and since, requires appeal to a wider context of cultural psychology, which configures such sentiment as *transeunt* effects of political, religious, national, and personal identity. In Newman's universe, convergence of these issues suggests the need for a cultural-linguistic analysis of English national psychology. One such study, which supplies just that, is by Salvador de Madariaga, who once declared, "A nation is a fact of psychology."[55] Amplified, that remark might more readily read, "Every nation is a psychology."

In a cultural study of three European peoples—English, French, and Spanish—Señor Madariaga proposed that, underpinning their apparent European commonality, there lies a stratum of "the subconscious underworld of instincts and tendencies . . . a distinctive attitude which determines . . . natural and spontaneous reactions towards life . . . [which] spring in each case from a characteristic impulse, manifesting itself in a complex psychological entity, an idea-sentiment-force peculiar to each of the three peoples, and constituting for each of them the standard of its behaviour, the key to its emotions and the spring of its pure thoughts."[56]

Supporting his argument, Madariaga directs attention to the perceptual-uniqueness and untranslatability of phrases which embody presumptive perceptions, such as are found in the English phrase, *fair play*, the French expression, *le droit*, and the Spanish affirmation, *el honor*. *Fair play* is a general term derived from sports, which regulates an Englishman's conduct vis-à-vis teammates and adversaries alike, and which provides equilibrium among individuals, or between an individual and a community. As fair play denotes a way of doing things, it is a procedural rule of action. By contrast, because *le droit* denotes an idea, it is a methodological rule of thought, and because *el honor* denotes a "patrimony of the soul," an imperative inner law, it is an existential rule of passion. Thus, English action, French thought, Spanish passion—three determining perceptual assumptions, each of which, says Señor Madariaga, makes possible a national life in "a different key" with a psychologically different "tone." Thus, Cromwell lived in the key of action, Voltaire, in the key of thought, and Santa Teresa of Avila, in the key of Passion.

ENGLISH PSYCHOLOGY

The idea of English action is evident in England's educational system. Action requires self-control, which is evident, not only in English education, but also in English life and in the English language. Self-control is thus a kind of weight, against which action contends, and because it is like a braking system, it is also a conservative force. A sense of weight is present in the English penchant for solid, massive, ponderous, gravitative furnishings, houses, menus, culinary habits. In Dickens's novels, for instance, the festive table is always "weighted down" with heavy foodstuffs—and heavy beverages such as ale and stout. As an English proverb remarks, "Good ale is meat, drink, and cloth."[57] Like tectonic plates, the English language in Newman's nineteenth century brought to bear great weight (as it still does), especially in matters of class, and in the social-psychological distinctions of English life. As George Bernard Shaw once put it in a preface to his play Pygmalion, "It is impossible for an Englishman to open his mouth without making some other Englishman despise him."

The English attraction to action may also explain English empiricism, which is "the blending of each instant of action with the minimum amount of thought," and defines both an attitude and a method. As Señor Madariaga says, "To thought [the Englishman] opposes the barrier of empiricism, to passion, the iron gates of self-control," but he also admits that "English thought is never more vigorous than when it is empirical."[58] Empirical bias in English temperament implies indifference to pure theory. And such indifference sheds light on English utilitarianism, which is "a tendency to exact from every moment of life a positive yield in action."[59] Even subterraneously, empiricism explains English anti-intellectualism. Says Senor Madariaga, "The empirical spirit of the [English] race manifests itself in the unpopularity of the intellectual boy, the 'brainy' fellow, as well as in the tendency to shun intellectual work and cultivate sports."[60] Empirical orientation equally explains English materialism. For, like a fulcrum,[61] action needs tangible and material objects to exert itself [and] . . . leads the Englishman to concentrate on matter. When the Englishman says, "That does not matter," he means, "that has no importance." "Immaterial" means without interest. Of English thought processes, Madariaga says, "The Englishman mistrusts abstract thought," and is not so much illogical as alogical. And he adds, "For logic is a thing he does not trouble about." This is because, as he says, "The Englishman does not seem to think with his brain. His ideas are not ideas properly speaking, but opinions, sentiments, sensations. He does not say 'I think,' but 'I feel.' His opinions do not seem to be emitted from his brain . . . but spread uniformly all over his nervous system."[62]

For the Englishman, life and thought are not synonymous, and thus do not coincide. Life is always irregular, always on the move, always unforeseen, and, therefore, necessarily opposed to thought, which is "regular, fixed, regulated in advance." In English thought, ideas are incarnated, and made into tangible objects. Thus, for example, while French students learn the theory of mechanics through the study of equations, English students learn it by building models.

BLURRED EDGES

To an Englishman, life is not only complicated, but complicating, because it is "blurred round its edges," and, consequently, only vaguely understood. This is why the Englishman is often driven to periphrasis and circumlocution, as witness Dickens's half-serious creation, in *Little Dorritt*, of a Circumlocution Office. Such vagueness is also encountered in the English experience of delays, because delays are always prompted by the "unexpected." Yet English vocabulary is conveniently and marvelously designed to deal with such conditions. Witness, for example, how easily English distinguishes dawdling from dillydallying, fiddling from twiddling, demurring from stalling, tarrying from lagging, or lingering from loitering—and filibustering from temporizing, reserving from shelving, detaining from retarding, even straggling from staying. Then, too, there are English dilatory and delaying tactics, as used in Parliament or committee, which express the accessible English "virtues" of procrastination and adjournment. The real enemy of "We'll cross that bridge when we come to it," is being confronted by a "cut-and-dried plan," or forced to follow a "hard-and-fast rule."

In light of Señor Madariaga's analysis, we suggest that the English mind-set can be portrayed as aspects of behavior, procedure, and attitude. Behaviorally, the English mind-set is characterized by action, fair play, self-control, and sports-centeredness. Procedurally, it is delineated by empiricism, materialism, and utilitarianism. Attitudinally, it is typified by anti-intellectualism, incertitude, and vagueness. These Madariaga-inspired behavioral-procedural-attitudinal traits may then approximate an operational definition of what it means, in Newman's nineteenth-century England, "to experience life like an Englishman." From this perspective, too, it is also understandable why the favored English philosophical bent is not towards metaphysics, but towards ethics—that is, towards modes of conduct rather than modes of being. Viewed descriptively and prescriptively, English ethical conduct may also be ethnic conduct.

ETHNIC CODE

John Henry Newman had said in an 1840 article in the *British Critic*, of which he was then editor, "We Englishmen like manliness, openness, consistency, truth." He then added, "Rome will never gain on us until she learns these virtues and uses them." This "solution" was, in effect, merely to say that, until Rome became an "Englishman's Rome," and thereby exhibited English ethnic-ethical traits, no one in England would pay her much mind. At that time, Newman believed that in order to win English fealty Rome would have first to acquire the English virtue of manliness. If she succeeded in such acquisition, "then she may gain us, but it will be by ceasing to be what we now mean by Rome."[63] By anyone's judgment, that would be a large order, which would implicitly involve an institutional revision of such immense political and spiritual magnitude that Rome would have to become schismatic to itself.

In 1840, of course, Newman was publicly just as much an English-man as any other Englishman. Like other Englishmen, he demon-strated his nationalism by being politically anti-Rome, a sentiment which, since Henry VIII's 1534 Act of Supremacy, had constituted the essential political adhesive by which Englishmen had been tenaciously glued to one another. An "anti-papal" persuasion had for so long, so strongly, so royally, so patriotically bound Englishmen together, be-cause, as folk wisdom and instinct instruct us, acquisition of a common enemy does wonders for binding up the political differences of any group. Also in his British Critic comments of 1840, Newman spoke in the unconditioned inflection of an Englishman who is dedicated to the ethnic-ethical ideals of manliness, openness, consistency, and truth. At the time, Newman was considered as manly as any other Englishman. Yet the following year, on 27 February 1841, Newman's Tract XC (90) appeared. Because of it, he was censured (but the document was not condemned) as being, indeed, unProtestant and unAnglican, and there-fore, unEnglish.

MANLINESS

Manliness and manly are terms which Newman continued to use, even long after 1840. For example, in The Idea of a University, he referred to manliness when he compared the "hard times" of the English past, when life demanded courage and endurance, to recent times of luxury, when "men congregate in towns . . . and good government robs them of courage and manliness." He praised John Locke for being a manly Eng-lishman, prizing good English qualities. "I have so high a respect for the character and ability of Locke," Newman confessed, "for his manly sim-plicity of mind and his outspoken candour." In A Grammar of Assent, Newman also argued that "Real Assents . . . form the mind out of which they grow, and impart to it a seriousness and manliness which inspires to other minds a confidence in its views."[64] Seriousness, then, is man-liness, and, conversely, manliness is seriousness. The implication that seriousness denotes manliness, should also resensitize us to the dis-tinction which Newman drew between the seriousness of the True Church and True University, as opposed to the lack of seriousness on the part of the feel-good church and the utilitarian university.

Terms already suggested, then, have defined English manliness, and done so by bracketing ethnic-ethical characteristics of—for instance—candor, confidence, generosity, openness, outspokenness, stability, steadiness, straight-forwardness, transparency, and truthfulness. Yet one other defining term, so far left unmentioned but of great English import, is that of simplicity.

SIMPLICITY

Simplicity particularly defines English ethnic-ethical traits, and has been of distinct service to the English mind. Everyday English preferences, everyday English choices are still characterized by an ideal of English simplicity—whether in styles of haberdashery or dress, demeanor, salutation, manners, letter-writing, or diurnal behavior. For example, English Puritans starkly invoked the spirit of simplicity in their dress, address, and linguistic conceits. This is clearly manifest if we compare English Puritans to the ornate Irani "puritans," who, after all, were the first to invent puritanism, catharism, and manichaeism. Simplicity is also especially emblematic of English philosophy and science. For example, William of Ockham, perceiving the singularity of things, devised a procedural rule—known as "Ockham's razor"—in order to guard against unnecessarily multiplying causes, beings, or even explanations.[65] As a consequence of such a "razor," the "truth" of things is therefore the truth of their simplicity, as in the formula: "The simpler, the truer."

SIMPLICITY AND COMPLEXITY

The simplicity motif of Ockham's razor also has consequences in the political assumptions of English national psychology. Because the converse of being English is being foreign, then the opposite of English simplicity must be foreign complexity. Complexity, of course, was for the Tudors and their successors the signature of England's continental enemies—the French, the Spaniards, the Italians—all of whom were, in addition, Catholic. To Elizabethans, for example, Jesuits were nationally advertised as sly, duplicitous, equivocating, and, in the bargain, foreigners. Especially since the Tudors, England has insularly viewed the world as being divided between *us* (simple English) and *them* (complex foreigners). As foreigners, they would "naturally" be subtle, sly, cunning, deceitful, duplicitous, underhanded, and therefore natural enemies of insular England. Should anyone be surprised, then, that Catholic-convert Newman, by turning towards Rome—foreign, enmitous power, political and religious enemy of the English State—should

be accused, not merely of being unmanly, but of having foreign sentiments—of being unEnglish.

According to Sir William Blackstone's nineteenth-century
Commentaries, "Where a person is reconciled to the See of Rome, or
procures others to be reconciled, the offense amounts to high treason."[66]
Converting to Rome, Newman could automatically be considered an
enemy of the State, and thus an enemy of the English people. Being
gratuitously dubbed a "Blackstone traitor," Newman would inevitably
become fair game for all kinds of attacks.

When it comes to manly-unmanly descriptors, however, Newman himself drew certain important distinctions, an action which
thereby suggests that the category *manly* is not really simple but, in fact,
is complex. In the 1840 *British Critic*, Newman praised the spirit of
"manliness, openness, consistency, truth." As manliness may uphold religion, so unmanliness will hinder religion: "I here mean by unmanliness the inability to do with ourselves what we wish . . . the saying fine
things, and yet slothfully lying on our couch [is he reminded of Richard
Whatley's encouched style of tutoring?], as if we could not get up,
though we ever so much wished it."[67]

But, even though Newman was supportive of music and poetry,
he observed that, in a certain kind of education, poetry and music "are
especially likely to make us unmanly," just as literary composition,
painting, and the like "have a tendency to make us trifling and unmanly,
and therefore are to be viewed by each of us with suspicion as far as regards himself." Here Newman is introducing a complex (not a simple)
representation, which qualifies "the danger of an elegant and polite education," which "separates feeling and acting; it teaches us to think,
speak, and be affected aright, without forcing us to practice what is
right."[68] And this view will precisely affect the complex manner by
which Newman, in Discourse VIII of *The Idea of a University*, will distinguish (a) the gentleman who, in perfection of the intellect, links moral
and intellectual action, and (b) the "gentleman" who, mirroring British
social psychology, does not. This latter figure is prompted to seek an
"over-jealousy of accomplishment," and has thus cultivated his mind,
but not his spirit; his head, but not his heart; his knowledge, but not his
virtue. Such a gentleman may therefore become "trifling" and "unserious." But, since religion is serious, it is clear that to be "trifling" about
religion is to be unserious, therefore unmanly and, ultimately, irreligious.

Newman argued that whenever "thinking aright" does not lead to "doing aright," then an implicit dichotomy exists between the capacity for action and the capacity for thought—and such dichotomy compromises both. But if, as Señor Madariaga proposes, action dominates the English mind-set, then English preference for sports, rather than for thoughts, will surely tend, as an English cultural condition, to magnify that same dichotomy. Better yet, as a cultural condition, it will be a temptation, to which Englishmen are especially prone. Hence, English cultural emphasis on action will not necessarily imply emphasis on right action. Thus, too, the English idea of fair play, which appears so central to English life, may, in fact, be more ethnic than ethical.

KNOWING OR DOING

Plato's Socrates resisted separation of knowing right from doing right, because he argued that really to know what is right, intellectually implies an actionable commitment to what is right and true, and thus to incarnating that commitment in action. Really to know what is true, Socrates suggested, is to act on that truth. St. Paul, on the other hand, unlike Socrates, underscored, as an everyday occurrence, the fact that there is a human weakness in attending to knowing and to acting on good resolutions. Such occurrence of moral weakness undoes the good that one would do, by doing the evil that one seeks not to do (Rom. 7: 19).

Perhaps, says Newman, one wishes to resist the temptation of cowardice. But, then, with full recognition of English style, he asks, "Shall we therefore do our duty, quitting ourselves like men? Rather, we are likely to talk loudly, and then run from the danger." He continues, "If we allow our feelings to be excited without acting upon them, we do mischief to the moral system within us, just as we might spoil a watch, or other piece of mechanism, by playing with the wheels of it. We weaken its springs, and they cease to act truly. . . . How, after destroying the connexion between feeling and acting, how shall we get ourselves to act when circumstances make it our duty to do so?"[69]

Bifurcating thought and action, Newman suggests, may occur in one kind of education. It may therewith inhibit "manliness," by inhibiting religion. And he underscores this point: "The refinement which literature gives, is that of thinking, feeling, knowing and speaking, right, not of acting right, and thus while it makes the manners amiable, and the conversation decorous and agreeable, it has no tendency to make the conduct, the practice of the man virtuous."[70]

Newman's solution to the psychological, intellectual, and moral split between right action and right thinking, however, is to follow the model of Scripture: "St. Paul and St. Luke show us, that we may be sturdy workers in the Lord's service, and bear our cross manfully, though we be adorned with all the learning of the Egyptians; or rather, the resources of literature, and the graces of a cultivated mind, may be made both a lawful source of enjoyment to the possessor, and a means of introducing and recommending the Truth to others."[71]

It is not education of itself, however, which inhibits religion—and thus proper human action. Rather, it is a certain kind of education which separates moral action from intellectual action. In another early sermon, Newman strikes a somewhat different note, thus shifting the emphasis in discourse about manliness. Sometimes so-called manliness (Kingsleyesque, jingoist manliness?) may also be downright dangerous to religion and faith. Newman put it this way: "But when our minds became more manly and the world opened upon us, then in proportion to the intellectual gifts with which God had honoured us, came the temptation of unbelief and disobedience. Then came reason, led on by passion, to war against our better knowledge. . . . A murmuring against the religious service . . . a rebellious rising against the authority of Conscience, and a proud arguing against the Truth . . . [these] are the beginnings of apostasy. Then come the affectation of originality, the desire to appear manly and independent."[72]

HEART AND MIND

In early sermons, Newman suggests that there are two dangers which one-dimensional manliness can embody: (1) cultivation only of the mind and not of the heart, and (2) hardening of the heart, and therefore hardening of the mind. By 1851, Newman had readjusted his assessment of manliness by emphasizing the implicit morality, which is present in true manliness. Also, in his *Lectures on the Present Position of Catholics*, given to lay members of the Oratory, he maintained that, while cultivation of mind is not the same as religious principle, such cultivation does, indeed, greatly enhance human nature. And it does so, through revision of the mind's "lesser defects."

Newman thus extols the view that, as we widen our intellectual horizon, and "as we mount up in the knowledge of men and things," so, in proportion, do we make progress in "those qualities and that character of mind which we denote by the word *gentleman*." Here, the term *gentleman* carries with it a sense of forthrightness, and therefore of manliness. When Newman revisits this theme in *The Idea of a University*, he will recall that division between knowledge and virtue, but without denying the possibility of having knowledge *and* virtue conjoined in the same person. In his Catholic University sermon of 1857, "Intellect, the Instrument of Religious Training," he will precisely reaffirm such a view.

Yet in the *Present Position* lectures, Newman urged upon his audience of lay Oratorians that, in their exchanges with English Protestants, it is they, the Oratorians, who must be manly. Such heroic acquisition will make them unlike the Protestants.

> "Your opponents, my Brothers, are too often emphatically not gentlemen: but it will be for you . . . to be manly and noble in your bearing towards them; to be straightforward in your dealings with them; to show candour, generosity, honourable feeling, good sense, and forbearance, in spite of provocations; to refrain from taking unfair or small advantages over them; not to fret at insults, to bear imputations, and to interpret the actions of all in the best sense you possibly can. It is not only more religious, more becoming, not only happier, to have these excellent dispositions of mind, but it is far the most likely way, in the long run, to persuade and succeed."[73]

Here is a clear desideratum for manliness to be exercised by Catholics:

> "I want a laity, not arrogant, not rash in speech, not disputatious, but . . . who know their religion, who enter into it, who know just where they stand, who know what they hold, and what they do not. . . . I want an intelligent, well-instructed laity. . . . I wish you to enlarge your knowledge, to cultivate your reason, to get an insight into the relation of truth to truth, to learn to view things as they are, to understand how faith and reason stand to each other, what are the bases and principles of Catholicism, and where lie the main inconsistencies and absurdities of the Protestant theory."[74]

DOUBLE IDENTITY

With a new twist, Newman formulates his version of English ethnic-ethical ideals. With it, there comes the distinct implication of a clear difference between two kinds of English identity—manly English Catholics and unmanly English Protestants. It is as if he were saying, for the first time, that there can be a clear difference between two kinds of gentlemanly identity. By acting in a manly fashion, Newman asserts, Catholics will demonstrate that they are truly Englishmen, while, at the same time, the bigoted English-Protestant counterparts will demonstrate just the opposite, and do so by their actively demonstrating that they are not truly dedicated to fair play, and so, not really acting like Englishmen ought to act.

At this point, then, Newman appears to have developed a new sense of what English manliness can mean. More than just declaring his own manly sense of English identity, he also provides new contexts for the term. For example, he considered Homer's poems "manly." [75] In contrast, in the subsequent Newman-Kingsley conflict, Kingsley tried to pass himself off as "the manly Englishman," an "advocate of chivalrous generosity," but all the while he was accusing Newman of being "the shifty Papist, the 'serpentine' dealer in 'cunning and sleight-of-hand logic.' " Of Kingsley, Newman would later say that, "Had he been a man of large and cautious mind, he would not have taken it for granted that cultivation must lead every one to see things precisely as he sees them himself." [76]

Manliness, unquestionably, is an important issue in English cultural life, and will later, disputatiously, become a central issue in Newman's public life. So, criticism of Newman, just before and after his conversion, often centered on his allegedly unmanly behavior, as expressed in "foreign" traits — *mendacity, slyness, ungentlemanliness.* Were these "foreign traits" alleged to suggest his "unmanliness"? Or just his *un*Englishness? And why would such allegations be suspended in solutions of such vitriol? And where would Charles Kingsley and "muscular Christianity" fit in? And what role, during the forthcoming contretemps between Kingsley and Newman, would be played by Newman's alleged "feminine traits"? Is there anything in that subsequent farrago of Victorian spite and enmity which can explain the significance of its rhetorical intensity? Of its being targeted on interpretations of English *identity* and gender *identity*?

IDENTITY AND IDEA

We will suggest that these issues were not abstractly suspended in Newman's life. Obversely, they also tell us something about the effects of Newman themes, such as "cultivation of mind," or about the binary "contrast between" versus "unification of," intellectual and moral values. Thus, Newman's intentions, as expressed in his University-Sermons and University-Lectures will also have bearing on the complex colloquy about English ethnic, ethical, and gender values of the time, as well as upon the theme of conscience and wisdom. Newman, a man of gentle manner, who was also resolute in action—*suaviter in modo, fortiter in re*—seems to have united in himself the very qualities which would be in dispute.

CHAPTER 5:
HEART AND MIND

"Literature which . . . represents
the abundance of the heart . . . approaches
to conversation."

"The Christian Creed . . . takes
possession of the intellect and heart."

"Throw yourself heart and mind
into what you are about."

The rich tapestry of Newman's varied life, woven from ordinary every-day experiences, was transfigured in his heart by being transformatively enlarged in his mind.

As Newman modulated ordinary speech into a gift for conversation, so he transfigured conversation into friendship, deflected grievance into kindness, and affection into clairvoyant vision. Because he lived consciously in the presence of providence, he had an abiding sense of the splendor of God's uplifting love. Newman was therefore a person of enlargement, enhancement, and abundance. Magnifying the ardor of his heart by the order of his mind, he leavened even his darkest trials, full measure, through concord, kindness, and prayer. Sensitive as he always was to the aspirations of his own mind and heart, he was pastorally devoted to the aspirations of the hearts and minds of others. Asked once by a Birmingham assemblage for his blessing, Cardinal Newman turned simple request into heartfelt response: "I bless you with all my heart, as I desire to be blessed myself. Each one of us has his own individuality, his separate history, his achievements and his future, his duties, his responsibilities, his solemn trial and his eternity."[1]

Newman held in especially high regard the individuality and unfathomable uniqueness of each human soul, as if he were identifying with St. Augustine's assertion that "God loves each of us as if there were only one of us." As Newman said in an early sermon, "Nothing is more difficult than to realize that every man has a distinct soul, that every one of all the millions who live or have lived is as whole and independent in being in himself, as if there were no one else in the whole world but he. . . . He has a depth within him unfathomable, an infinite abyss of existence."[2]

Even as Newman neared the end of his own life, he became more vividly conscious of the unique mystery of individual human identity.[3] If he paused in meditation, it was not so much over death (such as in *The Dream of Gerontius*) as over a final judgment. In light of that judgment, he sought, as early as 1843, to retract certain hard-edged anti-Roman remarks that he had previously published. Again, in 1871, he reprinted a two-volume collection of earlier essays, so that he could correct assertions which he had written largely as political expressions of his "Englishness."[4]

APOSTLE TO ENGLAND

The uniqueness of which Newman was always proud was being English. Consistently, he also took pride in the English Church, and in how it had been established by Pope St. Gregory the Great (540–604), Doctor and Father of the Church, Apostle of the English, who simply called himself the "servant of God's servants." Gregory's role in Christianizing England was recorded by St. Bede (672–735)—that Venerable "Candle," himself a Doctor of the Church, who told how, before elevation to the papacy, Gregory had passed one day through a Roman marketplace. There he "saw among other merchandise some boys exposed for sale," and asked who they were and whence they came? "They are called Angles [*Angli*] from the island of Britain." Fitting, replied Gregory, for "they have the faces of Angels [*Angeli*]."[5] In 596, six years after his election, Pope Gregory sent to England his trusted Benedictine companion, Augustine, together with forty monks, to inaugurate the English Church Catholic. Established first in Kent, with Augustine its first archbishop, the Church soon spread throughout the land from its episcopal center at Canterbury. It was a story which Newman himself reproduced.[6]

In the treasury of the English Church, Newman also discovered interfusing qualities and binary attributes, which he experienced in his

own mind as moral and intellectual integrity, which promoted confluence of heart and mind, convergence of virtue and knowledge, and conjunction of conscience and wisdom. Newman's fidelity to such relations
may explain why he believed that the human mind, by virtue of its
imago-nature (let us make mankind in image of us, in likeness of us),
is destined to dwell in divine society. For this reason, Newman intuited
that it is precisely such human destiny, based upon its *imago*-nature,
which invites the human mind to stretch, to expand, to enlarge its powers. With renewed sense of its need for spiritual abundance, the human
mind is invited to replicate a scriptural creativity, by fully responding to
God's genetic and exhortative commands (*mitzvoth*) to increase, to be
fruitful, and to multiply—to be, in short, creatively enlarging.[7]

Scriptural imagery also illustrates, for Newman, how *imago*-
theology can become theophanic theology—that is to say, a theology
of God's presence. It is this theology which anchors Newman's concept
of moral-intellectual life and prompts him towards recognition of the
integrative nature of religious experience, because religion binds together (*religare*) binomial aspects of human personality. Thus, as Newman prayerfully thought about God, he could thoughtfully pray to Him.
In so doing, he unified devotion and learning—through actions which
turn conscience into wisdom, and transform wisdom into love. A comprehension—that is, a "bringing-together" and "understanding"—of
Christian religion can then interpret religion as "education of the soul,"
which is dedicated to perfection of the intellect.

BINARY PATTERN

Such a view might also explain why Newman consistently focused his
genius on serving both Church and University—or (in different language) religion and education. Such a dual ministry recognizably typified the binary pattern of Newman's life.[8] This complemental similitude
of Newman's heart and mind amalgamated his commitment to devotion with learning, to faith with understanding, and bonded his sense of
moral action with intellectual accomplishment. Here, indeed, surfacing
anew, is Newman's sense of connections and interconnectedness, which
so pervades his enlarging approach to human experience. This is so because, as he suggested, intellect "takes a connected view of old and new,
past and present, far and near"; it "makes every thing in some sort lead
to every thing else." For Newman, connections between religion and

education also appear as expressions of the spiritual relation between the Church's empire of faith, and the University's empire of intellect. Such a vision of connectivity also signifies the kind of enlargement, which, in human educative terms, can reach out beyond itself, and, in consequence, can be said to presage, and to pledge, a conviction of the pleromaic promise of the Spirit.

The syntactic, systematizing idea of spiritual enlargement, so central to Newman's vocabulary, implicitly reflects Johannine-Pauline-Patristic tradition. For we need merely recall that the Gospel and Letters of John, the Epistles of Paul, and the writings of the Greek and Latin Fathers came easily to Newman's mind and tongue. His first contact with Patristic literature, as he tells us, was when he was fifteen years old:

> I read Joseph Milner's *Church History* [*History of the Church of Christ*, 3 vols., 1794–97], and was nothing short of enamoured of the long abstracts from St. Augustine, St. Ambrose, and the other Fathers which I found there. . . . The broad philosophy of Clement and Origen carried me away. . . . Some portions of their teaching . . . came like music to my inward ear, as if the response to ideas, which, with little external to encourage them, I had cherished so long. . . . Nature was a parable: Scripture was an allegory: pagan literature, philosophy, and mythology, properly understood, were but a preparation for the Gospel. The Greek poets and sages were in a certain sense prophets. . . . There had been a directly divine dispensation granted to the Jews; but there had been in some sense a dispensation carried on in favour of the Gentiles.[9]

PLEROMAIC THEOLOGY

Awareness of spiritual enlargement is consonant with Newman's boyhood apprehension of how Johannine-Pauline-Patristic theology, long intrinsic to Christian life and thought, reveals the filling and fulfilling relevance of Scripture to everyday experience. Through a sense of enlargement, for example, the Christian view of history discloses how the Divine Imperium, which St. Paul preached, has made known to mankind "a plan for the fullness () of time, to gather up all things" in Christ, both "in heaven and on earth" (Eph. 1: 10).

The filling, fulfilling, enlarging process in Johannine language is rooted in the fact that Christ is logos, light, and life. He is logos in that

"All things were made by him, and without him was not anything made that was made." (Jn. 1: 3). He is light, in that He is illuminator, teacher, source of wisdom, "light of men" (Jn. 1: 4), and "light of the world" (Jn. 11: 9). He is life, as his own words announce: "I am the pathway, the truth, and the life" (Jn. 14: 6), and "whoever believes in the Son has everlasting life" (Jn. 3: 36). John's Gospel also ascribes to Christ's Resurrection a continuing, filling presence, or inchoate parousia—an advent—which anticipates Christ's final Parousia. Through Christ's implicit parousia, Newman well understood, everyday experience becomes suffused and enlarged with sacramental possibilities.

PAUL'S UNKNOWN GOD

Addressing the Athenians, who were themselves dedicated to an unknown God ($\dot{\alpha}\gamma\nu\dot{\omega}\sigma\tau\omega$ $\theta\epsilon\tilde{\omega}$), St. Paul identified the True God, Whom they—now, at last, through Christ—could scripturally come to know (Acts 17: 23). Applying to the True God the words of seventh-century (BC) Cretan poet, Epimenides, St. Paul could then proclaim to the Athenians that it is the Christian God "in whom we live and move and have our being" (Acts 17: 28). Only to God, says Paul, does Power over all things belong, because "the Lord's is the earth and the fullness ($\pi\lambda\acute{\eta}\varrho\omega\mu\alpha$) thereof" (1 Cor. 10: 26). God the Father has likewise put all things under Christ's dominion, "and has made him the head over all things for the Church, which is his body, and the fullness ($\pi\lambda\acute{\eta}\varrho\omega\mu\alpha$) of him who fills ($\pi\lambda\eta\varrho\sigma\nu\mu\acute{\epsilon}\nu\sigma\nu$) all in all" (Eph. 1: 22–23). It is in Christ, St. Paul insists, that there "dwells all the fullness ($\pi\lambda\acute{\eta}\varrho\omega\mu\alpha$) of the Godhead bodily," and Paul can thus assure the Colossians that "you are complete ($\pi\epsilon\pi\lambda\eta\varrho\omega\mu\acute{\epsilon}\nu\sigma\iota$) in him" (Col. 2: 9–10). In many ways, Newman's pervasive sense of Christ's enlarging presence in experiential reality reflects Pauline theology that Christ

> is the image of the invisible God, the firstborn of all creation, for in him all things in heaven and on earth were created, things visible and invisible. . . . All things have been created through him and for him. He himself is before all things, and in him all things hold together. He is the had of the body, the church; he is the beginning, the firstborn from the dead: so that he may come to have first place in everything. For in him all the fullness ($\pi\lambda\acute{\eta}\varrho\omega\mu\alpha$) of God was pleased to dwell (Col. 1: 15–19).

THEOLOGY OF ENLARGEMENT

As God the Father is the source of all things, so, says Paul, it is He "for whom we exist." There is "one Lord, Jesus Christ, through whom are all things, and through whom we exist" (1 Cor. 8: 6). Ultimately, the reason all things are subjected to God is "so that God may be all in all" (ἵνα ᾖ ὁ θεὸς τὰ πάντα ἐν πᾶσιν — 1 Cor. 15: 28). Here, then, a new vista on experience opens up. And this is such as to express a theology of enlargement, to which Scripture gives witness, and of which philosophy also provides partial insight. Hence, St. Justin Martyr —Flavius Justinus (c.100–c.165)— announced that, while only Christianity provides the complete answer to questions posed by the philosophers, philosophy itself clarifies the path to the True God. Philosophy can then be viewed as an enlightenment, a spiritual enlargement, an educative journey towards the Truth—which is fully found only in divine revelation. Truth, observes Justin, is therefore Christian Truth, and whatever has been truly said is "the property of us Christians" (*Second Apology*, 10).

St. Ireneus of Lyons (c.130–c.200) also suggested that Christianity is the one, true philosophy. "The true Gnosis," he said, "is the teaching of the Apostles" (*Contra Haereses*, IV, 33, 8). Philosophy (as Joseph Milner, in his recitation, had made known to young Newman) is consequently God's extra-scriptural gift to the pagans. Philosophy proffered an enhancement, enlargement, and education, of the human spirit. Like all true learning, Philosophy is an enlarging function of Truth itself, which, ultimately, is Christian Truth.

Clement of Alexandria (c.158–c.215), a thinker particularly dear to Newman's heart, said that while philosophers always appeal to the logos, it is only Christians—those who actually believe in Christ—who already know the logos incarnate. Clement suggests that the God who gave the Old Covenant and the God who gave the New Covenant is, indeed, the same God who gave Greek philosophy (*Stromata*, I. 5). Philosophy is therefore God's extra-scriptural covnot merely an ornament of thought, but is, insofar as a man is capable of pursuing it, essential to Christian life (*Stromata*, I. 7, 8, 9). Philosophy has prepared the pagan world for Christ, in much the same way that Mosaic law had prepared the way toward Christ (Παιδαγωγὸς εἰς Χριστόν). Even before His incarnation, Christ is teacher and educator of the world. Philosophy, therefore, is one of God's works, because it can open men's minds, and prepare them for the Gospel. It follows, then, that Christian

Gnosis is, in fact, Christian faith as transformed into intellectual knowledge.

Origen (c.185–254), disciple of Clement of Alexandria, and most learned of the ante-Nicene Fathers, was Christianity's first synthetic thinker. Demonstrating that Platonic philosophy is consonant with Christianity, Origen provided Christian thought a philosophical structure. It is imperative, Origen's argument runs, to know thyself, and to know thyself is (as Newman reiterated) in some way to know God, because God demands to be known. The human desire to understand nature and experience is implanted in humankind by God, because God asks that humankind seek to learn of Himself. Knowledge of created things thereby bears within itself knowledge of the divine Creator of things. So, he who despises philosophy can have no genuine piety towards God. Since philosophy is the love of wisdom, he who rejects wisdom, also rejects God, who is wisdom itself (*De Principiis*, II, ii, 4).

Of course, this link between wisdom and God, or truth and God, would be indelibly inscribed by St. Augustine in his *Confessions*: "For wherever I found truth, there I found my God, who is truth itself. Thus from what I learned of you, you have remained in my memory and there I find you, whenever I recall you in memory, so that I am continually delighted in you" (Confessions X, 24).

EXEMPLARISTIC THEOLOGY

The Christic Word, said Origen, is mediator between the Father and creatures, because Christ is the exemplar, model, of creation. Desire to create resides in the Father, but in Christ the Logos (a variation on Plato's *Timaios*), all things are created. Perfection and fulfillment of creation comes through the action of the Holy Spirit. In this Patristic focus on the Trinity—later to be articulated by European medieval theologians—the whole process is one in which the Father wills, the Son makes, and the Holy Spirit makes perfect.

Similarly, St. Gregory of Nyssa (c.330–c.395), brother of St. Basil the Cappadocian, argued—as St. Anselm, after him, would also do—that the Christian message, though accepted on faith, not logic, is nonetheless fully intelligible. Together with Origen, Gregory proclaimed the "restoration of all things" (ἀποκατάστασις πάντων), and the ultimate enlargement of reality, or "fullness" (πλήρωμα) of all things in Christ. Gregory likewise set forth the principle that Christ is the really real (ὄντως ὄν), from whom all creatures have their being and truth-fulness, and through whom, by the Incarnation, mankind is restored to God's image. Gregory perceived a spiritual need for constant, personal enlargement of the soul towards God. Through love, God eternally draws the loving soul towards Himself, and thus clarifies the soul's spiritual ascent. His notion of ascent, unlike that of Plotinus, is thoroughly Christocentric, because he envisions Christ the Logos as intimately engaged in the Godward advance of the soul. The enlarging, developing, fulfilling advance is not, however, for the sake of some oriental solitary blending with the divine. Rather, it is for the sake of realizing—making real—the divine fullness, the pleroma of Christ.

St. Athanasius (c.296–373), greatest anti-Arian theologian, and the Father who especially influenced Newman's thinking, insisted that God does not have existence, but—as expressed in Exodus 3:14, "I Am Who I Am"—is *existence itself*. Athanasius added that the Logos seeks always to support creatures through a grace (χάρις)—a word, coincidentally, whose accusative plural, χάριτας, is identical with the Latin word for compassionate love, *caritas*.

ENLARGING REVELATION

Against the backdrop of such arguments by St. Athanasius, Newman understood how deeply embedded in nature is the enlarging message of revelation. In Scripture, as Newman observed, "The whole revealed scheme rests on Nature for the validity of its evidence. . . . There is no greater satisfaction to the Christian than that which arises from his perceiving that the revealed system is rooted deep in the natural course of things, of which it is merely the result and completion; that his Saviour has interpreted for him the faint or broken accents of Nature; and that in them, so interpreted, he has, as if in some old prophecy, at once the evidence and the lasting memorial of the truths of the Gospel."[10]

These words of Newman, envisioning grace as fulfilling and enlarging nature, as Henri de Lubac assures us, were "read eagerly" by Pierre Teilhard de Chardin, and produced therewith a marvelous effect upon his own cosmic vision.[11] In Teilhard's vision, enlargement of consciousness means "to see God everywhere, to see him in all that is most hidden, most solid, and most ultimate in the world. . . . [It is] a way of teaching how to see." For Teilhard, enlargement is historicized by means of the human attempt to be about a "divinization of activity" and a "sanctification of actions." Such actions add to reality, because, Teilhard would say, any addition of consciousness is an addition to being. Evolutionary enlargement of consciousness in the cosmos portends for Teilhard—in a sense, not distant from Newman's own intuitions—that something spiritual is constantly and educatively occurring. As Teilhard said, "Under the free and ingenious effort of successive intelligences, something . . . irreversibly accumulates, according to all the evidence, and is transmitted, at least collectively by means of education, down the course of ages. The point here is that this 'something' . . . ends up always by translating itself into an augmentation of consciousness, and consciousness in its turn, as we now know, is nothing less than the substance and heart of life in process of evolution."[12]

In like spirit, John Henry Newman, in the last of his *University Sermons*, asserted, "Realizing is the very life of true developments."[13] From Newman's perspective, Patristic tradition clarifies devotional practice as an essential condition of genuine thought. This is so, because devotion stretches, expands, extends, and raises up the mind to God. Such stretching can provide a psychological *and* theological context. For God, as Augustine said, "by deferring our hope, stretches our desire; by the desiring, stretches the mind; by stretching, makes it more capacious. . . . Let us therefore desire, for we shall be filled. Let us stretch ourselves unto Him, that when He shall come, He may fill us."[14]

Just so, stretching and enlarging the human heart and mind transforms interrogation into prayer, and transposes prayer into inquiry. Inquiry, as it relates to and communes with Truth itself, becomes another way of seeking God. To Newman, stretching and enlarging the mind is the beginning of wisdom, and so the beginning of a fundamental process of serious life. Reflecting the influence of Athanasius, Newman could then envision how God can draw up "the whole circle of creatures into divine adoption."[15]

COSMIC ENLARGEMENT

Though more implicit than explicit, there is still in Newman's thought an inherent sense of cosmic enlargement, which is reflective of Johannine-Pauline-Patristic tradition. That tradition is woven—like so many golden threads—into the rich tapestry of Newman's life and mind. Its presence explains his constant concern for scriptural "abundance of the heart" and mind, which, conceptualized as enlargement, is the necessary condition of religious and educative experience. Without enlargement, there can be no development. Without development, there can be no religious or educative process. Development is precisely what religion and education entail because they envision a rigorous unfolding of consciousness. Newman's *Essay on the Development of Christian Doctrine* suggested that enlargement and development are necessary for the educative life of Christian doctrine. Development of Christian teaching—which is exactly what doctrine means—is an educative process in the enterprise of the Church. This is another way of saying that development likewise constitutes the necessary condition of education.

Because religion itself "has its own enlargement," those who may hitherto have been untouched by the unseen world—as is "often remarked of uneducated persons"—may, when enlargement comes to them, begin "looking into themselves, regulating their hearts, reforming their conduct, and meditating on death and judgment, heaven and hell." So, Newman adds, "in point of intellect," they become different beings from what they had been. Prior to their renovation, says Newman, such people "took things as they came, and thought no more of one thing than another. But now every event has a meaning; they have their own estimate of whatever happens to them; they are mindful of times and seasons, and compare the present with the past; and the world, no longer dull, monotonous, unprofitable, and hopeless, is a various and complicated drama, with parts and an object, and an awful moral."[16]

ENLARGING VISION

In *The Idea of a University*, Newman constantly reverts to this theme of enlargement. Thus, the opposite of enlargement, he says in Discourse VI, is "the error of distracting and enfeebling the mind by an unmeaning profusion of subjects; of implying that a smattering in a dozen branches of knowledge is not shallowness, which it really is, but enlargement, which it is not."[17]

Again, in the following Discourse VII, he says that to imagine that we know intuitively, or at a glance, or at once, or by simple vision, is to mistake knowing. Rather, we know "by going round an object, by the comparison, the combination, the mutual correction, the continual adaptation, of many partial notions, by the employment, concentration, and joint action of many faculties and exercises of the mind."[18]

This "joint action of many faculties" is inquiry into creation. Hence, the sense and concept of enlargement of mind is a theme which constantly enlarged Newman's mind. He writes, for example, to Hurrell Froude (having won for himself the debate about going overseas with the Froudes): "But it may be a duty to consult for one's health, to enlarge one's ideas, to break one's studies, and to have the name of a travelled man." Again, in speaking of University lectures and discussion, he says that they issue in "a general exchange of ideas, and . . . an enlargement of mind, intellectual and social," and that "cultivation of the intellect is an end distinct and sufficient in itself, and . . . it is an enlargement or illumination."[19]

TRANSFORMATION

Enlargement of the mind imposes a transformational process, because it involves, not a mere addition, or accretion, or accrual—as simulated, say, by grains of sand, pebbles, rocks, or fungus. What it requires is growing, germinating, and enhancement, because enlargement is an inward process, which cannot merely be duplicated or imitated in the form of "respectable" behavior. The important contrast between enlargement and addition, appears, for instance, in a sermon in which Newman measures the true Christian against the "respectable" but uncaring person. Serious effort at personal enhancement by the Christian person is unmistakable, and cannot easily be imitated. The Christian is genuinely alive—reproductive of the spirit by producing real effects—and willing to grow spiritually. In contrast, one who is merely "respectable" is already spiritually necrotic—being unwilling to grow.

This was a contrast which Newman laid out in his sermon "Equanimity," where he drew—as if in a prefiguring of the "gentleman" of the *Idea*'s Discourse VIII—a distinction between Christian composure, and the "composure" of indifference. The Christian, says Newman, "is cheerful, easy, kind, gentle, courteous, candid, unassuming; has no pretense, no affectation, no ambition, no singularity. . . . He is serious, sober, discreet, grave, moderate, mild, with so little that is unusual or striking in his bearing, that he may easily be taken at first sight for an ordinary man."

In contrast, there is that "common-place state of mind which does show itself calm, composed, and candid, yet is very far from the true Christian temper. In this day especially it is very easy for men to be benevolent, liberal, and dispassionate. It costs nothing to be dispassionate when you feel nothing, to be cheerful when you have nothing to fear, to be generous or liberal when what you give is not your own, and to be benevolent and considerate when you have no principles and no opinions. Men nowadays are moderate and equitable, not because the Lord is at hand, but because they do not feel that He is coming."[20]

Inner Growth

The Christian, then, is very much alive, and enlarging, while the spiritual rival is inert and diminished. Enlargement, being a growth process, is consequently a life process, which, in traditional discourse, is "a self-perfective immanent activity." In such traditional language, inspired by St. Thomas, life is what makes matter a first step "towards a greater similarity with God."[21] Because growth is always from within, it can never be merely an accumulation from without. In noetic terms, then, Newman observes that enlargement of mind

> consists, not merely in the passive reception into the mind of a number of ideas hitherto unknown to it, but in the mind's energetic and simultaneous action upon and towards and among those new ideas which are rushing in upon it. It is the action of a formative power, reducing to order and meaning the matter of our acquirements. It is a making the objects of our knowledge subjectively our own, or, to use a familiar word, it is a digestion of what we receive into the substance of our previous state of thought; and without this no enlargement is said to follow. There is no enlargement unless there be a comparison of ideas one with another."[22]

Enlargement requires a noetically active comparison. Through purposeful comparing action, semantic adjustments are made, because the inquirer seeks fulfillment of conceptual involvement. Here, there is no room for passivity. There can be no dreaming, no dawdling, no deferral, no idling, no putting off, no waiting for inspiration, because there must be constant examination and systematizing. There must, in short, be an abundance of mental participation. Only when we are so fulfillingly involved, says Newman, can we "feel our minds to be growing and expanding then, when we not only learn, but refer what we learn to what we know already. It is not the mere addition to our knowledge that is the illumination, but the locomotion, the movement onwards, of that mental centre, to which both what we know, and what we are learning, the accumulating mass of our acquirements, gravitates."[23]

Moreover, only through active enlargement of mind can connections be made. This enlarging power to make connections of idea with idea, of meaning with meaning, of intelligibility with intelligibility, of reality with reality, is inherently the power of intellect. As Pierre Rousselot once put it, "Nothing has a title to reality except in function of intelligibility" because "mind comes first and all being is for mind."[24] This connective intellectual force bespeaks, simultaneously, the power to philosophize, for a truly great intellect "takes a connected view of old and new, past and present, far and near, and . . . has an insight into the influence of all these on one another; without which there is no whole, and no centre. It possesses the knowledge, not only of things, but also of their true and mutual relations; knowledge not merely considered as acquirement, but as philosophy."[25]

Because divine creation is the unity of a superabundance of events, then the essential characteristic of creation is connectedness, and interconnectivity. To see connectively is the "highest state to which nature can aspire, in the way of intellect."

Newman then proceeds to describe the spirit of interconnectedness:

> That only is true enlargement of mind which is the power of viewing many things at once as one whole, of referring them severally to their true place in the universal system, of understanding their respective values, and determining their mutual dependence. Thus is that form of Universal Knowledge, of which I have on a former occasion spoken, set up in the individual intellect, and constitutes its perfection. Possessed of this real illumination, the mind never views any part of the extended subject-matter of Knowledge without recollecting that it is but a part, or without the associations which spring from this recollection. It makes every thing lead in some sort to every thing else; it would communicate the image of the whole to every separate portion, till that whole becomes in imagination like a spirit, everywhere pervading and penetrating its component parts, and giving them one definite meaning. . . . [A]s the word "creation" suggests the Creator, and "subjects" a sovereign, so, in the mind of

the Philosopher . . . the elements of the physical and moral
world . . . are all viewed as one, with correlative functions,
and as gradually by successive combinations converging,
one and all, to a true centre.[26]

CONNECTIVE ENLARGEMENT

This conjunctive force, and connective energy, is the power to link, to
bring together—*religare*—various meanings and realities as presented
in creation. There consequently resides in this unifying force an implicit
reflection of a religious action, with authority and dominion, as is rev-
erently inherent in intellect as *imago Dei*. In this enlargement is a full
potentiality of the binary union of devotion and learning, of moral and
intellectual activity. This is the context, too, which clarifies the relations
of Church and University, religion and education, faith and understanding, conscience and wisdom. This binary unification makes Newman's insight consolidate with the tradition of exemplaristic theology,
as found in biblical and Patristic literature.

Because Newman believed that only an enlarged—and enlarging—mind can do justice to reality, he exhorted his Oratorian audience,
whom he addressed in his *Present Position* lectures, to take enlargement seriously: "I wish you to enlarge your knowledge, to cultivate your
reason, to get an insight into the relation of truth with truth, to learn to
view things as they are, to understand how faith and reason stand to
each other, what are the bases and principles of Catholicism, and where
lie the main inconsistencies and absurdities of the Protestant
theory. . . . Ignorance is the root of all littleness."[27] In 1859, at the insistence of Bishop Ullathorne and Cardinal Wiseman, Newman became
editor of *The Rambler*, which had been founded in 1848, but recently
had come under episcopal censure. Newman announced in his first issue
a spirit of enlargement: "In commencing a new series of the *Rambler*,
its conductors think it right to state, that they profess no other object in
their labours but that which has been the animating principle of the
Magazine hitherto, viz., to co-operate with Catholic periodicals of
higher pretentions in a work of special importance at the present day,—
the refinement, enlargement, and elevation of the intellect of the educated classes."[28]

Enlargement of mind and heart and spirit is thus a truly Christian task, and consubstantial with the scriptural motivation of Christ's

earthly appearance, which is precisely to provide enlargement of life—"I am come that they might have life, and that they might have it more abundantly" (Jn. 10: 10).[29] Other passages of Scripture also signify how the source of abundance reveals itself—out of the abundance of the heart the mouth speaks (Lk. 6: 45, Mt. 12: 34–35).

In *imago*-theology, just such enlargement also mirrors the scriptural mitzvah to be fruitful, increase, and multiply (Gen.-Ber. 1: 28). Once again, by applying these scriptural admonitions towards fecundity, augmentation, and abundance, enlargement can reflect theophanic theology. Because these scriptural invitations center the need to expand one's vision of the meaning of creation, it consequently requires that we must learn how to see. To see well is to see what needs to be seen in creation. Or, as Teilhard de Chardin phrases it, "By virtue of the Creation and, still more, of the Incarnation, nothing here below is profane for those who know how to see."[30]

SEEING

Having learned how to see, Newman existentially enlarged the relational meaning of religion and education as extensions of the powers of conscience and wisdom. Seeing the interrelation of religion and education, intertwined in the spiritually connective work of Church and University, Newman revealed a process which articulates spiritual enlargement. The Church can then be understood as fulfilling the hope of religion, just as, similarly, the University is conceptualized as satisfying the expectations of education.

Newman considered religion (even in the form of natural religion) to be universally available to mankind. Through religion, humankind develops a capacity for access to a providential God. How can this be explained? "This process of development," Newman said, "has been well delineated by a living French writer," and he cites Francois Guizot. The sources of religion, Newman quotes Guizot, lie in the need to elucidate the human problematic—"problems of our nature"—and to justify moral experience, "the necessity of seeking for morals a sanction." To Newman, religion means "the knowledge of God, of His Will, and of our duties towards Him," for which there are three sources which nature furnishes us, namely, our own minds, the voice of mankind, and the course of the world, that is, of human life and human affairs. And the most authoritative of these three means of knowledge, as being specially our own, is our own mind, whose informations give us the rule by which we test, interpret, and correct what is presented to us for belief, whether by the universal testimony of mankind, or by the history of society and of the world. . . . Our great internal teacher of religion is . . . our Conscience. Conscience is a personal guide, and . . . is nearer to me than any other means of knowledge.[32]

CONSCIENCE CONNECTION

Mankind's gift of conscience, says Newman, "is a connecting principle between the creature and his Creator; and the firmest hold of theological truths is gained by habits of personal religion."[33] Conscience leads towards a religious awareness, which, he says, "is a spirit afloat, neither 'in the secret chambers' nor 'in the desert,' but everywhere. It is within us, rising up in the heart where it was least expected, and working its way, though not in secret, yet so subtly and impalpably. . . . [It is] the spiritual awakening of spiritual wants. . . . All we insist on is, that religious opinion is deeper than mere caprice or than syllogistic conviction, and more enduring than excitement or passion."[34]

Precisely because of Christian experience, mankind's longing for the fulfillment of spiritual wants is not left unaided, because the Church, as the Body of Christ, re-frames, re-orders, and enlarges these deep, spiritually experiential meanings of religion. Through the Church, religion becomes devotionally concretized, and is provided with a "local habitation and a name." The Church is the visible Communion of the People of God, as well as the invisible Communion of the Saints. Religion—as a linkage, *religio*, which Lactantius called *vinculum pietatis*—requires the Church, and without the Church, it would be abstractive, homeless, and nameless. Without the Church, religion might become merely linguistic, conceptual, and clubby. But with the Church, religion is the Spirit enfleshed, communalized, and enlarged. The Church, says Newman,

> from an inward spiritual power or grace imparted directly from above, and of which she is the channel . . . has it in charge to rescue human nature from its misery . . . by lifting

it up to a higher level than its own . . . [to] set it free from earth . . . by exalting it towards heaven. It was for this end that a renovating grace was put into her hands. . . . [T]he Catholic Church, viewed in the concrete, as clothed and surrounded by the appendages of its high sovereignty . . . [is] a supereminent prodigious power sent upon earth to encounter and master a giant evil . . . brought together into one."[35]

EDUCATING THE SOUL

Only by the action of the Church's spiritual enlargement can there be brought about that renewal and reshaping which reside in the religious impulse. Revelation fulfills that impulse, which itself is a desire for enlargement. The Church is the vessel of revelation, which provides for religious education of the human soul. Perhaps, says Newman, "we might say that the object of revelation was to enlighten and enlarge the mind, to make us act by reason, and to expand and strengthen our powers;— or to impart knowledge about religious truth, knowledge being power directly it is given, and enabling us forthwith to think, judge, and act for ourselves . . . or to secure, what otherwise would be hopeless, our leading a religious life."[36]

For those who focus their attention and who listen, for those willing to learn how to see, Holy Scripture effects enlargement of thought, which becomes vision (Pro. 29: 18). To the spiritual and the devout, Newman observes, "to the disconsolate, the tempted, the perplexed, the suffering," Scripture provides "an enlargement of thought, which enables them to see in it what they never saw before."[37]

To traditional Catholics in England, Newman and his gospel of enlargement were, it seems strange to say, resented. In his *Journal*, he recorded how English Catholics may be deficient in sight, as well as in insight. As he said, "Catholics in England, from their very blindness, cannot see that they are blind. To aim then at improving the condition, the status, of the Catholic body . . . by giving them juster views, by enlarging and refining their minds, in one word, by education, is . . . more than a superfluity or a hobby, it is an insult."[38] The reason that Catholics in England were insulted by the thought of enlargement, so Newman believed, was that they were wanting in self-knowledge—wanting, that is, in the absolutely necessary condition for enlargement of mind. To lack self-knowledge is to lack consciousness of one's own identity, consciousness of the self as knower. Self-knowledge is an act of inquiry about who one really is. Because knowing is an activity, not a passivity—what one does, rather than what one undergoes—knowledge requires the involvement of one who is self-consciously knowing. Knowing is existential and personifying. Without self-knowing, as an act of personhood, there can really be no knowing at all, or, at least, no knowledge worthy of the name. For this reason, it is important to understand, as Newman said in a sermon, that "self-knowledge is at the root of all religious knowledge." He put it this way: "For it is in proportion as we search our hearts and understand our own nature, that we understand what is meant by an Infinite Governor and Judge. . . . God speaks to us primarily in our hearts, self-knowledge is the key . . . to Scripture."[39]

Regrettably, Newman observed, "multitudes called Christians go through life with no effort to obtain a correct knowledge of themselves." They prefer to know about the secret faults of others, rather than their own. They substitute vague and general impressions for exact systematic knowledge, and have no interest in attempting to alter anything about themselves. It is impossible, Newman admitted, fully to know ourselves, or, with any finality, even partially to know ourselves. But those who avoid any attempt whatever to know themselves—those who neglect the conscientious duty to examine their own lives—"are using words without meaning."[40] Without the enlargement initiated by self-knowledge, there also can be no devotion, as, equally, there can be no insight, no learning. Without self-knowledge, genuine mental life, authentic spiritual life, and veracious human life cease to exist. Thoughtless custom and habit, easily indulged in, will fill the empty space as thoughtless life—and take over as impersonal life. With simple straightforwardness, Newman asserted, "Without self-knowledge you have no root in yourselves personally."[41] Such rootlessness and lack of thought, Newman attributed to "the infidelity of the day." By living the gifted life of enlargement, however, Newman clearly demonstrated that it is at least possible to do so.

IS GENIUS ENOUGH?

Great geniuses, Ralph Waldo Emerson once assured us, have the shortest biographies. Perhaps he meant to say that genius itself suffices for any human life. But, a Newman biographer suggests, "People, honest, worthy, efficient people, look askance upon a man of genius. There is something strange, something odd about him that half scares and half repels." This, allegedly, is "why geniuses are not popular. They are not, as the phrase goes, clubbable men. They do not suffer mediocrities gladly; indeed, folly, so it be innocent and generous, is much more to their taste. . . . [F]rom the man of ideas they turn instinctively away in fear or dislike, regarding him as a menace or a nuisance. They band themselves together in a union to protect their mediocrity."[42]

Now, while history may be mute, historians assuredly never are. Together with certain commentators, some historians have long turned full scrutiny upon Newman's intricate, almost century-spanning life.[43] Some have sought to portray—even betray—its events, or to pretend to have deciphered the real meaning of each or any occurrence.

Newman "psychobiographers" have apparently sought to minimize his spiritual substance and personal achievement, making him appear reductively definable, therefore explainable, therefore understandable, and therefore dismissible—as if he were no different from any other man, perhaps even less of one. So, it is strange that Newman, apostle of spiritual enlargement, should be subjected to concerted belittlement of his genius. Cold contrarian invention appears to have replaced Newman's symmetrical vision with shallow diversion, an action which seems to typify Newman's principle: "Ignorance is the root of all littleness."[44] During the first-centenary celebration of the Oxford Movement (1833–1933), for example, Gertrude Donald detected an "inexplicable belittling" of "one of the greatest Englishmen of the nineteenth century." Was there any reason, she asked, for such treatment except "a desire to minimize an influence whose power they still fear"?[45] Scarred during his life by verbal assault upon his integrity, Newman was never—he has never been—irretrievably wounded. He remains today what he had, in fact, always been.

But looking back, more than a century after his death, who could seriously doubt the merits of this saintly man? What could be the mystery which enshrouds these curious attacks upon him and upon his integrity? Doubted in his lifetime, now lifetimes later, his sincerity is still doubted. Is it Newman's power, of whatever kind, as Gertrude Donald suggested, that is feared? Is it resentment of what such power has wrought, or is capable of producing? Is this fear currently magnified by Newman's veneration, his recently approved beatification,[1] and anticipated canonization, or the expectation that he will be declared a Doctor of the Church? Such nagging questions sustain repeated asking—Why should this be so?

Curiously, Newman himself, on one occasion, seems to have unraveled the mystery of such resentment. As he pointed out, supporters of the Establishment have their own doubts—and indulge those of others—about the integrity of their National Church. Do they not, asks Newman, "almost think better of a man for doubting it, providing he does not follow his doubts out, and end in disbelieving it?" Therewith, Newman unriddled the riddle: "Hence these very same persons, who speak so severely of any one who leaves the communion in which he was born, doubting of it themselves, are in consequence led to view his act as an affront done to their body, rather than as an evil to himself. They consider it as a personal affront to a party and an injury to a cause, and the affront is greater or less according to the mischief which it does them in the particular case. It is not his loss but their inconvenience, which is the real measure of his sin.[46]

DEFINING MOTIVES

Mischief? Personal affront? Injury? Inconvenience? These are classical psychological signs of emotional insecurity. Can such insecurity, proffered in high dudgeon, explain the intransigence and reveal the motive of Newman's adversaries? Here is motive enough to prompt spiteful intent, especially in view of the fact that, in the parlance of British outrage, it is a "perversion" to leave the Church, to abandon a party, and to do so with personal, injurious, and inconvenient affront. If nothing else, Newman's adversaries were invariably Establishment-proud —in title, position, and persuasion, in wealth, or eminence, or pretension.

Establishment friction that was created by Newman's conversion also falls into place, indeed, if we examine his earlier days when he was Tutor at Oriel. There was, for example, Oriel student James Howard Harris, third Earl of Malmsbury, known by the "prefatory-Fitz" as Lord FitzHarris. Ringleader of indulgent undergraduates, he was adept at flaunting rules, conjuring insidious pranks, and was wont to ambulate—to Newman's distinct distress—from champagne festivity to communion rail, and back again. In November, 1826, Newman wrote his sister, Harriet, about just such students: "I have some trouble with my horses [college pupils], for whenever they get a new coachman, they make an effort to get the reins slack. But I shall be very obstinate, though their curvettings and shyings are very teasing."[47]

Almost sixty years later, in 1884, Lord Malmsbury published *Memoirs of an Ex-Minister: An Autobiography*, in which he belittled Tutor Newman as "a helpless dummy," and as one whose future career "no one at that time would have predicted."[48] Newman, said Malmsbury, "used to allow his class to torment him with the most helpless resignation; every kind of mischievous trick was, to our shame, played upon him." And, "He remained quite impassive, and painfully tolerant."[49]

On publication of this memoir, Newman's friend and former pupil, Frederic Rogers, Lord Blachford, responded in the *Daily News*, and pointed out that Newman's conduct "was absolutely the reverse of what Lord Malmsbury describes. He was very kind and retiring, but perfectly determined (as might be expected from his subsequent history)—a tutor with whom men did not venture to take a liberty, and who was master of a formidable and speaking silence calculated to quell any ordinary impertinence."[50]

Malmsbury ignored Lord Blachford's riposte, and so Newman himself replied in the *Daily News*, noting that, as a Tutor, he had met resistance from gentlemen commoners, "who, relying on the claims of family and fortune, did their best to oppose me, and to spread tales about me." Thus, "what Lord Malmsbury calls 'helpless resignation' and 'a painful tolerance,' I interpret to have been the conduct of a gentleman under great provocation."[51] In a similar case, a gentleman-commoner, later Sir Charles Murray, was quoted in an 1898 memoir—too late for reply from Newman—with intent comparable to Malmsbury's reminiscence:

> Newman never inspired me or my fellow undergraduates with any interest, much less respect; on the contrary, we disliked, or rather distrusted him. He walked with his head bent, abstracted, but every now and then looking out of the corners of his eyes quickly, as though suspicious. . . . At lectures he was quiet, and what I should call sheepish; stuck to the text, and never diverged into contemporary history or made lessons interesting. He always struck me as the most pusillanimous of men—wanting in the knowledge of human nature; and I am always surprised, and indeed never can understand, how it was he became such a great man.[52]

Murray's final year at Oriel, 1826, coincided with Newman's first year as Tutor. During that period, Murray had staged a series of pranks against the young Tutor, but to which Newman did not react in kind. That, apparently, prompted Murray to conclude of Newman that "if he had been anything of a man, he would have come out of his room and caught us red-handed."[53]

Now it is well-known that frustration can turn to rage, as rage can change to fury. And these effects can be cryptically displayed, especially by the proud, but secretly cloaked in begrudgement, otherwise known as the capital sin of covetousness. Covetousness, Roman poet Horace once said, means never having enough, and always wanting more. Begrudgement or covetousness often reveals itself in acts of belittling (Oh, he's not so great) or grumbling (I can't stand that man). Backbiting, rumor mongering, gossip, and scorn are among its associates. Its theme—I don't want you to have what you've got (I want it)—invites the begrudger to examine every detail of another's walking, talking, dressing, and behaving. Begrudgement's consort is rivalry, or envy, which covets not what another has, but who another is. Its theme—I don't want you to be who you are (Stay in my shadow)—breeds suspicion, ill will, dissension, spite, and venom. In Scripture, the Greek for rivalry-envy (ὁ φθόνος) means "having displeasure at another's success or prosperity," while its Latin form, *invidia*, means "looking closely and maliciously at someone."[54]

DEMYTHOLOGIZING

Both rivalry-envy and begrudgement-covetousness seek to categorize, classify, and rank their targets—just as Murray and Malmsbury had sought to do. And, so far as Newman is concerned, the practice has not ceased. For example, during the last decade, it has become fashionable to judge, appraise, rank, and rate Newman's life, mind, work, and person—and these include attempts to demystify Newman's "mystery," or to demythologize his "myth."[55] Unadmiring attempts to expose Newman have become even notoriously frequent.[56] Even so, otherwise supportive commentators on Newman have equally sought to "understand the 'mystery' of Newman, and, to some degree, contribute to the process of demystification of his person."[57]

OLD WOMAN THEME

A further complication of commentary centers on Newman's so-called feminine characteristics. For instance, A. N. Wilson invokes this theme in a caption in one of his books. Under the 1889 Emmeline Deane portrait of octogenarian Cardinal Newman, he writes, "At this period, hobbling along the Hagley Road in Birmingham in his cassock, Newman was often mistaken for an old woman."[58] Not the first to describe Newman as an old woman, Wilson may have based his caption on a statement by Canon Scott Holland, who had paid a visit in 1877 to Newman's Oratory, on "a day that I can never forget." Curiously, however, in recalling the incident, Scott Holland remembered someone else's words: "I recall the swift sudden way in which I found him beside me. I turned at the sound of the soft quick speech, and there he was—white, frail and wistful, for all the ruggedness of the actual features. I remembered at once the words of Furse about him, 'delicate as an old lady washed in milk.' One felt afraid to talk too loud, lest it should hurt him."[59]

J. Lewis May also retells—perhaps, retails—this story, and in other vignettes, depicts Newman and Ambrose St. John on their first trip to Rome, like "a pair of High School misses doing the grand tour." He suggests other portraits of Newman when, after a dinner, "my Lord Bishop" handed Newman to a sofa, "as if he had been a lady. And indeed there was something ladylike about him . . . [an] almost effeminate gentleness and debonair refinement."[60] Again, in relating the story of Newman's being offered the cardinalate red hat, May wonders if Newman had been saying no, when all the while he meant yes—"for all the world like a woman returning a coy refusal and all the time expecting to be pressed?"[61]

Contrastingly, but with similar theme, Frederick Faber, 49-year-old nephritic Oratorian, recorded a periodic deathbed scene (Newman often asked Ambrose St. John, "How many times has Fr. Faber been a-dying?") of Newman's visit to him on 20 July 1863. Despite the fact that Faber and Newman had not spoken since a quarrel seven years previously, Newman nonetheless interrupted preparations for a trip abroad, and went directly to Faber's bedside. Faber later dictated: "Fr. Newman has been this morning and spent full twenty minutes with me—we went into everything—no woman could be tenderer than he was."[62] Meriol Trevor observes that "Faber felt guilty towards Newman," and, after the interview, "he felt he was forgiven and was happy and content."[63]

Similar gender-assignment occurs in a Newman dream which William George Ward recounted to his son, biographer Wilfrid Ward, a year before his death, at seventy:

The present writer's father—never one of the most intimate of the circle which surrounded Newman at Oxford—used to say that his heart would beat as he heard Newman's step on the staircase. His keen humour, his winning sweetness, his occasional wilfulness, his resentments and anger, all showed him intensely alive, and his friends loved his very faults as one may love those of a fascinating woman; at the same time many of them revered him almost as a prophet. Only a year before his death, after nearly twenty years of misunderstandings and estrangement, W. G. Ward told the present biographer of a dream he had had—how he found himself at a dinner party next to a veiled lady, who charmed him more and more as he talked. At last he exclaimed, 'I have never felt such charm in any conversation since I used to talk with John Henry Newman, at Oxford.' 'I am John Henry Newman,' the lady replied, and raising her veil showed the well-known face.[64]

In level-headed reaction to this revealing dream, Meriol Trevor (who also quotes the incident in her own work) observed:

The dream has been taken to give information about Newman, when it is surely a cardinal point in the interpretation of dreams that their information relates to the dreamer. That Ward identified Newman in his dream with a fascinating lady does not prove that Newman ought to have been one; it tells us nothing about Newman, but quite a lot about Ward. He was very much the intellectual, his mind concentrated on logical reasoning, and noticeably deficient in those qualities of imagination, intuition and sympathy which are associated with the feminine side of human nature and are often symbolized in the image of a woman. . . . It is commonplace that artists of all kinds have this 'feminine' side of their nature highly developed, and that the most balanced of people of either sex are those in whom these two energies of being act in unity, so that there is no knowing without loving and no loving without knowing.[65]

Then there is Shane Leslie (first cousin of Winston Churchill) who also depicts Newman in feminine terms, as being "in the ecclesiastical background," but playing the part "which the French assign to the femme fatale. He fascinated, influenced and changed men's lives. He was often inexplicable save on temperamental grounds."[66] Even supportive Martin D'Arcy referred to Newman's "sensitive and almost feminine temperament,"[67] a view perhaps based on Cardinal Wiseman's initial impression, which mistook Newman's caution for timidity. Wiseman wrote, "I think Mr. Newman is a timid man."[68] Attempting to fathom the Newman-Kingsley dispute, Charles Frederick Harrold likewise invoked the image of Newman's femininity: "Doubtless a certain feminine strain in Newman's complex character repelled him [Kingsley], and this, together with his mistrust of his opponent's argumentative subtlety, led him to say the unpardonable."[69]

To Harrold, that "certain feminine strain" became a significant reason for the Newman-Kingsley affair of 1864. Is it possible that such judgments were based on deeming gentleness, kindness-kindliness, consideration, loyalty, long-suffering—(admittedly found more frequently among women than among men)—as feminine, rather than as human traits?

Still, there are certain questions which naturally arise: Are there discernible psychological gender-traits? Are there factual gender descriptors which pertain more often to one gender than to the other? The answer is, certainly, yes. To explain how this theme may bear on Newman studies requires a closer inspection of such gender descriptors.

GENDER PSYCHOLOGY

During recent decades, gender studies have empirically identified neuroanatomical and psychosocial gender skills. Tending towards right-brain dominance, women possess linguistic superiority, which is not otherwise explainable by left-brain speech-syntactical centers (Broca's and Wernicke's areas). Similarly, men, tending towards left-hemisphere dominance, possess superior skills in mathematical and spatial tasks.[70]

Psychogender attributes are distinguishable along biopsychosocial axes of male and female behavior and attitude, or ethological patterns. In Western societies, males tend to perceive mutually exclusive predicates, such as independence *or* dependence, superiority *or* inferiority, dominance *or* submission. A game is therefore a contest, having, by definition, winners *and* losers, because players are antagonists engaged in a zero-sum competition—somebody wins, somebody must lose. In contrast, women tend to perceive non-exclusionary predicates, such as interdependence, interrelation, equivalence, concordance, connection. Their comparable matrix of a game is engagement, where parties are participants, involved in non-zero-sum alliances. Men prefer command, control, confrontation; women prefer cooperation, suggestion, intimacy.

Thus, too, whereas men incline towards asymmetrical challenge, competition, conflict, adversariness, women, contrastingly, incline towards symmetrical sharing, tolerance, harmony, agreement, reconciliation. Male predilection for non-engagement, and (protective) psychic distance, underlies transactions of aggressive power (boyish contests, such as King of the Hill) with expectations of entitlement. Among women, there is propensity for psychic closeness, love, and supportiveness. Where men tend to be deed-*agonistic*, women tend to be speech-*oralistic*, as suggested by an English proverb, "Deeds are males, but words are females."[71] Additionally, psychogender traits are contextualized by the concepts gender-identity and gender-identity/role, [72] terms first improvised by endocrinologist John Money. [73]

NEWMAN AND PSYCHOGENDER

In a vocabulary of psychogender distinctions, we have suggested that, like Shakespeare and Dante, Newman was endowed with right-brain and left-brain co-dominance, and could therefore respond from both ends of the psychic continuum. He preferred being straightforward at all times, but, where necessary, could be blunt, without being tactless, direct but reassuring, assertive but connective. He had a finely tuned and discriminating mind, and highly sensitive responses. Whereas, in earlier years, he had a male sense of ambition, later, he had a female sense of achievement.

As leader of the Oxford Movement, he seems to have preferred suggestion over command, and was not (as some colleagues pressed him to be) a manager. As Superior of the English Oratory, Newman's leadership style was to be engaged, but not confrontational. Adversarial power he saved for controversy, just as Cicero did. Judging by his letters, diaries, and disinterested witness, Newman was cautious, calm, sensitive, and low-key. And he knew how to "carry on business."

Newman could be gentle but, when warranted, brusk, and certainly brisk. So, it is curious—except by reason of hostility—that but one side of Newman's enlarging personality seems to have attracted critical comment. The binary, complemental character of Newman's mind and personality did, in fact, empower both his dialectical (left-brain) as well as his intuitive (right-brain) skills. Still, the adversarial nineteenth-century phrase, "feminine characteristics," appears to be— as, indeed, it was meant to be—denigrating, especially when descriptively used in connection with the 1864 Newman-Kingsley dispute.

That complicated affair was several layers deep. A surface dispute about moral epistemology—whether Newman was a truth teller—concealed other significant issues as well as bigotry and bias, clearly enough to turn the dispute into an entanglement. Still worse, Kingsley's secret grudge against Newman, combined with "muscular Christianity" and British Imperial State interests, aggravated the dispute. To account for this, requires a brief look backwards.

First of all, Britain's Imperium had, during Newman's lifetime, grown more expansive, even in population, which at Newman's birth in 1801 was 16 million, but was more than 40 million at his death in 1890. Britain's addiction to the "Great Game" of international intrigue and dissimulation (Muslims call it *taqīya*) had attracted English corsair adventurers in oriental pursuit of that sublime deceit.[75] Also, Britain had but recently extricated itself from the misadventurous Crimean War (1853–56), a piece of "Johnbullism" that Newman analyzed in a series of "Catholicus" letters, "Who's to Blame?" in the *Catholic Standard*, beginning in March 1854.[75] That conflict embarrassingly exposed the geopolitical importance of the Middle East and was triggered when, under pretense of protecting his Orthodox subjects in the Turkish-dominated Holy Land, Tsar Nikolay I of Russia moved against Turkey. In rapid response, England and France moved against Russia. Nikolay's underlying motive, of course, was to break his fleet out of the Black Sea, and into the warm waters of the Mediterranean.

Secondly, in France, Bonaparte's nephew, Louis Napoleon, had come to power by exchanging a populist mask for imperial identity as Emperor Napoleon III. With British connivance, Louis Napoleon was also promoting the coronation—it took place the same year as the Newman-Kingsley dispute—of Maximilian of Austria and his wife, Carlotta, as Emperor and Empress of Mexico. This was open meddling, not only in Mexican, but also in American affairs, where Britain had already been aiding the Southern Confederacy, and blatantly undermining Northern Union interests. Meanwhile, Prussia's Prince Otto von Bismarck was uniting Teutonic states into a German Nation, which could challenge Britain on the Continent. Italy was becoming a nation, also threatening the status quo territorial claims of the Papal States.

Thirdly, having expropriated the lucrative "white man's burden" from its nonwhite colonial clients, Britain had instituted governance of India, and hegemony on the Australian Continent, which it had already been seeding with its unwanted convicts. By making significant incursions, then, into two-thirds of the world—Africa, Asia, Latin America, the Middle East, and the Subcontinent—Imperial Britain needed to impress onlookers that it was, indeed, the ruling power.

PSYCHOLOGICAL ILLUSION

At the time Britain was projecting political, military, and economic power abroad, it also required, at home and abroad, a psychological illusion of being indomitable. With its former mercantilist policies now toothless and antiquarian, Britain was ceramically glazing a new, "masculinist-manly" imperious image.[76] While Victoria was no Queen Elizabeth, she was supported by Whitehall propaganda, and the determination of Prince Consort Albert (until his death in 1861). Innumerable resources of State power were consequently devoted to Britain's realpolitik, not excepting political use of State religion—engaged, for example, in 1841, when Anglican Britain and Lutheran Prussia carved out a joint bishopric in Jerusalem, an action to which Newman had so strongly objected.[77] On the international stage, British assumptions about white superiority, ethnic purity, and physical prowess were given more than cameo roles to play. And upon this stage, like a *minim* Descartes, Charles Kingsley advanced behind a mask.[78]

From 1857, Kingsley's mask had been that of "muscular Christianity," a cult movement with which he had been expressly identified by editors of the *Edinburgh Review*.[79] Indeed, "muscular Christianity" was synonymous with Britain's aggressive and (favored word) "hearty" imperialist policies. In keeping with those policies, Kingsley neurasthenically prided himself on being intense, xenophobically patriotic, adhesively royalist, and (paradoxically) "an extreme radical." Kingsley was a court favorite, Victoria's chaplain, and Prince Albert's preferred author. His intensely partisan writings assured his appointment as Cambridge's Regius Professor of Modern History and, later, as Canon of Westminster. His politics had been variously described as "Toryism tempered by sympathy, or as radicalism tempered by hereditary scorn of subject races."[80]

Embedded in such comfortably assured circumstances, Charles Kingsley undertook for the January 1864 edition of *Macmillan's Magazine*, to review volumes VII and VIII on Tudor Protestantism, which James Anthony Froude, youngest brother of Hurrell, had just published as part of a twelve-volume *The History of England*. While Froude eulogized Tudor-Protestant policy to explain Britain's then current world hegemony, Kingsley gratuitously aimed his review at Newman and the Catholic Church, in especially provocative language: "Truth, for its own sake, had never been a virtue with the Roman clergy. Father Newman informs us that it need not, and on the whole ought not to be; that cunning is the weapon which Heaven has given to the saints wherewith to withstand the brute male force of the wicked world which marries and is given in marriage. Whether his notion be doctrinally correct or not, it is at least historically so."[81]

On reading the review, Newman immediately wrote to Alexander Macmillan, the magazine's surviving partner, and he in turn, with Newman's letter in hand, secretly penned a note to Frederick Denison Maurice, characterizing Newman as "the great pervert." Receiving no satisfaction from Macmillan, Newman issued public rejoinder to Kingsley in weekly pamphlets, later published as a classic *histoire de l'âme, Apologia pro vita sua*.[82]

Effects of Newman's rejoinder were, however, devastating to Kingsley, who, as the hitherto favored party, paid a high price on his dignity. The British press, notably the magazine *John Bull*, switched sides, cheered that "defenceless" clergyman, Fr. Newman—now become a British bulldog—and railed at Kingsley as a "masculine and muscular Christian" who "is fain to shuffle, to hedge and to lurch."[83] Unsuccessful in altering the public chemistry of the exchange, Kingsley made matters worse by issuing yet another broadside: "What, then, does Dr. Newman mean?" Faced, finally, with controversial defeat, Kingsley bitterly let it be known that he had "nothing to retract."[84]

WHAT WAS THE MOTIVE?

Still, the question insinuates itself: Why had Kingsley, unprovoked, deliberately gone out of his way to attack, deprecate, belittle, and minimize Newman, as preferring cunning to truth? Was there something insecure in Kingsley's personality, one observer suggested, which hankered after "the frank expression of indignation"?[85] Perceiving how far the effects had exceeded the cause, Newman shrewdly divined that Kingsley had "some motive or other to be as severe with me as he can possibly be."[86] Had Newman, after all, suspected that Kingsley's hysterical tone appeared little bent upon truth or cunning, and was more concerned with the brute male force of the wicked world which marries and is given in marriage? Kingsley's gratuitous attack and subsequent response were also undergirded by "muscular Christianity," imperial-masculinist imagery, Protestant hostility, and his own temperamental bias. But there was another component—secretive, rancorous, vendettist—which he guardedly stated in a letter of 9 March 1864, just as the *Macmillan* affair was heating up: "I am answering Newman now and though of course I give up the charge of conscious dishonesty I trust to make him and his admirers sorry that they did not leave me alone. I have a score of more than twenty years to pay, and this is an installment of it."[87]

A score of more than twenty years to pay? That would date back to Kingsley's marriage to Fanny Grenfell. Five years older than Kingsley, fervently Tractarian, "buxom, Spanish-style,"[88] Frances Grenfell was to have become an Anglican nun. Cambridge undergraduate Kingsley, having ceased to believe in Christianity, met Fanny while cantering along riding paths of Oxfordshire, and thereupon rapidly changed his tune, his faith, and the course of his life. Irresistibly, even ironically, drawn to rekindle Kingsley's guttered faith, Fanny passed along to him copies of Newman's writings. But, as if signaling Fanny's success, 23-year-old Kingsley altered history by taking Holy Orders. Two years later, in 1844, he married Fanny.

But Kingsley's adherence to "muscular Christianity," and confusion of English "virility with truth and cunning with virginity,"[89] had enshrined an obsessive animus towards Newman. Kingsley considered virginity and celibacy addictively "unnatural" and associated them with un-virile villain-priests, whom he had obstinately depicted in a book about "religious" torture of St. Elizabeth of Hungary. Self-illustrated in a devil-haunted, dream-creatured, and overwrought style, the book reflected the tortured state of Kingsley's psychic experience. As Meriol Trevor perceptively says, "The same complex of feelings about virginity, sexual love, torture, and virility, appears in all Kingsley's works."[90]

Of itself, the Kingsley story is less important than its effects upon current Victorian scholarship, which is dedicated to exploring hypocrisy in Victorian self-denial. Discalced by scholars, Kingsley's sexual motive has led academic triumphalism to declare, "What was at issue in Kingsley's quarrel with Newman . . . was not so much mendacity as sexuality." [91] Because the current fashion in Victorian scholarship has largely focused on Newman's gender identity, that fashion seems to have turned The Venerable John Henry Cardinal Newman into The Vulnerable John Henry Cardinal Newman. Such a fashion has simply created new opportunities for Newman's belittlement. [92]

** Editor's note: In July 2009, Pope Benedict XVI approved Cardinal Newman's beatification.

CHAPTER 6:

EDUCATION AS DEVELOPMENT

> "Education is a high word. It is the preparation for knowledge, and it is the imparting of knowledge in proportion to that preparation. . . . But Education is a higher word; it implies an action upon our mental nature and the formation of character."

> "Education, and . . . the principles on which it must be conducted, has ever had a hold upon my mind. . . . Education has been my line. . . . Education is so much my line, not yours."

> "The image of God, if duly cherished, may expand, deepen, and be completed . . . by means of education."

> "In a higher world it is otherwise, but here below to live is to change, and to be perfect is to have changed often."

Education is a liberating word because it signifies a liberating promise. To John Henry Newman, this liberating promise found fulfillment in the idea of liberal education—a concept which, ever since the appearance of Plato, has encompassed enhancement of the intellect. Such enhancement, as understood by Newman and Plato, is initiated as an "ascent from below."

Even though derived from a Latin word, *education* has traditionally symbolized an idiosyncratic Greek idea—which was expressed in an idiosyncratic Greek word, *paideia* (παιδεία)—"culture."[1] For this reason, education is not merely a "schoolroom" term, because it actively stretches outward in an attempt to circumscribe, in all its transformative aspects, the semantics of human civilization. As a term and as an action, *education* is clearly differentiated from *instruction*, or from *indoctrination*. In its ideal sense, education is related to the Greek concept of *philosophy*, out of which, indeed, that ideal was created by Plato and Aristotle. *Education* and *philosophy* equally suggest that only by an intellectual vision of the (interrelated) everything of the world, can a truly perceptive understanding of a (discrete) anything in the world be attained. *Education* and *philosophy* are therefore essentially visionary terms, in the sense that they embody the means and methodologies by which humankind can learn to "see."

INTERCONNECTIONS

The Platonic-Aristotelian idea of education possesses a primal sense of interconnectedness, which, in Newman's words, "makes every thing in some sort lead to every thing else."[2] Historically, Western education, as both praxis and theory, refers principally to a process of development by which the human mind—intellect—is shaped and brought to its highest levels of human perfection.

As founder of the idea of education, Plato was the first to lay down general philosophical concepts upon which a theory of liberal education could be constructed, and he was, as well, the first to contemplate an ideal setting in which education could be pursued. Son of an illustrious, politically influential Athenian family, Plato was committed to the stratagem of educationally creating *ideal* rulers, empowered by wisdom to administer an *ideal* commonwealth, or *politeia*. To Plato, such education ($\pi\alpha\iota\delta\acute{\epsilon}\iota\alpha$) involved a philosophical meta-methodology—by which to "penetrate" experience, and to envision truth ($\acute{\alpha}\lambda\acute{\eta}\theta\epsilon\iota\alpha$) and justice ($\delta\acute{\iota}\kappa\eta$) as the ultimate criteria by which to "deal with" what we would call reality, and what Plato referred to as "being-meaning-truth-goodness-value."[3] For the express purpose, then, of educating good leaders to design, administer, and rule a good society, Plato devised (388/387 BC) an ideal environment, which he called the Academy ($\acute{\eta}$ $\acute{A}\kappa\alpha\delta\eta\mu\acute{\iota}\alpha$). There, in a cloistered olive grove on the green hills of Colonos, northwest of Athens, he became the first "chancellor" of the world's first "university."[4]

Another, but different kind of "university" was established by Plato's student, Aristotle, Macedonian Stagirite—forty-four years the junior, twenty of which he spent at the Academy. Aristotle's institute, called the Lyceum (*τò Λύκειον*), was situated in the groves of Apollo Lykeios, the wolf slayer, just outside the southeastern walls of Athens, and thus diametrically across the city from the Academy. Dedicated, not to training political leaders, but to amassing, exploring, and contemplating objects and ideas, the Lyceum sought to form a wisdom which projected a scientific picture of the universe. Aristotle might then be thought of as the first "director" of the world's first "research university."

Plato and Aristotle contributed substantially to the idea of liberal education, and to the formation of what eventually would become the seven liberal arts. The Platonic-Aristotelian concept of education involved ways by which to promote, and to understand, how the powers of human intellection can be ordered, shaped, heightened, ennobled—and therefore authenticated. As already suggested, both Plato and Aristotle did something correlatively significant by ordaining a special place, a distinctive environment, in which wisdom might relentlessly be pursued. This distinctive environment was the origin of what later, in medieval Europe, would become the University.

DEFINING LIBERAL EDUCATION

Still, the path to liberal education—which these founders, together with innumerable others, had laid out for posterity—has been less smooth than might have been imagined. Perhaps this is because recent debate about the meaning of liberal education has provoked more heat than light, more rancor than rigor. In Newman's nineteenth-century English-speaking universe, the idea of liberal studies seemed more congenial. Yet, even in *The Idea of a University*, Newman still needed to conceptualize the meaning, to identify the value, and to explain the motive for undertaking liberal education. The power of liberal training is, said Newman,

> the result of a scientific formation of mind; it is an acquired faculty of judgment, of clearsightedness, of sagacity, of wisdom, of philosophical reach of mind, and of intellectual self-possession and repose—qualities which do not come of mere acquirement. The bodily eye, the organ for apprehending material objects, is provided by nature; the eye of the mind, of which the object is truth, is the work of discipline and habit . . . [because] the human mind is made for truth, and so

> rests in truth, as it cannot rest in falsehood. . . . This process
> of training, by which the intellect . . . is disciplined for its
> own sake, for the perception of its own proper object, and
> for its own highest culture, is called Liberal Education. . . .
> And to set forth the right standard, and to train according to
> it, and to help forward all students towards it according to
> their various capacities, this I conceive to be the business of
> a University.[5]

Two pivotal points dominate Newman's characterization here, and they unite two basic themes—one of process and one of place. First, liberal education—which, for Newman, is education par excellence—involves a disciplined forming, shaping, and cultivating of the intellect. Secondly, liberal education remains the proper task of the University. Thus, liberal education is quite distinct from being persuaded by an advertiser, propagandized by a politician, inculcated by a cultist, informed by a news anchor, briefed by a government official, trained by a coach, drilled by a sergeant, quizzed by a catechist, or edified by an evangelist. Thus, too, University is not just "any old school," with "any old program," granting "any old degree." To Newman, it is essentially a place for cultivation of intellect.

To provide an amplified context for what Newman means here, let us stitch together several passages from *The Idea of a University* that will help define different aspects of liberal education. Newman says,

> That alone is liberal knowledge which stands on its own pre-
> tensions . . . [because] intellectual culture is its own end . . .
> [and] is the indispensable condition of expansion of the
> mind, and the instrument of attaining it . . . [and so produces]
> the force, the steadiness, the comprehensiveness and the ver-
> satility of the intellect, the command over our own powers,
> the instinctive just estimate of things as they pass before us,
> which . . . commonly is not gained without much effort and
> the exercise of years. This is real cultivation of mind. . . .
> Certainly a *liberal education* does manifest itself in a cour-
> tesy, propriety, and polish of word and action, which is beau-
> tiful in itself . . . but it does much more. It *brings the mind
> into form*. . . . When the intellect has once been properly
> trained and formed to have a *connected* view or grasp of
> things . . . it makes itself felt in the good sense, sobriety of
> thought, reasonableness, candour, self-command, and steadi-

ness of view . . . [as well as] the slow, silent, penetrating, overpowering effects of patience, steadiness, routine, and perseverance which characterize it. . . . In all it will be a faculty of entering with comparative ease into any subject of thought, and of taking up with aptitude any science or profession. . . . *A habit of mind is formed* which lasts through life, of which the attributes are freedom, equitableness, calmness, moderation, and wisdom; or what . . . I have ventured to call a philosophical habit . . . a habit of order and system, a habit of referring every accession of knowledge to what we already know, and of adjusting the one with the other . . . the actual acceptance and use of certain principles as centres of thought, around which our knowledge grows and is located. . . . This then I would assign as the special fruit of the education furnished at a University. . . . *This is the main purpose of a University.* . . . Liberal Education and *liberal pursuits are exercises of mind*, of reason, of reflection. . . . Liberal Education makes . . . the gentleman. It is well to be a gentleman, it is well to have a cultivated intellect, a delicate taste, a candid, equitable, dispassionate mind, a noble and courteous bearing in the conduct of life—these are the connatural qualities of a large knowledge; they are the objects of a University. . . . Liberal Education, viewed in itself, is simply the *cultivation of the intellect*, as such, and its object is nothing more or less than *intellectual excellence*.[6]

Surveying the expression of this dominant liberalizing process, which brings the mind into form through cultivation of the intellect, it seems possible to infer here two kinds of liberalizing effect—one noetic, the other psychological. The first can be called *dianoetic* which, being intellectually based, produces intellectual effects; the second can be called *diathetic* which, being psychologically based, synchronously and symmetrically produces attitudinal sequelae.[7] (See Schema "B.")

Now, so far as can be determined, no one other than Newman has ever developed such a persuasive case for, and broad outline of, how liberal education can holistically perfect the intellect through "dispositionally supportive" powers. Likewise, no one other than Newman has attempted to ascribe *noetic* with psychologically enhancing sequelae, which accompany the process of liberalizing education. We detect causative exchanges—or "complemental reciprocities"—between dianoetic (intellectual) and diathetic (attitudinal) effects. Sagacity of mind (dianoetic) reflects attitudinal clearsightedness (diathetic), just as intel-lective steadiness of mind (dianoetic) reflects attitudinal sobriety of thought (diathetic).

SCHEMA "B"

EFFECTS OF LIBERAL EDUCATION

DIANOETIC	*DIATHETIC*
Sagacity	Clearsightedness
Force	Courtesy
Steadiness	Propriety
Comprehensiveness	Polish of word and action
Intellectual versatility	Good sense
Command of power	Sobriety of thought
Inherent just estimate	Reasonableness
Freedom	Candor
Equitableness	Self-command
Moderation	Steadiness of view
Wisdom	Consideration
Calmness	Indulgence
Connected view	Generosity
Ease of entry	Large-mindedness
Intellectual self-possession	Gentleness
Philosophical reach of mind	Repose

Diathetic traits of *attitude* are reflective of dianoetic traits of *intellect*.

INTELLECT AND ATTITUDE

Thus, it can be said that, for Newman, the liberally "cultivated" or the "properly trained and formed" intellect produces attitudinal or disposi-tional consequences for the whole person. The attitudinal evidences are there in Newman's words, because such an intellect, he says, "makes it-self felt in the good sense, sobriety of thought, reasonableness, candour, self-command, steadiness of view, which characterize it," and it does "manifest itself in a courtesy, propriety, and polish of word and action," as also in "the slow, silent, penetrating, overpowering effects of patience, steadiness, routine, and perseverance," and yet more, in "a delicate taste, a candid, equitable, dispassionate mind, a noble and courteous bearing." In such liberal cultivation of intellect, there is formed "a habit of mind," a "habit of method," as well as "a habit of order and system."[8]

Scholastics might express this relation of intellectual causes with attitudinal effects in the renowned maxim, *agere sequitur esse*— roughly, "Behavior follows identity," or "A thing acts as what it is." Hence, a well-formed intellect *tends* to produce supportive psychological behavior. To elevate the meaning further, we might even suggest that a loyally cultivated intellect tends to produce moral behavior. And Newman suggests—in confutation of the "infidelity of the day"—that intellectual and moral actions can, indeed, be harmonious. Thus, the "good" (or valuative) intellect will tend to act for the good. This, of course, comes perilously close to what Socrates sought to portray by arguing that one who really knows the "good" will follow its path to "good action." On the other hand, St. Paul's more difficult but realistic observation is that we do not always do the good that we intend, nor turn from the evil we would avoid. Still, we must recall, St. Paul's was not an argument about the well-formed intellect, but about the ordinary weakness of those who, even with the best intentions, remain merely intentional.

Still, Newman notes, liberal education has the power—which is "excellent in itself" and "has a result beyond itself"—to form a "habit of mind." And this formative power, he has just told us, can issue in five attributes, which, curiously, have the appearance of classical virtues—freedom, equitableness, calmness, moderation, and wisdom (see Schema "B"). Setting aside, for the moment, the dyad of flanking attributes (freedom and wisdom), we can first interrogate, as it were, each of the inner triad—equitableness, calmness, and moderation.

This "inner" dianoetic triad of Newman's lexicon, we might just as easily have cited as diathetic attributes of disposition or attitude. Such categorization would be reminiscent of the way in which prudence has traditionally been accounted by Aristotle and St. Thomas as both an intellective and a moral virtue.[9] Here each member of this inner triad also suggests an emotive, dispositional, or attitudinal correlative. Such would be the case, for example, if *equitable* meant "pleasant," *calm* meant "unflappable," and *moderate* meant "mild." But, in Newman's use of these terms, on the contrary, these are primarily the attributes, not of disposition, but of intellection.

Thus, *equitableness*, in Newman's usage, appears to represent fairness and balance of mind, not just of emotion; to represent impartiality of mind, not just of sentiment; to represent an nonprejudicial mind, not just unbiased feeling. In addition, *calmness* appears as tranquility of mind, and not merely of attitude.[10] But finally, moderation, although dianoetic, also seems akin to the moral virtue, temperance, which is one of the four cardinal virtues.[11] Here, however, *moderation* refers to intellective balance—in an Aristotelian sense, avoidance of extremes of excess or deficiency—even though it also seems to have moral implications.

Completing the circle, there is the dyad of flanking attributes, freedom and wisdom. First, *freedom* (intellectively) means freedom from ignorance—that which, as Newman has often said, "is the root of all littleness."[12] Secondly, there is the connatural complement, wisdom, which, for Aristotle, is an intellectual virtue, being "the most perfect of the modes of knowledge."[13] Of course, even here we can be sensitive to that term *wisdom* in another universe of discourse, where it signifies a divine gift, rooted in religious experience. Apparently implicit as this may seem, such interpretation would be inconsistent with Newman's interest in education "simply on the grounds of human reason and human wisdom," because "philosophy of Education is founded on truths in the natural order."[14]

Newman's presentation and analysis of the idea of liberal education (implicitly including attitudinal effects) bespeak his long familiarity with its beau ideal. Newman reveals in the very first paragraphs of *The Idea of a University* that he has been on intimate terms with the topic of education. And we need but recall whence that intimacy originated, as he moved from brilliant student at Ealing Prep School, to Oxford student, Trinity scholar, and private tutor; to Oriel Fellow, Vice Principal of St. Alban's Hall, University Tutor, and University Examiner. These were the experiences which cemented his connection with the subject of liberal education. As he said, "Education and the principles on which it must be conducted have ever had a hold upon my own mind." And again, "The views to which I have referred have grown into my whole system of thought, and are, as it were, part of myself."[15]

INTELLECTUAL AUTOBIOGRAPHY

As Newman constructs *The Idea of a University*, we can intuit his self-knowledge as that of an implicit subject, who himself developed, cultivated, and perfected his own intellect. In this sense, the *Idea* may be understood as an intellectual testimonium, just as later, the *Apologia pro vita sua* would seem to follow the pattern of developmental witness to his religious opinions. Not surprisingly, the testimonium of the *Idea* and the *Apologia* parallel that of St Augustine's *Confessiones*, in which he attested to his own religious and intellectual development. If it can rightly be claimed that *The Idea of a University* is a testimonia to Newman's intellectual development, and so prefigures the *Apologia*'s testimonium to his religious development, then their combined testimonia contrive to evoke the central educative and religious transformations of Newman's life. By enlisting the spirit of devotion and learning, these works engaged the genius of his conscience and wisdom.

It seems at least plausible, then, to argue that *The Idea of a University* represents Newman's intellectual autobiography and furnishes us an implicit record of just how Newman perfected his own intellect. *The Idea of a University* thus contains an implicit scenario of Newman's narrative of his own intellectual life. In addition to the *Idea*'s discourses as autobiographical portrait, there are also in the work autobiographical subtexts and a pair of Newman self-portraits.[16] How else could Newman write so persuasively and convincingly of the perfection of the intellect, unless he himself had undergone the experience of just such a renovation? By means of his own liberating experience of University education, Newman could explain to others the several ways in which intellect can be perfected. Such, perhaps, is what Newman instructively, and (if we can legitimately infer) experientially, recorded. In that spirit of experience and instruction, Newman is unreservedly empowered to recommend similar efforts to others. Surely, this would explain just why—more than a century-and-a-half since his Dublin lectures on education—Newman's ideas about the shaping of the intellect continue to hammer at our hearts and renovate our minds.

PERSONALIZED INSIGHT

We also sense autobiographical effect in *The Idea of a University* because it is written with such deeply felt emotion, personalized insight, pervasive sincerity, and experiential clarity. Little wonder that the *Idea* has been called "a triumph of literary art, perhaps the finest example of nonfictional prose in the English language."[17] Like his other "perfect work," *The Present Position of Catholics in England* (which also has educational intent), the *Idea* reveals Newman as uncannily present for us, and as being in spiritual conjunction, even moral fusion, with so much of what he writes. Here, uniquely, Newman's personality does more than just shine through these works, because, in them, his personality mysteriously becomes surface and substance, style and message, text and subtext. In these "two most perfect works"—*Present Position* and *The Idea of a University*—Newman appears, as if he were companionably and companionately present with us. He dwells among us, speaks conversationally to us as individuals—as though we were known to him as he is known to us. In these two educational works, then, we hear him in our mind's ear, just as we see him in our mind's eye. We applaud what we enjoy and what we value; what we enjoy is his humor, his light touch, his panache, and what we value is his deep seriousness. We marvel at the ease with which he surmounts whatever resistance to his arguments we might retain. Yet, we are still struck by how, with his insight, he opens up for us the very heavens of intellectual, moral, and spiritual vision.

In these two works, Newman seems to surpass the actor on the stage, the conductor at the podium, the artist at the easel. This is because he himself becomes (as it were) the play, the music, the painting. Unifying idea and expression, thought and word, *verbum* and *sermo*, Newman simultaneously transforms them all. As the teacher he so often praises, with the voice that so often moves us, he persuades our hearts and convinces our minds. His artistry dissolves into art, as his art is transfused with truth. In the *Present Position* and in the *Idea*, Newman has rendered to us a magnificent bequest, by accounting these "my two most perfect works, artistically."[18]

As a treatise on education, however, *The Idea of a University* is neither abstract nor abstractive. Rather, it is a work of pragmatic force and existential intention. It does not suggest what "would be nice to have," but rather—if education is to renovate mind and spirit—"what must be done." It lays down, out of human promise and potentiality, how human beings can be brought to intellectual perfection. Unlike John Locke's 1693 *Some Thoughts Concerning Education*—the *Idea* is not a tract on political ideology, and—unlike Jean-Jacques Rousseau's

Emile of 1762—it is not a treatise on social psychology.[19] Instead, *The Idea of a University* is exclusively educational in purpose, because it explores, with spiritual intensity, the ascentive promise of the human mind.

PERSONAL DEVELOPMENT

But there is a more cosmic "self-portrait" implicit in *The Idea of a University*, and this concerns Newman's personal experience of the idea of development. It may be useful, then, to look back on the biographical origins of the idea of development, an idea very much Newman's own, because he discovered it in an inspired moment of religious concentration.

One day, while reading Thomas Scott's 1779 spiritual autobiography, *The Force of Truth*, Newman, with the enlightening clarity of spiritual inspiration, was confronted by two transfiguring exhortations—holiness rather than peace, and growth as the only evidence of life.[20] Throughout his subsequent life, these exhortative "revelations" lent to Newman's experience a deeper, indefectible meaning. To the rule of holiness, he dedicated the substance of his days, while to the lesson of growth, he surrendered the expansion of his mind. Instinctively, Newman perceived that the very purpose of spiritual life is growth in holiness, and that the very force of spiritual growth is development of personal identity.

For what is the purpose of time, except to develop? So too, development of time is precisely designed to develop ourselves—for what else is there for us to develop except ourselves? And is not development of intellect the singular way in which that occurs? Even development of our "heart" or of our conscience involves development of our "consciousness"—and therefore development of the *intellectual* identity of who we are.

In Newman's case, development—as *idea* and as *reality*—represents an autobiographic illustration of how he continued to enlarge his experience through a series of transfiguring ascensions. He must also have sensed that his mind had been refashioned by the idea of development, that his humanity was magnified by it, and that by it his work had been brought to fruition. Intuitively, he must have understood that development is not only appropriate to, but required of, all life, especially spiritual life; and that the "power of development is a proof of life, not only in its essay, but especially in its success."[21] He perceived that development is, in essence, historical, and thus provides the necessary condition for spiritual history—indeed, for all history. Because spiritual perfection is the goal of Christian life, Newman must also have sensed that spiritual development is its requisite expectation. This may be why he understood that "to live is to change, and to be perfect is to have changed often."[22]

EDUCATION AS DEVELOPMENT

Because the process of development is uniquely stipulated by the nature of the intellect, Newman considered that intellectual development is precisely the kind of experience which liberal education provides. Thus, he repeatedly says that liberal education undertakes the perfecting— that is, the developing—of the intellect. Given that premise, development ought to be qualitatively discernible in University life—itself the natural residence of liberal education.[23] It would seem fair also to suggest that development is clearly an educative idea. Yet in a far larger sense—a sense in which development goes well beyond the confines of University—it would be equally fair to suggest that development is essentially a religious idea. For without spiritual growth, educatively and religiously, there can be no human development, just as, without development, there can be no spiritual ascent. And, without ascent, there can be no perfecting of human life. Here again is another illustration of the confluence, in Newman's thought, of his educative-religious intuitions.

As Newman clearly sensed, spiritual development presupposes—while at the same time it intensifies—enlargement of heart and mind. This is because "increase and expansion . . . are the necessary attendants on any philosophy . . . which takes possession of the intellect and heart."[24] Spiritual development—meaning enlargement—explicates, unfolds, and reveals the nature of human nature. As if echoing here the thought of Pico della Mirandola, Newman stipulates that the nature of human nature is *openness*, since the human person

> is a being of progress with relation to his perfection and characteristic good. Other beings are complete from their first existence . . . but man begins with nothing realized . . . and he has to make capital for himself by the exercise of those faculties which are his natural inheritance. Thus he gradually advances to the fulness of his original destiny. . . . It is

his gift to be the creator of his own sufficiency; and to be emphatically self-made. This is the law of his being, which he cannot escape; and whatever is involved in that law he is bound, or rather he is carried on, to fulfil. . . . For this law of progress is carried out by means of the acquisition of knowledge.[25]

Synoptically, the concept of development of the intellect, and of its knowledge, by means of liberal education, implies the existence of two conditions: that there must be history, since everything cannot be given at once; and that there must be mystery, since everything cannot be understood at once. The first of these existential conditions arises because, "from the nature of the human mind, time is necessary for the full comprehension and perfection of great ideas." And the second existential condition arises because "the highest and most wonderful truths, though communicated to the world once for all by inspired teachers, could not be comprehended all at once by the recipients, but, as being received and transmitted by minds not inspired and through media which were human, have required only the longer time and deeper thought for their full elucidation."[26]

REFERENTS

Concealed within these existential conditions—history and mystery—we also discern the developmental prospect of perfection, because development is how perfection is actually existentialized. We further discern a linkage between the idea of perfection and those dual exhortations to which Thomas Scott riveted Newman's attention—namely, holiness rather than peace, and growth as the only evidence of life. These exhortations are mutually referential. As a developmental end-in-itself, that perfection called holiness is, simultaneously, the perfecting of spiritual growth. Only through spiritual growth can holiness be sustained. Only through holiness can spiritual life be said to grow.

Here then, shorn of ornament, is Newman's simple truth: perfection of the intellect requires development. Seriously developed, the human intellect also suggestively brings with it an implicit potential sanctification—a kind of hidden holiness—because what is being developed as the intellect is, precisely, *imago Dei*. Without development—which, after all, is the exclusive condition of perfection—intellect would cease to be what it truly is, because it would cease to be what it should be. Without (at least the possibility of) perfection, intellect would also lack finality, and hence fulfillment, thereby becoming purposeless—which is to say, without identity.

The nature of intellect is, after all, a life nature. This means that intellect must confront the requirement either to develop or to decay. In life there is no standing still, no protective "cone of safety" where, conveniently and risklessly, life can be frozen. Frozen life is dead life. Should intellect choose decay, not development—or corruption, not perfection—it would be choosing not to be what it really is. Those alternatives—development or decay, perfection or corruption—provide the only directions which intellect can follow. Like any other living reality, intellect, without development, ceases to live. Having ceased to live, and so having lost its life, intellect—like Dante's *le gente dolorose*—would have "lost its good."

Perhaps it could also be said that, like Newman's "living idea," intellect's "beginnings are no measure of its capabilities, nor of its scope." Along with the exigencies involved in its development, intellect, as it were, "changes with them in order to remain the same."[27] In other words, to remain what it really *is*, intellect needs to become what it *ought to be*. And this assertion, once again, is based upon the fact that intellect is *imago Dei*. The requirement that intellect develop in order to remain itself may also explain why Newman holds the University in such high regard as a social institution, because its fundamental task is precisely the cultivation and perfection of the intellect.[28] For like the creative commands of *Genesis-Bereshith* (1: 27–28)—which initiate "history as the eighth day of Creation"—the principle of development preconditions the growth of the human intellect. This means that the principle of development ought (1) to guide thinking about the role of intellect in higher education, (2) to foster reflection about the purpose of higher education, and (3) to support the intellectual integrity of University life.

Ironically, it was not Newman's intention to make the principle of development a means of assessing the scope of educational ideas. When he first articulated this principle of development, his interests lay elsewhere—indeed, they were riveted on the historical and ecclesiological nature and growth of Christian doctrine. In light of a developmental principle, Newman was attempting to provide a realistic account of the doctrinal integrity of the Catholic Church vis-à-vis other Christian Churches.[29]

Not surprisingly then, Newman first discovered the principle of development in Scripture.[30] He also understood that learning and enlargement of mind also follow the paradigm of devotional development of living Christian doctrine. Thus, Scripture anticipates "the development of Christianity" (he was saying), just as the mustard seed analogically anticipates the Kingdom of God (Mk. 4: 31, Lk. 13: 19). As an educational issue, the idea of a scriptural anticipation of the principle of development seems especially appropriate to Newman's mind-set. To accept this, we need only recall how often Newman links religion and education. We need only recall, too, how often Newman has emphasized that revelation is essentially educative of mankind: "Perhaps we may say that the object of Revelation was to enlighten and enlarge the mind, to make us act by reason, and to expand and strengthen our powers—to impart knowledge about religious truth, knowledge being power directly it is given, and enabling us forthwith to think, judge, and act for ourselves . . . or to secure what otherwise would be hopeless, our leading a religious life."[31]

WIDER REACH

The principle of development has wider reach than even Newman, at first, might have suspected. As he said, "I saw that the principle of development not only accounted for certain facts, but was in itself a remarkable philosophical phenomenon."[32] So, in rather a scriptural sense, the developmental nature of intellect already anticipates the insight that education is precisely and implicitly ordained for intellectual development. Such a principle will, indeed, become crucial to arguments which Newman carefully presents in *The Idea of a University*. There can be little cause for hesitation in asserting that Newman expected the principle of development to be, as it ought to be, at the center of any idea about education. This is because such an idea involves the process of intellectual growth.

Not unexpectedly, this same principle of development is also at the center of philosophy, which, par excellence, denotes intellectual growth. In Western culture, philosophy suggests that only through an intellectual vision of the (interrelated) everything of the world, can any truly perceptive view of a (discrete) anything be achieved. The same can be said of Western ideas about education. Intellectual vision, being congruently applicable to philosophy and education, is the power of generalization, which implicitly affirms the principle of connectedness.

The power of generalization and the principle of connectedness make "every thing in some sort lead to every thing else."[33]

EDUCATION AND PHILOSOPHY

If we advance this notion a further step, we must admit that, in Western culture, the idea of education tacitly reflects the idea of philosophy. Indeed, Western education has been suffused with the idea of philosophy, largely because it has been shaped by philosophical axioms, which articulate truths about the sheer penetrative power of the human mind. For this reason, the idea of education has, like that of philosophy, been fixed upon the goal of attaining intellectual excellence. Also like the Western idea of philosophy, the idea of education seeks to ascertain the most appropriate ways in which the human mind needs to—and thus ought to—conduct its business. If a grasp of wholeness is the classical ideal of Western education, it is only because that ideal embodies the basic philosophical insight into what Newman calls the "interconnectedness" of the whole fact of reality. Clearly enough, Newman reiterates his loyalty to that special connective power of the intellect, when he says that it

> seizes and unites what the senses present to it . . . gives them a meaning, and invests them with an idea . . . assigns phenomena to a general law, qualities to a subject, acts to a principle, effects to a cause. In a word, it philosophizes; for I suppose Science and Philosophy in their elementary idea, are nothing else but this habit of viewing, as it may be called, the objects which sense conveys to the mind, of throwing them into a system, and uniting and stamping them with one form. . . . When I speak of Knowledge, I mean something intellectual, something which grasps what it perceives through the senses . . . takes a view of things . . . sees more than the senses convey . . . reasons upon what it sees, and while it sees . . . invests it with an idea. It expresses itself not in a mere enunciation, but by an enthymeme; it is of the nature of science from the first, and in this consists its dignity . . . [which] is this germ within it of a scientific or a philosophical process. This is how it comes to be an end in itself; this is why it admits of being called Liberal.[34]

Tucked into the center of this passage is the assertion that

Knowledge expresses itself not as mere enunciation, but, as derived by intellective power, in a logic of intellect, of a reasoning which uncovers the connections of knowledge. Thus, intellect "speaks" not merely through a linguistic "word," but through a higher intellective "Word," or *Logos*.

Force of mind—or, as Thomas Scott would say, "the force of truth"—culminates, then, in the way that intellect thinks what it sees, and knows what it thinks. Intellect processes what it gathers to it, and makes connections with what it already knows. When disciplined to the "perfection of its powers," intellect "knows and thinks while it knows," because it "has learned to leaven the dense mass of facts and events with the elastic force of reason." This explains, Newman says, why having "even a portion of this illuminative reason and true philosophy is the highest state to which nature can aspire, in the way of intellect."[35]

INTELLECT'S POWERS

Intellect, then, represents itself in more than simple language, more than naked speech, more than mere enunciation, or what might be called categorically innocent verbal expression. Instead, intellect uses the force of spiritually perceptive sight, and generates an annunciation of that integral "Thought or Reason exercised upon Knowledge, or what may be called Philosophy."[36] When promulgated as thought or reason, the liberally disciplined mind is carried beyond rhetoric, into philosophy, where, kerygmatically, it is enfolded into intellective speech.

In that environment, liberal education attains philosophical integrity, because it inaugurates that "clear, calm, accurate vision and comprehension of all things, as far as the finite mind can embrace them."[37] By definition, then, liberal knowledge cannot be vague or ordinary knowledge, because, in a nontechnical sense, it is inspired by the spirit of philosophy. Liberal education, in imitation of its model, has donned a kind of philosophical raiment, and thus acquires the formative power of philosophical exactitude: Liberal knowledge really means thinking the way philosophy thinks. As a consequence of this edifying principle, Newman states that "whatever claims Knowledge has to be considered as a good, these it has in a higher degree when it is viewed not vaguely, not popularly, but precisely and transcendently as Philosophy. Knowledge, I say, is then especially liberal, or sufficient for itself, apart from every external and ulterior object, when and so far as it is philosophical. . . . Knowledge is called by the name of . . . Philosophy, when it is acted upon, informed, or if I may use a strong figure, impregnated by Reason [Intellect, (νοῦς).] . . . [which] is the principle of that intrinsic fecundity of Knowledge."[38]

Once again, Newman stresses, with clarifying force, that his theme is the philosophical integrity of liberal knowledge. In its acquisition, he says, "We are satisfying a direct need of our nature. . . . We start with an idea, we educate upon a type; we make use, as nature prompts us, of the faculty, which I have called an intellectual grasp of things, or an inward sense, and which I shall hereafter show is really meant by the word 'Philosophy.'"[39]

LIBERAL AS PHILOSOPHICAL

That "special Philosophy" to which Newman makes continued reference, clearly consists in "a comprehensive view of truth in all its branches."[40] Because it is the reflective image of philosophy, liberal education is, of necessity, concerned with truth, and "educates the intellect to reason well in all matters, to reach out towards truth, and to grasp it."[41] Truth, says Newman, "is the proper object of the intellect; its cultivation then lies in fitting it to apprehend and contemplate truth." Liberal enlargement, development, and comprehensiveness constitute a training, which "is not a mere application, however exemplary, which introduces the mind to truth, nor the reading many books, nor the getting up many subjects, nor the witnessing many experiments, nor the attending many lectures. . . . [The] power of discriminating between truth and falsehood . . . is the result of a scientific formation of mind . . . of clear-sightedness, of sagacity, of wisdom, of philosophical reach of mind."[42]

Seen from this viewpoint, says Newman, education "is a high word; it is the preparation for knowledge, and it is the imparting of knowledge in proportion to that preparation." At another point he adds that liberal education "is a higher word; it implies an action upon our mental nature, and the formation of a character; it . . . is a state or condition of mind."[43] To assure that we have caught Newman's point, let us "stitch together" an extended quotation of his words:

> The word "Liberal" and the word "Philosophy" have already
> suggested, that there is a Knowledge which is desirable,

though nothing come of it, as being of itself a treasure, and
a sufficient remuneration of years of labour. . . . In default of
a recognized term, I have called the perfection or virtue of
the intellect by the name of philosophy, philosophical knowledge, enlargement of mind, or illumination. . . . The enlargement consists, not merely in the passive reception . . . of
ideas hitherto unknown to it, but in the mind's energetic and
simultaneous action upon and towards and among those new
ideas. . . . It is the action of a formative power, reducing to
order and meaning . . . making the objects of our knowledge
subjectively our own. . . . There is no enlargement unless
there be a comparison of ideas with one another . . . and a
systematizing of them. We . . . not only learn, but refer what
we learn to what we know already. . . . And therefore . . . the
intellect . . . takes a connected view of old and new, past and
present, far and near, and which has an insight into the influence of all these one on another; without which there is no
whole, and no centre. It possesses the knowledge, not only
of things, but also of their mutual and true relations; knowledge not merely considered as acquirement, but as philosophy.[44]

This composite message appears, as well, in Newman's University Sermon XIV,[45] which he preached to an Oxford congregation on
Whit-Tuesday morning, 1 June 1841. That connective fact clearly tells
us that, prior to his 1852 discourses, Newman had already been thinking about this topic, and thinking about it for at least eleven years. It
further tells us that he apparently felt impelled to transfer that essential
Oxford message to his Dublin University *Discourses*.

Consequently, the mutually relational, intellectively interconnective power of knowledge, to which Newman refers, is the power of
"viewing many things at once as a whole," since "all knowledge forms
one whole because its subject-matter is one"; it is the power of realistically "viewing things as they are," and as being in "one and the same
circle of objects . . . one and all connected together . . . [which] at once
need and subserve each other."[46] It is the power of "referring them severally to their true place in the universal system"; it is the power of "understanding their respective values, and determining their mutual
dependence"; it is the power of "real illumination of the mind." Here,
then, in this universalizing and energizing action of intellect, lies the
power which is prepared to deal with absolutes. And it is for this reason

that "such an intellect cannot be partial, cannot be exclusive, cannot be impetuous, cannot be at a loss, cannot but be patient, collected, majestically calm, because it discerns the end in every beginning, the origin in every end, the law in every interruption, the limit in each delay; because it ever knows where it stands, and how its path lies from one point to another."[47]

ASCENT

Newman admits that "it is no easy matter to view things correctly." Therefore, whenever we seriously—intellectively—examine any issue, or any object, it becomes preconditionally necessary to ascend beyond that issue, or that object. We must ascend—rise up—to a higher plane in order to judge by principles, which are "higher" than things. To ratify this point, Newman appeals to the authority of Francis Bacon, who said, "No perfect discovery can be made upon a flat or a level."[48] Here, as if from practical as well as theoretic experience, Newman shrewdly observes the practice of experienced travelers who, as they arrive at an unfamiliar city, ascend to a high point from which to survey it. Analogically, he cites such advice when writing to a friend about someone who confused an issue: "When we have lost our way," he says, "we mount up to some eminence to look about us." Thus too, says Newman, "If we would improve the intellect, first of all, we must ascend; we can not gain real knowledge on a level; we must generalize, we must reduce to method, we must have a grasp of principles, and group and shape our acquisition by means of them. It matters not whether our field of operation be wide or limited; in every case, to command it, is to mount above it."[49]

Thus, the higher the mind ascends to universal principles and categories, the more it can perceive what is below it. Here is the law, not only of physical height, as every navigator knows, but also of spiritual height, as every thinker knows. Once again, Newman tells us that the well-disciplined mind

> never views any part of the extended subject-matter of
> Knowledge without recollecting that it is but a part, or without the associations which spring from this recollection. It
> makes every thing in some sort lead to every thing else; it
> would communicate the image of the whole to every separate
> portion, till that whole becomes in imagination like a spirit,

> every where pervading and penetrating its component parts, and giving them one definite meaning. . . . That perfection of the intellect . . . is . . . the true and adequate end of intellectual training and . . . is not Learning or Acquirement, but rather is Thought or Reason exercised upon Knowledge, or what may be called Philosophy.[50]

Here is what liberal education does par excellence, and this is what genuine education means. By being methodologically philosophical, education is the legatee of philosophy. In Western culture, philosophy had designed a "theory of Education,"which became a residence of philosophy's spirit of generalization. If the aim and intent of educational theory *and practice* is to instill the spirit of generalization, then education and philosophy do share an identity, not so much of scope, as of purpose. The intent of philosophy is to provide an overarching rational account of all human experience. Hence is explained philosophy's passion for the art of generalization which sees the world as participatively unified. This is the gift which philosophy bestows on the Western theory of education.

The West's theory of liberal education, moreover, is nothing short of a symbolic formulation of the ideal of philosophical perception. Liberal education can luxuriate, then, in a common purpose of shaping a well-developed, logically disciplined, reliably decisive mind, which is exquisitely suited to a life of deed and thought, performance and reflection, work and meditation. To achieve its goal, liberal education must undertake certain necessary actions—"to open the mind, to correct it, to refine it, to enable it to know, and to digest, master, rule, and use its knowledge, to give it power over its own faculties, application, flexibility, method, critical exactness, sagacity, resource, address, [and] eloquent expression."[51]

THREE TASKS

Embedded in these commanding and necessary actions are three implicit constituents of the educational process. First of all, there is motivation, which is the action to open the mind. Second, there is guidance, which is the action to correct it. Third, there is governance, which is the action to refine it. These actions are inherent in the developmental process of genuine education. Without motivation, the educative process could not commence. Without guidance, it could not continue. Without governance, it could not achieve completion and fulfillment.

This triadic Newmanesque complex is also suggestive of a parallel structure which Alfred North Whitehead has called the "three rhythmic phases of education"—*rhythmic* being "the conveyance of difference within a framework of repetition."[52] Real education, says Whitehead, essentially develops through three sequential stages. First, there is the stage of *romance* which is Whitehead's deliberately provocative term for the initiation of raw interest. Secondly, there is the stage of *precision* which, for raw interest, provides a rigorous discipline. Finally, there is the synthesizing stage of *generalization* which, in a dialectic of thetic-antithetic-synthetic action, conjunctively fulfills the preceding two stages. Whitehead also refers to this developmental complex as a sequencing of "freedom-discipline-freedom."

STRUCTURAL ROMANCE

In the process of development, then—a theme on which Newman and Whitehead concur—the mind first requires motivation or romance, which begins with the psychological need to open the mind—to motivate, to allure, to attract it. Such action reveals the magnetic importance of truth, by which alone intellect can achieve fulfillment. As Newman said, intellect "is made for truth, can attain truth, and, having attained it, can keep it, can recognize it, and preserve the recognition . . . and so rests in truth, as it cannot rest in falsehood."[53] Thus, there is need for a stage in which intellect confronts the romance of truth. Indeed, revealing to students just such a stage of allurement is the first task of all good teaching. The teacher who does not, or cannot reveal a subject-matter's attraction and interest has failed the primary test of productive teaching. By didactic instinct, effective teachers always know that, unless brought to perceive an initial stage of allurement or interest, a student will make no progress. This is especially so, says Whitehead, in view of the fact that all "valuable intellectual development is self-development." Moreover, he says,

> There can be no mental development without interest. Interest is the sine qua non for attention and apprehension. . . .
> [For] the natural mode by which living organisms are excited towards suitable self-development is enjoyment. . . .
> There is no comprehension apart from romance. . . . Without the adventure of romance, at the best you get inert knowl-

edge without initiative, and at the worst you get contempt of ideas—without knowledge. . . . The stage of romance is the stage of first apprehension. The subject-matter has the vividness of novelty. . . . Romantic emotion is essentially the excitement consequent on the transition from the bare facts to the first realisations of the import of their unexplored relationships.[54]

With Newman and Whitehead, we set it down that the educative process must begin with the psychological dynamics of motivation, or romance, which opens the mind, and dynamically releases, so to speak, increasing energies by which the mind, with continuing motivation or romance, opens itself. The same energy that opens the mind reveals to it the possibility of its cultivation and perfection. Motivation or romance thus represents a kind of initial insight, which discloses to the mind its own adventure in discovery.

In Whitehead's vocabulary, this first stage of allurement uncovers raw interest, which impels the mind to undertake the arduous task of exercising its inherent powers. Then, motivation (or romance) analogically becomes the "stage-prompter" which sets intellective action in motion, and focuses the mind upon a subject, which can then be apprehended in all its vividness. This stage, says Whitehead, is one of intellectual inspiration and provocation, where knowledge is kept alive, and thus prevented from becoming inert. By *inert ideas*, Whitehead means what is "merely received into the mind without being utilized, or tested, or thrown into fresh combinations."

A mind filled with inert ideas resembles a rabble rather than a disciplined regiment. Anesthetized by inert ideas, and thus lacking vividness of apprehension, the mind will be incapable of either precision or vision. As Whitehead phrases it, "Schools of learning, which at one epoch are alive with a ferment of genius, in a succeeding generation exhibit merely pedantry and routine. The reason is, that they are overladen with inert ideas. Education with inert ideas is not only useless: it is, above all things, harmful. . . . Every intellectual revolution which has ever stirred humanity into greatness has been a passionate protest against inert ideas."[55]

STRUCTURAL GUIDANCE

The mind requires guidance or precision, which is a disciplining action designed to correct it, to form its process, and to commit it to clarity. Left unattended, the mind is also left inexact, logically unnourished, and bereft of semantic care. To keep it on track in its explorations, mind essentially requires direction, reinforcement, exercise. As befits the demands of truth, the mind needs to be precise in perception, rigorous in procedure, strict in interpretation, and exact in formulation. Without a prior stage of motivation or romance, which opens the mind, the subsequent stage of guidance or precision would be barren. Similarly, without its consequent stage of guidance or precision, motivation or romance would be irrelevant.[56] These two stages stimulate and discipline the mind, and the mind is thereby prepared for the third stage of its development, in which the mind will master, rule, and use its knowledge.

STRUCTURAL GOVERNANCE

The mind requires governance or generalization, which inspires it to ascend to a higher level. As Newman says, "We must generalize. . . . We must have a grasp of principles, and group and shape our acquisitions by means of them."[57] Generalization, says Whitehead in concert with Newman, is "the fruition which has been the goal of precise training." It is the stage of "shedding details in favour of the active application of principles, the details retreating into subconscious habits."[58] Just as gold is refined from ores, and freed of alloys and purified, so too, the mind, emboldened by purifying discipline, enters upon a new freedom, in a new realm of governance or generalization, in which it discovers powers of clarification, comprehension, and insight.

To Newman, as to Whitehead, the spirit which should dominate higher education is precisely the spirit of vision. "A well-planned university course," Whitehead once said, "is a study of the wide sweep of . . . [generalization, in which] concrete fact should be studied as illustrating the scope of general ideas." The spirit of generalization—which is that of visionary principles—should "dominate a university." Whitehead goes on to explain,

> Your learning is useless to you till you have lost your text-books, burnt your lecture notes, and forgotten the minutiae which you learnt by heart for the examination. . . . The func-

> tion of a university is to enable you to shed details in favour of principles. . . . A principle which has thoroughly soaked into you is rather a mental habit. . . . It becomes the way the mind reacts. . . . Nobody can be a good reasoner unless by constant practice he has realized the importance of getting hold of the big ideas and of hanging on to them like grim death.[59]

Continuing Process

Implicitly with Newman, and explicitly with Whitehead, this ultimate stage of vision will act as a new platform of interest, and thus will lead to a new stage of discipline, which, in turn, will be completed on reaching a new and higher stage of vision. For Whitehead, every final stage of the enjoyment of generalization becomes a new starting point for romance, and then for precision, and then for a new level of generalization. Not unlike what Newman holds about the spirit of growth, Whitehead envisions each educational cycle as a unit cell, which conspires in the reproduction of further learning cells. This is why Whitehead believed that education consists in a continual repetition of such cycles, and of cycles of such cycles.

The learning process, in other words, is not a boundable event, but a complex of continued, continuing, and continuous events.[60] In consequence, there can be no "single moment"— for example, the graduation ceremony—at which education comes to an end point. This is because a little true learning invites a little more true learning, and this little more, a little more yet, lest it become, in the shopworn phrase of Alexander Pope, a dangerous thing.

Yet, unless a little learning does seriously produce a little more learning, and does so with steady, rhythmic assurance, Alexander Pope's warning is destined to be realized with a vengeance, and will continue to haunt those who are unprepared for the advent of such danger. Newman and Whitehead also concur in urging that educational development follow Rome's imperial maxim—*festina lente*—that is, "make haste without haste." Indeed, this maxim contains the secret of all sound educational theory. To that Roman maxim, Newman adds his own obliquely imperative caution, *multum, non multa*—"learn much, but not too much at one time."

LITTLE, BUT WELL

In the second half of *The Idea of a University*, the section "Elementary Subjects" features illustrative *dramatis personae*, consisting of Tutor Mr. White, the elder Mr. Black, and the promising young Mr. Black, who (like young Mr. Newman) possesses all the attributes of a person who is attitudinally prepared to undertake serious intellectual studies. Together, Mr. White and the elder Mr. Black articulate an important teaching principle: "[E]very sensible tutor will maintain . . . 'a little, but well'; that is, really know what you say you know: know what you know and what you do not know; get one thing well before you go on to a second. . . . Our rule is to recommend youths to do a little well, instead of throwing themselves upon a large field of study. . . . [If they] are to be taught well, they must be taught slowly, and step by step."[61]

Whitehead would add a caution: "We enunciate two educational commandments, 'Do not teach too many subjects,' and again, 'What you teach, teach thoroughly.' The result of teaching small parts of a large number of subjects is the passive reception of disconnected ideas, not illumined with any spark of vitality. Let the main ideas which are introduced into . . . education be few and important, and let them be thrown into every combination possible."[62]

Like Whitehead, Newman also perceived the inevitable chaos which awaits those who ignore such warnings. This is why he deplored "the error of distracting and enfeebling the mind by an unmeaning profusion of subjects; of implying that a smattering in a dozen branches of study is not shallow, which it really is, but enlargement, which it is not. . . . [Such] ill-used persons . . . leave their place of education simply dissipated and relaxed by the multiplicity of subjects, which they never really mastered, and so shallow as not even to know their shallowness."[63]

Hence, Newman argues, it were better that a student not know anything of a subject, rather than "to have a slender knowledge." He anticipates Whitehead's words by echoing Alexander Pope's advice:

> And here we see what is meant by the poet's maxim, "A little learning is a dangerous thing." Not that knowledge, little or much, if it be real knowledge, is dangerous; but that many a man considers a hazy view of many things to be real knowledge, whereas it does but mislead, just as a short-sighted man sees only so far as to be led by his uncertain

> sight over the precipice. . . . [I]t is better for a youth to know
> nothing of the . . . subject, than to have a slender knowledge
> which he can use freely and recklessly, for the very reason
> that it is slender. And here we have the maxim in corrobora-
> tion: "A little learning is a dangerous thing."[64]

A little learning is especially dangerous, not because it is little,
but, more importantly, because it is fraudulent. And it is fraudulent because it lacks the true enlarging dignity of learning, and thus is not learning at all. Learning is never minuscule, or, were it so, it could not then
really be learning. Learning precisely provides an enlarging experience,
and enlarges the person who takes it into his or her inner being. Dollops
of information, large or small—even an exaggerated "heaping up" of
data—are not the same as learning. Mere facts, whatever their quantity,
are devoid of that quality which distinguishes them from learning—
namely, interconnectedness.[65]

CAST OF CHARACTERS

Sketched in student cameo in *The Idea of a University*, are several fraud-
ulently pretentious claimants to knowledge. There is, for instance, the
youth who, with

> a litter of ideas heaped up into his mind anyhow . . . can utter
> a number of truths or sophisms . . . and one is as good as an-
> other. He is up with a number of doctrines and a number of
> facts, but they are all loose and straggling, for he has no prin-
> ciples set up in his mind round which to aggregate or locate
> them. He can say a word or two on half a dozen sciences,
> but not a dozen words on any one. He says one thing now
> and another thing presently, and when he attempts to write
> down distinctly what he holds upon a point in dispute, or
> what he understands by its terms, he breaks down, and is sur-
> prised by his failure. . . . And withal, he has a very good opin-
> ion of himself, and is well satisfied with his attainments.[66]

Such youths, whatever their mental attire, do but people the
pages of *The Idea of a University*. Sometimes they have names—there
is, for instance, the inadequate Mr. Robert Brown—but mostly they
spread themselves namelessly through the text. They especially include
those who look at the world

in that offhand, idle way, which we signify by the word *un-real*. "That they simply do not know what they are talking about" is the spontaneous silent remark of any man of sense who hears them. Hence such persons have no difficulty in contradicting themselves in successive sentences, without being conscious of it. . . . [They] have the most unfortunate crochets . . . can never look straight before them, never see the point, have no difficulties in the most difficult subjects . . . are hopelessly obstinate and prejudiced . . . intemperate and intractable . . . who, like blunt weapons, tear and hack instead of cutting clean, who mistake the point in argument, waste their strength on trifles, misconceive their adversary, and leave the question more involved than they find it. . . . Such minds cannot fix their gaze on one object for two seconds together.[67]

Furthermore, this is so, says Newman, because

the multitude of men have no clear view what it is they know, what they presume, what they suppose, and what they only assert. They make little distinction between credence, opinion, and profession; at various times they give them all perhaps the name of certitude, and accordingly, when they change their minds, they fancy they have given up points of which they had a true conviction. . . . [I]t is scarcely worth while to dwell upon the absurdities and excesses of the rude intellect . . . the prejudices, credulities, infatuations, superstitions, fanaticisms, the whims and fancies, the sudden irrevocable plunges into the unknown, the obstinate determinations—the offspring, as they are, of ignorance, wilfulness, cupidity, and pride—which go so far to make up the history of mankind.[68]

And this is also because such minds miss "the connection of fact with fact, truth with truth, the bearing of fact upon truth, and truth upon fact, what leads to what, what are points primary, and what secondary. . . . [E]very thing comes and goes like the wind, nothing makes an impression, nothing penetrates, nothing has its place in their minds. They locate nothing, they have no system."[69]

Inexactness Generalized

These sorts of minds, therefore, cannot see broadly, because they cannot see precisely. Thus, they do not understand that "exactness of idea" and "generalization of idea" are simply opposite sides of the same coin. Nor do they understand that, without precision, generalization is empty, just as, without generalization, precision is blind. Such a person of careless mind will also usually neglect to comprehend the regency and sovereignty of a sentence, and thus will not know "how the separate portions of a sentence hang together, how they form a whole, how each has its own place in the government of it, what are the peculiarities of construction or the idiomatic expressions in it proper to the language in which it is written, what is the precise meaning of its terms, and what the history of their formation."[70]

For this reason, Newman encourages students to attain commanding linguistic competence. There is benefit in learning, not just another language, but learning the mastery of how to translate that other language into one's mother tongue, along with the discipline of accurately turning one's mother tongue into that newly acquired language. Newman can therefore observe, "What a discipline in accuracy of thought it is to have to construe a foreign language into your own; what a still severer and more improving exercise it is to translate from your own language into a foreign language. . . . To translate an English sentence into Latin is to frame a sentence, and is the best test whether or not a student knows the difference of Latin from English construction; to construe and parse is to analyze a sentence."[71]

Being in similar company to Newman's view of translation, Whitehead can remark on the theoretic consequences of translation skills: "The philosophic instinct which Latin invokes, hovers between [logic and history] . . . and enriches both. The analysis of thought involved in translation, English to Latin or Latin to English, imposes that type of experience which is the necessary introduction to philosophic thought. If in your after life your job is to think, render thanks to Providence which ordained that, for five years of your youth, you did a Latin prose once a week and daily construed some Latin author."[72]

Thus commanding the genius of its mother tongue, the mind will say precisely, and articulate persuasively, what it actually means to convey.

VIRTUES OF TRANSLATING

One such case in point is Newman himself. From age seven, on first learning Latin, he spent some portion of each day of his subsequent life in translating to, or from, Latin, or writing out a Latin theme. Thomas Mozley, Newman's brother-in-law, recorded of Newman: "While at Oxford he never passed a day without writing a Latin sentence—either a translation, or an original composition, before he had done his morning's work."[73] Newman was therefore his own best advertisement for a practice to which he so often commended others.

Newman and Whitehead, then, would agree that any educational theory that fails to be as dynamic as the mind itself, leaves no room for growth and development, does not open up experience to inquiry, has no explanation for the effects of the universe on learning, or of learning upon the universe—such a "theory" is unworthy of the dignity of being considered educational.

Suggestively, the triadic complex of Newman's—motivation, guidance, and governance—also provides the mind certain forms of *moral* capacity. And this is because this triad (1) endows the mind with the moral capacity of seriousness, so that, when challenged by difficulties, the mind does not slip easily into doubt;[74] (2) accords the mind the moral capacity for self-exhortation, so that, when confronted by rigidity, or ideological simplicity, the mind does not falter; and (3) confers upon the mind the moral capacity of perseverance, confidence, and sound judgment, so that, when its operations are impeded, it does not surrender duty to convenience. Through such renewing actions, certain forms of sagacity, even wisdom, are then created. As the mind becomes reliantly and reliably capable of trusting in its own powers, it will beget new aptitudes of resourcefulness.

LIBERATING ARTS AND SCIENCES

Such powers and accomplishments will then illuminate the question of why liberal studies confer upon the mind a gift of intellectual freedom, by means of which the mind is redeemed of mental servility, or ideological indenture, and freedom from those states "in which the mind has little or no part."[75] For this reason, too, liberal studies have come to be known as the seven liberal (liberating) arts and sciences. Divided (as already mentioned) into Trivium, which led to the medieval degree Bachelor of Arts, and Quadrivium, which led to the degree Master of

Arts, they were distinguished as arts and sciences, not for the purpose of separation, but for the purpose of concentration and unification. They acquired distinction only because they possessed integrative character, such as might be portrayed in the formula, *Distinguer pour unir*.

We have previously said that Trivium comprised grammar, rhetoric, and logic. Grammar was the "science of observation" which disciplined one to say clearly what one intended to say. Grammar was, above all, the "art of statement," and was concerned with exact expression of its intention, with exact word for an intended meaning, with exact proposition by which to elucidate that intended meaning. Grammar's associate, a notch higher, was rhetoric. Building upon grammatical foundation, rhetoric fashioned, not just clear statement, but artful, persuasive, eloquent statement. Finally, there was logic, a notch higher still, which focused, not just on clear, or persuasive, but on coherent statement, and upon coherence among several statements. Logic was the instrument by which propositions could be elevated to the level of precision.

In contrast, Quadrivium comprised the sciences—in a sense not too distant from our own use of the term—as forms of "physics." They were divided into the science of arithmetic, or manipulation of magnitudes; of harmonics, or delineation of proportional relations among magnitudes; of geometry, or conceptual demonstration of magnitudes of dimension; and of astronomy, or articulation of patterns of magnitude in macro-physical motion.

Together, Trivium and Quadrivium therefore illustrated how one could master verbal and mathematical skills, otherwise known as the arts and sciences. Newman, however, had a somewhat different, perhaps more ambitious, sense of what constitutes arts and sciences, which he called "literature and science":

> The book of nature is called Science, the book of man is called Literature. Literature and Science . . . nearly constitute the subject-matter of Liberal Education. . . . Science . . . has to do with things, literature with thoughts; science is universal, literature is personal; science uses words merely as symbols, but literature uses language in its full compass. . . . Literature is the personal use or exercise of language. . . . Literature stands related to Man as Science stands to Nature; it is his history. . . . Literature is to man in some sort what autobiography is to the individual; it is his Life and Remains.[76]

THINKING AND WRITING

Education, in at least one of its many phases, is especially devoted to students' ability to exercise the art of "thinking well," and thus of "thinking for themselves." Precisely to think, and exactly to think well, have always constituted arduous tasks. Moreover, writing well implies first learning the art of thinking well. If a person cannot write well, it is because she or he cannot think well. Hence, in extension of what he has so far said, Newman points out, "The rule is, first think, and then write; don't write when you have nothing to say; or if you do, you will make a mess of it. . . . [C]ompare one idea with another; adjust truths and facts; form them into one whole, or notice the obstacles which occur in doing so. This is the way to make progress; this is the way to arrive at results."[77]

A device for estimating how well one knows what one claims to know is, as Newman suggests, writing it down, because the act of writing something down usually settles the issue. "Till a man begins to put down his thoughts about a subject on paper he will not ascertain what he knows and what he does not know, and still less will he be able to express what he does know."[78]

Writing becomes doubly important, because writing not only reveals what one claims to know, but also reveals the kind of thinking that accompanies such claims. Reading is also important—so long as, like writing, it is done well. It is precisely good writing and intelligent reading which liberal education promotes. But the proper function of liberal studies—and, therefore, of the University—is not just to produce women and men who are merely well-read or well-informed. John Henry Newman says of such people, "If they are nothing more than well-read ..., [or persons] of information, they have not what specially serves the name of culture, or fulfils the type of Liberal Education." And this is because "the very impulse which leads them to read at all, leads them to read on, and never stay or hang over any one idea."[79] Whitehead added his own version of the same caution: "The merely well-informed man is the most useless bore on God's earth."[80]

Education, then, is not, said Whitehead, "a process of packing articles in a trunk," because "its nearest analogue is the assimilation of food by a living organism."[81] As a living reality, the mind requires nutritious noetic sustenance, without which it cannot enlarge its intellective powers. The human mind—intellect—thrives, not on facts, information, ideology, or inert ideas, but on truth. Because truth "is the proper object of the intellect," cultivation of the intellect then "lies in fitting it to apprehend and contemplate truth."[82]

Education is not "stuffing birds or playing stringed instruments"; it is not amusements, because to amuse is to entertain, not to educate. Simply put, amusements "are not education."[83] Education is never successfully engaged in without hard-drawn commitment, attention, and application, by both teacher and student. We do not, in other words, attain intellectual objectives "without setting about it; we cannot gain them in our sleep or haphazard." We can reach intellectual goals only by an "accurate vision and comprehension of all things, as far as the finite mind can embrace them."[84]

To repeat Newman's counsel, the methodological trinity which governs education is (1) the development of the intellect, (2) by means of liberal studies, which are pursued (3) in the University. Liberal studies are thus the means by which—and the University is the place wherein—the intellect can reach its perfection, and attain an intellectual or philosophical grasp of things.[85]

CRITERIA OF LIBERAL STUDIES

In keeping with Newman's theme of philosophical grasp, there are three empowering characteristics which appear to signify how liberal studies shape, cultivate, and perfect the human mind. These characteristics are *orderliness*, *universality*, and *vision*.

Orderliness is the power of perceptual and conceptual concordance. Such orderliness reveals those qualities which reinforce its rule, the chief of these are three:

☐ accuracy, or the quality of correctness, which avoids falsity;

☐ exactitude, or the quality of definitional strictness, which avoids uncertainty; and

☐ precision, or the quality of semantic specificity, which avoids ambiguity.

Lacking qualities of accuracy, exactitude, and precision, less educated minds consequently lack characteristics of orderliness. Such minds, Newman says, wanting in "clearness of head," cannot "fix their gaze on one subject for two seconds together." Such minds "mistake the point in argument, waste their strength on trifles, misconceive their adversary, and leave the question more involved than they find it." By contrast, those who have mastered "acuteness, caution, and exactness," have also achieved "logical precision."[86]

Universality is the power of perceptual and conceptual amplitude. Universality builds upon the governing characteristic of orderliness, which—having brought the mind to "abstract, compare, analyze, divide, define, and reason correctly"[87]—now enables the mind to "look out into the world right forward, steadily and truly." This is the special trait of liberal education, which "brings the mind into form,"[88] and ratifies the mind's capacity for the powers "of clearsightedness, of sagacity, of wisdom, of philosophical reach of mind, and of intellectual self-possession."[89]

Vision is the power of perceptual and conceptual plenitude. It symbolizes the mind's achievement of both orderliness of methodological concordance and universality of perceptualconceptual amplitude, thus becoming a visionary habit of mind, which, says Newman, involves "the actual acceptance and use of certain principles as centres of thought, around which our knowledge grows and is located. Where this critical faculty exists, history is no longer a mere storybook, or biography a romance; orators and publications of the day are no longer infallible authorities; eloquent diction is no longer a substitute for matter, nor bold statements, or lively descriptions, a substitute for proof."[90]

John Henry Newman has said that the University "issues in the promotion of . . . enlargement of mind, intellectual and social, of an ardent love of the particular study, which may be chosen by each individual, and a noble devotion to its interests."[91] Liberal education is therefore no more and no less than "the cultivation of the intellect as such, and its object is nothing more or less than intellectual excellence."[92] Therefore, liberal education is that process "by which the intellect . . . is disciplined for its own sake. . . . And though there is no one in whom it is carried as far as is conceivable . . . yet there is scarcely any one but may gain an idea of what real training is . . . and make its true scope and result, not something else, his standard of excellence."[93]

197 A PRIVILEGE OF INTELLECT

It is true that liberal education may not always be carried as far as it is conceivable. The implication here which Newman takes seriously, however, is that liberal education is theoretically unboundable, being potentially as infinite as the human intellect is potentially infinite. For Newman, the figure of the "gentleman" personifies liberal studies—far enough, at least, to induce Newman to identify liberal studies as a "gentleman's knowledge."

CHAPTER 7
GENTLEMAN'S KNOWLEDGE

> "Liberal Education makes . . . the gentleman."

> "It is common to speak of 'liberal knowledge,' of the 'liberal arts and sciences,' and of a 'liberal education' as the special characteristic or property of a University and of a gentleman."

> "I speak of Knowledge which is its own end. . . . I call it liberal knowledge, or a gentleman's knowledge."

A gentleman was not all that Newman was, nor all he ever wanted to be. Yet he himself personified his liberally educated gentleman, by embodying "all that goes to constitute a gentleman—the carriage, the gait, address, gestures, voice, the ease, the self-possession, the courtesy, the power of conversing, the talent of not offending; the lofty principle, the delicacy of thought, the happiness of expression, the taste and propriety, the generosity and forbearance, the candour and consideration, the openness of hand."[1] In his own words, Newman autobiographically tells us that the liberally educated gentleman is distinguished by his appearance (bearing, ambulation, speech, gesture), his comportment (ease, self-possession, courtesy, consideration), and his demeanor (generosity, candor, conversational delight).

Such outward marks of the gentleman, however, are intended to portray his inner intellectual and moral powers. Thus, the gentleman mingles with those "most practised and earnest minds," who "converse sensibly" on literature and history, on politics, philosophy, and art. Such discussions denote, "with special appositeness, a gentleman's knowledge," or "liberal knowledge," or the "knowledge which I have espe-

cially called Philosophy, or, in the extended sense of the word, Science."
Liberal knowledge is "the special characteristic or property of a University and of a gentleman," or of one whose "intellectual horizon recedes," as he mounts ever higher towards "those qualities and that character of mind which we denote by the word 'gentleman.'"[2]

DEFINITIONS

Why, then, should it be considered unusual when Newman invokes the formula "gentleman's knowledge," sometimes placing greater weight on the substantive noun, *knowledge* than on the adjectival noun, *gentleman*? Why should it be thought illicit if he fuses the terms *knowledge* and *gentleman*, or conflates the terms, *University*, *liberal studies*, and *gentleman*. Yet there are those who imagine the former unusual, and the latter illicit.[3] To understand such meanings however, and to appreciate Newman's emphases, we need to *listen* to him.

Early on, in *The Idea of a University*, Newman admits that his use of the term *gentleman* may appear to some as restrictive, even unwelcome. He cautiously concedes that there are those who will "anticipate that an academical system, formed upon my model, will result in nothing better or higher than in the production of that antiquated variety of human nature and remnant of feudalism . . . called 'a gentleman.'"[4] Newman was naturally sensitive to the resonant echoes —particularly before a Dublin audience—reverberating in the English word *gentleman*. Yet remedially, he persuaded that same Dublin audience that the Pope, "the Vicar of Christ . . . when he suggests . . . establishment of a University, his first and chief and direct object is . . . some benefit or other, to accrue, by means of literature and science, to his own children; not indeed their formation on any narrow or fantastic type, as, for instance, that of an 'English Gentleman.'"[5] Yet, even while persuading his Dublin auditors of the gentleman's concerted intellectual, moral, and emotive powers—which inspire confidence in others, and thus gain influence in the world—Newman ironically addressed his listeners by that very same title, *Gentlemen*.[6]

In trying to come to terms with what Newman intended to convey by use of such an ambiguous term, we need, as it were, to distinguish the term's metaphysics from its sociology. That is to say, we need to differentiate Newman's concern with the traditional reality of the term, rather than concentrate on its class-centered English sociology.

Newman was, of course, familiar with gentlemanly English models delineated, say, by Englishmen William Harrison (1534–93) or Henry Peacham (1576–1643), or even by Mantuan Baldassare Castiglione (1478–1529).[7] But these were not his models.

Newman's vision, or version, of the liberally endowed gentleman was inspired by the highest cultural ideal of classical Greece, an ideal which saturates Greek literature from Homer onwards. That ideal was "beauty-goodness"—*kalokagathia*. The person who incarnated that ideal was the "gentleman"—*kaloskagathos*, a man of excellence, or virtue, or *Areté* (ἀϱετή). Uniting moral, intellectual, and physical capacity to "reach up" towards the highest values of human dignity and prowess, the Greek ideal (gentleman, *kaloskagathos*) represents not a social attainment, but a spiritual achievement.

That ideal was also lent special enhancement in the verbal and conceptual vocabularies of Plato and Aristotle. From Plato's *philosophos*, or "wisdom quester," for instance, Newman derived the deeply intellectual side of his *gentleman*. As one observer put it, Plato's *philosophos* "is simply the *kaloskagathos* resurrected and inspired by the spirit of Socrates." Like Plato's *philosophos*-gentleman, Newman's University-gentleman possesses a "gentleman's knowledge," acuteness, eagerness to understand, quick apprehension, good memory, perseverance, and great intellectual power. He is "friend and kinsman of truth," displays harmony of mind and character; he makes connections between things and ideas, and "sees things as a whole." For the deeply moral side of the gentleman, Newman appropriated Aristotle's *megalopsychos*, or "great souled." For, as Aristotle says, "Greatness of Soul (μεγαλοψυχία) [is] the crowning ornament of the virtues: it enhances their greatness, and cannot exist without them . . . [and] is impossible without moral nobility." In *The Idea of a University*, Newman recalls that "Aristotle, in his sketch of the magnanimous man, tells us that his voice is deep, his motions slow, and his stature commanding." And he expresses "lofty sentiments in lofty sentences" because he has developed "the inner man." Roman poet Juvenal also gave this ideal a certain Latin resonance, expressing it as a healthy mind (*mens sana*), with healthy temperament (*ingenium sanum*), residing in a healthy body (*corpore sano*).[8]

BINARY INTEGRITY

As portrayed in *The Idea of a University*, Newman's gentleman is stalwart of body, staunch of disposition, and vigorous of mind, because he unites corporeal, intellectual, moral, and emotive healthfulness—such that each strength reflects another, as each becomes, in turn, the symbol and the splendor of its alternate. Newman's gentleman is thus a person of binary spiritual-corporeal integrity, a creature of inner connections which replicate the material and spiritual interconnectivity that marks his mental experience of the world. The gentleman's physical traits— "strength, energy, agility, graceful carriage and action, manual dexterity, and endurance of fatigue"—mirror "in like manner general culture of mind."

To approximate Newman's idea of a gentleman—beyond a sentence here or there—invites extended citations, which can be "stitched together." A gentleman, therefore, is

> the man who has learned to think and to reason and to compare and to discriminate and to analyze, who has refined his taste and formed his judgment, and sharpened his mental vision . . . [who has] the force, the steadiness, the comprehensiveness, and the versatility of intellect, the command of . . . [his] own powers, the instinctive just estimate of things as they pass before [him] . . . [and] a connected view or grasp of things . . . good sense, sobriety of thought, reasonableness, candour, self command, and steadiness of view . . . a courtesy, a propriety, and polish of word and action,   a cultivated intellect, a delicate taste, a candid, equitable, dispassionate mind, a noble and courteous bearing in the conduct of life. . . . [He can] make a telling speech, or . . . write a good letter, or . . . fling in debate a smart antagonist. . . . [He can] state an argument or a question, or take a clear survey of a whole transaction, or give sensible and appropriate advice under difficulties, or do any of those things which inspire confidence and gain influence. . . . [He] takes a connected view of old and new, past and present, far and near . . . and has an insight into the influence of all these on one another; without which there is no whole, and no centre. . . [And he] possesses the knowledge, not only of things, but also of their mutual and true relations. . . . He apprehends the great outlines of knowledge, the principles on which it

rests, the scale of its parts, its rights and its shades, its great points and its little. . . . [He has] the clear, calm, accurate vision and comprehension of all things, as far as the finite mind can embrace them . . . which is the power of viewing many things at once as one whole, of referring them severally to their true place in the universal system, of understanding their respective values, and determining their mutual dependence. . . . Possessed of this real illumination . . . [his] mind never views any part of the extended subject-matter of Knowledge without recollecting that it is but a part, or without the associations which spring from this recollection. . . . [His] intellect, which has been disciplined to the perfection of its powers, which knows and thinks while it knows, which has learned to leaven the dense mass of facts and events with the elastic force of reason, such an intellect cannot be partial . . . exclusive . . . impetuous . . . [but is] patient, collected, and majestically calm. . . . To have even a portion of this illuminative reason and true philosophy is the highest state to which nature can aspire, in the way of intellect; it puts the mind above the influences of chance and necessity, above anxiety, suspense, unsettlement, and superstition, which is the lot of the many. . . . [Such a one has] a clear conscious view of his own opinions and judgments, a truth in developing them, an eloquence in expressing them, and a force in urging them. [He] see[s] things as they are. . . . [goes] right to the point . . . disentangle[s] a skein of thought . . . detect[s] what is sophistical . . . discard[s] what is irrelevant . . . accommodate[s] himself to others . . . throw[s] himself into their state of mind . . . bring[s] before them his own . . . come[s] to an understanding with them . . . bear[s] with them. He is at home in any society; he has common ground with every class; he knows when to speak and when to be silent; he is able to converse; he is able to listen; he can ask a question pertinently, and gain a lesson seasonably, when he has nothing to impart himself; he is ever ready, yet never in the way; he is a pleasant companion, and a comrade you can depend upon; he knows when to be serious and when to trifle, and he has a sure tact which enables him to trifle with gracefulness and to be serious with effect. He has the repose of a mind which lives in itself, while it lives in the world, and which has resources for its happiness at home when it cannot go abroad. He has a gift which serves him in public, and supports him in retirement without which good fortune is but vulgar, and with which failure and disappointment have a charm.[9]

EQUIPOISE

In this 700-word composite portrait—two-thirds of which signify noetic, and one-third behavioral predicates—there is poise and counterpoise of mind and body, of disposition and spirit, of being and action, of thought and feeling, of perception and contemplation. These denote graces of intellect (*mens sana*) and psyche (*ingenium sanum*) which extend to graces of the body (*corpore sano*). Such conjunction of poise and counterpoise synthesizes a principle of equipoise, which governs intellectual power (thinking, comparing, discriminating, analyzing); estimative competence (refinement of taste, just estimate of things, courtesy, propriety, polish, candor, self-command); and appreciative skill (gracefulness, tactfulness, steadiness, sobriety, pleasantness, sensibility, appropriateness). Together, like precious jewels, these are mounted in a diamond setting of tranquility and repose of spirit.

Newman's gentleman is further rooted in the Hellenic ideal of the "avoidance of extremes," as expressed in that Greek maxim "nothing too much" ($\mu\eta\delta\grave{\epsilon}\nu$ $\mathring{\alpha}\gamma\alpha\nu$), or its Roman equivalent *ne quid nimis*. These expressions typify harmony (symmetry, proportion, orderliness, composure, concordance) and balance—equipoise, geometric mean ($\mathring{\eta}$ $\mu\epsilon\sigma\acute{o}\tau\eta\varsigma$), mid-way point, middleness ($\mathring{o}$ $\mu\acute{\epsilon}\sigma\sigma\nu$), not-too-muchness). The Roman poet Ovid, being of similar mind and like spirit, added that one must always take the middle course, *medio tutissimus*, because it is the most modest, the most watched over, and the safest of passages.

With mental and spiritual tranquility, Newman's gentleman possesses psychic command and force of personality, which embody accuracy and discipline of mind, enabling him to envision far-reaching horizons of comprehension by means of the simple grace of sublime understanding. Such a gentleman maintains an authority in disentangling truths—and a sovereignty in declaring them. He retains poetic insight to apprehend, and rhetorical eloquence to reveal, the nature of things. Yet even such a wondrous portrait as this has been critically dismissed.[10]

TWO VERSIONS

Still, there remains for us to examine a more substantive issue. And it arises as soon as we begin to contrast this composite portrait with that portrait drawn by Newman in Discourse VIII, § 10. Approximating a thousand words, that portrait has encouraged some critics—supportive or adversative—to endow it with a finality, as representing "Newman's definition of a gentleman."[11] Such labeling, however, seems to ignore two important facts. First, there is the fact that Newman introduces this portion of the discourse by cautioning that "it is almost a definition of a gentleman"—which means that it is not completely the definition. Second, there is the fact that Newman concludes this same passage by saying, "Such are some of the lineaments of the ethical character, which the cultivated intellect will form, apart from religious principle." Saying "some of" means that not all of the lineaments have been included— and those that have been included are largely ethical, that is to say, behavioral. Because definitions presume universal attribution, that which is "almost" a definition, or contains only "some of" the predications, may not be intended as a definition.

To understand the status—and thus the meaning and significance—of Discourse VIII, § 10, as well as to estimate its comparison with our composite quotation, we need, as already suggested, to examine it more closely. We need also to take into account the contrast between the ethical intention of Discourse VIII, § 10, and the major intellectual theme, not only of our composite portrait, but of much of *The Idea of a University*. As contrasted with our composite portrait, the language of Discourse VIII, § 10, seems to contain dominantly behavioral patterns—social and psychological modes of conduct—which the gentleman personifies. (Only two nonbehavioral traits are mentioned there, namely, "intellectual discipline" and "clear-headedness.")

DISCOURSE VIII

That passage of Discourse VIII, § 10, often denoted "Newman's definition of a gentleman," begins by observing that the gentleman does not ever inflict pain. He removes obstacles which impede the freedom of others; he concurs with, rather than initiates, the free circulation of others whom he meets. He avoids whatever may jar or jolt the minds of others. He shuns all collision of feeling or opinion. He abstains from suspicion, gloom, and resentment. Rather, he is concerned with putting others at their ease. Therefore, the gentleman is accommodating, agreeable, amiable, and hospitable.

With concern and affection, the gentleman carefully and concernfully examines whatever company he is in. His eyes are on all; and so, he is tender towards the bashful, gentle towards the distant, merciful towards the absurd. He carefully recollects to whom he is speaking, just as he guards against inappropriate allusions. He is never prominent in conversation, and he is never wearisome. When he indulges others with gifts, he makes light of his gifts. Even as he gives, then, he appears to receive. Unless compelled to do so, the gentleman never speaks of himself. He does not boast, nor is he mock-modest. He never gives retort, and has no ear for gossip or scandal. He is scrupulous, and does not impute motives to others. He interprets everything for the best. He is never mean or little; he will not take unfair advantage of others, or indulge in ad-hominem argument. He does not mistake bons mots for true debate, and he never insinuates evil. Therefore the gentleman is congenial, indulgent, and cheerful; courteous, amenable, and generous; affable, cordial, and gracious; charitable, kind, and clement.

Never affronted by insult, because he is too busy to take account of injury, and too relaxed to bear malice, the gentleman, on philosophical principle, is patient, forbearing, and resigned. When he submits to pain, bereavement, or death, it is because he understands that these are inevitable, irreparable, and fated. He is too intellectually disciplined to be blundering or discourteous. Therefore, the gentleman is prudent and lenient; obliging, benign, and benevolent.

Too clear-headed to be unjust, he exhibits true simplicity, and true force. He is brief, but decisive. He is candid, but considerate. He is always compassionate. Because he throws himself into the minds of his opponents, he can account for their mistakes. He thus recognizes the strengths and weaknesses of human reason—its province and its limits. Too large-minded to ridicule, too wise to be dogmatic, too cautious to be intemperate, he respects religion, honors its ministers, supports its institutions, because he sees them as venerable and useful. He does not assail faith, or denounce its practitioners, but looks on them impartially. Therefore, the gentleman is regardful, benignant, well-disposed, and a friend to religious toleration.

Preserving Balance

Because Newman has already indicated (in Discourse VIII, § 10) that his general interest has been ethical or behavioral, his "definition," prima facie, need make no pretense that it is a full, self-sufficient, intentionally balanced portrait. If we compare the language of this section with the composite portrait we "stitched together," whose dominant theme is noetic, then we face an unusual series of problems: Which of these portraits, *if either*, can be accounted a complete "definition" of a gentleman? Are both portraits needed? Does one do what the other cannot do? Is the largely behavioral theme of Discourse VIII, § 10 important enough to nullify all other contenders—even though Newman qualifies it as being "almost" a definition, and claims only that it contains "some of" the gentleman's characteristics? How then shall we manage to understand the noetic motif of the composite portrait?

To explore these questions, we can construct a directory of gentlemanly predicate-adjectives, which are representative of Newman's gentleman. This directory we divide into three overarching categories representing the gentleman's qualities (each with three individuating features). These are noetic predicates, comprising traits that are mental, intellectual, and perceptual; prescriptive predicates, comprising traits that are spiritual, moral, and ethical; and behavioral predicates, comprising traits that are social, somatic, and locutory. Arranging these predicate-adjectives in tabulated form, we construct a directory of terms, labeled Schema "C" below.

Schema "C"

Characteristics of the Gentleman

MENTAL	INTELLECTUAL	PERCEPTUAL	SPIRITUAL
circumspect	accurate	compassionate	calm
cautious	attentive	disciplined	charitable
clear-sighted	clearheaded	holistic	compliant
commonsensical	complex	perceptive	concerned
concentrated	comprehensive	self-possessed	conscionable
cultured	disciplined	sensitive	constant
enterprising	dispassionate	tasteful	contemplative
experienced	intuitive	unaffected	contented

foresighted
healthy-minded
independent
intelligent
logical
masterful
mature
provident
reasonable
resourceful
seasoned
self-reflective
sensible
serious
thoughtful
unbiased
unemotive
urbane
versatile

learned
noble-minded
philosophical
precise
profound
ratiocinative
sagacious
studious

courageous
devout
empathetic
equanimous
faithful
forgiving
gentle
imperturbable
joyful
light-hearted
merciful
moral
patient
peaceful
serene
sincere
tender
true

CHARACTERISTICS OF THE GENTLEMAN

Moral	Ethical	Social	Somatic	Locutory
appreciative	balanced	accessible	agile	articulate
assiduous	candid	accommodating	alacritous	eloquent
benign	collected	admirable	comely	expressive
benignant	conciliatory	affable	dexterous	fluent
conscientious	deliberate	amiable	durable	linguistic
forthright	dependable	amicable	enduring	pithy
ingenuous	differential	anticipatory	energetic	polished
high-minded	diligent	charming	forceful	well-spoken
magnanimous	equitable	chivalrous	graceful	
mild	ethical	companionable	strong	
noble-hearted	forbearing	congenial	vigorous	
persevering	generous	conversationable		
pleasant	honest	cordial		
resolute	honorable	courteous		
respectful	judicious	delicate		
steady	just	delightful		
straightforward	loyal	discreet		
sympathetic	measured	engaging		
temperate	moderate	friendly		
truthful	modest	gallant		

virtuous	prudent	genteel
well-intentioned	quiet	hospitable
wholehearted	reposeful	magnetic
	resigned	personable
	self-composed	pleasant
	tactful	pliant
	veracious	receptive
	wise	refined
		relaxed
		respectful
		responsive
		sentient
		sociable
		supportive
		tender

HIERARCHIC CONFIGURATION

Tallying the total number of gentlemanly predicates in each of the above categories, we notice a shifting order of frequency. Reversing expectations, the distributional axis is now cluster-codified as (A) behavioral, (B) prescriptive, and (C) noetic. With parenthetic totals and original positions, the new format reveals the following order of precedence: social (35 terms; formerly in position #7), ethical (28; #6), mental (27; #1), spiritual (26; #4), moral (23; #5), intellectual (16; #2), somatic (11; #8), perceptual (8; #3), and locutory (8; #9).

Since behavioral and prescriptive clusters outrank the noetic cluster, the consequent predicates seem more in line with those of Discourse VIII, § 10. What has come to be known as "Newman's definition of a gentleman" may, then, not be too far off the mark. Yet the problem remains: Can we nonetheless justify dominance—as in Discourse VIII, § 10 and in the conclusions drawn from our predicate directory—of behavioral traits to define Newman's *gentleman*? How then shall we explain Newman's apparent concentration on "the gentleman's Knowledge," which *The Idea of a University* appears to dwell on? What then is the meaning of the gentleman's liberal knowledge, "which I have especially called Philosophy," and whose cultivation is "the essential business of a University?" What shall we make of the interchangeability of the terms *University*, *liberal studies*, and *gentleman*, or of the fusing of *knowledge* and *gentleman*, or of the very definition of *liberal knowl*edge as "the special characteristic or property of a University and of a gentleman?" And what of that sense of widening intellectual horizons and noetic skills which mark out "those qualities and that character of mind which we denote by the word *gentleman?*" Is intellect, then, less important than social or prescriptive behavior? Little wonder that, in referring to Discourse VIII, § 10, one observer believes that "it is ironic that this portrait [of the gentleman] should often be taken as a serious expression of Newman's positive ideal."[12] Perhaps we need to look more wisely at the "definitional" context, which, implicitly and explicitly, is embedded in Discourse VIII.

So far, we have said that the definition of a gentleman, as it occurs in Discourse VIII, §10, appears less intellectual than what Newman elsewhere portrays in the *Idea*; provides Newman's critics an opportunity to scoff; and challenges various attempts to defend it as the final definition, since it is first qualified by Newman as being "almost a definition" which contains only "some" of the gentleman's ethical traits.

We need, first of all then, to focus on the actual title of Discourse VIII. That title is "Knowledge Viewed in Relation to Religion." We need also to recall that Newman's underlying purpose in composing these discourses—and Archbishop Paul Cullen's reason for proposing them—were implicitly religious. Orientation towards religious interest is further revealed in the fact that the titles of almost two-thirds of these discourses are concerned with "ideal" and "existential" relations between religion-theology and University-education.[13]

SEMANTIC AMBIGUITY

We have assumed that Newman's University is the locus of liberal studies, and thus the proper residence of the noetic gentleman. Whatever ostensible conflict exists, then, between Newman's noetic gentleman and his behavioral gentleman may be shaped by two prevailing conditions. These are that *The Idea of a University* is imbued with a fundamentally religious theme, and that, for religious reasons, Newman also views the gentleman of Discourse VIII in a less-than-flattering light. Perhaps these two conditions may also explain what appears to be a factual ambiguity in Newman's portrait of the gentleman. In other words, in light of Discourse VIII, Newman may implicitly have drawn a dual, not a single or univocal, portrait of a gentleman. Focusing on such ambiguity, we cannot fail to appreciate Newman's genuinely approbative, as well as his genuinely disapprobative estimates. Moreover, failure to distinguish between distinct images of the gentleman—worse, fusing them into one image—will likely result in unfortunate and unnecessary confusion.

If a duality in Newman's portrait is a legitimate possibility, then we are faced with a double-layered, deceptively geminated gentleman. On one hand, there is a liberally endowed "gentleman A"—autobiographic image of Newman, we have called it—and, on the other, the sociopolitical English "gentleman B" who is contaminated by "unbelief" or "disbelief." If this is so, then we may infer that something, somewhere along the line, intervened to make "gentleman A" distinguishable from "gentleman B." Indeed (we shall suggest), something did intervene, and the clue to that intervention is to be found in the fact that Discourse VIII's "definition" of the gentleman comes, not at its beginning but at its end. What happens between the beginning and the end of this discourse may clarify the shift in Newman's "definitional" portrait. Such a shift suggests that each aspect of the portrait serves a distinctly different purpose. But before we consider the contextual problem of the gentleman at the beginning of Discourse VIII, it may be useful to review the concluding language of Discourse VIII, § 10, as well as the logical integrity with which that "definition" begins.

In such concluding language, Newman immediately asserts that a "gentleman . . . is one who never inflicts pain." This seems a faintly dissonant move, because it unexpectedly bends traditional protocol for cognitive-connotative definition. That protocol roughly requires (1) that a defining clause (*definiens*) contain the essential element of the term being defined (*definiendum*), meaning that there be (logical) equivalence between *definiendum* and *definiens*—between what is defined and how it is defined; (2) that a definition be straightforward, noncircular, nontautological; (3) that the definition be clear, and phrased in cognitive, not metaphoric, language; (4) that the definition be constructed relationally in reference to a class (*genus*) and a species (*differentia*), according to the traditional maxim "*definitio per genus et differentiam*"; (5) that the definition be phrased in affirmative, rather than negative, language; and (6) that the definition preserve grammatical consistency, which means, a noun defining a noun—rather than a nounal *definiendum* followed by some verbal-clause *definiens*, such as, "is when you . . . ."

It would, of course, be foolish to hold Newman's glorious rhetoric hostage to logical protocol. But suppose we invert the process. Suppose we ask: Why would a logician—such indeed as Newman was—offend against the spirit of logical definition? Our search for an answer might be instructive.

The first hint of the problem, then, is the contrast between the requirements of a logical definition and Newman's formulation of a definition—since he is the one who introduces the language, "almost a definition." Admittedly, this contrast is based on the assumption that when Newman invokes that formula, he intends to use (a) cognitive (rather than persuasive), (b) connotative (rather than denotative), and (c) logical (rather than rhetorical) language. By that assumption, Newman compromises, in various degrees, all six of the protocol criteria suggested above. By "definably" asserting what a gentleman does not do—that is, does not inflict pain—Newman begins his "definition" by compromising at least one of the rules of definition. The negative format—"one who never inflicts pain"—would also apply (which is the point) to a geranium or a light bulb. This negative format also includes one additional negatizing note, namely, that of pain. Why does Newman (who knew logical protocol) consider it permissible (perhaps imperative!) to establish, straight-off (but negatively), that the gentleman never inflicts pain? Is there an unexpressed antecedent?

In almost any of its senses—somatic, emotional, mental, even preventively—pain suggests a social, a physical, a psychological context, or all three. Yet in any context, pain is usually accompanied by a questioning sense of its moral relevance. This also implies that, to prevent pain may be as moral an action as to inflict pain can be deemed immoral. Newman's implicit argument seems to run, then, that the gentleman is one who, in no sense and in no degree, and under no circumstances, takes part in violence. For violence is what inflicting pain inevitably involves. Is Newman saying that only because he knows that violence, in any form, is directly antithetical to civilization? And is it not also contrary to civilizing action? Consequently, is it not likewise opposed to the very meaning of intellect?

Moreover, although preventing pain is not an intellective predicate, a cultivated intellect would obviously avoid any form of violence. A cultivated intellect is, in a word, empathetic. Newman seems, then, to be saying that what the gentleman does, he does "from the gentleness and effeminacy of feeling, which is the attendant on civilization."[14] This only affirms that intellect is civilized. Indeed, intellect is what makes civilization possible.[15] It may follow, then, that to cause pain—just as, a fortiori, to initiate war—is uncivilized action, and thus unworthy of a gentleman, because unworthy of the intellect.

SOCIOPOLITICAL GENTLEMAN

As Newman reaches this stage in portraying the gentleman, he carefully recollects the religious deficits of the sociopolitical gentleman, or what we have called "gentleman B." Newman ambiguously initiates this theme in the very first section of Discourse VIII. Intellectual culture, he says there, "which is so exalted in itself, not only has a bearing on social and active duties, but upon Religion also. The educated mind may be said to be in a certain sense religious; that is, it has what may be considered a religion of its own, independent of Catholicism, partly cooperating with it, partly thwarting it; at once a defence yet a disturbance to the Church in Catholic countries,—and in countries beyond her pale, at one time in open warfare with her, and another in defensive alliance."[16]

Here is an indication of a fundamental ambiguity in any human portrait, which contains the possibility of transcendence, but, equally, the possibility of profanation—a theme reminiscent of the perfectibility, or the corruptibility of intellect. Newman has also said, in this regard, that "the action of a University [is such as] to exhibit its general bearings on Religion." But is it not possible that he has already suggested an ambiguity, which may reside even at the center of University training itself? And is this not because ambiguity potentially lies at the center of intellect—and thus, at the center of human life?

On this score, Newman explores the implications of what he has said by distinguishing between *right reason* (responsible intellect) and *mere reason* (which may act without governance—and thus, irresponsibly). It is upon just such a distinction that Newman bases his concept of the power of the University ultimately to form the liberally endowed gentleman: "Right Reason, that is, Reason rightly exercised, leads the mind to the Catholic Faith, and plants it there, and teaches it in all its religious speculations to act under its guidance. But Reason, considered as a real agent in the world, and as an operative principle in man's nature, with an historical course and with definite results, is far from taking so straight and satisfactory a direction. It considers itself from first to last independent and supreme; it requires no external authority; it makes a religion of itself."[17]

With such ambiguity in mind, then, we should distinguish between two intentional forms of reason. The one, let us call, reason $_1$, and the other reason $_2$, these being precursors of an impending distinction between two intentional forms, philosophy $_1$, and philosophy $_2$; and between two intentional kinds, intellect $_1$, and intellect $_2$. Thus framed, Newman's remarks can only mean that reason, intellect, and philosophy can be subverted, because each inherently represents the ambiguity of finitude. Caution is necessary here, because while we may speak abstractly of reason, of philosophy, or of intellect, in doing so, we disregard the concrete fact that, behind every such abstraction, there is a person, in whose power such abstractions reside. Once again, it is the person, not the abstraction, who is responsible. Thus, Newman may already be implicitly defining two kinds of person, which we have called *gentleman A* and *gentleman B*, figures which have been silently present in his early sermons.

There seems little doubt that Newman has been fully committed to the need for refinement and enlargement of mind. There is also little doubt that he has said that philosophy (in its original usage) promotes such enlargement of mind since, as he said, knowledge when pursued for its own sake must have philosophy$_1$ as its form, for "such a philosophical contemplation of the field of Knowledge as a whole" leads to "an illumination" or "an enlargement of mind." And so, "if you would obtain a picture of contemplation . . . you could not have recourse to a better furnished studio than to that of Philosophy."

ARDOR AND ORDER

Newman has consistently maintained that, between enlargement of the well-formed mind and refinement of the well-intentioned heart, there exists reciprocal compact. And he accounts the influences "which intellectual culture exerts upon our moral nature" to be such as to acknowledge "how striking is the action of our intellectual upon our moral nature, where the moral material is rich, and the intellectual cast is perfect." But, of course, there is a radical difference between mental refinement and genuine religion. And this distinction, he very clearly says, is his "cardinal point."[18] If we expect that a gentleman will attain—and maintain—status as "ornament" of University education, then Newman has established the condition by which this is to be accomplished. That condition is the clear relation between the richness of moral material, and perfection of intellectual cast. Only this relationship bespeaks "real cultivation of mind," and "the characteristic excellences of a gentleman" which are included in it.[19]

When balance and harmony between the ardor of heart and the order of mind is interrupted, minimized, or destroyed, both heart and mind are equally affected. If "gentleman B" has no sensitivity towards balance of both—if he has (to use our former language) mind but no heart, he lacks the very harmony of spirit which the true "gentleman A" exhibits. This, indeed, is why he is merely "gentleman B." He exhibits what might be called a *prolapsed intellect.*

Here, we perceive Newman's realization that—in spite of surface similarities between English religion and "refinement of mind"—there are more serious, and more deeply submerged, differences. As he said in an early sermon, "Men of learning and ability are so often wrong in religious matters," for the adversaries of truth (of which there are many) will also include "highly endowed and highly cultivated minds." This simply asserts that "what is called ability and talent do not make . . . a Christian."[20] Between, on the one hand, "religious love of truth and goodness," and, on the other, "quickness, sagacity, depth of thought, strength of mind, power of comprehension, perception of the beautiful, power of language," there can also be discerned a dark and bottomless chasm. Gifts of intellect "are excellent gifts," says Newman. But they are "clearly quite of a different kind from spiritual excellences."[21] Upon just such differences, once again, everything else depends, including Newman's ambiguous—and thus, implicitly dual—concept of a gentleman.

As early as Discourse V of the *Idea*, Newman had set down the principle that "Liberal Education makes not the Christian, not the Catholic, but the gentleman." So here, in Discourse VIII, with perfect consistency, Newman can further assert, "At this day the 'gentleman' is the creation, not of Christianity, but of civilization."[22] And he acknowledges, "It is well to be a gentleman, it is well to have a cultivated intellect, a delicate taste, a candid, equitable, dispassionate mind, a noble and courteous bearing in the conduct of life. . . . [But] they are no guarantee for sanctity or even for conscientiousness."[23]

Prior to this statement, Newman had expressed a basic insight, and we should now clearly see with what eminent cause he did so. For theoretical and practical need, he had to separate intellectual from moral action: "Knowledge is one thing, virtue is another; good sense is not conscience, refinement is not humility, nor is largeness and justness of view faith. Philosophy, however enlightened, however profound, gives no . . . vivifying principles."[24]

Such a view, iterated in an otherwise intellectually focused Discourse V, becomes, at last, fully persuasive by the time it is revisited in Discourse VIII. How often had Newman urged clear distinction between kinds of persons? Even before *The Idea of a University*, he was aware that while preserving the distinction between what is moral and what is intellectual, there was a spiritual need eventually to unite them—hence, his proclamation that the separation of intellectual and moral actions constitutes the scandal of his age. In other words, Newman was willing to distinguish them, only in order to prepare for their ultimate unification. It was his *distinguer pour unir*.

Throughout his early sermons, Newman emphasized the principle that mind, apart from religion, is not self-sustaining. A God-neglecting mind is one which is oblivious of the fact that it is created as *imago Dei*. It is negligent of the fact that it incarnates the privilege of intellect. Early on, then, Newman had been struck by the fact that "learned men are so often defective Christians," and he soon saw just why this is so. He could then state the precursor of his formula, "Knowledge is one thing; virtue is another," by observing that "there is no necessary connection between faith and ability; because faith is one thing and ability is another; because ability of mind is a gift, and faith is a grace."[25] What Newman did not distinguish (although he may have implied it) is that both ability and grace—however different—are nonetheless gifts, the former perhaps by natural selection, but the latter by God's intervening kindness.

SURFACE EQUIVOQUE

Surface traits may make all gentlemen appear the same, like a night where all cats are black. But a surface can also be equivocal. We have said that there is ambiguity in intellect—the power of creativity or of corruption—ambiguity in being human, ambiguity in civilization. But there is no ambiguity in true religion, because religion already exposes its competitors. Granted, there is ambivalence in usage of the term *religion*, but there is no ambiguity in the relational reality of that term itself. In English, certain synonyms reveal an equivoque of denotation in the term *religion*, such as is the case of *religionism* or *religiosity*—where each conveys a negative sense of excessiveness or pretense. When Newman refers to the religion of those who are "polished in their manners, kind from natural disposition or a feeling of propriety," it is clear that he is not referring to true religion, which bears relation to God. It is not the religion of the mere gentleman to which he refers, because that version of religion is "based upon self and the world."[26]

Just as we have distinguished true Church from imposturous church, or true religion from "the religion of the day," so here we can distinguish true gentleman from apparent gentleman. Here is another reason to suggest that Newman implicitly constructs two portraits: (1) the liberally endowed "gentleman A," who is devotedly concerned with truth; and (2) the socially oriented "gentleman B," who is merely a political Englishman. Although "gentleman B" has been educated, he is essentially concerned with the interests of the world, which means with his own interests. He does not perceive the ultimate implications of intellect's being perfected. He seems quite satisfied with who he is, and who he is perfectly satisfied to be.

Again we ask—Why does Newman's implied difference between two kinds of gentleman appear so necessary? The answer is because (as previously suggested) something in his experience did intervene, which necessitated a need for him to distinguish (what we have called) "gentleman A" from "gentleman B." Indeed, such a distinguishing portrait opens Discourse VIII, which should elucidate why it also concludes Discourse VIII. It defines what is, in fact, "gentleman B." What intervened was Newman's penetrative awareness—arrived at long before the Dublin Lectures and the *Idea*—of the motivating office of a "religion of civilization," a "religion of reason," and a "religion of philosophy." These, in fact, barely differ from what Newman had already labeled "the religion of the day."[27]

Imposturous religion—like an imposturous church, imposturous university, or imposturous education—might magically alter "gentleman A" into "gentleman B." A "religion of reason" thus subverts intellect into an idol of itself. This transformation would produce a competitive "religion of civilized times . . . of the philosopher, scholar, and gentleman," because such figures accent the ambiguity of being human, of having intellect, and of residing in civilization.[28]

IMAGE ALTERED

A transmuted image of a gentleman—from "gentleman A" to "gentleman B"—was artfully influenced, even sponsored (as Newman believed), by several English spokesmen, especially by Edward Gibbon, by Lord Chesterfield, and by the Third Earl of Shaftesbury.[29] What had previously seemed a congenial figure of liberally endowed "gentleman A" now becomes, at Newman's easel, stippled in irresolvable, contaminating, and illiberally endowed outline. Under such illiberal influence, even the term *philosophy* can become semantically contaminated. It is no longer *noble philosophy*—which, for Newman, epitomizes the perfection of intellect—but, like a neoplasm, becomes corruptive. Not merely suspect of equivocity, such opportunistic "philosophy B" has become an equivocation, whose cognitive ambiguity and noetic ambivalence are transformed into a theory of fashionable irreligion.

This statement is justifiable as an assertion of that semantic split in Newman's gentlemanly images. For "gentleman B," religion is clearly severed from true morality, a disruption which Newman illustrated by the manner in which Edward Gibbon drew a gentlemanly portrait of a dying Julian the Apostate. By literary taste and hatred of Christianity, says Newman, Gibbon was superbly suited to be Julian's panegyrist, because Gibbon "paints with pleasure [the] sentiments of a godless intellectualism," which was "his own idea of moral perfection." The scene to which Newman refers is recorded by Gibbon when he narrates the wounding and subsequent death of Julian the Apostate. Laid upon a death couch, Julian begins his own funeral oration, as if he were the *Phaedo*'s dying Socrates redux. Metaphorically, Gibbon watches the scene, and interpolates the meaning of the dying words of Julian, emperor and apostate.[30]

Newman, however, said this of Gibbon's Julian: "I cannot but recognize in him a specious beauty and nobleness in moral deportment. . . . His simplicity of manners, his frugality, his austerity of life, his singular disdain of sensual pleasure, his military heroism, his application to business, his literary diligence, his modesty, his clemency, his accomplishments, as I view them, go to make him one of the most eminent specimens of pagan virtue which the world has ever seen. Yet how shallow, how meagre, nay, how unamiable is that virtue after all."[31]

To Newman, Gibbon's Julian simply reflected "the sentiments [of] godless intellectualism"—that "final exhibition of the Religion of Reason"—and "the insensibility of conscience," as well as an "ignorance of the very idea of sin . . . the simple absence of fear." In this sense, Gibbon was merely duplicating ideas presciently appearing in Lord Shaftesbury's *Characteristicks of Men, Manners, Opinions, Times.*[32]

What such portraits by Shaftesbury and Gibbon actually reveal is, for Newman, less important than what they omit. For they particularly omit the importance of conscience—that "great internal teacher of religion." Conscience is "implanted in the breast by nature." Conscience is "the guide of life . . . discriminating right from wrong, and investing right with authority and sway." Conscience "is a proof of the doctrine of a Moral Governor." Conscience is "the aboriginal Vicar of Christ, a prophet in its information, a monarch in its peremptoriness, a priest in its blessings and anathemas."[33]

With English aplomb, however, "gentleman B," like Gibbon and Shaftesbury, displaces conscience by sentiment, taste, benevolence, pleasantness. And, just so, he replaces morality with aesthetical English ethics, thereby crowning conduct with cordial sentiment. Aesthetical morality avoids whatever seems morally difficult to manage. Indeed, George Bernard Shaw once observed that an Englishman always confuses discomfort with morality.[34] Such a transformation from arduous morality to ardent aesthetics reveals the ethnic face of English ethics. Was not that the cautionary theme of Newman's early sermon, "The Religion of the Day"? Indeed, it was precisely in that sermon that, for the first time, in the first place, we were actually introduced to our "gentleman B."

In English aesthetical morality, there is found what seems to be "especially congenial" to "gentleman B," and to all those who possess "an imaginative and poetic cast of mind, who will accept the notion that virtue is nothing more than the graceful in conduct."[35] To such persons, appearance inevitably becomes reality. This is only because where "decency is virtue," detection is the only crime. "To seem becomes to be; what looks fair will be good, what causes offence will be evil; virtue will be what pleases, vice what pains."[36] Here is Newman's portrait of "gentleman B" who seems "morally" motivated towards avoidance of giving pain. Rematted, reframed, and reformatted, however, the portrait seems to fit the "definition" with which Discourse VIII, § 10 begins: "It is almost a definition of a gentleman to say he is one who never inflicts pain." Yet, is such reframing of "gentleman B" interpretable as no more than the gentleman's protest against pain and violence? Perhaps, in startling contrast, we can understand that Newman's implicit comparison is now unsheathed as a "moral fashion," not so much to be against pain, but to be in favor of a more fundamental pleasantness and benevolence. To be in favor, in other words, of an aesthetical morality which can, indeed, anesthetize the soul.

AESTHETICAL MORALITY

Using aesthetic logic, aesthetical morality codifies "gentleman B" as one who favors certain modes of behavior, which aesthetically, like Oscar Wilde's Dorian Gray, will sort out honor and dishonor, good and evil, right and wrong, virtue and vice. "Gentleman B" can then reason that if what is pleasant is good, then what is painful must be evil; if what is honorable is seemly, then the unseemly must be dishonorable; if what is reputable is noble, then the disreputable must be ignoble; if what is worthy is true, it follows that the unworthy must be false. Given such aesthetic logic, terms may also be altered—pride being no less than self-respect, avarice merely thrift, lust simply "the life force," gluttony only healthy appetite, envy and wrath nothing but assertiveness, sloth merely relaxation." Aesthetical morality also seems wondrously suited to England's nineteenth-century stratified, class-ridden, status-conscious society, in which the self-serving are also the self-served.

In England, too, as Newman observes, there can be found—reclining in "cloudless self-confidence . . . serene self-possession . . . [and] cold-satisfaction"—the figure of "the mere Philosopher."[37] As "mere Philosopher," Lord Shaftesbury might argue that "Christianity is the enemy of moral virtue, as influencing the mind by fear of God, not by love of good."[38] Where Newman seems to have been forced to admit that "the 'gentleman' is the creation, not of Christianity, but of civilization,"[39] he might just as easily have said, "the creation of English psychology." What, then, had become of Newman's bright representations, which extolled the "philosophical habit of mind"? What had become of intellectually renovating philosophy? The answer is not hard to find, for under the aegis of "gentleman B," all these had become self-contaminant—each an intellectual counterfeit of the true representative. So, in the spirit of "gentleman B," says Newman, philosophy has become something quite different, because,

> when it is strong enough to have a will of its own, and is
> lifted up with the idea of its own importance [thus ceasing to
> be Philosophy], and attempts to form a theory, and to lay
> down a principle, and to carry out a system of ethics, and un-
> dertakes the moral education of the man, then it does but abet
> evils to which at first it seemed instinctively opposed. . . .
> [This] intellectual counterfeit has no root in itself: it springs
> up suddenly, it suddenly withers   [and] falls under the do-

minion of the old Adam. Then, like dethroned princes, it keeps up a state and majesty, when it has lost the real power.[40]

If the excuse for philosophy is that it be merely polite, then the politely pleasant philosopher ceases to be philosophical. And where what is pleasant is bartered for pleasantries; where beauty can never be deeper than skin; where virtue is conformity, and Laws are but words; where deception is a vocation, and politics charming enmity; where "the very refinement of Intellectualism, which began by repelling sensuality, ends by excusing it,"[41] then, such wondrous opportunities open the gates of hypocrisy.[42] Thus shorn of moral power and moral companionship, intellect becomes morally corrupt, virtue becomes mindless behavior, wisdom, lacking conscience, is no longer wise. Conscience, disengaged from intellect and wisdom, is no longer a moral apostle.

THE TAMWORTH COVENANT

Unless conscience and wisdom are vividly present to, and in, the University, Newman is telling us, there will eventually be no University. True, the institutional shell will remain. Its buildings will stand; its assets, indemnities, appurtenances will repose in its ledgers, as will its debts, liabilities, and obligations. When the spirit of the University has vanished, only just another socially useless luxury will remain. Was not this the message that Newman delivered in his "Catholicus" dispatches of 1841 to *The Times* of London? In those "Tamworth" letters he articulated the relation between religion and education, saying, "Christianity, and nothing short of it, must be made the element and principle of all education. But if in education we begin with nature before grace, with evidences before faith, with science before conscience, with poetry before practice, we shall . . . misplace what in its place is a divine gift."[43]

On the other hand, Newman made it equally clear that the highest forms of intellectual excellences are fully compatible with religious faith. He said that "belief in revealed religion is not inconsistent with the highest gifts and acquirements of mind. . . . Men even of the strongest and highest intellect have been Christians."[44] He had to have been thinking of St. Luke and St. Paul; St. Athanasius, St. Basil the Great, St. Gregory Nazienzenus, St. Gregory of Nyssa, and St. Benedict; St. Jerome, St. John Chrysostom, St. Ambrose, and St. Augustine; St. Gregory the

Great, St. Anselm, St. Bonaventura, St. Thomas, St. Catherine of Siena, St. Teresa of Avila, and countless others.

CHRISTIAN GENTLEMAN

But Newman, all along, was anxious to put forward a Christian who clearly epitomized the true gentleman. At the conclusion of Discourse VIII—and notably of Discourse IX—he cited as just such a model for enlargement of the human mind and spirit his "own special Father and Patron, St. Philip Neri." Founder of the Congregation of the Oratory, St. Philip was the one person from whom Newman had learned "all the thought which I have been able to bestow upon the subject" of University education.[45] As for himself, Newman admitted that if he is to have "a share in the great undertaking, which has been the occasion and the subject of these Discourses, [then], whether or not I can do anything at all in St Philip's way, at least I can do nothing in any other."[46]

The mature Newman lived his life in the spirit of St. Philip. Doing so, he also enhanced that model through his own imitation of it. Applying his own genius, ardor, and spirituality, Newman was able (through grace) to enlarge the meaning of his own sanctity, which could not—as one critic charges of St. Philip's [47]—"erase" or diminish his own accomplishments. His life work—rhetorical skill, theological acumen, studies, publications, secular and churchly tasks—were not erased, but increased, heightened, and intensified by his sanctity. His life was spiritually interconnected because he fused his conscience and his wisdom in moral and intellectual splendor. His spirit of holiness simply raised up higher all those acts of his which, either recorded or forgotten, have filtered down to us. Sanctity does not abrogate nor eliminate intellectual gifts or spiritual identity; it roots them deeper and crowns them in grace. Through sanctity, Newman became who he wanted to be, who he should have been, and who, all along, he really was. Newman thereby intuited for us the truth that only by becoming who we should be, can we truly become who we really are. Spiritual development is the process of making real what, at any instant before its inception, might be merely promissory.

We can examine Newman's own modest statement of who he saw himself to be. It sounds very much like what we have called "gentleman A" and what he had called the liberally trained gentleman, a man who has ever been fair to the doctrines and arguments of his opponents; who has never slurred over facts and reasonings which told against himself; who has never given his name or authority to proofs which he thought unsound, or to testimony which he did not think at least plausible; who has never shrunk from confessing a fault when he felt that he had committed one; who has ever consulted for others more than for himself; who has given up much that he loved and prized and could have retained, but that he loved honesty better than name, and Truth better than dear friends.[48]

Apart from the model of St. Philip Neri, there was Newman's own dear friend of Oxford, John Keble, whom Newman once compared to St. Philip. Keble, too, had developed, enhanced, and integrated his own personal nature through spirituality. Writing of St. Philip, Newman mused, "This great saint reminds me in so many ways of Keble that I can fancy what Keble would have been had he been born in another place and age."[49]

St. Philip Neri, John Keble, and John Henry Newman mirrored the image of the true gentleman. They were gentle in spirit and imbued with the intense desire to develop, enhance, integrate, and perfect the intellect, and thus to ascend to spiritual reality. Such a definition seems worthy of a gentleman—perhaps even of a saint.

CHAPTER 8
A GRAMMAR OF ASCENT

> "I say then, if we would improve
> the intellect, first of all, we must ascend."

> "We attain to heaven by using
> this world well . . . we perfect our nature,
> not by undoing it, but by adding to it what
> is more than nature, and directing it to-
> wards aims higher than its own."

> "Scripture teaches us the duty of
> faith, it teaches quite as distinctly . . . lov-
> ing inquisitiveness."

The Newman narrative begins and ends with the idea of wholeness of mind and holiness of intellect. This is because being the image of God—*imago Dei*—is "the privilege of intellect." It signifies the scriptural invitation—in a mitzvah of fruitfulness—to bring the gift of human intellect closer to the wholeness and holiness of its divine model, which means closer to perfection and fullness ($\pi\lambda\acute{\eta}\varrho\omega\mu\alpha$). By virtue of the fact that perfection of human intellect involves enlargement and enhancement of its gift, it is rather like the scriptural parable of talents.

That parable is the narrative of a master of a large property who prepares for an extended journey abroad, before which he summons his three servants. In accordance with what he deems their competence ($\varkappa\alpha\tau\grave{\alpha}$ $\tau\grave{\eta}\nu$ $i\delta\acute{\iota}\alpha\nu$ $\delta\acute{\upsilon}\nu\alpha\mu\iota\nu$, Mt. 25:15), the Master commits to their care significant assets.[1] To the first, he gives five talents; to the second, two; to the third, one—which he expects will be wisely enhanced by each. Because the Gospel world has no investment banks, equities, or mutual markets, enhancement of funds will, on the part of each servant, require personal effort. It will have to be some enterprise—perhaps trading or building or setting up a business—in which each servant will have to take a direct and responsible hand. Certainly, it will have to be more than consulting moneylenders, which the master himself could have done.

During the long period of the master's absence, the first servant doubles the value of his talents, and will give back to the master enhancement of twice what he was originally given. Likewise, the second servant accomplishes a comparable yield of twice what was originally given to him. But the third servant, being suspicious of the master's motives, dug a hole in the ground, and buried his talent. The Gospel says that he hid it, or concealed it (ἀπέκρυψεν). He was taking no chances. He was not about to risk anything, least of all himself.

When, at last, the master returns from his journey, he is truly gratified by the success of his faithful and creative servants, who, by increasing the value of the talents he had given them, had productively increased the wealth of his property, and brought to it abundance and fullness. The first two servants come forward, and each says, "Master, you gave me these talents, and I return to you twice what you have given me." And so the Master commends these inventive and faithful servants, and invites them to draw near and to share in the delights of his wealth. But, at his turn, the third servant stands apart, defensively berating the master as hard-hearted (σκληρός), and unforgiving of failure—which, had he not shrewdly saved the talent by burial, might have been his own lot. So, to the master, he hands back the talent that had been given him, as though he were saying, "Here, you get back just what you gave me." But by not investing what he was given—essentially, by not wishing to invest himself[2]—the third servant invited his own disaster. He not only lost more than he was willing to risk, but, being discharged from his master's service, he lost everything else as well—most importantly, his own feared-for safety.

Of course, the parable is about faith, which itself involves risk and investment. As Newman often put it in sermons, if we are not willing, and ready, to venture ourselves in faith—because faith is a venture—we can have no business with faith. The Gospel message is that to fail to use what God has faithfully entrusted into our care, is to fail the creative challenge—and its spiritual commandment, mitzvah—to increase, to be fruitful (Gen.-Ber. 1:28). That command holds, whether we are speaking of faith or of intellect. Little wonder that the master bestowed upon the faithful servants extra abundance (περισσεία), due to their being "large-hearted" (περίσπλαγχνος). For failure of Gospel expectation, the indolent (ἀχρεῖος) servant will experience an outer darkness of "the weeping and the gnashing of the teeth."

PARABLE OF ASCENT

The parable also reflects that Newmanesque message of enlargement, development, and integration of human intellect and of human life. If we are unwilling to advance, to expand, and to enhance our mind; unwilling to connect, to unify, to fuse disparate parts of our genuine experience; unwilling to welcome the implications of, as well as the responsibility for, being *imago Dei*—and so possessing the privilege of intellect—then we shall have failed the only test worth passing. We shall have failed to ascend.

Newman dedicated many of his sermons—and certain portions of *The Idea of a University*—to preaching this message of ascension, which draws together the arts of knowing and of acting. He stressed the simple truth that "if we would improve the intellect, first of all, we must ascend."[3] Because Newman understood the nature of intellect, he took seriously its need for cultivation and perfection, and, thus, its need for ascentive fulfillment. The need for intellect to ascend is precisely rooted in the creative fact that intellect is *imago Dei*.

Newman also understood the prismatic physics of intellect, in all its glorious promise and resurrective majesty, as "a living spontaneous energy within us." For, as he says, "[It] ranges to and fro, and spreads out, and advances forward with a quickness which has become a proverb, and a subtlety and versatility which baffle investigation. It passes on from point to point . . . and thus it makes progress not unlike a clamberer on a steep cliff, who, by quick eye, prompt hand, and firm foot, ascends."[4]

Intellectual education, Newman so often said, remolds, reshapes, remakes the mind, and refocuses the mind's eye, empowering that mental eye "to look out into the world right forward, steadily, truly; to give the mind, clearness, accuracy, precision."[5] Such subtlety, versatility, and precision are all, by the very ascentive nature of the human mind, necessary—and thus, necessarily to be desired. Truth and error are often difficult to distinguish, and thus difficult to judge correctly—correct judgment requiring a higher, more eminent elevation. Indeed, perceptually, truth and error are not black and white, nor as easily and effortlessly discernible as is often imagined. In the manner in which Newman identifies this issue, truth and error "do not meet each other here by harsh lines; there are ten thousand varieties of intermixture between them."[6] To an undeveloped mind, the differences between truth and error—unwisely judged from insufficient height—may appear imperceptibly confused.

TRUTH AND KNOWLEDGE

Of course, despite what Newman conceived of as "the infidelity of the age," or "the moral weakness and the intellectual confusion of the majority" of people, it would, for him, always be the case that, because of its essential eminence, "Truth will prevail in the end." And it would equally be the case that "the only effect of error ultimately is to promote truth."[7] Still, it is not an effortless task to mark off error from truth. Distinction does not come by request, nor is it realized by wish or by expectation, but only by a concentrated and faithful intellectual assent to ascend.

As the object of knowledge, truth is also, after all, the function of knowledge. In inquiry of what is meant by truth, Newman once supposed, "It is right to answer that Truth means facts and their relations." But it means, as he very well knew, something more than that. It means connections. And this, Newman said, is steeped in this perception:

> All knowledge forms one whole, because its subject matter is one. . . . All belong to one and the same circle of objects .
> . . one and all connected together. . . . All branches of knowledge are connected together, because the subject matter of knowledge is intimately united in itself, as being the acts and the work of the Creator. . . . All that exists, as contemplated by the human mind, forms one large system or complex fact, and this of course resolves itself into an indefinite number of particular facts, which, as being portions of the whole, have countless relations of every kind, one towards another. Knowledge is the apprehension of these facts, whether in themselves, or in their mutual positions and bearings. . . . All taken together form one integral subject for contemplation.[8]

TRUTH-BEARING CONNECTIVITY

Knowledge, as encompassing the truth of things, is, therefore, essentially concerned with the truth-bearing connectivity of things. To say this is to declare the subliminal and ultimate relevance of God to the act of implicative perception. Newman was keenly aware, as Anselm put it, that God demands of us all that we are and have and can become. To see the world by means of such connectivity and interconnectivity is not only to see God in the world—in His Creation—but also, and in a Christian sense, to see the world in God. It was in this spirit, for example, that Robert Grosseteste detected an identity between a physics of light and a theology of Light.[9]

As there is a higher, more perceptive way to see the world, so too and regrettably, there can also be a lower, less perceptive way to regard the world. Equally, then, the contrast is between an ascentive mode of engaging knowledge, and a descentive, unengaged, and careless mode of seeing. And this means, Newman said, that "there are two ways of using Knowledge . . . two ways of reading Nature . . . two methods of Education; the end of the one is to be philosophical, of the other to be mechanical; the one rises towards general ideas, the other is exhausted upon what is particular and external . . . [and so] ceases to be Knowledge."[10]

One mode of engaging knowledge, nature, and education, therefore, keeps the whole circle of creation distinctively but distinguishably in view. It is integrative, fulfilling, and ascentive because it aims towards fulfillment ($\pi\lambda\acute{\eta}\varrho\omega\mu\alpha$), and thus towards a "sacramental" vision of the whole reality. One mode of knowledge is empowered to go higher since it is intentionally ascentive. Contrastingly, the other mode is partial, particled, broken in fragments, like pebbles sinking to the bottom of a deep lake, where, because of the absence of light, there is also absence of vision.

When Newman says "exhausted upon what is particular and external," he means that such "knowledge" ultimately becomes irrelevant. And when he says "particular" in this context, he does not mean "singular." He means exhausted of amplification and connection; he means what has been severed from the living branches of being. In cutting down trees, this mode of knowing would lose sight of the forest. By making much ado about nothing, it will not do much about the world's interconnectivity. This kind of "philosophy sets up a system of universal knowledge and teaches . . . about all things imaginable except one—about God."[11] To people of "exhausted" knowledge (G. K. Chesterton might have said), everything matters—except everything.

ENCAPSULATING REALITY

We must keep clearly in view, then, that knowledge has ambassadorial duty for the whole universe, or the whole reality. It is capable, in great measure, of encapsulation, as if it were an embassy of the "comprehensive view of truth in all its branches."[12] For, once again, this kind of knowledge "makes every thing in some sort lead to every thing else."[13] Any instance of knowledge, therefore, is an intellective mirror, and represents truth microcosmically. This is why Newman's "true representative" of the University's "imperial intellect" will be faithful to the principle of connectivity, because he aims at "following out, as far as man can, what in its fulness is mysterious and unfathomable. Taking into his charge all sciences, methods, collections of facts, principles, doctrines, truths, which are the reflexion of the universe upon the human intellect, he admits them all. . . . If he has one cardinal maxim in his philosophy, it is that truth cannot be contrary to truth."[14]

Unless a sense of connectivity is also linked to an ascentive power to act in truth, there will be no vision of the ultimate interconnectivity of reality. Mere knowledge, of course, will not suffice. Hence, the utilitarian notion of "knowledge as information"—manipulated by the Robert Peels of the world—assumes that information can instantly redeem human beings of their inadequacies. But, to assume, as Newman phrased it, "that the mind is changed by discovery, or saved by a diversion, and can thus be amused into immortality . . . by an examination of shells or grasses, or inhaling of gases, or chipping of rocks, or calculating the longitude, is the veriest of pretences which sophist or mountebank ever professed to a gaping auditory."[15] Knowledge without ascentive action—like words without deeds, prayer without intention, life without purpose—ceases to be knowledge worthy of the name. If to know is one thing, and to do is another; if, as Newman observed, "knowledge is one thing, virtue is another," then only ascentive, deed-centered knowledge comports with the intellective nature of faith. "Life is for action. . . . To act you must assume, and that assumption is faith."[16]

LOSS OF VISION

In contrast, Sir Robert Peel and Henry Lord Brougham, in order, through utilitarian conjury, to forestall civil upheaval in mid-nineteenth-century industrial England, minimized knowledge as information, so as to enchant it into an instrument of social psychology. By stripping knowledge of visionary urgency, as well as by detaching it from Christianity, Peel and Brougham simply "deconstructed" knowledge into ideology, which is to say, into a "faith" which has no faith. Newman, however, repositioned the question of knowledge by observing that, "Christianity is faith; faith implies a doctrine; a doctrine propositions; propositions yes or no; yes or no differences. . . . When, then, Sir Robert Peel calls such differences points of 'party feeling,' what is this but to insult Christianity?"[17]

It is precisely by choosing a standpoint that is of greater eminence than mere information that knowledge can actually ascend to a height from which, authentically and authoritatively, the world can be viewed. Change the standpoint and you change the view. Minimize the view and you have already minimized the viewpoint.

RELIGION AND THEOLOGY

Here, then, we can relate to the first ascentive theme in *The Idea of a University*, which is that the University ought necessarily include in its curriculum the study of theology. Why is this necessary? That answer is grounded in the connectivity inherent in knowledge: "All that exists, as contemplated by the human mind, forms one large system or complex fact." It is grounded, too, in the interconnectivity inherent in a God-created universe: "The subject-matter of knowledge is intimately united in itself, as being the acts and the work of the Creator."[18]

Two spiritually ascentive ways accredit these connective aspects, and are to be found, first, in the existential practice of real religion, and, secondly, in the intellective study of notional theology. Religion is existentially real and personal,[19] because it is the worship of God. Theology is intellectively notional, because it is the science of God. Newman stipulates that "by Theology, I simply mean the Science of God, or the truths we know about God put into system; just as we have a science of the stars, and call it astronomy, or of the crust of the earth, and call it geology."[20]

Distinctly motivated, and distinguishably experienced, religion and theology are directly concerned with God—either, in a knowledgeable worship of God, or in a worshiping knowledge about God. In Newman's words, "Religion has to do with the real, and the real is the particular; theology has to do with the notional, and the notional is the general and systematic."[21] In the practice of religion, and in that ascentive "loving inquisitiveness" of theological study, there is the consciousness-enhancing perception that "all that is good, all that is true, all that is beautiful, all that is beneficent, be it great or small, be it perfect or fragmentary, natural as well as supernatural, moral as well as material, comes from Him. ... . . [Therefore,] Religious Truth is not only a portion, but a condition of general knowledge. To blot it out is nothing short . . . of unravelling the web of University Teaching."[22]

When we understand, as Newman did, that religious truth is "a condition of general knowledge," we have made an ascentive passage towards appreciating the implications of knowing. And that appreciation can give further credence to the University policy, which Newman makes explicit in his view that "the great principle of the University . . . [is] the indissoluble union of philosophy and religion."[23]

Possession of any truth implicitly involves an interconnective appreciation of the whole truth. This, in turn, generates a recognition that the genius of revealed truth ought to be included in University studies. As Newman indicated, "Revealed truth enters to a very great extent into the province of science, philosophy, and literature." Such truth can truly become ascentive: "Revelation itself may be viewed as one of the constituent parts of human knowledge, considered as a whole, and its omission is the omission of one of those constituent parts. Revealed religion furnishes facts to the other sciences, which those sciences left to themselves would never reach; and it invalidates apparent facts, which, left to themselves, they would imagine."[24]

Newman contends that the decision to omit any kind of knowledge from the University curriculum, whether human or divine, represents "not knowledge, but ignorance."[25] In saying this, as one observer remarked, Newman only "claimed a place for Theology in education on general grounds."[26] Hence, "the systematic omission of any one science from the [University] catalogue prejudices the accuracy and completeness of our knowledge altogether."[27] As a consequence, Theology ought not—and rightfully cannot—be excluded from the University curriculum. To restrict the curricular entry of theology would diminish knowledge, and, therefore, alter the definition of knowledge:

> I cannot so construct my definition of the subject-matter of
> University Knowledge, and so draw my boundary lines
> around it, as to include therein the other sciences commonly

studied at Universities, and to exclude the science of Religion. For instance, are we to limit our idea of University
Knowledge by the evidence of our senses? then we exclude
ethics; by intuition? we exclude history; by testimony? we
exclude metaphysics; by abstract reasoning? we exclude
physics. Is not the being of a God reported to us by testimony, handed down by history, inferred by an inductive
process, brought home to us by metaphysical necessity,
urged on us by the suggestion of our conscience? It is a truth
in the natural order as well as in the supernatural.[28]

Excluding theology from University study not only prejudices
the completeness of the University curriculum, but would "invalidate
the trustworthiness of all that is actually taught." Furthermore, "all sciences being connected together, and having bearings one on another, it
is impossible to teach them all thoroughly, unless they are all taken into
account, and Theology among them." Otherwise, "if Theology is not
allowed to occupy its own territory, adjacent sciences which are quite
foreign to Theology, will take possession of it."[29]

THEOLOGY AND INTEGRITY

In the introductory Discourse of the *Idea*, Newman argues that theology,
being ascentive, is essential to the integrity of a University, and in making his case, uses his rhetorical and logical skills. Clearly, any policy
which excludes theology from University education is, he says, absurd.
He frames the first of two logically supportive arguments this way:

Such a procedure . . . seems to me an intellectual absurdity;
and my reason for saying so runs, with whatever abruptness,
into the form of a syllogism: A University, I should lay down,
by its very name professes to teach universal knowledge:
Theology is surely a branch of knowledge: how then is it
possible for it to profess all branches of knowledge, and yet
to exclude from the subjects of its teaching one which, to say
the least, is as important and as large as any of them? I do not
see that either premiss of this argument is open to exception.[30]

Of course, neither premise, of itself, is open to exception. But
the form in which that argument is expressed is open to exception. First,

the premises appear not as in a syllogism, but as in an enthymeme, since his language—"how then is it possible . . .?"—is not a conclusion, but a commentary. Second, although the intent of the argument is uncompromised, it is formally impossible to state a conclusion.[31]

In the second formulation of his argument, Newman chooses a hypothetical framework, and he says,

> So I will throw my argument into a more exact form. I say, then, that if a University be, from the nature of the case, a place of instruction, where universal knowledge is professed, and if in a certain University, so called, the subject of Religion is excluded, one of two conclusions is inevitable. Either, on the one hand, that the province of Religion is very barren of real knowledge, or, on the other hand, that in such University one special and important branch of knowledge is omitted. I say, the advocate of such an institution must say this, or he must say that, he must own, either that little or nothing is known about the Supreme Being, or that his seat of learning calls itself what it is not.[32]

These inferences which Newman draws hypothetically appear (as in the categorical) essentially intuitive (right hemisphere) rather than only formal (left hemisphere). This simply reinforces a sense of the breadth of Newman's experience, and perhaps demonstrates, once again, the complementarity of his intellectual vision.

ENHANCING CONSCIOUSNESS

Complementarity lends further substance to—as it provides further sustenance for—the ascentive nature of his mind. Indeed, one could argue, with Newman as model, that there is confirmation that every act of ascentive knowing is an implicit act of worship. Such an act, replicating the parable of talents, returns to God the knowledge of creation, but now with this unique difference—it has been invested in, and has been enhanced by, a new consciousness, and, through perception of the meaning of the creation, it has acquired personalized ownership.[34]

A prerequisite of such new consciousness as ascentive knowing is what Newman has called self-knowledge. We might also think of it as self-identity-knowledge, which issues in the spiritual-intellectual revelation to ourself, of who, uniquely, we are. This is precisely why Newman's notion of the perfection of the intellect is ultimately and so crucially important. In other words, each of us is called to reveal—to make real, and so to fulfill—her or his own identity. This is because, in Newman's terms, we are images, uniquely, of God—*imagines Dei*. Each of us is a potential revelation, which personally, educatively, religiously requires pleromaic realization. Newman, in his life, made known, and continues to make known, the revelation of his spiritual identity. And so ought we of ours. In this process, we would affirm a kind of covenantal acknowledgment. In affirmation, we can then see, and envision covenantally what ought to be seen. Reprised, in the words of William James, this means that "when we see all things in God, and refer all things to Him, we read in common matters superior expressions of meaning. The deadness with which custom invests the familiar vanishes, and existence as a whole appears transfigured."[35]

In light of ascentive and universalizing insight, it is interesting that in his lecture, "Christianity and Letters," Newman envisions the University's arts curriculum both historically and theologically. He consequently suggests both a teleology and eschatology of liberal arts.[36] In that lecture, Newman accounts the history of Western culture as the "civilization of intellect." Over its long history, he notes, Western civilization has united religious and secular knowledge, wherein, "Jerusalem is the fountain-head of religious knowledge, as Athens is of secular . . . [as] two centres of illumination, acting independently. . . . To separate those distinct teachings, human and divine, which meet in Rome, is to retrograde. . . . [For] sacred learning and profane learning are dependent on each other, correlative and mutually complementary, [because] faith operates by means of reason, and reason is directed and corrected by faith."[37]

CIVILIZATION OF INTELLECT

Since the beginning of history, says Newman, from time immemorial, there has arisen in countries which surround the Mediterranean "the seat of an association of intellect and mind, such as to deserve to be called the Intellect and the Mind of the Human Kind." Such a commonwealth, he adds, is "pre-eminently and emphatically Human Society, and its intellect the Human mind . . . and the territory on which it lies the *orbis terrarum*, or the World." But joined to this "seat of Civilization" will be found "the seat also of the supernatural society and system which our Maker has given us directly from Himself, the Christian Polity." Thus, there emerges "the civilization which began in Palestine and Greece."[38]

Then, of civilization and Christianity he says, "There is nothing else like the one, and nothing else like the other. Each is the only thing of its kind." As Western Civilization forms "one organized whole," so also does Christianity which "coalesces into one vast body, based upon common ideas."[39] Out of the ancient secular Civilization of Greece, there arose a "blind old man [who] lives in steep Chios." As "the first Apostle of Civilization," he "was invested with the office of forming the young mind of Greece to noble thoughts and bold deeds. To be read in Homer soon became the education of a gentleman."[40] From such beginnings, there came other great literary figures. Thence was formed "the course of liberal education. . . . The studies . . . which are known by the name of the Seven Liberal Arts. And thus a definite school of intellect was formed, founded on ideas and methods of distinctive character, and . . . of the highest and truest character." Thereupon, Newman adds, the literature of Greece, which was enriched by "the literature of Rome . . . has been the instrument of education, and the food of civilization, from the first times of the world down to this day." And thus these literatures have turned out "to be the best instruments of mental cultivation, and the best guarantees for intellectual progress."[41]

With the rise of the sacred city of Jerusalem and the humanist city of Athens, there also arose two standpoints, one being the sacred and the other being the secular. The relation between these two standpoints made possible their integrative connection. Culturally and historically, the connection was formed, and, in this fact, there actually occurred a cultural fusion between these two cities. This made possible the West's Judeo-Christian humanist civilization. The metaphoric alliance of the cities occurred as a conjunction of spiritual references and of distinct offices incorporated in the Roman Empire. Newman says, "The grace stored in Jerusalem, and the gifts which radiate from Athens, are made over and concentrated in Rome. This is true as a matter of history. Rome has inherited both sacred and profane learning; she has perpetuated and dispensed the traditions of Moses and David in the supernatural order, and of Homer and Aristotle in the natural."[42]

THE TWO CITIES

Describing the spiritual and cultural environment of the West, Newman is also describing here the civilization in which, through Christian religion and Christian education, ascentive knowing is made possible. Yet, conversely—given the ambiguity of being human—that same Western culture also makes possible, but inversely, a descentive knowing. Is this not a reminder of the dual-cities message of St. Augustine? Does it not, on one hand, sparkle with affirmative bonds and links, gussets and welds, yokes and pairings, of the genuine city? On the other hand, does it not also dissemble with disinheriting rifts and partings, cracks, and rents, the divisions of the negative society?

Augustine's envisioned cities—as if he had reframed them as a Gospel parable of wheat and faux wheat sown in the same field—are being created in the very same civilization. One city will be ascentive, and loving; the other, descentive, and destructive. Augustine describes these two standpoints as political entities, existing in the very same environment. But he does so with an evident Gospel clarity: "Two loves have brought about two cities—that is, the earthly city is brought about by the love of self and the defiance of God; but the glorified city, by the love of God and the diminution of the self. One city takes pride in itself, whereas the other exults in the Lord."[43]

Surely, it is obvious that whatever standpoint we take will determine what we see. Augustine understood this. So did John Henry Newman. Both comprehended that it is important to position ourselves in order truly to see. Otherwise we will fail to see.[44]

But an important paradoxical distinction has yet to be drawn. The paradox is that—even when we are positioned well and see what we ought to see—we can never see everything, nor can we see ultimately. We can never, as seventeenth-century Sir Thomas Browne imagined, "see things as in themselves they really are." For however much, however far, however high we see, our perspective will always remain finite. Thus, we need constantly to modify our sense of knowing, according to its present condition, which is that of mystery.

APPROXIMATIONS

No matter how bright, or how clear the glass we look through; no matter how sharp or accurate our vision; no matter the eminence from which we take our view—here below, as St. Paul affirmed—what we see will always remain enigmatic. (I Cor. 13:12). Intellectually, we can ascend to great heights. Yet, despite the height, there will always be a horizon, and every horizon is, by definition, finite, and always entails another. In this spirit, for example, Nicolaus Cusanus (1401–64) once observed that a polygon, inscribed in a circle, despite increase of the number of its sides, will only approximate, and never coincide with the circle. From this he drew an epistemological parallel that the mind never fully coincides with truth, but only approximates it (*De docta ignorantia*, I, 3).

Newman was keenly aware of this insight.[45] He appreciated the fact that our most precise expressions, our deepest intuitions, our hardest of "hard sciences," can never exceed the finite condition of approximation. Thus, we clearly do not see things as in themselves they really are, nor can we know, as Leopold von Ranke imagined it, a historical event as it actually occurred—"*wie es eigentlich gewesen.*" We observe, not history itself, not nature itself, but, as Werner Heisenberg remarked, a nature or a history that is exposed to approximating methods of questioning. As evolutionary biologist Ernst Mayr suggests, scientific inquiry approximates what is probably, not necessarily, believable. Thus, in all scientific inquiry, intellectual pride is not only untenable, unrealistic, and self-defeating. It is also anti-intellectual.

Since finitude is the human condition, we need seriously to reflect on our glorious strengths and hobbling insufficiencies. Captured by our own special "now-moment" in history, we are also captive of our special cultural constraints. We do not arrive here on earth as if from some Rousseauesque nature, and out of some indefinite nowhere. We come the way that mankind is given to come, with our own unique genetic identity, born on a specific day and year, and "appointed" to leave our special specific moment on earth as unequivocally as we came into it—but in a different direction.

Indeed, our everyday life suggests just how captive we are to our own times, and to our own civilization. It perhaps suggests, too, how much what we call reality becomes a mimetic function of our civilization. How well we see depends, of course, on our willingness to see widely, and upon our resolution to "mount up higher." But even this will be determined by the cultural perspective available to us. Perhaps we can make the point another way. And this requires a slight detour.

CULTURAL PERSPECTIVES

As a result of the introduction of perspective drawing in the late Renaissance, the classical view that "art imitates nature" was gradually rearticulated to apprehend that "nature imitates art." By making objects appear to recede in parallel planes that converge at one or more vanishing points, Genoese humanist Leon Battista Alberti (1404–72) set down, for the first time, theoretic formulations to represent a three-dimensional world on a two-dimensional plane. With profound consequences for painting and perception, he codified ideas of Florentine architect Filippo Brunelleschi (1337–1446), with whom he worked, and Florentine painter Paolo Uccello (1397–1475). Through intervention of a new perspective geometry, the European eye and imagination were brought to recast, revise, and revision nature. Ocular depth revised painting, as the European eye created a new sense of geometrical distance. What before had been flatly seen as nature, disappeared like an old illusion, to be replaced by a new illusion.[46]

If we can borrow this reference to linear perspective, we can rephrase the view that "culture imitates reality" into the statement that "reality imitates culture." Culture makes possible new ways of thinking, on condition, at least, that the old ways have first been mastered. Thus, if our culture determines our reality, then what we confront in everyday experience, as well as in our most reflective moments, is not bare, unconditional, absolute reality—although that remains within the background mystery—but rather a historical and cultural version of that reality.

This is the message of St. Paul, of St. Augustine, and of John Henry Newman. For no one looks on the world "with pristine eyes."[47] Rather, we look at the world with eyes accustomed to perceiving a prepared cultural reality, and according to laws, as it were, of a conceptual ocularity. In a special sense, it would follow that cultures and cultural phenomena are, in effect, illusions of a deeper reality. For however many statements we can make about any known reality, they can never be more than approximations. Here below, we are looking through a dark and enigmatic lens. On the other hand, we also need to recognize that our approximations, and cultural illusions, are necessarily perceived against a background of the truly real.[48] And this is the abiding mystery. If this were not the case, we could not speak about cultural illusions. And St. Paul could not speak of the difference between what we "know now," and what we will "know then."[49] As Cardinal Dulles—in the spirit of Cardinal Newman—has already told us, "We know more than we can say."

RELATIVE ERROR

Perception and expression, therefore, being finite and thus conditional, are subject to some relative error, which is another name for approximation. As F. H. Bradley once suggested,[50] every error entails some amount of illusion. In the human condition, every cultural image of (unrevealed) truth inevitably converts to possession of what is, somehow, less than the truth. But, once again, there is the other side of the coin. Despite its corrigibility and relativity, a cultural truth nonetheless remains a "truth." In no matter what guise such a truth comes, it ennobles and honors us.

Truth, of course, does not break into the human premises like a second-story cutpurse. On the contrary, it gradually grafts itself, culturally and historically, on previous consciousness. This is precisely the meaning of the patristic view about the making of the Kingdom of God. Truth is a lure for the culturally and historically disposed mind, and— Newman would add—for the spiritually prepared mind, in the same way that faith lures the "religious mind" and the scripturally "renewed heart."[51] Truth is that in which we are basically interested. Made for truth, as we are, we now possess, not so much a lie, as a proxy of truth. But even that proxy, because of its promissory face, prepares us for further truth. Our deepest experiences, then, are culturally, linguistically, socially, and historically conditioned as "real." But they are not yet real enough. Whenever, said Josef Pieper, we pierce through the dome of cultural and historical conditions, it can never be more than a probing. St. Paul still reminds us that we see, here and now, in a dark glass. We still fall short of God's glory (Rom. 3:23), and of our expectations of vision.

Cultural experience always anticipates more than it can express, and hopes for more than it perceives. Without attaining an order that transcends its own conditions, experience nonetheless points to transcension. And it is the pointing which is symbolically significant; pointing implies the existence of both an order from which pointing can be made, and an order to which pointing is addressed. And it is this order of transcension which we experience in religious life and worship. As Christopher Dawson once said, for those who lack understanding of the religious undergirding of culture, culture is destined to remain a closed book.[52] T. S. Eliot likewise remarked on the connection between lived religion and culture.[53] Josef Pieper similarly observed that "culture . . . is not possible unless it has a durable and consequently living link with the *cultus*, with divine worship."[54] Without culture—so pervasive is it in any sense—there could be no "human experience." This is because culture is the condition of human experience. And this is why it is important to recognize that cultural experience is also—implicitly and potentially—educative and preparative. In other words, education, though conditioned here and now, has consequences for eternity.

It has become commonplace, of course, to say that the success—or rather the failure—of the religious experience of the Ionians in the sixth century BC became an invitation to philosophy. Since that time, religion and philosophy (and perhaps its Western stand-in, education) have been closely linked. They have appeared variously in discursive alliance, and in competition. But whatever their relation, they each—religion, philosophy, and education—appeal to an order other than what immediately confronts each. They appeal to the order of mystery. Philosophy prospers on mystery, while religion is based on it. The prophet, the poet, and the philosopher are related because they are all concerned with *mirandum*—wonder.[55] Plato and Aristotle could verbalize this experience in their wonder verb, *thaumazein (θαυμάζειν)*.[56] What binds together prophet, poet, and philosopher is a reverential power, which Plato suggested was—combined with intellectual acumen—a prerequisite for the practice of philosophy.[57] For Plato, philosophizing was, indeed, the antechamber of religious intuitions, and a means of perceiving the ultimate in the proximate.

ORDER OF MYSTERY

What religion, philosophy, and education share most completely is their distinct desire to step out of what Josef Pieper has already described for us as the "workaday world."[58] It would be crude as well as inaccurate to assume that philosophy expresses what religion leaves unspoken.[59] The world's mystery makes philosophy plausible, as well as possible. And if philosophy no longer confronts mystery, it ceases to be philosophical, because it ceases to be itself.

Mystery, Whitehead once said, is what makes the world interesting. Indeed, mystery is the ontological side of what Whitehead once called our "delightful ignorance of important truths."[60] Now, a mind reformed by intellectual discipline, reshaped by ascentive vision, committed to perfection, and therefore to perfecting love—which St. Paul calls the "bond of perfection"[61]—provides a new platform from which to view mystery. Such a platform modifies our ignorance, and enables us, as Emerson once put it, to draw a "new circle" around our experience. A new circle enables us to focus on ultimate, as well as on proximate, aspects of the world's mystery. It enables us to magnify implications which our ignorance overlooks, or which our habits take for granted.

In this sense, for each of us as human beings, Newman boldly suggests, intellectually to ascend involves the moral employment, and thus the spiritual enjoyment, of using our own intellect. For it is our intellect which signifies that unique spiritual endowment—and therefore that privilege—which allows us to enter into the world's mystery of reality. In that entrance, we also become suppliants of the mystery of grace. And that, in turn, allows us existentially to refocus in our own lives a Newmanesque binary theme of Christian life, by which nature is transfigured by Grace.

GRACE AND PERFECTION

It is through grace, as has often been noted, that our privilege of intellect becomes our power to communicate with the Divine—for therein, divine grace consequently becomes the exaltation of our intellect. This is the message about the world's background of mystery which John Henry Newman, through his "heart metaphor" of intellect, so precisely and eloquently expressed: "Grace is lodged in the heart; it purifies the thoughts and motives, it raises the soul to God, it sanctifies the body, it corrects and exalts human nature."[62]

To become truly human, each of us needs to ascend towards her or his own special, unique identity. We cannot stand still. We cannot simply run in place. We cannot merely remain who we have been, because to do so would substitute habit for ascent, and thus turn mental torpidity into moral turpitude.

So too, in evolutionary theory, no species can afford simply to run in place, for that would abrogate the evolutionary process. As the Red Queen advises Alice, in Lewis Carroll's *Through the Looking Glass*, "If you want to get somewhere else, you must run as least twice as fast as that!" In keeping with such a theme, John Henry Newman would probably counsel that because Christians seek, in a patristic sense, "to get somewhere else," and in order to further the cause of creation, then, like Lewis Carroll's Alice, we "must run at least twice as fast." Otherwise, we are subjected to the laws of spiritual inertia. So that we may become who we are, we need to transfigure who we have been, and thereby continue to search for our unique spiritual identity. Perhaps, with Newman as model, we can come to understand that he changed from what he had been, only in order to become more truly himself. Doing so, he illustrated the principle that action can affect thought.

Indeed, there is neuroscientific support for just such a principle.[63] It suggests that there is a fundamental link between body behavior and brain behavior, as expressed in the formula: What we do can influence what we think. That is, action can determine thinking, or thinking follows action—*cogitare sequitur agere*. We might of course, expect the inverse to be true. We might expect that what we think automatically influences what we do, thinking determines action, or action follows thinking—*agere sequitur cogitare*. Still, by comparison, this neuroscientific principle implies that right action can influence right reason just as much as right reason can influence right action.

This same principle would support the notion that learning can influence devotion, as much as devotion can influence learning. Newman might say, "True Devotion increases true Learning," and equally, "True Learning increases true Devotion." Indeed, such a principle seems to support the claim that intellectually ascending to our own spiritual identity involves much more than maintaining mere legal identity.

True identity is individual and unique, not generalizable and replicable. True identity represents, as it were, a unique intellectual DNA, within a metaphoric spiritual genome. Unique DNA is the variation, which singularizes each of us. If interpreted as a spiritual metaphor, our unique mental DNA would ultimately record our intellectual identity.

SPIRITUAL GENOME

Within a metaphoric spiritual genome, unique identity would, consequently, be not only essential, but redemptive. In behavioral genetics, variation is what keeps the evolutionary process alive. Likewise, in metaphoric terms, our unique personal variation in becoming our unique intellectual reality might be said to be what can keep humankind spiritually alive. Our unique intellectual identity is necessarily achieved self-consciously, and is acknowledged self-affirmatively. In an almost patristic sense, such action would be what endows, clarifies, and elevates an evolutionary process of the human spirit, working in cooperation with Divine Spirit.

Therefore, as Newman seems to imply, bringing about the Kingdom of God becomes the responsibility of each of us—which is to say that unique personal identity can be developed only through the fusion of our moral and intellectual action. Being merely human, being merely enrolled in our own temporal time and cultural place, is not enough. Such enrollment represents the biblical talent, which each of us is given at birth. What each of us is biblically and providentially expected to do, therefore, is uniquely to invest that talent. Only by following Newman's example of developing, expanding, enhancing, unfolding, and realizing that talent—rising to that which we ultimately are—can we become who we are meant to be. Clearly, this is not a Gnostic doctrine.

PERFECTION AND IDENTITY

Following the example of John Henry Newman, we can achieve the goal of becoming perfectly ourself, by perfecting our intellect. Accomplishing that task, we will have changed only in order to become more perfectly who we really are—which means, who we are called to be. This is never an easy task. And there are few more painful challenges that anyone can apprehend than those which ask, "What do you want to do? What will you do with your life? Who are you going to be?" Such challenging questions are rooted in an imperative premise: Find out who you are.

Thus, the perfection to which we are called can be achieved in doing what we ought daily to do, by doing well whatever we are doing. If we seek to be perfect—to become perfectly ourself, then, in Newman's words, "we have nothing more to do than to perform the ordinary duties of the day well."[64] In that "ordinary" process, Newman has told us how faith expands understanding, revelation enhances reason, and grace develops nature just as devotion magnifies learning, religion matures education, and conscience integrates wisdom. Such a process will continue to summon us, not to our past, but to our present, and thus towards our future.

In this narrative, we have attempted to explore and to apprehend various aspects of Newman's splendorous spirit and personality. Our task was undertaken on the assumption that insight into Newman begins from a compassionate appreciation of his spiritual genius. Whenever we are attracted to Newman, and to the spirit he so well personalized, it is not because of the facts of his life, but because of the deeper truths it contains. We will never apprehend the significance of those deeper truths, nor venerate their implications, until we have made them a part of our own life.

It seems appropriate, then, to conclude this narrative by quoting a revealing truth which a well-known biographer has found in the many lives he has recorded. He says it this way: "A life only becomes real for us when it is interiorized, only when we find those connective threads of meaning and make the link to ourselves."[65]

NOTES

INTRODUCTION: THE NEWMAN NARRATIVE
NEWMAN EPIGRAPHS:

"Grace is lodged"—"Nature and Grace," *Discourses to
Mixed Congregations*, p. 151.
"A well-trained"—Letters and Diaries, XVI, p. 563.

1. John Henry Newman, *Discourses Addressed to Mixed Congregations*,
Westminster, MD, Christian Classics, 1966. "Mankind was created in the image
of God, and that image is in his soul" (p. 324). See also his *The Arians of the
Fourth Century, Their Doctrines, Temper and Conduct Chiefly Exhibited in
the Councils of the Church between A.D. 325 and A.D. 381*, London, Longmans, Green, 1895. "There never was a time when God had not spoken to Man"
(p. 790).

2. John Henry Newman, *The Idea of a University, Defined and Illustrated*,
London, Longmans, Green, 1898, VI. 6, pp. 136–37. Newman's connective
principle, being essentially ontological, represents more than mere pedagogic
epistemology. Founded in a philosophy and theology of "Creational Integrity,"
it is based upon the Creation story of Genesis-Bereshith.

3. More remains to be said in this book on this topic. Here, it may be useful to note recent emphasis on the fact that the human person is explicitly gendered, with gendered powers. For example, females tend to be dominantly
right-brained, and have sharper night vision, as males tend to be dominantly
left-brained, and have sharper day vision.

It is acknowledged that gentleness, sensitivity, caringness, and spiritual
nurturing—although identified as right-brain aspects of psychology—are
nonetheless human traits, not just feminine traits. Implications of this view for
Newman studies are clear. Briefly, Newman, in his own day, prophetically embraced gentleness and other spiritual gifts of interpersonal maturity. For acknowledging what, for his own times, were considered strictly feminine
attributes of personality, he was attacked by English male chauvinists, who
seem to have equated masculinity with brutality.

4. See Thomas Hobbes, *Leviathan, or the Matter, Form, and Power of a
Commonwealth Ecclesiastical and Civil*, Part I, chapter XIII. Hobbes (1588–
1679) proposed "three principal causes of quarrel. First, competition; second,
diffidence; thirdly, glory. . . . The first [type] use violence to make themselves
masters of other men's persons. . . . [T]hey are in that condition which is called
war; and such a war as is of every man against every man. For war consisteth
not in battle only . . . not in actual fighting, but in the known disposition

thereto" (cited in *The English Philosophers from Bacon to Mill*, (ed.) Edwin A. Burn, New York, Random House, 1939, pp.160–61).

5. John Henry Newman, *An Essay on the Development of Christian Doctrine*, New York, Image/Doubleday, 1960, p. 63.

6. A computer paradigm of Education has put computers "in every classroom"—a hint that an educational revolution is underway, which is apparently determined to substitute the computer as model for how people ought to "think" and "react." While computers expand the baseline of information, education is not just about "information." Thus, Newman's idea of educatively cultivating the intellect is perhaps more important now than it has ever been before.

7. Ian Ker, *The Achievement of John Henry Newman*, London, Collins, 1990. Fr. Ker adds the fact that Newman's work "has been surprisingly misunderstood and even ignored" (pp. ix, 2).

8. J. E. Raven suggests that Socrates's subsequent satirical praise of this sentiment by Agathon as much as brands it "high-sounding insincerity." See Plato's *Thought in the Making: A Study of the Development of his Metaphysics*, Cambridge, Cambridge University Press, 1965, p. 110.

9. Jean Guitton, *The Guinon Journals 1952–1955*, (trans.) F. Forrest, Baltimore, MD, Helicon, 1963, p. 242.

10. The late Vincent Ferrer Blehl, S. J., often told the story of how French philosopher Jean Guitton once inquired of Pope Pius XII if Newman might be canonized. Pope Pius replied sotto voce, "Don't worry. Newman will one day be made a Father of the Church." By such assurance, the Pope implied an affirmative response, for in order for Newman to become a Doctor of the Church he would already have to be a canonized saint. (Personal communication to the author from Fr. Blehl, 29 March 2001.)

CHAPTER 1:   UNIVERSITY
NEWMAN EPIGRAPHS:

"A University seems"—*Rise and Progress*, p. 6.
"Greatness and unity"—*Rise and Progress*, p. 16.

1. See C. J. B. Gaskoin, *Alcuin: His Life and His Work*, New York, Russell & Russell, 1966 [1904]; Eleanor Shipley Duckett, *Alcuin, Friend of Charlemagne: His World and His Work*, New York, Macmillan, 1951.

2. See Andrew Fleming West, *Alcuin and the Rise of Christian Schools*, New York, Scribner's, 1892; Albrecht Diem, "The Emergence of Monastic Schools: The Role of Alcuin" (pp. 27–44), and Mayke de Jong, "From Scolastici to Scioli: Alcuin and the Formation of an Intellectual Elite" (pp. 45–57), in *Alcuin of York, Scholar of the Carolingian Court*, (edd.) L. A. J. R. Houwen and A. A. MacDonald, Gronigen, Egbert Forstein, 1998.

3. See *Patrologia Latina*, 101. 952ff.

4. Charles Homer Haskins, *The Rise of Universities*, Ithaca, NY, Cornell University Press, 1957, p. 39. This phrase is used by Dankwart A. Rustow, "The Political Impact of the West," in *The Cambridge History of Islam*, 2 vols., (edd.) P. M. Holt, Ann K. S. Lambton, Bernard Lewis, Cambridge, Cambridge University Press, 1970, I, pp. 673–97. See F. Gabrieli, "The Transmission of Learning and Literary Influences to Western Europe," ibid., II, pp. 851–89. (The latest edition of this source was republished in four volumes in 1980.) See also, Gustave E. von Grunebaum, "Creative Borrowing: Greece in the 'Arabian Nights,'" in his *Medieval Islam: A Study in Cultural Orientation*, 2nd ed., Phoenix/University of Chicago Press, 1961, pp. 294–319; G. M. Wickens, "What the West Borrowed from the Middle East," and "Khatimah," in R. M. Savory (ed.), *Introduction to Islamic Civilization*, Cambridge, Cambridge University Press, 1976, pp. 120–25, and pp. 189–94; Werner Gaskel, "Western Impact of Islamic Civilization," in Gustave E. Von Grunebaum (ed.), *Unity and Variety in Muslim Civilization*, Chicago, University of Chicago Press, 1955, pp. 335–60; W. Montgomery Watt, "The Expansion of the Islamic Worldview," in his *What is Islam?* New York, Praeger, 1968, pp. 170–84; also "The Replacement of Christian Culture by Islamic," in his *The Majesty That Was Islam*, New York, Praeger, 1974, pp. 257–60. See also, A. J. Arberry, "Wisdom from the East," and "Science from the West," in his *Aspects of Islamic Civilization*, Ann Arbor, University of Michigan Press, 1967, pp. 72–154. See also H. A. R. Gibb and J. H. Kramers, *Shorter Encyclopedia of Islam*, Leiden, Netherlands, E. J. Brill, 1961, notably, "Azhar," pp. 50–52; "Madrasa," pp. 300–320; and "Masdjid," pp. 330–53.

5. Bernard Lewis, *The Muslim Discovery of Europe*, New York, Norton, 2001.

6. See Richard Walzer, *Greek into Arabic*, Oxford, Oxford University Press, 1962. See also, Etienne Gilson, H*istory of Christian Philosophy in the Middle Ages*, New York, Random House, 1955, pp. 540–42, and p. 803, note 82. Gilson emphasizes the important medieval confluence of Christianity and Greek philosophy. From that union, he says, came a "blossoming of theological and philosophical speculation," such that "the philosophical speculation of the middle ages appears as a sort of appendix to the history of Greek philosophy." To this, he adds, "This is one of the main reasons why the sixteenth-century Renaissance was a continuation of the Christian civilization of the middle ages."

7. Charles Homer Haskins, *The Renaissance of the 12th Century,* New York, Meridian, 1957, p. 368. A comparative word appears necessary here in order to place Newman's historical University essays in proper historical perspective, and to distinguish the history of education from the history of the University. While the latter history is part of the former, the former does not determine the course of the latter. Thus, Pierre Marique in his *A History of Chris-*

tian Education (3 volumes, New York, Fordham University Press, 1924) tells the story of education from ancient to medieval times, but he does not pretend to write a history of the University. The University, then, is not an inevitable unfolding of the history of education. Rather, its history denotes a psychological and cultural corporate development in the history of Europe. Without European recovery of its own cultural genius (by means of the Islamization of the West), there would be little difference between the "schools" of Athens, Alexandria, Rome, and Cairo and the "schools" (per saltum) of Paris, Salerno, Bologna, and Oxford. Such, however, is not the case. The University—as we know it, with its strictly medieval, unique title, universitas—is not just an outgrowth of Athens, or of other ancient schools, as some Newman scholars plead. Concerning the rise and progress of the University, whatever significant differences do exist between John Henry Newman's and, say, Hastings Rashdall's views, these ought not to be accounted matters of mere interpretation. See especially, Hastings Rashdall, *The Universities of the Middle Ages*, 3 vols., (edd.) F. M. Powicke and A. B. Emden, London, Oxford University Press, 1936. Newman wrote twenty essays/articles for Dublin's *Catholic University Gazette* (1854–56), which were republished (1856) as *Office and Work of Universities*. Later still (1872), these essays were re-titled *Rise and Progress of Universities*, and reprinted on three occasions [London, B. M. Pickering, 1872, and 1881; London, Longmans, Green, 1913] as part of Newman's three-volume *Historical Sketches*. Recently, *Rise and Progress of Universities* has appeared separately. See Newman, *Rise and Progress of Universities and Benedictine Essays*, Notre Dame, IN, University of Notre Dame Press, 2001. These essays have, on occasion, been construed as recording the history of the University. But the School of Athens was not a University, but rather an "ideological prototype." Further, prior to the rise of medieval studies in the late nineteenth and early twentieth centuries, historical documentation of the University, as provided by Hastings Rashdall, Charles Homer Haskins, and others, was unavailable. Technically, then, Newman's *Rise and Progress* does not constitute a history of Europe's universities, but does provide an anticipatory intellectual typology of the University. Newman was, plausibly, imaginatively constructing—rather than recording—University history.

8. Quoted in Pierre J. Marique, *A History of Christian Education*, I, p. 188. See especially, Hastings Rashdall, *The Universities of the Middle Ages*, I, pp. 4–20.

9. Hastings Rashdall, *The Universities of the Middle Ages*, III, p. 442.

10. Sheldon Rothblatt, *The Modern University and Its Discontents: The Fate of Newman's Legacies in Britain and America*, Cambridge, Cambridge University Press, 1977. Allowing that his "is not a work about John Henry Newman," the author asserts that Newman's name should be mentioned in the title because "every educational ideal" that Newman held is "irrelevant" to the modern world.

11. Owen Chadwick, "The University of Mount Zion," in *The Spirit of the Oxford Movement: Tractarian Essays*, Cambridge, Cambridge University Press, 1990: "If he had a real university to run, the *Idea of a University* could not have been written with a straight face" (pp. 99–100). Jaroslav Pelikan, *The Idea of a University: A Reexamination*, New Haven, CT, Yale University Press, 1992. Roy Jenkins, Lord Jenkins of Hillhead, "Newman and *The Idea of a University*," in *Newman: A Man for Our Time*, David Brown (ed.), London, SPCK, 1990, p. 157. J. M. Roberts, "*The Idea of a University* Revisited," in *Newman after a Hundred Years*, (edd.) Ian Ker and Alan G. Hill, Oxford, Clarendon Press, 1990, pp. 193–222. This author assumes Newman to be "a great apostate, or . . . an austere saintly teacher" (p. 219). Robert's implication is this: What Newman tells us we already know, and what we need to know, he doesn't bother to tell us. Contrast such words with those of Pope John Paul II in his centenary letter, which says that Newman's "remarkable life . . . continues to inspire, to uplift, and to enlighten" (letter of 18 June 1990, *L 'Osservatore Romano* [English edition, 16 July 1990, 1149]). On 22 January 1991, Cardinal Newman was declared Venerable by Pope John Paul II (*L 'Osservatore Romano*, 28 January 1991).

12. John Henry Newman, *The Idea of a University, Defined and Illustrated*, London, Longmans, Green, 1898, Discourse V. 1, pp. 101–102.

13. Ibid., V. 6, p. 139; VII. 10, p. 178.

14. Trivium and Quadrivium constituted the medieval liberal arts and sciences. Trivium comprised grammar, rhetoric, and logic, whereas Quadrivium consisted of geometry, arithmetic, astrology-astronomy, and harmonics. They were popularized in a fifth-century prose-verse work, *De Nuptiis Mercurii et Philologiae*—"Wedding of Mercury [prosperity] and Philologia [love of learning, scholarship]," by North African, Martianus Minneus Felix Capella. For Martianus, see *De Nuptiis Mercurii et Philologiae*, (ed.) A. Dick, Leipzig, Germany, Teubner, 1925. See also Hastings Rashdall, *The Universities of the Middle Ages*, I, pp. 34–37; E. K. Rand, *Founders of the Middle Ages*, New York, Dover, 1957, pp. 228–30. For educational background, see H. I. Marrou, A *History of Education in Antiquity*, (trans.) George Lamb, New York, Mentor / New American Library, 1964, pp. 369–99. See also R. R. Bolgar, *The Classical Heritage and Its Beneficiaries, from the Carolingian Age to the End of the Renaissance*, New York, Harper & Row, 1964, pp. 30–45. For the rhetorical influence of Cicero on liberal arts, see Charles Norris Cochrane, *Christianity and Classical Culture: A Study of Thought and Action from Augustus to Augustine*, New York, Galaxy/Oxford University Press, 1957, pp. 38–61, 146.

15. *The Idea of a University*, VI. 8, p. 142, VI. 10, p. 149.

16. Ibid., V. 2, p. 103.

17. Ibid., V. 2, p. 104. Compare this language with the statement that "a University does but contemplate a necessity of our nature" (*Rise and Progress of Universities and Benedictine Essays*, p. 6).

18. *The Idea of a University*, VI. 8, pp. 144–45.

19. Ibid., VI. 8, p. 145.

20. *Rise and Progress of Universities and Benedictine Essays*, pp. 6–8.

21. Ibid., pp. 8–9.

22. Ibid., p. 10.

23. Ibid., pp. 14–15.

24. Ibid., p. 16.

25. *The Idea of a University*, pp. xv–xvi, VI. 1, pp. 125–26.

26. Ibid., VI. 4, p. 130. "The pages which follow," says Newman in a footnote, "are taken almost verbatim from the author's 14th (Oxford) University Sermon" [Sermon XIV, "Wisdom, as Contrasted with Faith and with Bigotry"]. This borrowing should not be surprising, if only because the Idea is not merely an instructional title, but a pastoral tract. Pastoral teacher, and teaching pastor, Newman was interested in both the "sanctification of learning," and the "learning of sanctification."

27. *Fifteen Sermons Preached Before the University of Oxford*, Notre Dame, IN, University of Notre Dame Press, 1997, p. 293.

28. *The Idea of a University*, VI. 6, p. 139.

29. See below, Chapter 2, note 2.

30. *The Idea of a University*, VI. 6, p. 137.

31. "Poetry, with Reference to Aristotle's Poetics," in *Essays and Sketches*, 3 vols., (ed.) Charles Frederick Harrold, Westport , CT, Greenwood Press, 1970, I, p. 74.

32. See Etienne Gilson, *History of Christian Philosophy in the Middle Ages*, pp. 535–36. Christian sensitivity to the notion of infinity, says Gilson, "is at the core of the metaphysics of Nicholas of Cues. . . . In short, the infinite is the absolute and perfect coincidence of contraries" (*De doctrina ignorantia* I. 2).

33. Wilfrid Ward, *Men and Matters*, Freeport, NY, Books for Libraries, 1968, pp. 287–88.

34. See Jan H. Walgrave, O. P., *Newman the Theologian*, (trans.) A. V. Littledale, New York, Sheed & Ward, 1960. Fr. Walgrave uses the phrase "unstable equilibrium" (p. 327), and there quotes Paul Sobry's formula of "deep-seated dualism." See also Terrence Merrigan, *Clear Heads and Holy Hearts: The Religious and Theological Ideal of John Henry Newman*, Louvain, Peeters Press, 1999. As a disciple of Fr. Walgrave, this author uses the terms polarity and unity-intension (pp. 7ff.). See, too, Lee H. Yearly, *The Ideas of Newman: Christianity and Religiosity*, London, Pennsylvania State University Press, 1978. The author says Newman "tries to stand in both a traditional and a modern world," and "reflects the tensions of these two worlds," which requires "using polar oppositions" (pp. ix–x).

35. Ian Ker, *John Henry Newman: A Biography*, Oxford, Oxford University Press, 1990, p. viii. What Homer says of Odysseus, in the first line of

the Odyssey, also applies to Newman as a man of "many-layered mind" (πολύτροπος).

36. "Intellect, the Instrument of Religious Training," in *Sermons Preached on Various Occasions*, Westminster, MD, Christian Classics, 1968, p. 8.

37. See Geoffrey Faber, *Oxford Apostles*, London, Faber & Faber, 1933. Faber (later Sir Geoffrey, great-nephew of the orator, Frederick W. Faber) charges Newman with inconsistency, including that of probably being Jewish (p. 4), and of "suspect" gender (p. 32). He makes much of alleged inconsistencies of Newman's personality. Owen Chadwick, "The University of Mount Zion," pp. 177–78, asserts "a chief contradiction in Newman's personality," first suggested by Henri Bremond. (*Newman: Essai de biographie psychologique*, Paris, Librarie Bloud, 1906; translated, *The Mystery of Newman*, [trans.] H. C. Corrance, London, Williams & Norgate, 1907.) Chadwick seems also to imply that Newman suffered a "personality disorder," or "dissociative disorder," first popularized in 1888 by French neurologist Pierre Janet. (See John H. Talbot, M.D., et al., *Textbook of Psychiatry*, Washington, DC, American Psychiatric Press, 1988, pp. 557–85.) Propositions and positions may be contradictory or have contradictions. Personality, however, is neither propositional nor positional, and to apply logical categories to psychological phenomena denotes a fundamentally flawed technique. Chadwick also charges Newman with separating "mental from ethical development" (p. 103). [See also "severance" argument, see below, note 52.]

38. Garry Wills, *Papal Sin, Structures of Deceit*, New York, Doubleday/Image, 2000, p. 262. See also his *Why I Am a Catholic*, Boston, Houghton Mifflin, 2002, pp. 285ff.

39. Louis Bouyer, *Newman: His Life and Spirituality*, (trans.) H. F. Davis, London, Burns Oates & Washbourne, 1958, p. 387.

40. Sean O'Faòlain, *Newman's Way*, New York, Devin-Adair, 1952. "This youth, for whom the world was a shadow, had a character of iron" (p. 63).

41. For more than a century, language centers have been identified in the brain's left hemisphere, specifically in that area at the foot of the third frontal convolution of the cerebral cortex, known as Broca's area, named for Parisian surgeon Paul Broca (1824–80), and that area at the posterior third of the upper temporal convolution, known as Wernicke's area, named for the German neurologist Carl Wernicke (1848–1905). The former controls expressive language, the latter, semantics and language comprehension. The language genius of the right brain, however, awaits further investigation.

42. See below, Chapter 5, notes 58–70.

43. John Henry Newman, *An Essay on the Development of Christian Doctrine*, New York, Doubleday/Image, 1960, p. 311.

44. For example, Newman's contrastive statement: "As prayer is the voice of man to God, so revelation is the voice of God to men" (*An Essay in Aid of a Grammar of Assent*, London, Longmans, Green, 1947, p. 307).

45. *The Idea of a University*, V. 9, p. 120.

46. Ibid., VII. 5, pp. 163–64.

47. Ibid., p. 164.

48. Ibid., VII. 6, p. 165.

49. Ibid., p. xvi.

50. Ibid., VII. 6, pp. 165–66.

51. Ibid., VII. 9, pp. 177–78; IX. 8, p. 232.

52. Dichotomy, rather than congruence, says one critic, shapes Newman's contrast of intellectual-moral aspects of University life. See Timothy Corcoran, S. J., "Liberal Studies and Moral Aims: A Critical Study of Newman's Position," in Thought 1 (1926), 54–71, and also *Newman: Selected Discourses on Liberal Knowledge*, Dublin, University College, 1929. Newman's alleged "severance" of moral and intellectual aspects of education, he says, makes it impossible for the University to become "an instrument of the Church." In contrast, John E. Wise, S. J., "Newman and the Liberal Arts," *Thought* 20 (1945), 253–70, persuasively argues the opposite case. Reprinted in *American Essays for the Newman Centennial*, (edd.) J. K. Ryan and E. D. Benard, Washington, Catholic University of America Press, 1947, pp. 133–50. A similar supportive argument for congruence was advanced by Fernande Tardivel, *John Henry Newman, Éducateur*, Paris, Beauchesnes, 1937.

53. Conscience symbolically refers to moral power, as contrasted with wisdom, symbolic of intellectual power. The terms also "understudy" other contrasts—e.g., between devotion and learning, religion and education, faith and understanding, and Church and University.

CHAPTER 2:   INTELLECT
NEWMAN EPIGRAPHS:

> "Intellectual culture"—The Idea of a University, VII. 4, p. 162.
> "Cultivation"—The Idea of a University, V. 2, p. 103.
> "Faith"—*Development of Christian Doctrine*, p. 311.
> "No one can deny"—University Sermons, IV, p. 57.

1. Aristotle asserts that "the intellectual part [τοῦ γὰρ διανοητικοῦ] . . . appears to be a man's real self" [ὅπερ ἕκαστος εἶναι δοκεῖ, *Ethica Nicomachia*, 1166a 16–17]. Again, "if then the intellect is something divine [εἰ δὴ θεῖον ὁ νοῦς] in comparison with man . . . it may even be held that this is the true self of each (1177b 31–32, 1178a 2–3)." St. Augustine argued similarly in saying that "mind and spirit are not names of relations, but denominate the essence (*De Trinitate*, 9.2; *Patrologia Latina*, 42. 962A)."

St. Thomas thought otherwise, and argued that the human "intellect is a power of the soul, and not the very essence of the soul. . . . In God alone is His act of understanding the same as His very Being. Hence in God alone is His intellect His essence ... in other creatures the intellect is a power (*Summa theologiae*, I, q. 79, a.1 Resp.)." Previously, he observed (*Summa theologiae*, I, q. 54, a.3 Resp.) that "in every creature the essence differs from the being, and is compared to it as potentiality is to act, as is evident from what has been already said" (a reference to *Summa theologiae*, I, q. 44, a. 1). He also acknowledged that the "crowning" attribute of the human person—and thus of the human intellect—is its possibility of "beatitude." The human intellect's potential is to "acquire universal and perfect goodness, because he [man] can acquire beatitude (*Summa theologiae*, I, q. 77, a. 2)." He then asserts (against St. Augustine and St. Bernard of Clairvaux) that "the intellect, in itself and absolutely, is higher and nobler than the will," because "the Philosopher holds the intellect to be the highest power of the soul (Summa theologiae, I, q. 82, a. 3)." The Philosopher he refers to is Aristotle, who, in the *Ethica*, says that "the intellect is the highest thing in us, and the objects with which the intellect deals are the highest things that can be known" :--καὶ γὰρ ὁ νοῦς τῶν ἐν ἡμῖν. καὶ τῶν γνωστῶν, περὶ ἃ ὁ νοῦς, *Eth. Nic.*, 1177a21-22.

Unlike Aristotle, St. Thomas regards the human intellect as being "in the lowest degree, according to his [man's] nature, of those to whom beatitude is possible (*Summa theologiae*, I, q. 77, a. 2)." That is to say, farthest displaced from the perfection of the divine intellect: *Humanis intellectus est infimus in ordine intellectuum et maximae remotus a perfectione divini intellectus (Questiones disputatae de anima*, qu. un. art. I, ad Resp.), quoted in Etienne Gilson, *The Philosophy of St. Thomas Aquinas*, (trans.) Edward Bullough, New York, Dorset, 1948, p. 217. St Thomas's view that intellect "can acquire beatitude" suggests St. Bonaventura's conception of the human person (intellect) as *capax Dei*, "capable of God" (*Comm. in II Libr. Sent.*, 19, I, I, resp.).

In *Bereshith-Genesis* (1:26–27) God (divine intellect) is what mankind (human intellect) is created "in image of." The term image—*ts'lehm*, (צלם)—carries a sense of "shadow or shade," and something "cut out." See Brown-Driver-Briggs, Hebrew and English Lexicon, Peabody, MA, Hendrickson, 1979, p. 853b, which renders image as "Schnitzbild," or "scissored-out illustration." The *Genesis-Bereshith* phrasing, "in image of us," *b'tsalmaynu* (בצלמנו) and "in image of God," *b'tsehlehm Eloheem* (בצלם אלהים) appear equivalent to what St. Thomas means by divine intellectus.

In his *Oxford Sermons*, Newman could not slip into Thomistic formulation because, at that period, he believed that intellect meant "refined pagan intellect," and that "in the Old Testament scarcely any mention is made of the existence of the reason as a distinct and chief attribute of the mind," since there is a "silence of Scripture concerning intellectual excellence . . . and intellectual gifts." See Sermon IV, "The Usurpation of Reason," in *Fifteen Sermons Preached Before the University of Oxford*, Notre Dame, IN, University of

Notre Dame Press, 1997, pp. 55–58. Hebrew has absolutely no word for intellect; intellect is a Greco-Roman word *and* idea. In this light, it is interesting to compare Newman's intellectual growth from the period of his Oxford University sermons (1826–43) to his Dublin University sermons. From age 25 to age 42, Newman had not reached the point where he could cite (so casually it seems now) the phrase, "the cultivation of intellect," as appears in his Dublin University Discourses at age 51.

We suggest, then, that the phrase "the privilege of intellect" implies the power (1) to fulfill the vocation of being aware of the presence of God, and (2) to acknowledge intellect as being capax Dei, or "capable of beatitude." For our ensuing argument, the phrase "the privilege of intellect"—together with its religious subtext of "using the mind well"—provides the foundation upon which Newman's idea of "perfecting the intellect" might have been constructed. This, indeed, the argument of this book.

2. Intellect has both Latin (*legere*) and Greek (*legein*—λέγειν; logos—λόγος) roots. See *Freund's Latin Dictionary*, (edd.) Charlton T. Lewis and Charles Short, Oxford, Clarendon Press, 1958. Latin legere is a compound concept for collecting-reading (pp. 1047–48). See also Henry George Liddell and Robert Scott, *Greek Lexicon*, Oxford, Clarendon Press, 1984, which suggests that the Greek λέγειν (*gathering-counting-speaking*) includes the meanings (1) lay-lie, (2) arrange-gather, (3) reckon-count, and (4) recount-relate-say (p. 408). The related root in Greek λόγος includes the meanings (1) word, and (2) thought (pp. 416–17). See also Eric Partridge, *Origins*, New York, Greenwich House, 1983, which distinguishes a phylum *legere-legein* terms under lead-word legend (pp. 345–48), comprising derivatives such as *diligent, selection, lexicon, analogy, dialogue, logic*, and *syllogism*. Another phylum of juridical legere words, under lead-word legal (pp. 344–45), includes *college, colleague, legitimate, legacy*, and *loyalty*. For *privilege*, Partridge's lead-word is *private* (p. 527), whereas, *Freund's* describes *privilegium* as *privus-lex*, "a bill or law in favor of, or against, an individual (p. 1447)." *Freund's* lists primary intellectus terms (p. 974). See also *Oxford English Dictionary*, 2nd ed., Oxford, Clarendon Press, 1989. *OED* does not speculate on origins, but simply lists usages. For intellect, see *OED*, VII, 1067; for privilege, see OED, XII, 522. *The Compact Edition of the Oxford English Dictionary*, Oxford, Oxford University Press, 1983, lists *intellect* in I, 1455–56, and *privilege* in II, 2307.

3.   *le gente dolorose*
        c'hanno perduto il ben de l'intelletto
                        —Inferno, 3. 17–18.

Newman characterized the most painful experience of Hell as perhaps being solitary. See his *Sermon Notes*, (edd.) Fathers of the Birmingham Oratory, Notre Dame, IN, University of Notre Dame Press, 2000, pp. 199, 251.

4.   *mai non si sazia nostro intelletto, se 'l ver non lo*
                illustra di fuor dal qual nessun vero si spazia
                              —*Paradiso*, 4. 124–28. See also Canto 33:

I was confronted with the Infinite Treasure. . . .
In its profundity I saw, internalized, Clasped by love, as if in
    a single space,
What in the universe is scattered abroad.
                              —*Paradiso*, 33. 81, 85–87.

5. John's Gospel (1:9) identifies that light as the Logos-Christ—"He was the true light which enlightens every human being."

6. John Henry Newman, *The Idea of a University*, Defined and Illustrated, London, Longmans, Green, 1898, VIII. 3, p. 186.

7. The iconic language of Genesis-Bereshith 1:26 is this: "Then God said 'let us make humankind in image of us, in likeness of us'"; *v'yohmer Eloheem n'ehseh 'adam b'tsalmaynu keedmotnu*—

ונתומרב זנמלצב סרא השענ סיהלא רמאיו:

The verse which follows this P (Priestly-text) formula (1:27) is unquestionably bi-gendered: "So, God created the humankind in image of him, in image of God he created him, male and female he created them"; *veyeebrah' Eloheem at hah'adam b'tselmoh b'tselem Eloheem bahrah' 'otov zakar vu n'qayvah bahrah' 'otahm*—

סתא ארב הבקנו רבז ותא סיהלא סלצב ומלצב סראה תא סיהלא ארביו:

Eloheem-God creates humankind ('*adam*, סרא) gendered as *male* (zakar, רבז) and female (*n'qayvah*, הבקנ). This bi-gendered icon, *zakar-n'qayvah*, provides the original foundation of Imago Dei doctrines, in Judaism and in Christianity. The more popular J (Yahveh-text) formula (2:18 ff.) stipulates that the female is taken from Adam's rib (mankind-rib, *hatsaylah'*, עלצה), which is made into woman (*l'eeshah*, השאל). Thus, in word play on 'eesh /'eesha (השיא/ שיא) [man / woman], mankind-Adam, as a man [vir; 'eesh] (שיא), calls her woman ('eesha, אישה), because she was "taken" from a man (*may'aheesh*, מאיש). Also, while mankind ('adam) is generic, that same generic name (hah 'adam, red-earth-mankind) will become, in fact, a proper name—Adam. Subsequently—that is, after the Fall—the woman-wife ('eesha, השיא /שיא) will, by Adam, be called Eve (khavah, חוה), meaning "life"—"because she would become the mother of all the living" (3:20).

8. Three points need to be made about intellective and infra-intellective knowing. (1) Intellect is mankind's sole agency of semantic—or meaning-in-

tensive—knowing, including self-knowing and self-reflection. In a parallel sense, like other animals, mankind has a capacity to be aware neuro-somatically or infra-intellectually, which is why we speak of "animal intelligence," but do not speak of "animal intellect." Neuro-somatic awareness (roughly, knowing), however, is absolutely distinct from human knowing. Such a difference was doubtless in Newman's mind when he refused to predicate knowledge "of the brute creation." (See *The Idea of a University*, V. 6, pp. 112–13.)

(1) One specialized kind of human infra-intellectual awareness is found in the limbic (or "border") cortex, described by Paul Broca in 1878, which, surrounding the human brain stem, determines certain autonomic or motor responses. It administers (through the amygdala) a repertoire of behavioral-emotive functions (e.g., fear-anger). Neuroanatomy, with its electro-ionic activity, is the basis for processing neuro-somatic information, which a mammalian body requires for its reaction and survival skills, as in the case of fight or flight. See Peter Brown, M. D., *The Hypnotic Brain: Hypnotherapy and Social Communication*, New Haven, CT, Yale University Press, 1991.

(2) All human knowing involves intellect in however indirect a manner, and reaches above and beyond sense experience. See J. F. Donceel, S. J., *Philosophical Anthropology,* New York, Sheed & Ward, 1967). He says, "The intellect . . . although it needs the collaboration of the senses, transcends the domain of the senses and can reach suprasensory reality. . . . The point of view of the intellect is not relative but absolute" (p. 350). Fr. Donceel is also helpful in clarifying usage of the terms, *intellect, reason,* and *understanding,* by noting that the ancients referred to the lower aspect of mind as ratio (reason), and the high aspect as *intellectus* (intellect), while the moderns, in this same respect, use the terms *understanding* and *reason.* He suggests calling (with the moderns) the lower aspect *understanding,* and (with the ancients) the higher aspect intellect (See J. F. Donceel, S. J., *Philosophical Anthropology*, p. 349, note 13; p. 364.)

(3) Human knowing of the intellect necessarily functions through the human brain's 10 billion to 13 billion cells, in conjunction with the Central Nervous System (CNS). See Sir Charles Sherrington, *Man on His Nature: The Gifford Lectures*, 2nd ed., Cambridge, Cambridge University Press, 1951, pp. 186, 208. Clearly, the brain is not intellect, nor is intellect the brain. Nor is the brain's frontal lobe—usually considered the executive area of the cerebral cortex—the same as intellect. The brain, however, in an evolutionary sense, is the condition for the existential presence of human intellect. We can say—as we, ironically, are driven back upon our own metaphor—that the human intellect takes up "residence" in the neural complex of the brain. Which means that the highly organized CNS structure provides, for intellect, a neurological habitat.

9. *The Idea of a University*, IV. 1, p. 72. *An Essay in Aid of a Grammar of Assent*, London, Longmans, Green, 1947, p. 174.

10. See John Henry Newman, *The Letters and Diaries of John Henry*

Newman, (ed.) Charles Stephen Dessain, London, Thomas Nelson, 1962. Because he was an Englishman, Newman in his correspondence often employed the symbolism of heart. At the time of his conversion (October 1845), a letter to his aunt Elizabeth says, "He alone knows how much you are in my heart, or how it pierces my heart so to distress you." To his sister Jemima, he writes, "There is One who knows how much it has lain upon my heart to pain you." To Maria Giberne, "I have received most abundant cordial simple-hearted kindness." To the Marquise de Salvo, "Your letter announcing your conversion gave me the most heartfelt satisfaction." To Ambrose St. John, "Faber's pamphlet . . . is the recipe, the specific, to close simply and entirely the hearts of such as Pusey." To Pusey, "A number of persons are making great sacrifices [and] . . . their brethren, who feel called to remain . . . have the heart to scrutinize the details of their manner." To Mrs. Bowden, "There are many individual hearts who feel a sympathy with me." Newman's close friend, H. W. Wilberforce, also writes him on 5 October 1845, that "my heart has been full of you all day," while Faber writes, "The bishop seems out of heart." *The Letters and Diaries*, XII, pp. 4, 14–15, 102, 105, 117–18, 124, 126.

11. "Intellect, the Instrument of Religious Training," in *Sermons Preached on Various Occasions,* Westminster, MD, Christian Classics, 1968, pp. 5–6.

12. Ibid., pp. 6–7.

13. Ibid., pp. 7–8.

14. Ibid., p. 12.

15. Ibid., p. 13.

16. John 1:1—". . . and the Word was God," and John 1:9—"He was the true light which enlightens every man." There is also 1 John 1:5–7, with the reaffirmation of the theme of light: "God is light . . . if we live our lives in the light, as he is in the light, we are in union with one another." The Love theme— "God is Love"—is in 1 John 4:8 and 1 John 4:16.

17. St. Thomas uses *ex aequo* the terms *intellect, reason,* and mind— "Therefore reason, intellect, and mind are one power" (Summa theologiae, I, q 79, a 8, Resp.). For our purpose, intellect (*intellectus*) is preeminently the center of the human mind's semantic luxuriance. In contrast, reason (*ratio*) ambiguously connotes both the "lower" form of mind, and the instrument of logical reasoning. Although reason derives its power from intellect, it is not precisely the same as intellect.

18. St. Anselm (1033–1109) observes that "truth in an affirmation is simply its rectitude" (V: 178, 25). Thus, he says, "We can define truth as the rightness perceptible only to the mind" (V: 191, 19–20). See also V: 191, 27–31; 192, 2–3, 6–8. S. *Anselmi Opera Omnia*, 2 Tom. (ed.) Franciscus Salesius Schmitt, Stuttgart, Friedrich Fromann, 1968. For Anselm, the noetic linkage of truth and justice (oughtness) is often referred to as "moral epistemology." He rephrased an insight of his mentor, Lanfranc, that "Truth is justice in words"— based on Rom. 3:4, "In all you say your justice shows"—into the phrase "Jus-

tice is truth in action." See R. W. Southern, *St. Anselm: Portrait in a Landscape*, Cambridge, Cambridge University Press, 1990, p. 42, note 5; p. 172.

19. "Faith and Love," in *Parochial and Plain Sermons*, San Francisco, Ignatius Press, 1987, IV.21, p.924.

20. There are psychiatric occurrences of disconnection between mind and reality, which range from relatively mild (e.g., "slip of the tongue," *lapsus linguae, parapraxis*, or misaction, which Freud considered symptomatic of something more significant) to severe delusional states, as in schizophrenias or schizoform/schizotypal disease—that is, from neurosis (reality-testing unimpaired, with no underlying severe abnormality of personality) to psychosis (gross impairment of reality-testing, because of organic brain damage or functional impairment). Now, because neuroses generate defense mechanisms, a parallel point needs to be made. One defense mechanism is called "intellectualization" (the opposite of what it seems to mean), which substitutes psychologically "safe ideas" for "dangerous ideas." Furthermore, intellectualization is, by definition, unconscious, and thus repressional. It is thus distinctly at odds with the term *intellect*, as we have so far used it. A similar distortion is contained in the term *rationalization* which gives a bad name to serious actions otherwise considered rational. See Sigmund Freud, SE XII, pp. 109–120. See also Robert Jean Campbell, M.D., *Psychiatric Dictionary*, 6th ed., New York, Oxford University Press, 1989.

21. *My Campaign in Ireland*, edited by William P. Neville, printed for private circulation, Aberdeen, A. King & Co., 1896, p. 120.

22. *An Essay in Aid of a Grammar of Assent*, p. 83.

23. *The Idea of a University*, IV. 3, pp. 74–75.

24. True, there are meteorological forms of energy which are independent of life. But these are conditionally initiated, and are not self-initiators. A hurricane, for example is an energy system, provided it has the proper conditions of elevated water and air temperatures, vast expanses of water, and appropriate steering winds. The hurricane is formed by such conditions. It does not, like a heartbeat, initiate itself.

25. In the self-activating pumping muscle of the heart (really two self-activating pumps), the sinoatrial node—a small bundle of specialized muscle fiber (myocardium) in the rear wall of the right atrium—spontaneously initiates an electrical excitation, which activates a systolic/diastolic, contraction/expansion motion of the heart, and, by means of the vascular system, moves nutrient blood through the body. Contraction/expansion is detectable as a pulse in several peripheral bilateral parts of the human body—e.g., carotid, brachial, radial, femoral, popliteal, dorsal-pedal, and posterior-tibial pulse.

26. See *The Idea of a University*, V. 1, p. 102.

27. Ibid., VI. 6, pp. 137, 138. This passage contrasts with one from Newman's University Sermon XIV, "Wisdom, as Contrasted with Faith and Bigotry" (See *Fifteen Sermons Preached Before the University of Oxford*, p. 292).

Set side by side (below), they illustrate how Newman recrafted the original text. A. represents the University Sermon text, and B. is the *Idea* text:

A. But Philosophy

B. *But the intellect, which has been disciplined to the perfection of its powers, which knows and thinks while it knows, which has learned to leaven the dense mass of facts and events and the elastic force of reason, such an intellect*

A. cannot be partial, cannot be exclusive, cannot be impetuous,

B. *cannot be partial, cannot be exclusive, cannot be impetuous,*

A. cannot be surprised, cannot fear, cannot lose its balance, cannot be at a loss, cannot but be patient, collected, and majestically calm,

B. *cannot be at a loss, cannot but be patient, collected, and majestically calm,*

A. because it discerns the whole in each part, the end in each beginning,

B. *because it discerns the end in every beginning, the origin in every end,*

A. the worth of each interruption, the measure of each delay,

B. *the law in every interruption, the limit in each delay,*

A. because it always knows where it is, and how its path lies from one point to another.

B. *because it ever knows where it stands, and how its path lies from one point to another.*

28. In Gal. 5:22, St. Paul cites patience ($\mu\alpha\kappa\rho o\theta\upsilon\mu i\alpha$ —i.e., *longanimitas*) as the fourth of the fruits of the spirit ($\dot{o}\ \delta\dot{\varepsilon}\ \kappa\alpha\rho\grave{o}\varsigma\ \tau o\hat{\upsilon}\ \pi\nu\varepsilon\acute{\upsilon}\mu\alpha\tau\acute{o}\varsigma$). Paul's term for patience combines the idea of "far stretching" ($\mu\alpha\kappa\rho\acute{o}\varsigma$) and "sacrifice" ($\tau\acute{o}\ \theta\hat{\upsilon}\mu\alpha$, from the verb $\theta\acute{\upsilon}\omega$, "I sacrifice"). See Walter Bauer (trans. Arndt-Gingrich), *A Greek-English Lexicon of the New Testament*, 2nd ed., Chicago, University of Chicago Press, 1979, pp. 488, 365. In *Galatians*, the virtue of patience is in impressive company, namely, that of love, joy, peace, and faith. Cf. other *New Testament* references to patience (Lk. 21:19; *Rom.* 15:4–5; *Col.* 1:11; 1 *Thes.* 1:3; 2 *Thes.* 1:4; 1 *Tim.* 6:11; 2 *Tim.* 3:10). That John Henry Newman chose this term, patience, may indicate, once again, his willingness to associate a *moral* term with an *intellective* power.

29. *The Idea of a University*, VIII. 4, pp. 189–90.

CHAPTER 3:   CHURCH AND UNIVERSITY
NEWMAN EPIGRAPHS:

"The Catholic Church"—*The Idea of a University*, I. 2, p. 7.

"To maintain"—"Christianity and Scientific Investigation," Idea, p. 457.

"University . . . [is]"—*The Idea of a University*, IX. 1, pp. 214–15.

"University is an intellectual"—*Rise and Progress*, XIX, p. 231.

1. See *John Henry Newman Autobiographical Writings*, (ed.) Henry Tristram, New York, Sheed & Ward, 1957. "In the Church of England, I had many detractors; a mass of calumny was hurled at me; my services towards that Church were misrepresented by almost everyone in authority in it. . . . I was oppressed and lost hope. And now the cheerfulness I used to have has almost vanished." As a Catholic priest, he recorded the hostile rumor and backbiting of Rome, "so far from being thought engaged in any good work, I am simply discouraged and regarded suspiciously by the governing powers as doing an actual harm" (pp. 247, 259).

See also *The Letters and Diaries of John Henry Newman*, (ed.) Charles Stephen Dessain, et al., London, Thomas Nelson, 1963. Newman writes Ambrose St. John, "I go to Rome to be snubbed. I come to Dublin to be repelled by Dr. Hale [Archbishop of Tuam] and worn away by Dr. Cullen [Archbishop of Dublin, Irish Primate]. The Cardinal [Wiseman, English Primate] taunts me with his Dedications and Fr. Faber [head of the Brompton Oratory in London] insults me with his letters" (XVIII, p. 426).

See also Wilfrid Ward, T*he Life of John Henry Cardinal Newman, Based on His Private Journals and Correspondence*, 2 vols., London, Longmans, Green, 1912. Newman advises Henry Wilberforce, in 1870, that Catholic critics "say that this remark was illogical, and that unheard of, a third realistic, a fourth idealistic, a fifth sceptical, and a sixth temerarious, or shocking to pious ears" (II, p. 454). The "most dangerous man in England" remark occurs in a letter from Msgr. George Talbot, English papal chamberlain in Rome, to Archbishop Henry Edward Manning. See, Wilfrid Ward, II, p. 147; and pp. 145–50. See also Ian Ker, *John Henry Newman: A Biography*, Oxford, Oxford University Press, 1990, pp. 597–600, 611–12, 715–18; Meriol Trevor, *Newman: Pillar of the Cloud*, New York, Doubleday, 1962; *Newman: Light in Winter*, London, Macmillan, 1962.

2. Newman knew much about courage because, in many ways, he personified it. He said, "Courage does not consist in calculation, but in fighting against chances," Sermon XI, "The Nature of Faith in Relation to Reason," in *Fifteen Sermons Preached Before the University of Oxford*, Notre Dame, IN, University of Notre Dame Press, 1997, p. 210.

3. Much disinformation about Newman concerns his genealogy. See *The Cambridge Guide to Literature in English*, (ed.) Ian Ousby, Cambridge, Cambridge University Press, 1988, which cites "John Henry Newman, Theologian. Of Huguenot and Jewish descent" (p. 713). But see Louis Bouyer, Newman, *His Life and Spirituality*, London, Burns Oates & Washbourne, 1958. Fr. Bouyer meets this issue head-on: "The notion that he was of Jewish descent, which rests on nothing more substantial than the contour of his nose and his father's line of business, may be dismissed as the purest fantasy" (p. 1). See Geoffrey Faber, *Oxford Apostles: A Character Study of the Oxford Movement*, London, Faber & Faber, 1933. He speculates thus: "It is not easy to dismiss the

idea that there was Jewish blood in the Newman of some of the Oxford-period portraits. . . . It is borne out—at least it is not contradicted—by his own aptitude for business and for figures, his habit of closely scrutinizing tradesmen's accounts, and by his father's profession, which was that of a banker" (pp. 4–5). See also William Barry, *Newman*, London, Hodder & Stoughton, 1904. Barry (perhaps the initiator of this "genealogy") states that Newman was "this clerical Fellow of Oriel, who was not by origin either Catholic or English" (p. 8). After an unpalatable litany, Barry states,

> These particulars . . . will prepare us for the fact that in an earlier generation the family had spelt its signature "Newmann"; that it was understood to be of Dutch origin; and that its real descent was Hebrew. The talent for music, calculation, and business, the untiring energy, legal acumen, and dislike of speculative metaphysics, which were conspicuous in John Henry, bear out this interesting genealogy. A large part of his character will become intelligible if we keep it in mind. That his features had a strong Jewish cast, is evident from his portraits, and was especially to be noted in old age. It may be conjectured that the migration of these Dutch Jews in England fell within a period not very distant from the death of Spinoza in 1675. [Spinoza died in 1677.] But the qualities he inherited from his mother's family cannot be left out of account. The Fourdriniers were French by descent and Huguenots into the bargain (pp. 9–10).

This is speculation disguised as evidence. But Barry proceeds,

> We smile at these things; all the more if there was scarcely in the veins of our great genius one drop of English blood . . . for his views are English-Hebrew, and, in the long run, his method is not Greek. This should be clearly understood. Drawing out refined trains of argument, subtle in exposition, he seems to wield a dialectic borrowed from the Porch or the Academy; but it is not so. . . . [H]is pages are composed in the forecourt of the Temple. . . . In minds unsympathetic, [there is] a suspicion that [his] . . . sentiments are too beautiful to be true. . . . To strangers he seems cold and distant (pp. 231–32, 234–35, 259).

See also Wilfrid Ward, *The Life of John Henry Cardinal Newman*. Newman's "Jewish genealogy" disturbed Ward, who "was at pains to ascertain the evidence for the alleged Jewish descent of the Newman family, and it proved to be a curious instance of how stories grow out of nothing." Ward contacted Barry, who "in answer to my inquiries, referred me to the article on J. H. Newman in the Encyclopedia Britannica as his authority." Ward then says, "I happened to know personally the writer in the Encyclopedia Britannica and communicated with him. In reply he pointed out that he had in his article never alleged Jewish descent as a fact, but only suggested its possibility. 'There is no evidence of it,' he added, 'except the nose and the name.' For those, then, who agree with the present writer that the nose was Roman rather than Jewish, the evidence remains simply that the name *Newman* betokens Hebrew origin—a bold experiment in the higher criticism" (I, pp. 27–29, note 2).

Wilfrid Ward also appended to his Life a genealogical summary of the Fourdrinier family (I, pp. 614ff.). See also (his daughter) Maisie Ward, *Young Mr. Newman*, New York, Sheed & Ward, 1948, who likewise considered the genealogy issue (p. 1). For other genealogy charts, see Sean O'Faòlain, *Newman's Way: The Odyssey of John Henry Newman*, New York, Devin-Adair, 1952, pp. xv, 328.

The Newmans were farmers, grocers, tailors. John Henry Newman's great-great grandfather, William Newman of Swaffham Bulbeck, married Alice Farrow of Swaffham Prior in 1689; his great-grandfather, Francis Newman, married Elizabeth Rolph, both of Swaffham Bulbeck, in 1733; his grandfather, John Newman I (1734–99), married Elizabeth Good (1733–1825) in 1763; and his father, John Newman II (1767–1824), married Jemima Fourdrinier (1772–1836) in 1799. She, by the way, brought with her a then not-unsubstantial dowry of £5,000. John Henry Newman himself was therefore John III.

The Fourdriniers were Huguenots (French Protestants), who came to England some time after revocation (1685) of the 1598 Edict of Nantes, devised by Henri IV for royal protection of the Huguenots. In England, the Fourdriniers became paper manufacturers, and eventually "solid London merchants of the Thackeray type." Like the Newmans, they merged with non-committal Anglican persuasion. There is no evidence, on either side of the family, of Evangelical forebears. See Sean O'Faòlain, *Newman's Way: The Odyssey of John Henry Newman*, pp. 1–12, 329–30.

4. See *Letters and Correspondence of John Henry Newman during His Life in the English Church*, 2 vols., (ed.) Anne Mozley, London, Longmans, Green, 1911, I, p. 72. See also John Henry Newman, *Apologia pro vita sua: Being a History of His Religious Opinions*, New York, Longmans, Green, 1948, p. 1; *An Essay in Aid of a Grammar of Assent*, New York, Longmans, Green, 1947, p. 43.

5. Early-childhood reading ability is a sign of intelligence. Samuel Taylor Coleridge read an Arabian Nights before he was five, John Stuart Mill read Greek when barely six, Camillo Cavour read at four, while Samuel Johnson and Jeremy Bentham were readers before they were speakers.

6. The phrase "grave majestic English" is Newman's. Tyndale's transla-

tion constitutes about nine-tenths of the King James Bible (KJV) of 1611, and about eight-tenths of its revision (RSV). One-time Franciscan "skilled in seven tongues," William Tyndale (1490–1536) studied at Oxford and Cambridge. In gracefully cadenced English, translated directly from Greek and Hebrew, he was using a freshly minted language, soon to be gloriously voiced by Shakespeare's genius. See J. F. Mozley, *William Tyndale*, Westport, Greenwood Press, 1971, p. 108; see also Alister E. McGrath, *In the Beginning: The Story of the King James Bible and How It Changed a Nation, a Language, and a Culture*, New York, Doubleday, 2001, esp. pp. 68–88; *The Cambridge History of the Bible*, 3 vols., (edd.) P. R. Ackroyd, C. F. Evans, G. W. H. Lampe, and S. L. Greenslade, Cambridge, Cambridge University Press, 1963, III, pp. 141–74. See also, F. F. Bruce, *History of the Bible in English*, 3rd ed., New York, Oxford University Press, 1978, pp. 28–52; Jack P. Lewis, *The English Bible from KJV to NIV: A History and Evaluation*, Grand Rapids, MI, Baker Book, 1982, pp. 17–68.

7. England's "Bible Religion" meant reading the Bible and leading a correct life. As Newman said, it was "not a religion of persons and things, of acts of faith and direct devotion; but of sacred scenes and pious sentiments" (*A Grammar of Assent*, p. 44).

8. Closure of Ramsbottom, Newman, Ramsbottom on 8 March 1816, being the result of post-Waterloo monetary jitters, heralded the onset of an investment-sluggish, peace-time economy. To appreciate how drastic this financial squeeze must have been for the Newmans, one need only read the novels of Charles Dickens, Jane Austen, or Anthony Trollope.

9. Young Newman, "left at school by myself, my friends gone away," and "terrified at the heavy hand of God which came down upon me," was spiritually supported by Ealing's Evangelical Reverend Walter Mayers, who was also brother-in-law to Maria Giberne. She would later ally herself with Newman and his family. See *Autobiographical Writings*, p. 150. The seriousness of Newman's teenage situation—financially, emotionally, existentially—bore intimately on Newman's conversion, as he felt "the heavy hand of God which came down upon me." That he should turn to Evangelicalism—known for its emotive intensity—simply underscores how much Newman then needed emotional support. Later, he would assert that such emotionally charged religious fervor was foreign to him and not in his nature.

10. Newman's family were in no way evangelical, and in the family line between Newman's great-great-grandfather and his own father, there is no evidence of such a persuasion. Yet it is "fashionable" to call the Newmans evangelical. See Noel Annan, *The Dons*, Chicago, University of Chicago Press, 1999. He says of Newman, "He was brought up Evangelical" (p 44). See also Frank M. Turner (ed.) *The Idea of a University*, New Haven, Yale University Press, 1996. He asserts that Newman "grew up in a moderately evangelical family" (p. xii). Although Professor Turner records a debt to Ian Ker's edition

of Newman's Idea, which "has been invaluable to the present editor" (p. xi), Turner apparently neglected to read Fr. Ker's biographical words, which stated that Newman "had been brought up as an ordinary member of the Church of England. His parents were in no way Evangelical, but belonged to what their son was later to call 'the national religion of England'" (*John Henry Newman: A Biography*, p. 3).

Meriol Trevor states the case just as strongly: "The Newmans have often been described as Evangelicals; they certainly were not. Evangelicals of the day frowned on theaters and dancing and would have considered the banker's household worldly and frivolous," (*The Pillar of the Cloud*, p. 7). This being so, John Henry Newman's "psychological" move towards Evangelicalism is worthy of note.

11. *Letters and Correspondence*, I, p. 27. Officially founded in 1554 by Sir Thomas Pope, Trinity College had, in fact, been erected on the ruins of Durham College, built in 1289 by Durham's bishop, Richard de Bury. See Hastings Rashdall, *The Universities of Europe in the Middle Ages*, 3 vols., (edd.) F. M. Powicke and A. B. Emden, London, Oxford University Press, 1936, III, pp. 186–88. At the time of Newman's matriculation, Trinity College under Dr. Lee was attempting to "rise in the University," by imitating what Provost John Eveleigh had done for Oriel College between 1781 and 1814 in making it Oxford's intellectual leader. See *Autobiographical Writings*, pp. 30–39. See also Meriol Trevor, *The Pillar of the Cloud*, pp. 23–31; Ian Ker, *John Henry Newman: A Biography*, pp. 6–13.

12. *Letters and Correspondence*, I, p. 38.

13. "Theology," (ibid., I, p. 21). "I was very fond," he wrote, "of [Bishop William] Beveridge's 'Private Thoughts' at this time." "University bells," (ibid., p. 45).

14. *See Autobiographical Writings*, "hard reading," (p. 51); "stumbling block," (p. 37); "alone honours," (p. 39); "under the line," (p. 47). *Letters and Correspondence*, "going too soon to Oxford" (I, p. 34). The books which Newman presented for examination included Aristotle's *Ethics, Poetics, and Rhetoric*; Homer's *Iliad*; Greek dramas of Aeschylus and Sophocles; Greek and Roman histories of Thucydides, Herodotus, Polybius, and Livy; the poetry of Virgil, Horace, Juvenal, and Cicero. Mathematics offerings included Euclid's *Elements*, algebra, conic sections, and trigonometry; Newton's Principia and (pre-calculus) fluxions; mechanics; hydrostatics; astronomy; and optics. See Henry Tristram, *The Idea of a Liberal Education: A Selection from the Works of Newman*, London, George Harrap, 1952, p. 18.

15. See Newman *Family Letters*, (ed.) Dorothea Mozley, London, SPCK, 1962, p. xix.

16. Newman quotes from his *Loss and Gain*; see *Autobiographical Writings*, pp. 49–50.

17. *Letters and Correspondence*, I, pp. 42, 56.

18. Oriel is the fifth Oxford college, outranking all others except Merton. On 1 January 1326, somewhat more than a year after its founding by Adam de Brome, Oriel was "surrendered into the King's [Edward II's] hands," and "re-established with the King as its nominal founder." It likewise assumed the royal arms of three lions rampant in "bordure engrailed argent." See Hastings Rashdall, *The Universities of Europe in the Middle Ages*, III, p. 204. Books on Oxford continue to use the "king's date" for Oriel; see A. R. Wooley, *The Clarendon Guide to Oxford*, London, Oxford University Press, 1971, p. 28; Peter Heyworth, The Oxford Guide to Oxford, Oxford, Oxford University Press, 1981, p. 92.

19. *Letters and Correspondence*, I, p. 61.

20. Ibid.

21. Ibid., I, pp. 62, 63. See also, Maisie Ward, Young Mr. Newman, New York, Sheed & Ward, 1948, p. 73.

22. *Apologia pro vita sua*, Whately, p. 10; Hawkins, pp. 7–8. On 3 November 1834 Newman gratefully wrote to Dr. Whately: "Much as I owe to Oriel in the way of mental improvement, to none, as I think, do I owe so much as to yourself. I know who it was first gave me heart to look about me after my selection, and taught me to think correctly, and—strange office for an instructor—to rely upon myself. Nor can I forget that it has been at your kind suggestion that I have since been led to employ myself in the consideration of several subjects, which I cannot doubt have been very beneficial to my mind" (*Letters and Correspondence*, I, p. 343).

23. *Prayers, Verses, and Devotions*, San Francisco, Ignatius Press, 1989, "VII Snapdragon," (p. 470); *Autobiographical Writings*, "live and die," (p. 63); *Apologia pro vita sua*, "snapdragon," (p. 215); "tender ties," (p. 84), "stars," (p. 85).

24. Newman writes from Littlemore to a friend, 20 January 1846, "'Obliviscere populum tuum et domum patris tui,' has been in my ears for the last twelve hours. I realize more that we are leaving Littlemore, and it is like going on the open sea" (*Apologia pro vita sua*, p. 214).

25. See *Letters and Diaries of John Henry Newman*, XI, p. 12. Newman records the previous night's arrival of the Passionist Fr. Dominic Barbieri: "He has now gone to Mass at Oxford—on his return I am to complete [my Confession] . . . and . . . shall be received this evening into what I believe to be the One and Only fold of Christ." His diary entry for that day reads thus: "Completed my Confession † admitted into the Cath. Ch. with Bowles and Stanton." See also, Jude Mead, C. P., *Shepherd of the Second Spring: A Life of Blessed Dominic Barbieri, C. P., 1792–1849*, Patterson, NJ, St. Anthony Guild Press, 1968.

26. Trained in the Vatican habit of "one-room intrigue" (what Spaniards call *camarilla*), Archbishop Paul Cullen, being distrustful of everyone but himself, was intractable, impenetrable, silent. Although Irish himself, he despised

the movement for Irish freedom from British domination, known as "Young Ireland," which he identified with Giuseppe Mazzini's "Young Italy." But Newman, as Rector of Dublin's Catholic University, developed many friendships with Fenians and members of "Young Ireland," and was sympathetic to the cause of Irish political freedom. He knew that "Cromwell, and others have, by their conduct to the Irish, burned into the national heart a deep hatred of England" (Wilfrid Ward, *The Life of John Henry Cardinal Newman*, II, p. 517). "If I were an Irishman," Newman wrote, "I would be (in heart) a rebel" (Ibid., II, p. 527).

27. The difficulties these Lectures represented, which Newman recorded in private letters and public announcements, included the following:

Uncertainty—"I am out on the ocean with them," and "out of sight of land," with "nothing but the stars," he writes to Bernard Dalgairns in July, 1852. (Quoted in A. Dwight Culler, *The Imperial Intellect: A Study of Newman's Educational Ideal*, New Haven, CT, Yale University Press, 1955, p. 152.)

Trouble—"My lectures have taken me more trouble than any one could by a stretch of the imagination conceive," he confides to Robert Ornsby, 14 April 1852. "I have written almost reams of paper, finished, set them aside—then taken them up again, and plucked them—and so on. I have no security to myself that the lectures will not be, from beginning to end, a failure from my not knowing my audience" (quoted in Fergal McGrath, S.J., *Newman's University: Ideal and Reality*, London, Longmans, Green, 1951, p. 142).

Oppression—"These lectures have oppressed me more than anything else of the kind in my life," he writes to F. W. Faber, in June, 1852 (McGrath, p. 162).

Pain—"The Discourses, now (thank God) all but finished, have been the most painful of all [my writings]," he reveals to Sr. Mary Imelda Poole on 22 October 1852 (Culler, *The Imperial Intellect*, p. 152).

Exhaustion—"My *University Lectures* have taken out of me no one can say how much, and I am fit for nothing but to lie on a sofa," he tells T. W. Allies, on 2 November 1852 (Culler, p. 304).

Defeat—"My Lectures in Dublin in May 1852 . . . were a flash in the pan," he believes (McGrath, p. 212).

Anxiety—"The following Discourses . . . belong to a time when ... [the Author] was tried both by sorrow and anxiety [in the Achilli affair], and by indisposition also, and required a greater effort to write, and gave him less satisfaction when written, than any other of his volumes," he says in the advertisement of the 1859 edition of the Lectures (McGrath, p.289).

Debilitation—"My lectures have cost me no one knows how much thought and anxiety, and again and again I stopped, utterly unable to get on with the subject. . . . For three days I have sat at my desk nearly from morning to night, and put aside as worthless at night what I had been doing all day," he writes Charles Newsham on 15 June 1852 (McGrath, p. 162).

Discovery—"I have just discovered how I ought to have written the lecture, what would have been the true rhetoric, and how I have plunged into a maze of metaphysics from which I may be unable to heave myself," he tells Ambrose St. John, on 17 May 1952 (McGrath, p. 160).

Exhilaration—"My two most perfect works artistically are my two last. The former of them [*Present Position of Catholics*] put me to less trouble than any I ever wrote, the latter [*University Lectures*] to the greatest of all," he reveals in February, 1853, to H. W. Wilberforce (McGrath, p. 175).

Newman expended enormous amounts of effort in anything he wrote. To his sister Jemima, on 29 January 1838, he explained, "My book on Justification has taken incredible time. I am quite worn out with correcting." He adds, "I write, I write again: I write a third time. . . . Then I take the third: I literally fill the page with corrections. . . . I then write it out fair for the printer. I put it by; I take it up; I begin to correct again: it will not do. Alterations multiply, pages are re-written, little lines sneak in and crawl about. The whole page is disfigured; I write again; I cannot count how many times this process is repeated" (*Letters and Correspondence*, II, pp. 223–24).

28. A certain consternation has been registered about Newman's exclusion of the original Discourse V from the 1859 edition of *Discourses on the Scope and Nature of University Education*, as well as from the 1873 *The Idea of a University*. One observer suggests, "If [Discourse] V was later dropped, it was because it never was needed in the first place. But Newman did not drop it as condemning anything in it" (A. Dwight Culler, *The Imperial Intellect*, p. 316, note 66).

29. See Ian Ker's edition of *The Idea of a University*, Oxford, Clarendon Press, 1976, pp. xxxiv–xxxix.

30. Ibid. (Ker's edition), p. 419.

31. Ibid., p. 421.

32. *Rise and Progress of Universities and Benedictine Essays*, Notre Dame, IN, University of Notre Dame Press, 2001, pp. 6, 13.

33. *The Idea of a University* (Ker's edition), p. 423.

34. To appreciate the Newtonian force of Newman's argument for structural coherence in the University, we need to recall that he lived in an age predating the Michelson-Morley experiments on the speed of light (1887), which demolished Newtonian theory. Einstein's *Restricted Field Theory* (1905), premised upon Michelson-Morley, declared the relativity of any physical motion to any other physical motion, measured by the absolute yardstick of the velocity of light (300,000 km/sec [299,743 km/sec; 186,282 mi/sec]).

Also, typographical errors are sometimes prescient. Thus, a recent Oxford University Press advertisement for Ian Ker's edition of Newman's *The Idea of a University* (printed on the dust jacket of Brian Martin's *John Henry Newman: His Life and Work*, New York, Oxford University Press, 1982) was recorded as The Idea of a Universe.

35. The Idea of a University (Ker's edition), p. 423.

36. Coherence (as well as singleness of purpose and effort) is, for Newman, the distinguishing mark of the genuine University. In describing the University, Newman uses both a (physical) planetary metaphor and a (political) imperium metaphor.

37. In "Christianity and Scientific Investigation," Newman identifies the singular difference between "the special character of the Philosophy I am speaking of" and "the method of strict science or system." Unlike physics, he says, philosophy "is not founded on one idea, or reducible to certain formulae." Hence, Newtonian mechanics, although it "might discover the great law of motion in the physical world, and be the key to ten thousand phenomena," is merely an approximation, because "the great Universe itself, moral and material, sensible and supernatural, cannot be gauged and meted by even the greatest of human intellects, and its constituent parts admit, indeed of comparison and adjustment, but not of fusion" (The Idea of a University, p. 460). The only One who fully knows the Universe is the One who created it. Any analogy we draw here is, then, between the University and the "Newtonian Universe." Similarly, Newman's analogy of an empire as approximation of Church and University only compares what we know of them.

38. The Idea of a University, VI. 8, p. 144.

39. In July, 1841, Newman published, in the British Critic, an essay titled "Private Judgment." In it, he cautioned the English Church that it was failing the test of catholicity. "How can any Church," he wrote, "be called Catholic, which does not act beyond its own territory? And when did the rulers of the English Church ever move one step beyond the precincts, or without the leave, of the imperial power?" ("Private Judgment," in Essays and Sketches, 3 vols., Westport, CT, Greenwood, 1970, II, pp. 137–70; p. 163).

40. The Idea of a University (Ker's edition), pp. 422–23.

41. During February 1841 (ironically coincidental with the condemnation of his "pro-Catholic" Tract XC [90]), Newman, at the suggestion of London Times editor John Walter, wrote seven letters (signed "Catholicus") to rebut ideas on popular education, as put forward by Sir Robert Peel. Newman was later amused that "My Catholicus in The Times was ascribed to [Henry] Phillpotts"—Bishop of Exeter (Letters and Diaries, letter of 28 March 1855 to Henry Wilberforce, XVI, p. 429, note 2). Sir Robert Peel thought of knowledge as information, which was a "wonderful instrument" of "refinement," useful (he asserted) to "calm" the passions of England's social and political discontents, particularly among the "lower classes."

42. A "patch" of our animal past is a poetic way of distinguishing three levels of brain growth, which develop through stages of fetal development, and (conveniently) replicate the human evolutionary past. There is (1) the reptilian brain (basal ganglion, or "old brain"), which governs sleeping-waking and autonomic movements, such as breathing and body temperature, and retains

animal "hostility." Then, there is (2) the paleomammalian brain, which contains the limbic system (and another form of hostility), which governs coordination and survival. Finally, there is (3) the neomammalian brain, or cortex, which fine-tunes lower functions and achieves abstract thinking and planning. (The mysterious cerebellum, meanwhile assumes the tasks of balance, motor, and geo-positioning guidance.)

43. *The Idea of a University*, V. 6, p. 114.

44. See *The Idea of a University* (Ker's edition), pp. 435–92. The appendix of the original Discourse V is designated, in Ker's edition, "Appendix II", and contains "illustrations" of Newman's first five discourses. Running in all about 22,000 words, its last few pages (about 1,000 words) reproduce parts of Newman's sermon, "The Religion of the Day," originally published (March 1834) as the first volume of his *Parochial and Plain Sermons*. In Discourse IX, Newman uses the language: "Religion of Civilization."

45. The argument, as stated here, directly conflicts with that of Fergal McGrath, S. J. (*Newman's University: Idea and Reality*). That author asserts, "In a sense, *The Idea* . . . is a misleading title, and the original title, *Discourses on the Scope and Nature of University Education*, is more accurate" (p. 281). The problem, voiced in this way, is that by 1873, Newman's emphasis in The Idea clearly shifts to the University as locus of education, in its highest sense, or as agent of such education. Otherwise, why would he re-title that work? That Newman did re-title makes it (at least) plausible to infer a reconceptualization in that action, which, therefore, makes possible a reinterpretation of his action. Furthermore, that apparently new emphasis may also suggest—indeed, make possible (as is here proposed)—a useful additional contrast between Church, as *Ecclesia docens*, and University, as *Universitas docens*.

46. Summary contrast between the original Discourse V and its present version reveals the following amplification:

1. All branches of knowledge are connected, and sciences have multiple bearings on one another, and thus correct one another. Each science has its own story.

2. It is important to enlarge the studies of a University, in order to represent the whole circle of knowledge. Such action creates an atmosphere which faculty and students breathe.

3. Liberal education apprehends the great outlines of knowledge, and thus forms a lasting habit of mind, whose attributes are freedom, equitableness, calmness, moderation, and wisdom. It thus becomes a philosophical habit.

4. Knowledge is its own end or reward, which comports with the nature of the human mind. Liberal education thus differs from commercial or professional education. What is liberal stands on its own, informed by no other than itself, and tends to enjoyment. Such knowledge is philosophical.

5. Thus there are two methods of education: philosophical or mechanical; the former is acquired as being illuminative, and provides an inner endowment. Providing just such illumination is the task of the University, which provides, not instruction, but education.
6. Philosophy, like education, is its own end. It should not be burdened with virtue or religion or mechanical arts. Liberal education is thus the cultivation of the intellect.
7. Liberal education perfects our nature, adding to it, directing it to higher aims.

47. "The Religion of the Day" (1834), in *Parochial and Plain Sermons*, San Francisco, Ignatius Press, 1987, 1. 24, pp. 196–205.
48. Ibid., pp. 196–98.
49. *The Idea of a University*, VIII. 10, p. 211.
50. "The Religion of the Day," pp. 198–99.
51. The name Friedrich Nietzsche (1844–1900) has acquired such unfortunate resonance, that it may seem risky to mention him in the same breath with Newman, even though both are linked, however loosely, by a mutual respect for moral values. We need to get past the opportunistic Nazi re-tooling of Nietzsche—as designed by his sister, Elisabeth Forster-Nietzsche—in order to understand how, like Newman, Nietzsche viewed modern "respectability" as a corruption of valuation, which thus required transvaluation of values. Like Newman, Nietzsche drew attention (but for different reasons) to a new worldliness in Christendom, wherein "the Christian acts like all the world," who are "all alike, all very puny, very round, very sociable, and very boring," and who, in Karl Marx's words, "settle everywhere, nestle everywhere, everywhere establish connections." For Nietzsche, modern morality was actually *ressentiment* (embitterment) which, he said, "is at the core of our morals." Hence, Nietzsche said of Christianity, "What remains is not God, Freedom, and Immortality [the Kantian trio], but benevolence, a feeling of decency, and the belief that throughout the universe, too, benevolence and feelings of decency will become prevalent. We are witnessing the euthanasia of Christianity." See *The Basic Writings of Nietzsche* (ed., trans.) Walter Kaufmann, New York, Modern Library, 1968, pp. 732ff.; Walter Kaufmann, *Nietzsche: Philosopher, Psychologist, Anti-Christ*, New York, Meridian, 1956, p. 94ff.; Friedrich Nietzsche, Beyond Good and Evil, (trans.) Marianne Cowan, Chicago, Regnery/Gateway, 1955, esp. pp. 135–36.
52. *Rise and Progress of Universities and Benedictine Essays*, Chapter XIX, "Abuses of the Colleges, Oxford," p. 230.
53. Even prior to his (1845) conversion, Newman believed that Catholicity was the fundamental mark of the Christian Credo—*unam sanctam catholicam et apostolicam Ecclesiam*. In 1834, (precisely three centuries after the Act

of Supremacy), such a Credo also exposed a cultural and psychological difference between Canterbury and Rome—English Crown and Christian Church.

54. Optimism/pessimism denotes a contrastive, reciprocal relationship—
like up/down and parent/child. Each contains its counterpart. Thus, if everything were up, and there were no down, if everyone were a parent, but there
were no children, then nothing could be said to be up, and no one could be said
to be a parent. Similarly, when everything is optimistic, then nothing is optimistic.

55. *The Idea of a University*, Ker's edition, p. 429.

56. Ibid., p. 434.

57. See *Life and Works of St. Bernard, Abbot of Clairvaux*, (trans.) S.
Eales, London, Hodges, 1889–96. This "symmetry argument" parallels the argument of St. Bernard of Clairvaux (in *Cant. Cant.*) on "intentional indistin-
guishability" between divine and human wills, when a person's will coincides,
and acts in accordance with the divine will, or divine purpose, but also preserves the order and identity of respective "substances" (71, pp. 9–10). See
also Etienne Gilson, *The Mystical Theology of St. Bernard*, (trans.) A. H. C.
Downes, New York, Sheed & Ward, 1940, pp. 123–25. The argument here can
be re-phrased: "Where realities share the same intentionality, then, in respect
of intentionality, they become indistinguishable; but, in respect of reality, they
maintain distinction, and are therefore separate. Hence, it is possible for two realities to be separate but indistinguishable."

58. *Apologia pro vita sua*, p. 229.

59. Ibid., pp. 225, 227.

60. See Josef Pieper, Leisure, *The Basis of Culture*, New York, New
American Library, 1963, pp. 70–75. In the sense intended, neither religion nor
education, neither Church nor University, though "in the world," is completely
bound to "the workaday world" of "doing things for useful ends."

61. Ian Ker, *John Henry Newman: A Biography*, argues that, for Newman, there is a "resemblance between his idea of the Church and his earlier
idea of the University, a similarity which suggests if not influence at least a
common source in a unified vision" (p. 396). Fr. Ker's remark, however, refers
to Newman's view of the Church, in his ecclesiological writings, after 1858. In
the present context, I suggest that what Fr. Ker perceptively calls "a unified
vision" may already be implicit in the *Discourses* themselves, and as early as
1852.

62. *Letters and Correspondence*, I, p. 417.

63. C. S. Dessain, "The Biblical Basis of Newman's Ecumenical Theology," in *The Rediscovery of Newman: An Oxford Symposium*, (edd.) John Coulson and A. M. Allchin, London, Sheed & Ward, 1967, p. 100. Root of the Latin
word pastor, is *pascere*, "to feed," which, in turn, is based on *panis*, "bread."
The associated Greek is "to feed on" ($\pi\alpha\tau\acute{\epsilon}o\mu\alpha\iota$—future tense: $\pi\acute{\alpha}\sigma o\mu\alpha\iota$).
There is also a related term, companion (*cum pane*, in Latin)—"one with whom
one breaks bread."

64. Quoted in A. Dwight Culler, *The Imperial Intellect*, p. 72, Culler suggests, "Newman regarded his office as a pastoral one and he believed its pastoral character would be largely destroyed if he were made into a lecturer on books rather than a teacher of men." Newman's letter to Hawkins is quoted ibid., p. 292, note 96. Culler adds, "The pastoral conception of the tutor's office is the most distinctive feature of Newman's work" (ibid., p. 74). Yet, Culler seems somehow dubious as to how seriously one ought to take Newman's words, and he seems to wonder "how well did he manage in this ordinary kind of instruction?" (ibid., p. 75).

65. See John Henry Newman, *Sermon Notes*, Notre Dame, IN, University of Notre Dame Press, 2000. The Introduction, by James Tolhurst, D. D., uses the phrase "an Empire of Faith" (pp. xxxvi, xxxviii). The phrase, "an imperial intellect," occurs in Newman's rectorial address, "Christianity and Scientific Investigation," in *The Idea of a University*: "an imperial intellect, for such I am considering a University to be" (p. 461).

> What an empire is in political history, such is a University in the sphere of philosophy and research. ...It is . . . the high protecting power of all knowledge and science, of fact and principle, of inquiry and discovery, of experiment and speculation; it maps out the territory of the intellect, and sees that the boundaries of each province are religiously respected, and that there is neither encroachment nor surrender on any side. It . . . assigns to all their due order of precedence. It maintains no one department of thought exclusively. . . . In this point of view, its several professors are like the ministers of various political powers at one court or conference. They represent their respective sciences, and attend to the private interests of those sciences respectively; and, should dispute arise between those sciences, they are the persons to talk over and arrange it, without risk . . . of angry collision or of popular commotion. A liberal philosophy becomes the habit of minds thus exercised; a breadth and spaciousness of thought, in which lines, seemingly parallel, may converge at leisure, and principles, recognized as incommensurable, may be safely antagonistic (pp. 459–60).

In the Introduction to his edition of *The Idea of a University*, Ian Ker rightly says that "Newman's idea of the Church is couched in terms noticeably similar in some respects to his idea of a university" (p. lxxiii). We have here suggested just such a relation. Also, Newman's sermon, "The Christian Church an Imperial Power," in *Sermons Bearing on Subjects*

of the Day, establishes that it is "the peculiarity of an imperial state to bear rule over other states." See *Sermons and
Discourses*, (ed.) Charles F. Harrold, London, Longmans,
Green, 1949, p. 57. Newman also says that "the Church is the
representative of the religious principle," and the University
acts "as the representative of the intellect" (*The Idea of a
University*, p. 215). The Church is thus an "Empire of Faith,"
as the University is an "Empire of Intellect."

More importantly, the institutional University—and not, indeed, any particular individual—is the imperial intellect. Misunderstanding Newman's imperial metaphor in this respect serves to misrepresent Newman's view. By
referring to "the various eulogies of man's 'imperial intellect,'" for example,
Fr. Ker appears to do that (see Ker's edition of *The Idea of a University*, p.
xlviii). He also notes that Newman's "*Elementary Studies*" (Part Two of Idea)
is a highly practical application of Newman's concept of the kind of intellectual training that leads to the formation of an "imperial intellect." He says,
"Thus we find that the 'imperial intellect' is formed not by lofty generalities but
by 'accuracy of thought,'" (*John Henry Newman, A Biography*, p. 396).
    But the referent of Newman's imperial phrase is not a particular person,
but only the University itself. A person does not have "an imperial intellect."
Rather, the University is "an imperial intellect." As an "intellectual confeder-
ation," the University has command of others. Also, no single science is imperial, but, confederated with other sciences under University rule, it
participates in the University's empire of intellect.
    66. "Christianity and Scientific Investigation," in *The Idea of a Univer-
sity*, p. 457.
    67. Ibid., pp. 457–58.
    68. *My Campaign in Ireland*, pp. 120, 290; *The Idea of a University*, pp.
101, 493, 186, 189. *Autobiographical Writings*, p.259; *Letters and Diaries*,
XVI, Appendix, p. 563, being Newman's remarks of Sunday, 5 November
1854, at University House to the first enrolled students at Dublin's Catholic
University.
    69. *The Idea of a University*, pp. 459–61.
    70. Newman is a person who "takes things as they are"—which means
that he is essentially a realist. In Discourse IX of *The Idea of a University*, he
advised his listeners to "take things as they are, not as you could wish them"
(ibid., p. 232). In Discourse I, he said, "I take things as I find them" (ibid., p.
7). To Richard Hurrell Froude, 22 June 1835, he wrote, "We must take things
as they are and make the most of them" (*Letters and Correspondence*, II, p. 98).
In *The Grammar of Assent*, he wrote, "We are in a world of facts. We do not
quarrel with them, but we take them as they are" (p. 263), and later he observed, "What is left to us but to take things as they are, and resign ourselves

to what we find?"(p. 266). In the *Lectures on the Present Position of Catholics in England*, he tells his Oratorian audience, "I wish you to . . . learn to view things as they are" (p. 390). In "Christianity and Letters," he said, "I take things as I find them on the surface of history" (*The Idea of a University*, p. 252).

71. Giovanni Perrone, Rome's leading theologian of the time, to whom Newman had once sent a list of statements about faith and reason, accused Newman of "mixing up and confusing everything together" (*Newman miscet et confundit omnia*). Maisie Ward, who cites this instance, comments appropriately that Perrone's reaction was "an admirable summary of the effect of genius on the tidy and uninspired" (*Young Mr. Newman*, p. 239).

72. *The Varieties of Religious Experience: Gifford Lectures*, New York, Random House, 1929, p. 465.

73. "Doing Glory to God," in *Parochial and Plain Sermons*, VIII. 11, pp. 1648–49. Newman provides a corollary in another sermon, "Attendance at Holy Communion," where he says, "If then a man does not seek Him where He is, there is no profit in seeking Him where He is not," (ibid., p. 1493).

74. William James, *The Varieties of Religious Experience*, p. 479. James also approximated Newman's view that, in education, any separation between knowing and doing, between intellectual and moral actions, is essentially wrong-minded. Newman also looked to the separate colleges of the University complex to undertake moral and intellectual guidance of students. As he said, "College is for the formation of character, intellectual and moral, for the cultivation of the mind, for the improvement of the individual" (*Rise and Progress of Universities and Benedictine Essays*, pp. 228–29). His view is reflected in the widespread work of "Newman Clubs." See, John Whitney Evans, *The Newman Movement: Roman Catholics in American Higher Education, 1883–1971*, Notre Dame, IN, University of Notre Dame Press, 1980.

75. *Young Mr. Newman*, p. 228.

76. J. Lewis May, *Cardinal Newman: A Study*, London, Geoffrey Bles, 1945, p. 159. May's terms *genius* and *gentleman* are linguistic siblings, being etymologically derived from the same Greek and Latin (*genus*) roots. Other such cognates significantly include (among many others) the terms *gender, generous, gentle, genial, general, genetics, gentry, gentility, genuine, genesis, ingenious, progeny, indigenous*, and *engineer*.

CHAPTER 4:   GENIUS AND GENTLEMAN
NEWMAN EPIGRAPHS:

> "I wish"—Letter 5 May 1841 [Dr. Chas. Russell], *Apologia*, p. 171.
> "I am" - Letter 20 Nov 1842, May Holmes, Ker, *Biography*, p. 256.

"My smile"—Verses, XXX, "The Scars of Sin," p. 507.
"I have been"—Letter 6 Feb 1868, Fr. [H. J.] Coleridge,
   Ward, *Biography*, II, p. 205.
"Those sad"—*Letters and Diaries*, XII, p. 223.
"I have not lost"—*Autobiographical Writings*, p.247.

1. Complimented in 1879 on being theologian, preacher, historian, poet, and philosopher, Cardinal Newman lightly parried the compliment by saying, "To be various is to be superficial." See *The Idea of a Liberal Education: A Selection from the Works of Newman*, (ed.) Henry Tristram, London, George G. Harrap, 1952, p. 35.

2. See Ian Ker, *The Genius of John Henry Newman: Selections from His Writings*, Oxford, Clarendon Press, 1989. He rightly regards Newman as "the very greatest writer of non-fiction prose in the language" (p. xiii).

3. John Henry Newman, "Literature," in *The Idea of a University*, London, Longmans, Green, 1898. The great author, says Newman,

> writes passionately, because he feels keenly; forcibly, because he conceives vividly; he sees too clearly to be vague; he is too serious to be otiose; he can analyze his subject, and therefore he is rich; he embraces it as a whole and in its parts, and therefore he is consistent; he has a firm hold of it, and therefore he is luminous. When his imagination wells up, it overflows in ornament; when his heart is touched, it thrills along his verse. He always has the right word for the right idea, and never a word too much. If he is brief, it is because few words suffice; when he is lavish of them, still each word has its mark, and aids, not embarrasses, the vigorous march of his elocution. He expresses what all feel, but all cannot say; and his sayings pass into proverbs among his people, and his phrases become household words and idioms of their daily speech (pp. 291–92).

4. "Poetry, with Reference to Aristotle's Poetics" [January, 1829], in *Essays and Sketches*, 3 vols., Westport, CT, Greenwood Press, 1970, 1, p. 71.

5. Ibid., pp. 64–65. The "poetical mind," he adds, "speaks the language of dignity, emotion, and refinement." Because "figure" is the medium of its commu nication, "the adoption of metaphorical language is the only poor means allowed it for imparting to others its intense feelings."

6. Sean O'Faòlain, *Newman's Way: The Odyssey of John Henry Newman*, New York, Devin-Adair, 1952. Characterizing Newman's intellect as "exceptional," because it "attaches to everything he wrote," O'Faòlain also argues that Newman "is not primarily a theologian or a philosopher but an artist" (p. 111).

7. "Doing Glory to God," in *Parochial and Plain Sermons*, San Francisco, Ignatius, 1987, VIII. 11, pp. 1648–49.

8. See *Letters and Correspondence of John Henry Newman during His Life in the English Church*, 2 vols., (ed.) Anne Mozley, London, Longmans, Green, 1911. "Those who make comfort the great end of their preaching," Newman notes in a memorandum of 16 September 1824, "seem to mistake the end of their ministry," which is holiness. "Comfort is a cordial, but no one drinks cordials from morning to night" (I, p. 76). He wrote that he would strive in every pulpit to preach Christian doctrine, "and to warn people that it is quite idle to pretend to faith and holiness" without "a pure disinterested upright line of conduct" (I, pp. 76, 78).

9. "A Short Road to Perfection," in *Prayers, Verses, and Meditations*, San Francisco, Ignatius Press, 1989, p. 328.

10. See Ian Ker, *John Henry Newman: A Biography*, London, Oxford University Press, 1990. Letter of 20 November 1842 to Miss Mary Holmes, p. 256; see also *The Idea of a University*, p. 177; Charles Stephen Dessain, *John Henry Newman*, London, Thomas Nelson, 1966, p. 157; "Knowledge of God's Will without Obedience," in *Parochial and Plain Sermons*, I. 3, p. 28.

11. William Ralph Inge, *Outspoken Essays*, Freeport, NY, Books for Libraries, 1971, p. 204. Dean Inge considered Newman an anti-intellectual (p.183), but nonetheless "clever" (p. 175), who was possessed of a "self-centered" nature which "has always something hard and inhuman about it" (p. 182). In his Apologia, said Inge, Newman "could feel and show the true Catholic ferocity, the crudest spirit on earth" (p. 178), yet was also "the most docile and credulous of converts" (p. 174). Newman "will live in history" only "as the real founder and leader" of Anglo-Catholicism, "which he created and then tried in vain to destroy" (p. 173).

12. Richard Holt Hutton, *Cardinal Newman*, London, Methuen, 1905, pp. 2, 231.

13. Christopher Hollis, *Newman and the Modern World*, New York, Doubleday, 1968, pp. 30, 213. Hollis says that Pope John XXIII, *il papa di passagio*, adopted the "spirit of Newman."

14. Principal J. C. Shairp, "Essay on Keble," in *Studies in Poetry*, London, Longmans, 1868, p. 273; Wilfrid Ward, "John Henry Newman," in *Ten Personal Studies, London*, Longmans Green, 1908, pp. 220–22; R. D. Middleton, *Newman at Oxford*, London, Oxford University Press, 1950, p. 93. The phrase "most transparent of men," is in James Anthony Froude's *Short Studies on Great Subjects*, also cited in Middleton, p. 96.

Roman Catholic treatment of Newman was mixed, sharp, unyielding, and obstinate. In July, 1864, Newman wrote James Hope-Scott, "One cannot speak ten words without ten objections being made to each." See Wilfrid Ward, *The Life of John Henry Cardinal Newman: Based on His Private Journals and Correspondence*, 2 vols., London, Longmans Green, 1912, II, p. 43. For the Manning–W. G. Ward combination against Newman, see Ward, *The Life of John Henry Cardinal Newman*, I, pp. 546–49. See also Edward Sheridan Purcell, *The Life of Cardinal Manning, Archbishop of Westminster*, 2 vols., New York, Macmillan, 1896, II, pp. 564–65. He quotes the *Pall Mall Gazette* on the hostility of Ultramontane (pro-Vatican) English Catholics toward Newman: "For many years they had done their best to forget, and to make others forget, Dr. Newman's existence" (Purcell, *The Life of Cardinal Manning*, II, p. 564). Archbishop (later Cardinal) Manning once tried to persuade Bishop Ullathorne, Newman's ordinary, that Newman was not to be trusted: "You do not know Newman as I do. He simply twists you around his little finger; he bamboozles you with his carefully selected words, and plays so subtly with his logic that your simplicity is taken in." Ullathorne had full confidence in Newman, and did not trust Manning. See Meriol Trevor, *Light in Winter*, London, Macmillan, 1962, p. 555. On publication of Frank Newman's *Contributions Chiefly to the Early History of the Late Cardinal Newman*, Manning was asked if he agreed with its "very negative portrait." He replied, "It is a photograph, a photograph" (H. L. Stewart, *A Century of Anglo-Catholicism*, London, J. M. Dent, 1929, p. 126). Manning's sermon at Newman's funeral alleged that they were lifelong friends ("for sixty years and more"), a claim which Purcell, using Manning's own letters, brands as hypocrisy. See Purcell, *The Life of Cardinal Manning*, II, pp.763, 754. See also Robert Gray, *Cardinal Manning*, London, Weidenfeld and Nicolson, 1985. He tries to restore credibility to Manning's image, and his harsh words for Newman are interlayered with inaccuracies—for example, that "Newman insisted the mind played no essential part in the genesis and maintenance of faith," and that "faith, in fact, is a branch of morality. That was the somewhat smug principle that lay at the root of the stern ethical strain in Newman's sermons" (pp. 51–52).

15. See *Letters and Diaries of John Henry Newman*, (ed.) Charles Stephen Dessain, Toronto, Thomas Nelson, 1961, XI, p. xxvii. Richard William Church (1815–90), himself onetime Oriel Fellow, was among the most devoted of Newman's younger colleagues. As University proctor, he had posted the veto that saved Newman's *Tract XC* (90) from condemnation. With Newman at Littlemore, he cut off contact after Newman's 1845 conversion to Rome, but with the publication of Newman's Apologia, renewed their friendship. In 1871, Newman dedicated to Dean Church the second edition of his *Oxford University Sermons*. See Meriol Trevor, *Pillar of the Cloud*, pp.199, 279, 346, 369, and *Light in Winter*, pp. 366, 490, 500.

16. R. W. Church, St. Anselm, London, Macmillan, 1888, pp. v, vi, 7. See also B. A. Smith, Dean Church: The Anglican Response to Newman, London, Oxford University Press, 1958. He remarks on a parallel between the story of Anselm and the story of Newman and the Oxford Movement: "Church himself, being at that time strongly moved by the claims of holiness as Newman was presenting them, obviously saw in the Prior of Bec [St. Anselm] . . . a hero

after his own heart. . . . The ordeals of leadership into which Newman was entering had been experienced by Anselm centuries before" (p. 63).

17. *Preces privatae*, or "personal devotions" (from prex—"request, entreaty, prayer, or devotion") was arranged anew from its 1675 edition, and translated by Newman in 1843. See Louis Bouyer, Introduction to John Henry Newman, *Prayers, Verses, and Devotions*, San Francisco, Ignatius, 1989. This work "should be considered," says Fr. Louis Bouyer, "the fundamental inspiration of all Newman's devotional writings" (p. xvii).

18. See *Rise and Progress of Universities and Benedictine Essays*, Notre Dame, IN, University of Notre Dame Press, 2001. Newman mentions Anselm three times in as many pages of a single chapter, "The Schoolmen"—pp. 171, 175, and 176. See also John Henry Newman, *Lectures on Certain Difficulties Felt by Anglicans in Submitting to the Catholic Church*, London, Burns and Lambert, 1850. Anselmian influence shows in a passage where Newman weighs whether it were better "to commit one single venial sin" or "one wilful untruth" than to have "the sun and moon . . . drop from heaven, for the earth to fail, and for many millions who are upon it to die of starvation" (p. 190). A similar choice was suggested by St. Anselm, in his *Cur Deus Homo*, in which he contrasts "physical disaster" with the disaster of "one look contrary to the will of God" (*unus aspectus contra voluntatem dei, Cu*: 88, 15). Anselm poses, "What if it were necessary that the whole universe, except God himself, should perish and fall back into nothingness, or else that you should do a small thing against the will of God? (*Quid si necesse esset aut totum mundum et quidquid deus non est perire et in nihilum redigi, aut te facere tarn parvam rem contra voluntatem dei? Cu*: 89, 1–3.) Both Anselm and Newman elected physical disaster, rather than moral defection. See also R. W. Southern, *Saint Anselm: A Portrait in a Landscape*, Cambridge, Cambridge University Press, 1990. He asserts that *Cur Deus Homo* "inspired Newman," because "the tragic emotion is the same in both passages," but gratuitously adds that "Newman's words have a rhetorical exaggeration, even (if one may say so) an absurdity, which is never found in Anselm" (pp. 217–18, 380).

19. The ontological argument—named by Leibniz's disciple Christian Wolff and Immanuel Kant—is interpretively based on confusion between Anselm's theological insight and the *Aufklärung*-metaphysics of "existential predicates." Anselm's argument for God's existence is not, strictly speaking, a priori because it does not precede experience—but, in its cultural-theological context, is encased within Christian experience. As St. Thomas observed, "I say that this proposition, *God exists*, of itself is self-evident, for the predicate is the same as the subject, because God is His own existence" (*Summa theologiae*, I, q. 2, a. 1, Resp.), and also because "God is not only his own essence . . . but also His own being" (q. 3, a. 4, Resp.). See Karl Barth, *Anselm: Fides Quaerens Intellectum: Anselm's Proof of the Existence of God in the Context of His Theological Scheme*, (trans.) Ian W. Robertson, Richmond, VA, John

Knox, 1960: "That Anselm's *Proof of the Existence of God* has repeatedly been called the 'Ontological' Proof of God, that commentators have refused to see that it is in a different book altogether from the well-known teaching of Descartes and Leibniz, that anyone could seriously think that it is even remotely affected by what Kant put forward against these doctrines—all that is so much nonsense on which no more words ought to be wasted" (p. 171).

20. See "The Immortality of the Soul," in *Parochial and Plain Sermons*. Newman refers to "the clear vision we have, first, of our own existence, next of the presence of the Great God within us, and over us, as our Governor and Judge, who dwells in us by our conscience, which is His representative" (I. 2, p. 17). See also Ian Ker, *Newman the Theologian*, Notre Dame, IN, University of Notre Dame Press, 1990. In his *A Letter to the Duke of Norfolk*, as prompted by W. E. Gladstone's attack on the Vatican I's doctrine of papal infallibility, Newman stated his view that conscience "is the voice of God," and "a divine voice, speaking within us" (Ker, Newman the Theologian, pp. 232, 236).

21. Psalms 26: 8, which St. Anselm quotes in *Proslogion* (pp. 97, 9–10). See Franciscus Salesius Schmitt, S. Anselmi, Opera Omnia, Stuttgart, Friedrich Frommann, 1968, I, p. 97.

22. "Secret Faults," in *Parochial and Plain Sermons*, I. 4, p. 32. Newman also says, "Man was created in the image of God, and that image is in his soul" (*Discourses Addressed to Mixed Congregations*, Westminster, MD, Christian Classics, 1966, p. 324). Newman sensed the renovating nature of imago-theology, and was aware of Augustine's contribution to it. As he once put it, "The great luminary of the western world is, as we know, St. Augustine; he . . . had formed the intellect of Christian Europe" (*Apologia pro vita sua*, New York, Longmans, Green, 1947, p. 241).

23. Henri Brémond, *The Mystery of Newman*, (trans.) H. C. Corrance, London, Williams and Norgate, 1907, p. 358.

24. See Harriet Newman Mozley, *Family Adventures*, 1852, in A. Dwight Culler, *The Imperial Intellect: A Study of Newman's Educational Ideal*, New Haven, CT, Yale University Press, 1955, pp. 2, 279. See also *Letters and Correspondence of John Henry Newman during His Life in the Anglican Church*, I, p. 14.

25. *John Henry Newman Autobiographical Writings*, (ed.) Henry Tristram, New York, Sheed & Ward, 1957, p. 29.

26. Sean O'Faòlain, *Newman's Way: The Odyssey of John Henry Newman*, pp, 64, 63, 41.

27. See Meriol Trevor, *The Pillar of the Cloud*, New York, Doubleday, 1962, pp. 8–9. Even Newman's senses were "keen and perceptive," says Ms. Trevor. He had an eye for color, landscape, and wide views; he had an ear for music, a nose for scents, and a tongue for flavors. Edward White Benson, future Archbishop of Canterbury, heard Father Newman at St. Chad's with the ears of a nineteen-year-old, and thought he heard "a kind of Angel eloquence

... sweet, flowing, unlaboured language. . . . You could not but have felt your heart turn towards him" (Ibid., pp. 431–32). See also John Halloway, *The Victorian Sage*, London, Macmillan, 1953, p. 165; see also Ian Ker, *John Henry Newman: A Biography.* A young woman, meeting the elderly Newman, said that "his voice was low and very sweet; it had a wonderful ring of sympathy in it" (p. 697).

28. Richard Holt Hutton, *Cardinal Newman*, London, Longmans, Green, 1891, pp. 207–208.

29. *Letters and Diaries*, XI, p. 138. Robert Coffin writing to Manuel Johnson, 21 March 1846. See also Fergal McGrath, S. J., *Newman's University: Ideal and Reality*, London, Longmans, Green, 1951; John Hungerford Pollen, writing in the *Month*, September, 1906, p. 369.

30. John Henry Newman, "The Scars of Sin," in *Prayers, Verses, and Devotions*, p. 507. It was written at Iffley, 29 November 1832, just before Newman's departure on his Mediterranean trip. Here is the first stanza:

> My smile is bright, my glance is free,
> My voice is calm and clear;
> Dear friend, I seem a type to thee
> Of holy love and fear.

31. See J. M. Flood, *Cardinal Newman and Oxford*, London, Ivor Nicholson & Watson, 1933, pp. 141–44.

32. See Rev. Thomas Mozley, *Reminiscences, Chiefly of Oriel College and the Oxford Movement*, 2 vols., Boston, Houghton Mifflin, 1882, I, p. 205. He adds, "His dress—it became almost the badge of his followers—was the long-tailed coat, not always very new," (p. 206). John Augustus O'Shea is quoted in Fergal McGrath, S. J., *Newman's University: Ideal and Reality*, p. 429.

33. See *Letters and Correspondence*, letter to Frederic Rogers, 22 November 1832, I, p. 247. Mozley quote, ibid., p. 246. In a letter to his mother from Falmouth, 5 December 1832, he wrote, "I am quite ashamed of this scrawl, yet since I have a few minutes to spare, I do not like to be otherwise employed than in writing" (ibid., p. 250).

34. Pierre LeRoy, S. J., "Teilhard de Chardin: The Man," in Pierre Teilhard de Chardin, *The Divine Milieu*, (trans.) Bernard Wall, London, Collins, 1960, p. 13.

35. *Letters and Diaries*, XII, p. 223; XX, p.409. Newman is clearly aware of that youthful inner feeling, which often accompanies advancing age.

36. See *Letters of James Russell Lowell*, 2 vols., (ed.) Charles Eliot Norton, New York, Harper & Brothers, 1984, II, p. 281. Lowell was 65 when he met 83-year-old Cardinal Newman.

37. *Apologia pro vita sua*, p. 171. See Meriol Trevor, *Pillar of the Cloud*;

she identifies the recipient of Newman's communication as Dr. Charles Russell.

38. *Contemporary Review*, May, 1885, p. 667; quoted in Wilfrid Ward, *The Life of John Henry Cardinal Newman*, II, p. 505.

39. Wilfrid Ward, *The Life of John Henry Cardinal Newman*, II, pp. 507–508, note 2. Newman's choice of nous clearly exonerates him from any possibility of scepticism. Anyone committed to ($\nu o\tilde{u}\varsigma$) (Latin: *intellectus*) could not, by definition, be a sceptic.

40. Richard Holt Hutton's rebuttal constitutes the final chapter of his *Cardinal Newman*, pp. 253–68.

41. Gaius Glen Atkins, *Life of Cardinal Newman*, New York, Harper & Brothers, 1931, p. 305. Atkins says of Newman, "He surrounded himself with wonders and legends he was too much a poet to disturb and too much of a rationalist to accept" (p. 308).

42. See (on Carlyle) James Anthony Froude, *Thomas Carlyle's Life in London*, 2 vols., London, Longmans, Green, 1884, II, p. 247; (on Jowett) Margot Asquith, *The Autobiography of Margot Asquith*, 2 vols., London, Butterworth, 1920, I, p. 123; (on Leslie Stephens) Cyril Bibby, *T. H. Huxley: Scientist, Humanist, Educator*, London, Watts, 1959, p. 181; (on Frederick Denison Maurice) A. F. Hort, *Life and Letters of Fenton John Anthony*, 2 vols., London, Macmillan, 1896; (on Thomas Huxley) Leonard Huxley, *Life and Letters of Thomas Henry Huxley*, 2 vols., London, Macmillan, 1900, I, p. 126. English men of letters, being neither gentle nor generous to adversaries, often disregarded their own ideal of fair play.

See also Stephen Neill, *Anglicanism*, 4th ed., New York, Oxford University Press, 1977. He records that F. D. Maurice was, in his lifetime, branded a "muddy mystic." J. B. Mozley said of Maurice that he "has not a clear idea in his head," while Benjamin Jowett said of Maurice that he "was misty and confused" (p. 252).

43. See John Henry Newman, "Catholicity of the Anglican Church," in *Essays and Sketches*, 3 vols., Westport, CT, Greenwood, 1948; rebuttal of alleged scepticism, II, p. 115.

44. Meriol Trevor, *Light in Winter*, London, Macmillan, 1962, p. 296. See *Letters and Correspondence*, letter from Oriel to Tom Mozley, 13 May 1832, to which he added, "It is one especial use of times of illness to reflect about ourselves" (I, p. 228).

45. See C. H. E. Smyth, *Church and Parish*, London, SPCK, 1955: "Newman didn't have what it takes" (p. 164); "Letter to the Editor," in *The Living Church*, 222.11 (18 March 2001), "Why did he leave?" (p. 26); Stephen Neill, *Anglicanism*, "ruthless quote," p. 256.

See also, Walter E. Houghton, *The Art of Newman's Apologia*, New Haven, CT, Yale University Press, 1945. He contends that Newman converted to Catholicism from "a growing sense of isolation, rejection, and resentment, which finally led to conversion as an act of revenge," (p. 98), claiming that such a view is "borne out by a careful study of the *Apologia*," (ibid., p. 99), although his "careful study" is actually based on remarks by Frank Leslie Cross, *John Henry Newman*, London, P. Allan, 1933, p. 143. Houghton adds, "The very title of Newman's life . . . 'Apologia' suggests distortion, and consciously intended" (ibid., p. 96). See, too, William Robbins, *The Newman Brothers: An Essay in Comparative Intellectual Biography*, Cambridge, MA, Harvard University Press, 1966. Robbins lays (unpersuasive) claim to "multiple instances" of Newman's scepticism (pp. 119–68), and quotes "an impatient remark by Cannop Thirlwall in 1867: "I believe him [Newman] to be at bottom far more sceptical than his brother Francis; and the extravagant credulity with which he accepts the wildest Popish legends is, as it appears to me, only another side of his bottomless unbelief" (ibid., p. 119). See also Gertrude Himmelfarb, *Victorian Minds*, New York, Knopf, 1968. The author remarks, "If he had been willing to settle . . . for a religion that was mystically inspired or a church that was justified in terms of social expediency—he would have spared himself much labor and anguish" (p. 313).

Scepticism, a term derived from Greek words—σκέπτομαι and σκοπείν—that variously mean "looking carefully, examining, seeing, spying, and a place to watch from." The word scope derives from the Greek term for "a watcher, spy, scout"—ὁ σκοπός. A sceptical attitude is quite appropriate for anyone reviewing ambiguous materials, which is quite different from a sceptical position, which is self-confuting. To argue that there is no truth (Is this statement true?), or that nothing is certain (Is this statement certain?), is to use self-referential criteria which implicitly appeal to truth and certainty. Or to say that every statement must be doubted implies, at the same time, that that statement must be held in doubt.

46. Algernon Cecil, *Six Oxford Thinkers*, London, John Murray, 1909, pp. 117–20. Arthur Quiller-Couch, *On the Art of Reading*, New York, Putnam's, 1920, p. 146. His remark on "stern and masculine minds," is in *On the Art of Writing*, New York, Putnam's, 1916, p. 38. "Q" (as he preferred to be called) tirelessly recommended Newman's *The Idea of a University* to his Cambridge "Lit. students": "The book is so wise—so eminently wise—as to deserve being bound by the young student of literature for a frontlet on his brow" (ibid., p. 37).

47. See Meriol Trevor, *Pillar of the Cloud*, p. 589.

48. *Apologia pro vita sua*, p. 386. In contrasting the "high points of the Italian character" with those of the English, he asserted, "I like the English rule of conduct better" (ibid., p. 248).

49. Henry Tristram (ed.), *The Idea of a Liberal Education: A Selection from the Works of Newman*, p. 14.

50. *Apologia pro vita sua*, p. 80. Having shown that Paley and other Englishmen—such as Johnson, Milton, and Taylor—defended lying under "cer-

tain circumstances," Newman asked his opponents, "Since you would not scruple in holding Paley for an honest man, in spite of his defence of lying, why do you scruple at holding St. Alfonso honest?" (ibid., p. 250). The answer is implicit: St. Alfonso was not an Englishman, and not a Protestant.

51. For Talbot's remark, see E. S. Purcell, Life of Cardinal Manning, II, pp. 322–23. Bishop Ullathorne, blunt Yorkshireman and Newman's ordinary, said that Manning's backstairs intrigues were "unEnglish." See Meriol Trevor, *Light in Winter*, p. 555. It is ironic that, in the index to Ian Ker's John Henry Newman: A Biography, Cardinal Manning is listed as "Archbishop of Canterbury," p. 749.

52. See *Letters and Correspondence*, Newman's letter to J. F. Christie, March 1833, called Rome "the most wonderful place in the world," adding ominously, "but then, on the other hand, the superstitions, or rather, what is far worse, the solemn reception of these as an essential part of Christianity. . . . Really this is a cruel place." To R. F. Wilson, 18 March, Newman confided that "Christian Rome is somehow under a special shade, as Pagan Rome certainly was. . . . Not that one can tolerate for an instant the wretched perversion of the truth which is sanctioned here" (I, pp. 324–25, 329).

See also John William Burgon, *Lives of Twelve Good Men*, New York, Scribner & Welford, 1891. Newman wrote Rev. Hugh James Rose, "It cannot be doubted that Rome is one of the four monsters of Daniel's vision. . . . I am approaching a doomed city" (*Letters and Correspondence*, p. 89). Again to Rose, Newman says of the Roman Catholic Church, "She may be said to resemble a demoniac" (ibid., p. 136). Dean Burgon then glosses this passage: "What else does he assert but that the Church of Rome—forsaken by the Holy Spirit of GOD—is under the usurped dominion of Satan; and therefore, as a Church, awaits a tremendous doom?" (ibid., p. 89).

See *Letters and Correspondence*, in a letter to his sister Harriet from Naples in February, Newman says, "We find such despicable frivolity so connected with religious observances, as to give the city a pagan character." And to his sister Jemima, also from Naples the same month, he writes, "The whole city offends me. It is a frivolous, dissipated place" (I, pp. 300, 304–305).

53. John Henry Newman, *Lectures on the Present Position of Catholics in England*, Notre Dame, IN, University of Notre Dame Press, 2000, pp. 1–2, 2–4. He said that controversies are constructed of ambiguous terms—like specific cultural constructs—because "half the controversies in the world are verbal ones. . . . When men understand each other's meaning, they see, for the most part, that controversy is either superfluous or hopeless" (Sermon X). "Faith and Reason, Contrasted as Habits of Mind," in *Fifteen Sermons Preached Before the University of Oxford*, 200–201. See also William James, A Pluralistic Universe, New York, Longmans, Green, 1909. He was close to the notion of cultural constructs in philosophy. As he put it, "Place yourself at the center of a man's philosophical vision and you understand at once all the dif-

ferent things it makes him write and say. But keep outside . . . and of course you will fail. You crawl over the thing like a myopic ant over a building" (p. 26).

54. See *Newman Family Letters*, (ed.) Dorothea Mozley, London, SPCK, 1962. This would especially include his father, John Newman II—"an unpretending, firm-minded Englishman, who had learned his morality more from Shakespeare than the Bible" (pp. xiv–xv); his sister Harriet; his aunt Betsy Good Newman; and Evangelical-secular, youngest brother Frank. Harriet, forthrightly establishment-minded, broke off all relations with her elder brother John Henry three years *before* his conversion to Catholicism.

55. Salvador de Madariaga, *Englishmen, Frenchmen, Spaniards: An Essay in Comparative Psychology,* London, Oxford University Press, 1928, p. xi. Salvador Madariaga y Rojo (1886–1978), well-known diplomat at the League of Nations, scholar-historian, author of a life of Don Cristobal Colon, was fluent in English, German, French, and Spanish. He taught at Oxford and later founded the College of Europe in Bruges.

56. Salvador de Madariaga, *Englishmen, Frenchmen, Spaniards*, p. 3. See also John Henry Newman, *An Essay on the Development of Christian Doctrine*, New York, Doubleday/Image, 1960. With special sensitivity, Newman refers to "the history of national character" as supplying an analogy for the close connection "between the development of minds and ideas," V. 1.6, p. 180.

57. See Selwyn Gumey Champion, M. D., *Racial Proverbs: A Selection of the World's Proverbs Arranged Linguistically,* London, Routledge & Kegan Paul, 1938, p. 20.

58. Salvador de Madariaga, *Englishmen, Frenchmen, Spaniards*, pp. 17, 57.

59. Ibid., p. 15.

60. Ibid., p. 144. See also Jacques Barzun, *The House of Intellect*, New York, Harper & Brothers, 1959. The "bookish boy" at English schools, says Barzun, is treated like Socrates, and with like hostility, pp. 7–8.

61. Salvador de Madariaga, *Englishmen, Frenchmen, Spaniards*, pp. 16–17.

62. Ibid., pp. 57, 62. See John Henry Newman, *An Essay in Aid of A Grammar of Assent*, New York, Longmans, Green, 1947. Newman speaks of the distinction between "ratiocination as the exercise of a living faculty" and "mere skill in argumentative science," which distinction explains "the prejudice which exists against logic in the popular mind, and the animadversions which are leveled against it . . . that Englishmen are too practical to be logical, that an ounce of common-sense goes farther than many cartloads of logic" (p. 230).

63. *Apologia pro vita sua*, p. 115.

64. *The Idea of a University*, VIII. 4, p. 189; *A Grammar of Assent,* pp. 122, 67. The conclusion of Newman's reference to Locke is this: "I feel no pleasure in considering him in the light of an opponent to views which I myself have ever treasured as true, with an obstinate devotion."

65. As expressed in the well-known formula, *entia non sunt multiplicanda sine necessitate*. The "razor" of William of Ockham (1285–1349) is still invoked in scientific theory—for instance, as illustrated in how Einstein's relativity mechanics was devised to simplify Newtonian mechanics, and dispense with Newton's "unnecessary" competing forces.

66. See Sir William Blackstone, *Commentaries on the Laws of England*, 4 vols., Chicago, University of Chicago Press, 1991, IV, p. 56.

67. "The Danger of Accomplishment," in *Parochial and Plain Sermons*, II. 30, pp. 460, 458.

68. Ibid., p. 459.

69. Ibid.

70. Ibid., p. 460.

71. Ibid., p. 461.

72. "The Self-Wise Inquirer," in *Parochial and Plain Sermons*, p. 140.

73. *Lectures on the Present Position of Catholics in England*, p. 392.

74. Ibid., p. 390.

75. John Henry Newman, "Poetry with Reference to Aristotle's Poetics," *Essays and Sketches*, I, pp. 55–81, 79.

76. See Wilfrid Ward, Life of John Henry Cardinal Newman, "manly Englishman," II, p. 15. *Apologia pro vita sua*, "Had he been a man," p. 375.

CHAPTER 5:   HEART AND MIND
NEWMAN EPIGRAPHS:

"Literature"—*Historical Sketches*, II, p. 222.
"Increase"—*Development of Christian Doctrine*, Intro. 21,
    p. 53.
"Throw"—"*Elementary Studies*," 3, Idea, p. 371.

1. See John Moody, *John Henry Newman*, New York, Sheed & Ward, 1945, p. 325.

2. "The Individuality of the Soul," in *Parochial and Plain Sermons*, San Francisco, Ignatius, 1987, pp. 778–79.

3. See "The Infinite Knowledge of God" and "The Bodily Sufferings of Our Lord," in *Prayers, Verses, and Devotions*, San Francisco, Ignatius, 1989, pp. 432, 455. See also, "Mental Sufferings of Our Lord in His Passion," XVI, *Discourses Addressed to Mixed Congregations*, Westminster, MD, Christian Classics, 1966, p. 328.

4. See *Letters and Correspondence of John Henry Newman during His Life in the English Church*, (ed.) Anne Mozley, 2 vols., London, Longmans, Green, 1911. On Wednesday, 25 January 1843, Newman wrote from Littlemore to J. R. Hope that certain retractive statements of his would appear "next Saturday" in Oxford's *Conservative Journal*, and that he would "eat a few dirty

words of mine" (II, p. 363). (That statement was later reprinted in his *Essays Critical and Historical*, 2 vols., London, Longmans, Green, 1907,1, pp. vii, viii–ix.) The following month, his sister Jemima said that the published letter "bears every mark of belonging to you except your name" (*Letters and Correspondence*, II, p. 364).

5. See Venerable Bede, *A History of the English Church and People* [*Historia ecclesiastica gentis Anglorum*], rev. ed., (trans.) Leo Sherley-Price, New York, Dorset, 1968, p. 94; Angli/Angeli, p. 100.

6. See John Henry Newman, *Rise and Progress of Universities and Benedictine Essays*, Notre Dame, IN, University of Notre Dame Press, 2001: "With what pertinacity of zeal does Gregory send his missionaries to England! With what an appetite he waits for the tidings of their progress! With what relish he dwells over the good news, when they are able to send it!" (p. 135).

7. As in Gen.-Ber. 1: 26–28, a scriptural command (*mitzvah*, מצוה; plural, mitzvoth, מצוה), is invariably preceded by a blessing (*b'rahkah*, בדבה). Such a "command-blessing" (מצוה-בדבה) becomes "injunctive invitation" to enlargement of "fruitfulness" and "growth." New Testament parables of enlargement promote similar images—the parable of seeds in various soils (Mk. 4: 2–9, 13–20; Mt. 13: 3–9, 18–23; Lk. 8: 4–8, 11–14); mustard seed (Mk. 13: 28–29; Mt. 24: 32–33; Lk. 21: 29–31); and talents (Mt. 25: 14–30; Lk. 19: 12–27).

8. See A. Dwight Culler, *The Imperial Intellect: A Study of Newman's Educational Ideal*, New Haven, CT, Yale University Press, 1955. He rightly remarks of Newman that "the intersection between educational and his religious interests . . . provides the central pattern of his entire life" (p. xii).

9. See John Henry Newman, *Apologia pro vita sua, Being a History of His Religious Opinions*, New York, Longmans, Green, 1947, pp. 6, 24. See also Vincent F. Blehl, S. J., "Newman, the Fathers, and Education," in Thought 45 (1970), pp. 196–212: Fr. Blehl notes, "In the Long Vacation of 1828 Newman began to read the Fathers chronologically, beginning with St. Ignatius and St. Justin" (p. 197). See also, Fr. Blehl's "The Patristic Humanism of John Henry Newman," in Thought 50 (1975), pp. 266–74.

10. See "The Influence of Natural and Revealed Religion Respectively," Sermon II, in *Fifteen Sermons Preached before the University of Oxford*, Notre Dame, IN, University of Notre Dame Press, 1997, p. 31.

11. Henri de Lubac, S. J., *Teilhard de Chardin: The Man and His Meaning*, (trans.) René Hague, New York, Hawthorn, 1965, p. 184.

12. See Pierre Teilhard de Chardin, *The Divine Milieu*, (trans.) Bernard Wall, New York, Harper & Row, 1960, "teaching how to see," p. 46; see also *The Phenomenon of Man*, (trans.) Bernard Wall, New York, Harper & Brothers, 1959, p. 178. Says Teilhard, of a converging universe, "This state is obtained not by identification (God becoming all) but by the differentiating and communicating action of love (God all in everyone). And that is essentially orthodox and Christian" (ibid., p. 308).

13. "The Theory of Developments in Religious Doctrine," Sermon XV, in *Fifteen Sermons Preached before the University of Oxford*, p. 337.

14. In *Epist. Joannis ad Parthos*, Tr. V, 7; quoted in *An Augustine Synthesis*, (ed.) Erich Przywara, New York, Harper & Brothers, 1958, pp. 77–78. It is interesting that the Greek root of the Latin *largus*, "abundant," is the verb "to desire, to long for" (λιλαίομαι), which suggests that, in Augustine's sense, enlargement is implicitly participative and reciprocal, and thus requires motivation.

15. *Select Treatises of St. Athanasius*, II, London, Longmans, Green, 1895, p. 465; quoted in George A. Maloney, S. J., *The Cosmic Christ: From Paul to Teilhard*, New York, Sheed & Ward, 1968, pp. 132, 298.

16. *The Idea of a University, Defined and Illustrated*, London, Longmans, Green, 1898, VI. 4, p. 133. The passage closely parallels a portion of Sermon XIV, "Wisdom, as Contrasted with Faith and with Bigotry," in *Fifteen Sermons Preached before the University of Oxford*, pp. 284–85:

> It is often remarked of uneducated persons, who hitherto have lived without seriousness, that on their turning to God, looking into themselves, regulating their hearts, reforming their conduct, and studying the inspired Word, they seem to become, in point of intellect, different beings from what they were before. Before, they took things as they came, and thought no more of one thing than of another. But now every event has a meaning; they form their own estimate of whatever occurs; they recollect times and seasons; and the world, instead of being like the stream which the countryman gazed on, ever in motion and never in progress, is a various and a complicated drama, with parts and with an object.

17. *The Idea of a University*, VI. 8, p. 142.

18. Ibid., VII. 1, pp. 151–52. Contrast the language—we cannot reflect on an idea "except piecemeal"—which he also employs in Sermon XV, "The Theory of Developments in Religious Doctrine," in *Fifteen Sermons Preached before the University of Oxford*, p.331.

19. See *Letters and Correspondence*, letter of 4 October 1832, I, p. 243. See also, "What Is a University?" in *Rise and Progress of Universities and Benedictine Essays*, p. 13. Also *The Idea of a University*, VI. 2, p. 126.

20. John Henry Newman, "Equanimity," in *Parochial and Plain Sermons*, pp. 995–96.

21. See J. F. Donceel, S. J., *Philosophical Anthropology*, New York, Sheed & Ward, 1967, p. 43. Similar language, characterizing life as "self-perfective immanent action," is used by Raymond J. Anable, S. J., *Philosophical Psychology*, New York, Fordham University Press, 1945, p. 9.

22. *The Idea of a University*, VI. 5, p. 134.

23. Ibid. Once again, it is instructive to compare this passage with its parallel in Sermon XIV, in *Fifteen Sermons Preached before the University of Oxford*: "It is not the mere addition . . . which is the enlargement, but the change of place, the movement onwards, of that moral centre, to which what we know and what we have been acquiring . . . gravitates" (p. 287). The change of place is a distinctive characterization of such "enlargement" because it alters mental space, and because it "renovates" mental habitation, or mental environment.

24. Pierre Rousselot, S. J., *The Intellectualism of St. Thomas*, London, Sheed & Ward, 1935, p. 34.

25. *The Idea of a University*, VI. 5, p. 134.

26. Ibid., VI. 6, pp. 136–37.

27. *Lectures on the Present Position of Catholics in England*, Notre Dame, IN, University of Notre Dame Press, 2000, pp. 390–91.

28. See Charles Stephen Dessain, *John Henry Newman*, London, Thomas Nelson, 1966, p. 112.

29. Because William Tyndale had translated, not the Greek positive adverb of Jn. 10: 10 ($\pi\varepsilon\rho\iota\sigma\sigma\tilde{\omega}\varsigma$, "*abundantly*"; Latin, abundanter), but Jerome's Vulgate Latin (Biblia Sacra Vulgata) comparative adverb (*abundantius*, "more abundantly" [Greek, $\pi\varepsilon\rho\iota\sigma\sigma\acute{o}\tau\rho\sigma\nu$]), KJV picking it up from Tyndale, used this form (an interesting theological grace note) with which Newman was so familiar. Revised Standard Version (RSV) now omits the comparative and retrieves the original Greek adverb, abundantly.

30. Pierre Teilhard de Chardin, *The Divine Milieu*, p. 66.

31. John Henry Newman, *An Essay on the Development of Christian Doctrine*, New York, Doubleday/Image, 1960. Newman footnotes the quotation, "Guizot Europ. Civil. Lect. v, Beckwith's Translation" (p. 71), referring to the 1837 translation of François Guizot's *Histoire de la civilisation en Europe* (1828). See François Pierre Guillaume Guizot, *General History of Civilization in Europe*, New York, Appleton, 1896, pp. 171–72.

32. *An Essay in Aid of a Grammar of Assent*, pp. 295–96.

33. Ibid., pp. 87–88, 89.

34. John Henry Newman, "Prospects of the Anglican Church," in *Essays and Sketches*, 3 vols., Westport, CT, Greenwood, 1970, I, pp. 341, 344.

35. *Apologia pro vita sua*, pp. 225, 227, 229.

36. John Henry Newman, "The Visible Church for the Sake of the Elect," in *Parochial and Plain Sermons*, IV. 10, p. 820.

37. *An Essay in Aid of a Grammar of Assent*, p. 60.

38. See Wilfrid Ward, *The Life and Times of Cardinal Wiseman*, 2 vols., 2nd ed., London, Longmans, Green, 1897. There was a "papistic" party, supporting Rome in all things, and a Gallican-spirited party of old Catholic families and clergy, which claimed the right to elect their own bishop and Vicar Apostolic (I, pp. 204, 512–14). See also "The Journal, 1859–1879," in *John Henry Newman Autobiographical Writings,* p. 259.

39. "Secret Faults," in *Parochial and Plain Sermons*, I. 4, p. 32.

40. Ibid., p. 31.

41. Ibid., p. 39.

42. J. Lewis May, *Cardinal Newman: A Study*, London, Geoffrey Bles, 1945, pp. 78, 171.

43. See John R. Griffen, *Newman: A Bibliography of Secondary Studies*, Front Royal, VA, Christendom Publications, 1980. He says, "The literature on Newman is so vast that no bibliographer, however zealous, could hope to do more than collect much of what has been written about the man or his work" (p. 1). See also Vincent Ferrer Blehl, S. J., *John Henry Newman: Bibliographical Catalogue of His Writings,* Charlottesville, University Press of Virginia, 1978. Newman's work has been translated into thirteen languages.

44. *The Present Position of Catholics in England*, p. 391.

45. Gertrude Donald, *Men Who Left the Movement*, Freeport, NY, Books for Libraries Press, 1967, p. 13.

46. John Henry Newman, "Illuminating Grace," Discourse IX, in *Discourses Addressed to Mixed Congregations*, p. 182.

47. *Letters and Correspondence*, I, p. 125.

48. Meriol Trevor, *Newman: The Pillar of the Cloud*, New York, Doubleday, 1962, p. 62.

49. See A. Dwight Culler, *The Imperial Intellect*, pp. 55, 290.

50. Ibid., p. 56.

51. See Meriol Trevor, *Newman: The Pillar of the Cloud*, pp. 62–63. See also Ian Ker, *John Henry Newman: A Biography,* Oxford, Oxford University Press, 1990, p. 740.

52. Sir Herbert Maxwell, *The Honourable Sir Charles Murray, K.C.B., A Memoir,* London, William Blackwood, 1898, p. 56, quoted in Bertram Newman, *Cardinal Newman: A Biographical and Literary Study*, New York, Century, 1925, p. 28.

53. See Culler, *The Imperial Intellect*, p. 55.

54. The Greek word for "covetousness" ($\pi\lambda\varepsilon\text{ove}\xi\acute{\iota}\alpha$), often used in the Bible, is based on the word for "more" ($\pi\lambda\acute{\varepsilon}\omega\nu$). In Hebrew, the term for envy-rivalry *(quhnah',* קנא); in Pi'el, it means to become red, hence, it is pictorially represented as a mind inflamed by envy. See, for example, Ps. 73:3.

55. Demythologizing does not simply strip bare a myth, revealing it in its nakedness. Rather, it attempts to dissolve the myth, so that nothing remains as residue. Demythologizing is premised on the assumption that the myth contains something other than the myth, which can then be exposed. But what the myth contains is itself.

56. See Oliver S. Buckton, *Secret Selves: Confessions and Same-Sex Desire in Victorian Autobiography,* Chapel Hill, University of North Carolina Press, 1998; David Hilliard, "UnEnglish and Unmanly: Anglo-Catholicism and Homosexuality," in *Victorian Studies* 25 (1982), 181–210; *Muscular Christi-*

anity: Embodying the Victorian Age, (ed.) David E. Hall, Cambridge, Cambridge University Press, 1994; Norman Vance, *The Sinews of the Spirit: The Ideal of Christian Manliness in Victorian Literature and Religious Thought,* Cambridge, Cambridge University Press, 1985 (esp. pp. 31–40, 78–103); Heather Henderson, *The Victorian Self: Autobiography and Biblical Narrative,* Ithaca, NY, Cornell University Press, 1989; *Approaches to Victorian Autobiography,* (ed.) George P. Landon, Athens, Ohio University Press, 1979. Clinton MacHann, *The Genre of Autobiography in Victorian Literature,* Ann Arbor, University of Michigan Press, 1994; Jonathan Loesberg, Fictions of Consciousness, New Brunswick, NJ, Rutgers University Press, 1986.

57. See Terrence Merrigan, *Clear Heads and Holy Hearts: The Religious and Theological Ideal of John Henry Newman,* Louvain, Belgium, Peeters, 1991. The author asserts that it "seems reasonable to regard Newman as an introvert" in a Jungian sense (p. 23). See also his "Newman's Progress towards Rome: A Psychological Consideration of His Conversion to Catholicism," in *Downside Review* 104 (1986), pp. 95–112, and "*Numquam Minus Solus, Quam Cum Solus*—Newman's First Conversion: Its Significance for His Life and Thought," in Downside Review 103 (1985), pp. 99–118. See also J. H. Walgrave, O. P., *Newman the Theologian: The Nature of Belief and Doctrine as Exemplified in His Life and Works,* (trans.) A. V. Littledale, New York, Sheed & Ward, 1960. Fr. Walgrave first suggested that "it is very tempting to see in Newman one of Jung's introverted types." Describing Newman's "Platonic tendency," and "continual, painful sense of isolation," he allowed that "all this is characteristic of the introverted type described by Jung" (pp. 19–20).

58. A. N. Wilson, *Eminent Victorians*, New York, Norton, 1989, p. 177. See also *Prayers, Poems, Meditations,* (ed.) A. N. Wilson, London, SPCK, 1989. He says, "For most people in the English-speaking world he is remembered as a poet" (p. xvii).

59. See Wilfrid Ward, *The Life of John Henry Cardinal Newman: Based on His Private Journals and Correspondence*, 2 vols., London, Longmans, Green, 1912, II, p. 369. See also Geoffrey Faber, *Oxford Apostles: A Character Study of the Oxford Movement,* London, Faber & Faber, 1933, p. 34; J. Lewis May, *Cardinal Newman: A Study,* London, Geoffrey Bles, 1945, p. 63.

60. J. Lewis May, *Cardinal Newman*: A Study, pp. 65, 70–71.

61. Ibid., p. 187. This reveals more of May's estimate of women than it does of Newman.

62. See Meriol Trevor, *Light in Winter*, p. 301.

63. Ibid., p, 307.

64. Wilfrid Ward, *The Life of John Henry Cardinal Newman*, II, pp. 348–49. See also Geoffrey Faber, who cites this "very remarkable passage" as indicating that "Newman's 'feminine' characteristics were closely associated, in the minds of his disciples and admirers, with his personal charm" (Oxford Apostles, p.33).

65. Meriol Trevor, *Light in Winter*, pp. 517–18.

66. Shane Leslie, *Studies in Sublime Failure*, Freeport, NY, Books for Libraries, 1970, p. 57.

67. Martin C. D'Arcy, S. J., "John Henry Newman," in *The English Way: Studies in English Sanctity from St. Bede to Newman,* (ed.) Maisie Ward, Freeport, NY, Books for Libraries, 1968, p. 325. Encyclopedia Britannica (14th ed.) reproduces the phrasing in its article on Newman thus: "His character may be described as strong, with an almost feminine sensitiveness to impressions" (XVI, p. 316).

68. See Wilfrid Ward, *The Life and Times of Cardinal Wiseman*, I, p. 395. This remark, prefaced by the assertion, "We may be running a great risk," is in an 1841 letter by then Bishop Wiseman to Ambrose Phillipps de Lisle—heir of a wealthy family, a Catholic at age fifteen—regarding rumors of English reunion with Rome.

69. Charles Frederick Harrold, *John Henry Newman: An Expository and Critical Study of His Mind,* Thought and Art, London, Longmans, Green, 1945, pp. 304–305.

70. Right-hemisphere linguistic skills require further investigation. But the hemispheres are not completely isolated, being connected by a cylindrical bundle of nerve fibers called corpus callosum. Still, right-hemisphere dominance also provides women better night vision, sharpened acoustical skills, better fine motor coordination (as in penmanship), and faster information processing. Female linguistic skills further reflect relative infrequency—but high male incidence—of dyslexia, stuttering, autism, delayed speech record, and hyperkinesis, and attention deficit hyperactivity disorder (ADHD). Idiosyncratic language skills are consonant, too, with other neuro-somatic female traits, including greater sensitivity to situational and existential variables, increased ability to focus, greater contact-sensitivity to touch, better social skills, higher levels of emotive sensitivity, and more interpersonal and independent behavior. Left-hemisphere dominance provides males higher competence in mathematics, architectonic and architectural skills, and spatial coordination, including better daytime visual acuity, and the capacity to maneuver objects in three-dimensional space.

See Eleanor E. Maccoby and Carol Nagy Jacklin, *The Psychology of Sex Differences*, Stanford, CA, Stanford University Press, 1974; M.A. Wittig and A. C. Peterson, *Sex-Related Differences in Cognitive Functioning*, New York, Academic Press, 1979; Jo Dourden-Smith and Diane Desimone, *Sex and the Brain*, New York, Arbor House, 1983, esp. pp. 21–93; Edwin B. Steen and J. H. Price, *Human Sex and Sexuality,* 2nd rev. ed., New York, Dover, 1988; John Money and Herman Musaph, M.D., *Handbook of Sexology*, Amsterdam, Excerpta Medica, 1977; A. E. Beal and R. J. Sternberg, *The Psychology of Gender,* New York, Guildford , 1993; *Sex Differences: Cultural and Developmental Dimensions,* (edd.) P. C. Lee and R. S. Steward, New York, Orizen, 1976;

Handbook of Sexuality, (ed.) B. B. Wolman, Northvale, NJ, Aranson, 1993.

See also Gayle Rubin, "The Traffic in Women," pp. 157–210; and Lila Leibowitz, "Perspectives on the Evolution of Sexual Differences," in *Toward an Anthropology of Women*, (ed.) Rayna R. Reiter, New York, Monthly Review Press, 1975, pp. 20–35; Joan Kelly-Gadol, *Women, History, Theory,* Chicago, University of Chicago Press, 1984, pp. 19–50; Catherine Belsey, "Constructing the Subject: Deconstructing the Text," pp. 45–64, in *Feminist Criticism and Social Change: Sex, Class and Race in Literature and Culture,* (edd.) Judith Newton and Deborah Rosenfelt, New York, Methuen, 1985; Judith Butler, *Gender Trouble: Feminism and the Subversion of Identity*, London, Routledge, 1990; *The New Feminist Criticism: Essays on Women, Literature and Theory,* (ed.) Elain Showalter, New York, Pantheon, 1985; Helene Cixous, "The Laugh of the Medusa," in *The Signs Reader: Women, Gender & Scholarship,* (edd.) Elizabeth Abel and Emily K. Abel, Chicago, University of Chicago Press, 1983; *A History of Women in the West*, Vol. I, (ed.) Pauline Schmitt Pantel, Vol. II (ed.) Christiane Klapisch-Zuber, Cambridge, MA, Harvard University Press, 1992.

For Psycholinguistic "gender descriptors," see Deborah Tannen, *I Only Say This Because I Love You*, New York, Random House, 2001; The Argument Culture, New York, Random House, 1998; *Gender and Discourse*, New York, Oxford University Press, 1994; *You Just Don't Understand: Women and Men in Conversation*, New York, William Morrow, 1990; *Talking Voices: Repetition, Dialogue, and Imagery in Conversational Discourse*, Cambridge, Cambridge University Press, 1989.

71. See Selwyn Gurney Champion, M.D., *Racial Proverbs*, London, Routledge & Kegan Paul, 1938, p. 25.

72. See E. M. Patterson, M.D., "Gender Identity," in *Encyclopedia of Psychology,* (ed.) D. G. Benner, Grand Rapids, MI, Baker, 1985, pp. 442–46. He says, "We should speak of psychogender identity, since sexuality is an expression of gender sense."

73. See John Money and Patricia Tucker, *Sexual Signatures: On Being a Man or a Woman*, Boston, Little Brown, 1975, pp. 86–118. These authors define gender identity as "the sameness, unity, and persistence of one's individuality as male, female, or ambivalent . . . especially as it is experienced in self-awareness and behavior." Gender role is everything "that a person says or does, to indicate to others and to the self the degree to which one is either male, female, or ambivalent. . . . Gender role is the public expression of gender identity." John Money and Anke A. Ehrhardt, *Man and Woman, Boy and Girl: The Differentiation and Dimorphism of Gender Identity from Conception to Maturity,* Baltimore, MD, Johns Hopkins University Press, 1972, p. 4.

74. See Edward Rice, *Captain Sir Richard Francis Burton*, New York, Scribner's, 1990. Sir Richard Burton, proficient in twenty-nine languages and dedicated to the "Great Game" of espionage, was once introduced at Oxford to

John Henry Newman, by Newman's friend, William Alexander Greenhill. Even years later, Burton meditated on that meeting, p. 20.

75. See *Letters and Diaries*, XVI, p. 340. See also Wilfrid Ward, *The Life of John Henry Cardinal Newman*, I, pp. 352–54; Ian Ker, John Henry Newman: A Biography, pp. 412–14. See also *Letters and Correspondence*, I, p. 275. As early as 1832, Newman perceptively saw through the hidden intentions of Russia, as he suggested in a letter to his sister Jemima: "Russia is at the bottom of these troubles [Mediterranean piracy], in order to gain the part of arbitration and then of sovereignty."

76. See C. J. W.-L. Wee, "Christian Manliness and National Identity," in *Muscular Christianity: Embodying the Victorian Age*, (ed.) Donald E. Hall, Cambridge, Cambridge University Press, 1994.

He says, "A dynamic Anglo-Saxon spirit coalesced with a nationalist Protestantism to form a triumphant national identity" (p. 68).

See also Norman Vance, *The Sinews of the Spirit: The Ideal of Christian Manliness in Victorian Literature and Religious Thought*, Cambridge, Cambridge University Press, 1985; David Rosen, *The Changing Fiction of Masculinity*, Urbana, Illinois University Press, 1993; Manliness and Morality: *Middle-Class Morality in Britain and America* 1800–1940, (edd.) J. K. Mangan and James Walvin, Manchester, Manchester University Press, 1987; George J. Worth, "Of Muscles and Manliness: Some Reflections on Thomas Hughes," in *Victorian Literature and Society, Essays Presented to Richard D. Altick,* (edd.) James R. Kincaid and Alberet J. Kuhn, Columbus, Ohio State University, 1984.

For "sub-text attitudes," see Thomas Hughes, Tom Brown's *Schooldays,* London, J. M. Dent, [1857] 1949, who says, "After all, what would life be without fighting, I should like to know? From the cradle to the grave, fighting, rightly understood, is the business, the real, highest, honestest business of every son of man. Every one who is worth his salt has his enemies, who must be beaten. . . . The world might be a better world without fighting for anything I know, but it wouldn't be 'our World' and therefore I am dead set against crying peace when there is no peace, and isn't meant to be" (pp. 250–51).

77. See Ian Ker, *John Henry Newman: A Biography*, pp. 234–39.

78. See C. J. W.-L. Wee, "Christian Manliness and National Identity." He says, "The late-Victorian national imperialism which develops with help from Kingsley's work is an attempt to confront urban-industrial circumstances as well as the anxieties raised by the increasing competition between the United States and Germany" (p. 71).

Professor Wee likewise suggests that the political image which Britain sought to project to the observing world was, on one hand, decorated in psychological and Establishment-religious icons, but, on the other, rooted in economic and political Hobbesianism.

79. See *The Compact Edition of the Oxford English Dictionary*, 2 vols.,

Oxford, Oxford University Press, 1988, which quotes the *Edinburgh Review* (January 1858): "It is a school of which Mr. Kingsley is the ablest doctor; and its doctrine has been described fairly and cleverly as 'muscular Christianity'" (I. p. 1880, col. A). See also *Muscular Christianity*, (ed.) David Hall, Cambridge, Cambridge University Press, 1994. The editor asserts that "muscular Christianity is shown to be at the heart of issues of gender, class, and national identity in the Victorian age" (p. 4).

80. See *Encyclopedia Britannica*, 14th ed., XIII, p. 349.

81. See *Apologia pro vita sua*, p. 358. Kingsley may have followed the advice of his own best-selling book, *Loose Thoughts for Loose Thinkers.*

82. See G. Egner [P. J. Fitzpatrick], *Apologia pro Charles Kingsley,* London, Sheed & Ward, 1969. See also Michael Ryan, "A Grammatology of Assent: Cardinal Newman's *Apologia pro vita sua,*" in *Approaches to Victorian Autobiography*, (ed.) George P. Landow, Athens, Ohio University Press, 1979, pp. 128–57. An instance of some current methodologies, it confuses apologia (ἀπολογία), "defense" (from ἀπολογέομαι, "to speak in defense of a fact") with apologos (ἀ), "story" or "fable." Methodological *conclusions* drawn from this error are alarming.

83. See Meriol Trevor, *Light in Winter*, p. 324.

84. Ibid., p. 344.

85. See Richard H. Hutton, *Cardinal Newman*, London, Methuen, 1905: "But there was something headlong about Kingsley as there was something essentially reserved and reticent about Newman, and there, I fancy, was the secret of the repulsion between them" (p. 228).

86. See "Mr. Kingsley's Method of Disputation" (Pamphlet of 21 April 1864), included in *Apologia pro vita sua*, p. 373.

87. See Meriol Trevor, *Light in Winter*, pp. 325–26. See also Frances Grenfell Kingsley, *Charles Kingsley: His Letters and Memories of His Life, Edited by His Wife*, 2 vols., London, Henry S. King, 1877. Mrs. Kingsley omits the letter of 9 March 1864. Its Chapter XXIII, "Controversy with Dr. Newman," avoids detailed mention of the Newman-Kingsley affair, except to say that it was about "whether the Roman Catholic priesthood are encouraged or discouraged to pursue 'Truth for its own sake'" (p. 191).

88. See Brenda Colloms, *Charles Kingsley: The Lion of Eversley,* London, Constable, 1975, p. 43. Fanny's also devout sister, Charlotte, had once become a Catholic, but recanted when she met James Anthony Froude, whom she later married. In Kingsley's mind, Charlotte may have been another Vestal Virgin saved from unspeakable danger. Of Kingsley's review of Froude, Ms. Colloms says, "What had begun as a piece of slipshod writing by Kingsley was turned into a time bomb, ready to explode in his face" (p. 273). She also believes that "Newman did not share Kingsley's high regard for women" (p. 271). But see Joyce Sugg, *Ever Yours Affly: John Henry Newman and His Female Circle,* London, Fowler Wright, 1997. See also "Newman and the Intellectual

Advancement of Women," in *Personality and Belief: Interdisciplinary Essays on John Henry Newman,* (ed.) Gerard Magill, Lanham, MD, University Press of America, 1994, pp. 53–62; and *A Packet of Letters: A Selection from the Correspondence of John Henry Newman,* (ed.) Joyce Sugg, Oxford, Clarendon, 1983.

89. See Meriol Trevor, *Light in Winter*, p. 328.

90. Ibid., p. 327. Newman, although unaware of Kingsley's subtexts, was certainly not unaware of the sort of person he was dealing with in Kingsley. By 23 April 1864, when Newman was fending off the Kingsley attack, he wrote to R. W. Church, Rector of Whatley in Somerset, with whom he had not spoken since Church's leaving Littlemore in 1845. Newman's purpose was to ask for help with previous correspondence and events. Here is what Newman said (in *Letters and Diaries*, XXI, p. 100):

> I know well that Kingsley is a furious foolish fellow—but he has a name—nor is it anything to me that men think I got the victory in the Correspondence several months ago— that was a contest of ability—but now he comes out with a pamphlet bringing together a hodge podge of charges against me all about dishonesty. Now friends who know me say: "Let him alone—no one credits him," but it is not so. . . . Therefore, thus publicly challenged, I must speak, and, unless I speak strongly, he won't believe me in earnest. I need hardly say that I shall keep secret anything you do for me, and the fact of my having applied to you.

91. James Eli Adams, "Pater's muscular aestheticism," in *Muscular Christianity*, pp. 215–38.

92. See Noel Annan, *The Dons, Mentors, Eccentrics and Geniuses,* Chicago, University of Chicago Press, 1999. He depicts Richard Hurrell Froude thus: "a handsome, dashing young man of a wellborn Devon family and Newman fell in love with him" (p. 49). Newman's sermons were "so bitter and characteristic of Newman's self-pity and anger that he and his minority of believers are scorned by the great and good and by the multitude. . . . Newman provoked an era of controversy, bitterness and intolerance which hung like a cloud over Oxford for the next thirty years . . . [and] had become the most notorious don in Oxford" (pp. 47, 52). Newman's was "the voice of a doctrinaire—indubitable, incontestable; and the reverberations were disagreeable" (pp. 59–60). See also Geoffrey Faber, *Oxford Apostles: A Character Study of the Oxford Movement*, London, Faber & Faber, 1933. He asserts that in Newman "the mating instinct never developed. . . . [H]e had made a discovery about himself, from which he concluded that he was not likely to marry. . . . But there can be no possible doubt of its nature. . . . Both Froude and Newman may have

derived the ideal of virginity from a homosexual root. . . . This is the unmistakable language of conflict with sexual temptation" (pp. 30–31, 218). See also Christopher Dawson, *The Spirit of the Oxford Movement*, New York, Sheed & Ward, 1933, p. vii, note 1; he angrily challenged Faber's assertion that Hurrell Froude was probably homosexual (in Geoffrey Faber, *Oxford Apostles*, pp. 217–19, 222–28).

See Oliver S. Buckton, *Secret Selves: Confessions and Same-Sex Desire in Victorian Autobiography*, Chapel Hill, University of North Carolina Press, 1998. He places Newman as first of five Victorians—with John Addington Symonds, Oscar Wilde, E. M. Forster, and Walter Pater, all self-assertedly gay—in his first chapter entitled, "An Unnatural State: Secrecy and 'Perversion' in John Henry Newman's *Apologia pro vita sua*." He asserts that Kingsley's distrust of Newman "stemmed not merely from widespread concern about Newman's 'honesty' but also from hostility toward his 'perversion'—a term that included his religious transgression as well as his perceived sexual ambiguity" (p.23). His thesis: "I want to argue, in fact, that 'perversion' is closer than any other term to being a catchall for the various layers of Newman's 'otherness,' . . . his allegedly secret Catholicism, his celibacy, his perceived gender transgression, or 'effeminacy,' and relatedly, his possible homosexuality" (p. 24). See Havelock Ellis, *Studies in the Psychology of Sex*, New York, Random House, 1937 [1st ed., London, University Press, 1897]. He was the first to use the fourteenth-century religious term *perversion* in a sexual context.

See also W. S. F. Pickering, *Anglo-Catholicism: A Study in Religious Ambiguity*, London, Routledge, 1989; John Boswell, *Christianity, Social Tolerance, and Homosexuality: Gay People in Western Europe from the Beginning of the Christian Era to the Fourteenth Century*, Chicago, University of Chicago Press, 1980. For response, see Glen W. Olsen, "St. Anselm and Homosexuality," in *Anselm Studies: An Occasional Journal*, II, (edd.) J. C. Schnaubelt, O.S.A., et al., White Plains, NY, Kraus International, 1988, pp. 93–141, and "The Gay Middle Ages: A Response to Professor Boswell," in Communio 8 (1981), pp. 119–38; J. R. Wright, "Boswell on Homosexuality: A Case Undemonstrated," in *Anglican Theological Review* 66 (1984), pp. 79–94.

CHAPTER 6:   EDUCATION AS DEVELOPMENT
NEWMAN EPIGRAPHS:

"Education is"—*The Idea of a University*, VI. 8, p. 144.
"But Education is"—*The Idea of a University*, V. 6, p. 114.
"Education and"—*The Idea of a University*, I. 1, p. 1.
"Education has been"—*Journal* 15 Dec 1859, *Autobiographical Writings*, p. 259.

"Education is so much"—*Letters and Diaries*, XVI, p. 428.
"The image"—*Grammar of Assent*, V, 1, p. 88.
"In a higher"—*Development of Christian Doctrine*, I, 7, p. 63.

1. See Freund's *Latin Dictionary*, (edd.) Charlton Lewis and Charles Short, Oxford, Clarendon, 1958. Latin root of education appears in both third (*educere*) and first (*educare*) conjugations—educere (from ducere, "lead"; dux, "leader") meaning "to lead forth, to summon, to produce," but also "to rear a child," whereas educare specifically means "to rear a child, physically or mentally." Second conjugation (*docēre*) means "to teach," while *edocēre* means "to teach thoroughly," its adverb (*edocenter*) meaning "instructively." The third conjugation verb (*edere*) means both "to eat" and "to bring forth, to raise up, to elevate."
2. *The Idea of a University*, Defined and Illustrated, London, Longmans, Green, 1898, VI. 6, p. 137.
3. Greek-Latin term for "being" does not express our term "reality"—which itself is based on the Latin for "thing" (res). *Reality*, in Greek-Latin, employs the terms truth (ἀλήθεια / *veritas*). Cardinal Newman's self-authored epitaph, "*ex umbris et imaginibus in veritatem*" (entablatured in Birmingham's Oratory Church), is often translated, "From shadows and images to truth." But, since *umbra* and *imago* are synonyms for "copy, representation, imitation, echo" (hence, "unrealities"), an appropriate translation might be "Out of unrealities into reality."
4. See J. E. Raven, *Plato's Thought in the Making*, Cambridge, Cambridge University Press, 1965. Raven describes the Academy as "the prototype of all universities" (p. 73). The Academy (named for the hero Hekkademos) lasted almost a millennium—until Byzantine Emperor Justinian, for political reasons, shut it down in 529 AD. Of Greek words for "form," two (τὸ εἶδος · ἡ ιδέα) are related to the English word idea, and would be enough to suggest a direct line to Newman's Platonic title, *The Idea of a University*.
5. *The Idea of a University*, VII. 1, pp. 152–53. *An Essay in Aid of a Grammar of Assent*, London, Longmans, Green, 1947, p. 167.
6. *The Idea of a University*, V. 4, p. 108; VII. 4, p. 162; VI. 3, p. 129; pp. xvi–xviii; V. 1, pp. 101–102; "Discipline of Mind," p. 502; V. 3, p. 107; V. 9, pp. 120–21; "Discipline of Mind," p. 493. Compare Plato, Epistle VII, 344A–344B, Thirteen Epistles of Plato, (ed.) L. A. Post, Oxford, Clarendon, 1925, pp. 98–99.
7. The terms *dianoetic* and *diathetic* are based on Greek words (ἡ διάνοια · ἡ διάθεσις) for "thought" and "attitude."
8. *The Idea of a University*, pp. xvi–xviii, 493, 120, xix, 101, 502.
9. See Aristotle, *Ethica Nicomachia*, VI, xiii, 1144b30–32 – 1 145a2–3. He says, "It is not possible to be good in the true sense without Prudence

[φρόνησις], or to be prudent without Moral Virtue. . . . For if a man have the one virtue of Prudence he will also have all the Moral Virtues together with it." See also St. Thomas, *Summa theologiae* I-IIae, q. 58, a. 3, Resp. 1. He asserts, "Prudence is essentially an intellectual virtue. But considered on the part of its matter, it has something in common with the moral virtues for it is right reason about things to be done. . . . It is in this sense that it is reckoned with the moral virtues."

10. See St. Augustine, *De civitate Dei*, XIX, xiii, 10. *Tranquillitas* (serenity) is linked there with *pax* (peace); in this famous *ordinata* passage (presaging Newman's rhetoric), Augustine displays a wide array of contexts—theological, metaphysical, psychological, and political.

11. See Plato, *Politeia* (The Republic), IV, 428A–433B. See also Aristotle, *Ethica Nicomachia*, III, 1115b–1119b17); V, 1129a–1138bl0; VI, 1140a25–1145all. See also *Summa theologiae*, I-IIae, q. 61, a. 2.

12. John Henry Newman, *Lectures on the Present Position of Catholics in England*, Notre Dame, IN, University of Notre Dame Press, 2000, p. 391.

13. See Aristotle, *Ethica Nicomachia*, VI, 1141a16–17: "Hence it is clear that Wisdom must be the most perfect of the modes of knowledge" (ὥστε δῆλον ὅτι ἡ ἀκριβεστάτη ἂν τῶν ἐπιστημῶν εἴη ἡ σοφία); see also, 1141a19, which notes that wisdom must be a combination of intellect and scientific knowledge (νοῦς καὶ ἐπιστήμη).

14. See *The Idea of a University*, I. 2, p. 5; I. 3, p. 7. "I shall consider the question simply on the grounds of human reason and human wisdom." See also Isaiah, 11: 2, which lists six "Spirits of the Spirit of Yahveh" (*ru-akh* Yahveh, הוהי חור)—the Spirit of wisdom and understanding, the Spirit of counsel and power, the Spirit of knowledge and fear of Yahveh. With the addition of piety, these became Christianity's "Seven Gifts of the Holy Spirit," which reside in the soul with habitual grace. See also St. Thomas, *Summa theologiae*, I-IIae, q. 68, a. 1, aa.

15. *The Idea of a University*, I. 1, pp. 1, 4.

16. See Charles Frederick Harrold, *John Henry Newman: An Expository and Critical Study of His Mind, Thought and Art*, London, Longmans, Green, 1945, p. 97. See also "*Elementary Studies*," *The Idea of a University*, pp. 331–71; VII. 10, p. 177. See also John Henry Newman, *Autobiographical Writings,* (ed.) Henry Tristram, New York, Sheed & Ward, 1957, p. 219.

17. See Ian Ker, *The Achievement of John Henry Newman*, Notre Dame, IN, University of Notre Dame Press, 1990, p. 2.

18. See *Letters and Diaries*, XV, p. 226. Newman writes Henry Wilberforce (February 1853): "My two most perfect works, artistically, are my two last. The former of them [*Present Position*] put me to less trouble than any I ever wrote, the latter [*The Idea of a University*] to the greatest of all."

19. See John Locke, *Some Thoughts Concerning Education*, (ed.) Peter Gay, New York, Bureau of Publications, Columbia Teachers College, 1964, p.

65. See also Jean-Jacques Rousseau, *Émile*, (trans., ed.) William Boyd, New York, Bureau of Publications, Columbia Teachers College, 1962, pp. 17, 166. Everything that Newman argued for in the Idea, excepting a common concern for Nature, was totally at odds with Locke's views. To Locke, nature is the condition in which teaching takes place; to Rousseau, it (*La nature*) is the very teacher and agent of education.

20. See John Henry Newman, *Apologia pro vita sua*, Being a History of *My Religious Opinions*, New York, Longmans, Green, 1947, pp. 4–5.

21. John Henry Newman, *An Essay on the Development of Christian Doctrine*, New York, Doubleday/Image, 1960, p. 190.

22. Ibid., p. 63.

23. See *The Idea of a University*, V. 4, p. 106; V. 5, p. 111; V. 1, p. 102; V. 6, p. 113.

24. *An Essay on the Development of Christian Doctrine*, p. 53.

25. *An Essay in Aid of a Grammar of Assent*, p.265. Compare Giovanni Pico della Mirandola, "On the Dignity of Man," (trans.) Elizabeth Livermore Forbes, in *The Renaissance Philosophy of Man,* (ed.) Ernst Cassirer et al., Chicago, University of Chicago Press, 1948. In his *De hominis dignitate oratio,* Pico (1463–94) argues for a concept (similar to that of Newman's "openness") of human nature as "indeterminate." Here is how he depicts it:

> At last the best of artisans ordained that the creature to whom He had been able to give nothing proper to himself should have joint possession of whatever had been peculiar to each of the different kinds of being. He therefore took man as a creature of indeterminate nature and . . . addressed him thus . . . "The nature of all other beings is limited and constrained within the bounds of laws prescribed by Us. Thou, constrained by no limits, in accordance with thine own free will, in whose hand We have placed thee, shalt ordain for thyself the limits of thy nature. . . . Thou shalt have the power to degenerate into the lower forms of life, which are brutish. Thou shalt have the power, out of thy soul's judgment, to be reborn into the higher forms, which are divine" (pp. 224–45).

See also, Avery Dulles, *Princeps concordiae: Pico della Mirandola and the Scholastic Tradition*, Cambridge, MA, Harvard University Press, 1941.

26. See *An Essay on the Development of Christian Doctrine*, p. 53. See also *Letters and Correspondence*, II, pp. 389, 412. "What a very mysterious thing the mind is," Newman writes his sister Jemima in August 1844. Seven months later, he adds in another letter to her, "Of course the human heart is mysterious." See also *Prayers, Verses and Devotions*, San Francisco, Ignatius, 1989, p. 536. In a variant context, Shakespeare gives voice, in Ophelia, to a

comparable mystery: "Lord, we know what we are, but know not what we may be" *Hamlet*, IV. 5, 42–43.

27. *An Essay on the Development of Christian Doctrine*, p. 63.

28. *The Idea of a University*, VI. 1; VI. 6, pp. 125, 139.

29. See *Letters and Correspondence*, II, p. 93. In January 1843, Newman informs his sister, Jemima, that he had "now for twelve years been working out a theory, and . . . it has this recommendation that it is consistent." See also ibid., II. p. 363. In 1818, as he listened to a sermon by Edward Hawkins, Newman had discerned the principle of doctrinal development; in 1824–25, in his conversations with Edward Hawkins, he had discussed this idea under the title "Christian Tradition"; in 1832, the idea had shaped his *The Arians of the Fourth Century*; in 1833, in Italy, he meditated on the idea; in 1836, in *Home Thoughts Abroad*, he had written on it; in 1844, he was writing his *An Essay on the Development of Christian Doctrine*. See *Apologia pro vita sua*, pp. 73, 101, 178, 212.

30. *See An Essay on the Development of Christian Doctrine*, II, 1. 10, p. 86; II, 1. 8, p. 85. "The whole Bible, not in its prophetical portions only, is written on the principle of development . . . [because] the prophetic Revelation is, in matter of fact . . . a process of development; the earlier prophecies are pregnant texts out of which the succeeding announcements grow; they are types. It is not that first one truth is told, and then another; but the whole truth or large portions of it are told at once . . . and they are expanded and finished in their parts, as the course of revelation proceeds."

31. John Henry Newman, "The Visible Church for the Sake of the Elect," in *Parochial and Plain Sermons*, San Francisco, Ignatius, 1987, IV. 10, p. 820.

32. *Apologia pro vita sua*, p. 179.

33. *The Idea of a University*, VI. 6, p. 137.

34. Ibid., IV. 3, pp. 74–75; V. 6, p. 113.

35. Ibid., VI. 6, pp. 138, 137.

36. Ibid., VI. 6, p. 139.

37. Ibid.

38. Ibid., V. 4, p. 111.

39. Ibid., V. 2, p. 104; See Ian Ker's edition, Oxford, Clarendon, 1976, p. 423.

40. *The Idea of a University*, V. 2, p. 103.

41. Ibid., VI. 1, pp. 125–26.

42. Ibid., VI. 1, pp. 151–52.

43. Ibid., VI. 8, p. 144; V. 6, p. 114.

44. Ibid., V. 6, p. 114; VI. 1, p. 125; VI. 5, p. 134.

45. See John Henry Newman, Sermon XIV, "Wisdom, as Contrasted with Faith and with Bigotry," in *Fifteen Sermons Preached before the University of Oxford,* Notre Dame, IN, University of Notre Dame Press, 1997, pp. 287, 290–91.

46. *The Idea of a University*, III. 4, pp. 50–51.

47. Ibid., VI. 6, p. 138.

48. Ibid., IV. 11, p. 90; VI. 7, pp. 139–40; VII. 6, pp. 166–67.

49. Ibid., IV. 3, p. 76; IV. 11, p. 90; VI. 6, pp.140, 139; VII. 6, pp. 166–67. See also *Letters and Diaries*, XI, p. 69.

50. *The Idea of a University*, VI. 6, pp. 137–39. See also John W. Donohue, S. J., *Jesuit Education: An Essay on the Foundations of Its Idea*, New York, Fordham University Press, 1963, p. 124.

51. *The Idea of a University*, V. 9, pp. 122–23.

52. Alfred North Whitehead, *The Aims of Education, and Other Essays*, New York, New American Library, 1949, p. 29.

53. *An Essay in Aid of a Grammar of Assent*, pp. 168, 167; see also John Henry Newman, *The Via Media of the Anglican Church*, (ed.) H. D. Weidner, Oxford, Clarendon, 1990, pp. 8, 70.

54. *The Aims of Education,* pp. 13, 42, 44, 29.

55. Ibid., pp. 13, 17.

56. Ibid., p. 30.

57. *The Idea of a University*, VI. 6, p. 139.

58. *The Aims of Education*, pp. 48, 30.

59. Ibid., pp. 38, 37, 90–91.

60. Ibid., p. 47: "The secret of success is pace, and the secret of pace is concentration."

61. *The Idea of a University*, "*Elementary Studies*," pp. 335, 352, 356.

62. *The Aims of Education*, p. 14.

63. *The Idea of a University*, VI. 8, p. 142; VI. 10, p. 149.

64. Ibid., "Discipline of Mind" and "*Elementary Studies*," pp. 501, 375.

65. See *Letters and Diaries*, XI, p. 279.

66. *The Idea of a University*, "Discipline of Mind," pp. 499–500.

67. Ibid., p. xvii, VIII. 10, p. 210, "*Elementary Studies*," p. 341.

68. *An Essay in Aid of a Grammar of Assent*, pp. 178, 177.

69. John Henry Newman, *Loss and Gain: A Story of a Convert*, New York, Sheed & Ward, 1935, pp. 16–17.

70. *The Idea of a University*, "*Elementary Studies*," I. 1, p. 335.

71. Ibid., "Discipline of Mind," p. 501; "*Elementary Studies*," p. 335.

72. "The Place of Classics in Education," in *The Aims of Education*, p. 73.

73. See Rev. Thomas Mozley, *Reminiscences, Chiefly of Oriel College and the Oxford Movement,* 2 vols., Boston, Houghton, Mifflin, 1882, I, p. 402. See also A. Dwight Culler, *The Imperial Intellect, A Study of Newman's Educational Ideal,* New Haven, CT, Yale University Press, 1955, pp. 30, 285–86, notes 48 and 50. See also, Vincent Ferrer Blehl, S. J., "John Henry Newman on Latin prose style: A critical edition of his *Hints on Latin Composition,"* *Classical Folia* 15 (1961), 1–12 (text, pp. 5–10).

74. See *Apologia pro vita sua*, p. 217. "Ten thousand difficulties do not make one doubt."

75. *The Idea of a University*, V. 3, p. 106.

76. Ibid., IX. 2, p. 219; "Literature," p. 275; IX. 6, p. 227. In contrast, see C. P. Snow, *The Two Cultures and the Scientific Revolution*, New York, Cambridge University Press, 1959.

77. *The Idea of a University*, "Elementary Studies," II. 3, p. 361; I.1, p. 336.

78. Ibid., "University Preaching," p. 422.

79. Ibid., VI. 5, p. 135; "*Elementary Studies*," I. 3, p. 341.

80. *The Aims of Education*, p. 13.

81. Ibid., p. 44.

82. *The Idea of a University*, VII. 1, p. 151.

83. Ibid., VI. 8, p. 144.

84. Ibid., VI. 6, p. 130. Compare Allan Bloom, *The Closing of the American Mind: How Higher Education Has Failed Democracy and Impoverished the Souls of Today's Students*, New York, Simon & Schuster, 1987, pp. 337–46. See also Mortimer J. Adler, *Reforming Education: The Opening of the American Mind*, New York, Macmillan, 1989.

85. *The Idea of a University*, Ker's edition, Discourse V, p. 423.

86. *The Idea of a University*, pp. 341, 349, 358; VIII. 10, p. 210; p. 501.

87. Ibid., "*Elementary Studies*," p. 332.

88. Ibid., p. xvi.

89. Ibid., VII. 1, p. 152.

90. Ibid., "Discipline of Mind," p. 502.

91. John Henry Newman, "What is a University?" in *Rise and Progress of Universities and Benedictine Essays,* Notre Dame, IN, University of Notre Dame Press, 2001, p. 13.

92. *The Idea of a University*, V. 9, p. 121.

93. Ibid., VII. 1, pp. 152–53.

CHAPTER 7: GENTLEMAN'S KNOWLEDGE
NEWMAN EPIGRAPHS:

"Liberal Education"—*The Idea of a University*, V. 9, p. 120.
"It is common"—*The Idea of a University*, V. 3, p. 106.
"I speak of"—*The Idea of a University*, V. 5, p. 111.

1. *John Henry Newman, "What is a University?" in Rise and Progress of Universities and Benedictine Essays,* Notre Dame, IN, University of Notre Dame Press, 2001, p. 10.

2. John Henry Newman, *An Essay in Aid of a Grammar of Assent,* New York, Longmans, Green, 1947, p. 42; *The Idea of a University, Defined and Illustrated,* London, Longmans, Green, 1890, pp. 111, 106; *Lectures on the Present Position of Catholics in England,* Notre Dame, IN, University of Notre Dame Press, 2000, p. 392.

3. See Fergal McGrath, S. J., *The Consecration of Learning: Lectures on Newman's Idea of a University,* New York, Fordham University Press, 1962. McGrath asserts that Newman "provides two instances of a defect that is fairly often found in the *Discourses* . . . the throwing in casually of some new idea or distinction, which creates confusion"—"two new names for liberal knowledge [being] a gentleman's knowledge" [the author calls it a dangerous phrase], and the term "Science" (pp. 126–27).

4. *The Idea of a University,* p. x.

5. Ibid., pp. x, xi.

6. See *Letters and Diaries,* XV, p. 84. "There were a number of ladies in the room," Newman wrote to Fr. Ambrose St. John, 11 May 1852 (the day after his first Discourse in Dublin's Rotunda), "and I fancied a slight sensation in the room, when I said, not Ladies and Gentlemen, but Gentlemen." In *The Idea of a University,* Newman uses that same form of address 27 times.

7. See William Harrison, *Harrison's Description of England in Shakspere's Youth, Being the Second and Third Books of His Description of Britaine and England,* (ed.) Frederick J. Furnivall, London, N. Trübner, 1877, esp. pp. 105, 123–24. [Alternate edition, William Harrison, *The Description of England,* (ed.) Georges Edelen, Ithaca, NY, Cornell University Press, 1968, pp. 94,110.] See also Henry Peacham, *The Complete Gentleman: The Truth of Our Times, and The Art of Living in London,* (ed.) Virgil B. Heltzel, Ithaca, NY, Cornell University Press, 1962, p. 2. See also [Bishop] William Stubbs, *The Constitutional History of England in its Origin and Development,* 3 vols., 5th ed., Oxford, Clarendon Press, 1896, esp. III, p. 563; Baldassare Castiglione, *The Book of the Courtier,* (trans.) Charles S. Singleton, New York, Doubleday/Anchor, 1959, pp. 29–67, 206–19.

8. See "Literature," in *The Idea of a University,* pp. 280–81. See also Plato, *Politeia (The Republic),* 535A–36B; compare *Gorgias,* 499E–514; Aristotle, *Ethica Nicomachia,* 1124al–5; Werner Jaeger, *Paideia: The Ideals of Greek Culture,* (trans.) Gilbert Highet, 3 vols., 2nd ed., New York, Oxford University Press, 1945, I, pp. 2, 276, 318, 416, n. 4; II, pp. 194, 267–68, 411–12, n. 343. Jaeger sees Sophocles and Pericles as "the Athenian gentlemen of the fifth century" whose "aristocratic origin in classical Greece is as clear as that of the gentleman of England." See also Juvenal, *Satires,* viii, 356–59.

9. *The Idea of a University,* VII. 6, pp. 165–66; pp. xvii–xviii; V. 9, p. 120, "*Elementary Studies,*" I. 2, p. 342; VI. 5, p. 134; V. 1, p. 101; VI. 6, pp. 139, 137–38; VII. 10, p. 178.

10. See William E. Buckler, "Newman's *Apologia* as Human Experi-

304 A PRIVILEGE OF INTELLECT

ence," in *Thought 39* (1964), 77–88. He asserts that *The Idea of a University* "is, ultimately, a devastating indictment of the educated man; and the 'gentleman' which is education's best end product is a figure with which no man of truly imaginative vision would allow himself willingly to be identified" p. 78. See also John R. Griffin, "In Defence of Newman's 'Gentleman,'" in *The Dublin Review* 239 (1965), 245–54, which takes the contrary view. This article (regrettably) is by-lined "John Triffin"; regrettably, too, it cites "Timothy Corcoran, S. J." as "Fr. Cormican" (pp. 249, 252). See also John R. Griffin, *Newman: A Bibliography of Secondary Studies,* Front Royal, VA, Christendom College Press, 1980, which lists the same Timothy Corcoran, S. J., as "Corcoran, R," p. 117.

11. *The Idea of a University*, VIII. 10, pp. 208–211.

12. See A. Dwight Culler, The Imperial Intellect: A Study of Newman's Educational Ideal, New Haven, CT, Yale University Press, 1955, p. 238.

13. *The Idea's* nine discourses (and preface) approximate 90,000 words, about two-thirds of which are of religious or theological import, with one-third knowledge-centered. Running heads and chapter titles also reveal the dominance of religious themes—"I. Introductory"; "II. Theology a Branch of Knowledge"; "III. Bearing of Theology on Other Knowledge"; "IV. Bearing of Other Knowledge on Theology"; "VIII. Knowledge and Religious Duty"; and "IX. Duties of the Church Towards Knowledge." The noetically titled chapters include these: "V. Knowledge Its Own End"; "VI. Knowledge Viewed in Relation to Learning"; and "VII. Knowledge and Professional Skill."

Discourses V through VII constitute a volume roughly equal to that of Discourses II through IV. But, if we include the other discourses, and the preface, and then measure the resulting volume, Discourses V through VII will take up only about a third of the book's total printed pages. The proportion of religion/theology titles to knowledge-centered titles thus approximates the ratio of two to one.

14. *The Idea of a University*, VIII. 10, p. 210. See Charles L. O'Donnell, *Newman's "Gentleman,"* New York, Longmans, Green, 1916. The author asks, "Does Knowledge make a man morally good? This is the problem of Discourse VIII" p. 7. In the process of his argument, he (negatively) suggests that Newman's contrast of knowledge and virtue constitutes a contrast between culture and religion.

15. Compare Sigmund Freud, *Civilization and Its Discontents,* in *Standard Edition of the Complete Psychological Works of Sigmund Freud* (trans., edd.) James Strachey, Anna Freud, et al., 24 vols., London, Hogarth Press, 1953–74, XXI (SE 1930A 21).

16. *The Idea of a University*, VIII. 1, pp. 180–81.

17. Ibid., VIII. 2, p. 181.

18. Ibid., VIII. 1, p. 179; VIII. 4, p. 190.

19. Ibid., p. xxvi. See also John Henry Newman, "Basil and Gregory," in

The Church of the Fathers, Essays and Sketches, 3 vols., Westport, CT, Green-wood Press, 1970, III, pp. 62–65.

20. John Henry Newman, "Truth Hidden When Not Sought After," *in Parochial and Plain Sermons*, San Francisco, Ignatius, 1987, VIII. 13, pp. 1660–62.

21. Ibid., pp. 1661–62.

22. *The Idea of a University*, V. 9, pp. 120–21, 203.

23. Ibid., p. 121.

24. Ibid., V. 9, p. 120.

25. "Truth Hidden When Not Sought After," in *Parochial and Plain Sermons*, VIII. 13, p. 1662.

26. "Knowledge of God's Will without Obedience," *Parochial and Plain Sermons*, I. 3, p. 24. See also *The Idea of a University*, VIII. 2, p. 181.

27. "The Religion of the Day," in *Parochial and Plain Sermons, I. 24, pp. 196–205.

28. *The Idea of a University*, VIII. 2, p. 182.

29. Edward Gibbon (1737–94), author of *The History of the Decline and Fall of the Roman Empire,* greatly influenced Newman's literary style, but was bereft of religious belief, and credited the fall of the Roman Empire to the advent of Christianity. See Edward Gibbon, *Memoirs of My Life,* (ed.) Betty Radice, London, Folio Society, 1991, esp. pp. 88–89.

Philip Dormer Stanhope, Fourth Earl of Chesterfield (1694–1773), author of *Letters to His Son*, and *Letters to His Godson,* recommended that a notable life is found in having "good manners," and in pleasing the world's powerful people. See A. Dwight Culler, *The Imperial Intellect;* he argues that Newman confused Chesterfield's *Advice to His Son* with James Forrester's *The Polite Philosopher,* and therefore considers Forrester "ironically" to be the true creator of Discourse VIII's conception of the "gentleman" (pp. 239–40). See also Dr. Johnson, *His Life in Letters,* (ed.) David Littlejohn, Englewood Cliffs, Prentice Hall, 1965, p. 28; James Boswell, *The Life of Samuel Johnson LL.D.,* Chicago, Encyclopedia Britannica, 1952, p. 73.

Anthony Ashley Cooper, Third Earl of Shaftesbury (1671–1713), foremost of English deists, argued in his *Characteristicks of Men, Manners, Opinions, Times* (1711) that "moral sense" is not derived from religion, but from nature.

30. *The Idea of a University*, VIII. 7, p. 196.

31. Ibid., VIII. 6, p. 194.

32. Ibid, VIII. 6, pp. 195–96; VIII. 7, p. 196.

33. *A Grammar of Assent*, p. 296; *The Idea of a University*, VIII. 5, p. 191; *Rise and Progress of Universities and Benedictine Essays*, p. 79; *Essay on the Development of Christian Doctrine*, New York, Doubleday/Image, 1960, p. 70; *Letter to the Duke of Norfolk* quoted in *The Rediscovery of Newman,* (edd.) John Coulson and A. M. Allchin, London, Sheed & Ward, 1967, p. 208. See

also Bernard Haring, *Christian Renewal in a Changing World*, New York, De-sclée, 1964, pp. 92–173.

34. See George Bernard Shaw, *Man and Superman*, in *The Theater of Bernard Shaw*, 2 vols., New York, Dodd, Mead, 1961. "Devil" says, "But the English really do not seem to know when they are thoroughly miserable. An Englishman thinks he is moral when he is only uncomfortable" (I, p. 387).

35. *The Idea of a University*, VIII. 5, p. 193.

36. Ibid., VIII. 8, p. 201.

37. Ibid., VIII. 6, p. 196.

38. Ibid., VIII. 7, p. 197.

39. Ibid., VIII. 8, p. 203.

40. Ibid., VIII. 8, p. 202.

41. Ibid.

42. See Francois, duc de la Rochefoucauld, *Réflexions ou Sentences et Maximes Morales, Dictionnaire des Citations de langue française,* (ed.) Pierre Ripert, Paris, Bookking International, 1995; he defines *hypocrisy* as "the tribute which vice pays for wishing to appear as virtue" *(L 'hypocrisie est un hommage que le vice rend a la vertu)*, p. 202. See also St. Thomas, *Summa theologiae*, IIa–IIae, q 111, 2, c.

43. "The Tamworth Reading Room," in *Essays and Sketches*, II, p. 190.

44. "Truth Hidden When Not Sought After," in *Parochial and Plain Sermons*, VIII. 13, pp. 1660–68, 1663.

45. *The Idea of a University,* IX. 9, p. 234. See Meriol Trevor, *Apostle of Rome: A Life of Philip Neri 1515–1595*, London, Macmillan, 1966; Theodore Maynard, *Mystic in Motley: The Life of St. Philip Neri,* Milwaukee, WI, Bruce, 1946. The influence of Filippo Romolo de' Neri on John Henry Newman was profound. Educated by Dominicans and Benedictines, Philip Neri studied philosophy and theology in Rome, wrote poetry, and established an apostolate dedicated to the poor. Sent to San Girolamo, he built an oratory, from which—with music by Palestrina—there developed the Oratorio. In 1575, he founded the Congregation of the Oratory. He was canonized in 1622.

46. *The Idea of a University,* IX. 10, p. 238.

47. See A. Dwight Culler, *The Imperial Intellect;* he says, "St. Philip, if he had not been a saint might well have been a courtier or a philosopher instead, or rather he already was these things and then erased them in the superaddition of saint" p. 242.

48. *Apologia pro vita sua*, p. 384.

49. *Letters and Diaries*, XII, p. 25.

CHAPTER 8:   A GRAMMAR OF ASCENT
NEWMAN EPIGRAPHS:

"I say then"—*The Idea of a University,* VI, 7, p. 139.

"We attain"—*The Idea of a University,* V. 10, p. 123.
"Scripture teaches"—*Development of Christian Doctrine*
VIII, 3, 2, p. 321.

1. See D. A. Carson, "Matthew," in The Expositor's Bible Commentary, (ed.) Frank E. Gaebelein, 12 vols., Grand Rapids, MI, Zondervan, 1984, VIII, p. 516. "Talent" (τὸ τάλεντον) refers to the weight (58 to 80 lbs.), in local currency, of copper, silver, or gold, equivalent to 6,000 denarii, representing a twenty-year labor cost.

2. See Abraham H. Maslow, *Toward a Psychology of Being,* 2nd ed., New York, Van Nostrand, 1968, pp. 60–67. Maslow wrote about "those who need to know," but to protect self-esteem, fear to know. See also William James, *Principles of Psychology,* Cleveland, OH, World Publishing, 1948, who argued, "All narrow people *entrench* their Me, they *retract* it,—from the region of what they cannot securely possess. . . . Sympathetic people, on the contrary, proceed by the entirely opposite way of expansion and inclusions" p. 189.

3. *The Idea of a University,* Defined and Illustrated, London, Longmans, Green, 1890, VI. 6, p. 139.

4. Sermon XIII, "Implicit and Explicit Reason," in *Fifteen Sermons Preached Before the University of Oxford,* Notre Dame, IN, University of Notre Dame Press, 1997, p. 257.

5. *"Elementary Studies,"* in *The Idea of a University,* p. 332.

6. "Prospects of the Anglican Church," in *Essays and Sketches,* 3 vols., Westport, CT, Greenwood Press, 1970, I p. 346.

7. "Christianity and Scientific Investigation," in *The Idea of a University,* pp. 479, 478.

8. Ibid., III. 4, p. 50–51; V. 1, p. 99; III. 2, p. 45.

9. See R. W. Southern, Robert Grosseteste, *The Growth of an English Mind in Medieval Europe,* Oxford, Clarendon, 1986, p. 135. Theologian, astrophysicist, mathematician, Oxford's first chancellor, and Bishop of Lincoln, Robert Grosseteste (c. 1170–1253) founded a systematic experimental scientific method, and translated Greek texts. By linking Aristotelian empiricism and Augustinian epistemology with theology and mathematics, his arguments for connection between nature and supernature were influential in his own time. He saw, says Southern, that "the light which shone on the natural world had the same source as the light which shone in Revelation and Redemption" p. 135. See also Etienne Gilson, *History of Christian Philosophy in the Middle Ages,* New York, Random House, p. 360. He muses on the relation of Platonism, patristic spirituality, mathematics, and scientific studies, which are "more frequently met together in thirteenth-century England than on the Continent." He adds,

> "One would like to follow the history of this particular culture; one would particularly like to know if it was by chance

that Oriel College gave us Joseph Butler in the eighteenth
century and, in the nineteenth, [John] Henry Newman" p.
360.

10. "The Tamworth Reading Room," in *Essays and Sketches*, II, p. 210;
The Idea of a University, V. 6, p. 112.

11. *The Idea of a University*, II. 5, p. 33.

12. Ibid., V. 2, p. 103.

13. Ibid., VI. 6, p. 137.

14. Ibid., "Christianity and Scientific Investigation," p. 461.

15. "The Tamworth Reading Room," in *Essays and Sketches*, II, p. 185.

16. Ibid., pp. 206, 180; *The Idea of a University*, V. 9, p. 120.

17. "The Tamworth Reading Room," p. 197. Sir Robert Peel and Henry
Lord Brougham were concerned with politically thwarting the probability of
mid-century civil upheaval in England. Interpreting knowledge as information,
they saw it as a means of social planning. Their goal, as Newman put it, was
"the easy working of the national machine." The old bond of religion, once "a
living power, kindling hearts, leavening them with one idea, moulding them on
one model, developing them into one polity" (pp. 198–99), is replaced by the
goal of "unified sentiment," which proved to be as transient as summer wind.
Christian doctrine was caricatured "under the name 'controversy'" (p. 195),
while faith was nicknamed "opinion" or "controversial divinity" (p. 193).

18. *The Idea of a University*, V. 1, p. 99; III. 2, p. 45.

19. See John Henry Newman, *An Essay in Aid of a Grammar of Assent*,
London, Longmans, Green, 1947, p. 43.

20. *The Idea of a University*, III. 7, p. 61.

21. *An Essay in Aid of a Grammar of Assent*, p. 106.

22. *An Essay on the Development of Christian Doctrine*, New York, Dou-
bleday/Image, 1960, p. 321; *The Idea of a University*, III. 7, p. 66. For theological propositions about the nature of God, see pp. 62–66.

23. *See Letters of John Henry Newman: A Selection*, (edd.) Derek Stanford and Muriel Spark, Westminster, MD, Newman Press, 1957, p. 137.

24. *The Idea of a University*, IV. 1, pp. 72–73.

25. Ibid., p. 73.

26. See Charles Stephen Dessain, *John Henry Newman*, London, Thomas
Nelson, 1966, p. 103. Fr. Dessain says of Newman, "He made the basis of his
Discourses as broad as possible, emphasizing that he claimed a place for Theology in education on general grounds, without introducing pleadings that applied to any particular religion." Cardinal Newman's "most magisterial writing
in my judgment," observes Rev. Dr. Theodore M. Hesburgh, C. S. C., "is what
he said about the place of theology and philosophy in a university" (personal
communication, 10 May 2001).

27. The Idea of a University, III. 4, p. 51.

28. Ibid., II. 3, p. 25.

29. Ibid., III. 10, p. 69; IV. 15, p. 98; IV. 14, p. 96.

30. Ibid., II. 1, pp. 19–20.

31. Newman's formulation of the argument (in his own words) is as follows:

> (Major premise) "A University . . . [is what] professes to teach . . . universal knowledge; (Minor premise) Theology is . . . a branch of knowledge;
>
> (Conclusion) how then is it possible for it to profess all branches of knowledge, and yet to exclude from the subjects of its teaching one which, to say the least, is as important and as large as any of them?"

But this "conclusion" is invalid, for the undistributed middle means that no valid conclusion is possible. To see why this is so, let us recall that the categorical syllogism consists of three, and only three propositions—a major premise, a minor premise, and a conclusion, and has three, and only three, terms—major term, minor term, and middle term. The major term appears in the major premise, the minor term, in the minor premise, and logical comparison between the premises, is made possible because they share a middle term. This is the basis of categorical comparison. (See *The Grammar of Assent*, p. 203, where Newman explores the fact that the logician's business is "to find and dress up middle terms.")

In any categorical syllogism, the minor term will become the subject of the conclusion, while the major term will become predicate of the conclusion. The middle term, being no longer needed, will have vanished in the process. Prescinding from other aspects of the categorical syllogism—*figure* (position of the middle term in the premises) and *mood* (affirmative or negative quality of premises)—it is necessary to be absolutely clear that the middle term, as it appears in the premises, must be distributed at least once, because comparison can be made only if the middle term, in at least one instance, represents all members of a class. In a universal affirmative proposition (*all*, stated or implied), the subject term is distributed, but its predicate term is undistributed, since it does not refer to all—but only to some—members of a class. In Newman's argument, *University*, the major term, is subject of the major premise, and distributed; *Theology,* the minor term, is subject of the minor premise, and distributed. But *knowledge,* the middle term, is undistributed in each premise. Hence, no conclusion can be drawn.

Had Newman cast his syllogism (enthymeme) otherwise, with the middle term as subject of the major premise, a conclusion would validly follow: See the following examples:

[1]

(Major premise)   All knowledge is within the purview of a University;

(Minor premise)   Theology is knowledge;
(Conclusion)   Theology is within the purview of a University.

[2]
(Major premise)   Every form of knowledge (is what) should be taught at a University;
(Minor premise)   Theology is a form of knowledge;
(Conclusion)   Theology (is what) should be taught at a University.

Yet Newman may have been intuiting the conclusion—and thus validly implying—his conclusion by means of the analytic principle, *dictum de omni et nullo,* or "axiom of universal affirmation and negation," which states, "Whatever is affirmed of a logical whole can be affirmed of a logical part of that whole, and whatever is denied of a logical whole can be denied of a logical part of that whole" *(Quod dicitur de omni dicitur de singulis; quod dicitur de nullo negatur de singulis).* This means that when Newman affirms of all knowledge—that it should be taught in a University—it can also be affirmed of a part of knowledge; thus, if a University claims to teach all knowledge, then theology, which is knowledge, should also be taught at a University.

32. *The Idea of a University,* II. 1, p. 21.

33. The hypothetical syllogism consists of three, and only three, propositions—major, minor, and conclusion. The distinctive difference between the hypothetical and categorical forms is that, while the categorical syllogism compares propositions, the hypothetical syllogism is an explication of the major premise. That major premise has two components—an *if-clause,* antecedent, or protasis; and a then clause, consequent, or apodosis; and is expressed, "p implies q," or, "If p, then q."

The procedural rule is this: Either affirm the antecedent *(ponendo ponens,* "by affirming the antecedent, we affirm the consequent") or, deny the consequent *(tollendo tollens,* "by denying the consequent, we deny the antecedent").

See *The Idea of a University,* II. 2, p. 24, for Newman's four conclusions, as follows:

[1]
IF a University is a place of teaching universal knowledge and omits religion, THEN religion is barren of real knowledge;
BUT the University is such a place, and does omit religion.
CONCLUSION: *Religion is barren of real knowledge.*

[2]
IF a University teaches all knowledge yet does not teach religion,

THEN it omits a branch of knowledge;
BUT the University does not teach religion.
CONCLUSION: *The University omits a branch of knowledge.*

[3]
IF a University teaches knowledge but nothing about the Supreme Being,
THEN nothing is known about the Supreme Being;
BUT the University teaches nothing about the Supreme Being;
CONCLUSION: *Nothing is known about the Supreme Being.*

[4]
IF a University calls itself a seat of learning yet excludes religion,
THEN it calls itself what it clearly is not;
BUT the University does call itself a seat of learning and excludes religion.
CONCLUSION: *The University calls itself what it is not.*

Here, then, is *a hypothetical* format for Newman's original *categorical* formulation:

> IF a University is a place of instruction in universal knowl-
>   edge,
> THEN it must teach theology;
> BUT the University does not teach theology;
> CONCLUSION: *The University is not a place of instruction
>   in universal knowledge.*

For another side of an immediacy argument, see Avery Cardinal Dulles, "Foreword," to Martin X. Moleski, S. J., *Personal Catholicism: The Theological Epistemology of John Henry Newman and Michael Polanyi,* Washington, DC, Catholic University of America Press, 2000. Cardinal Dulles asserts that John Henry Newman "came to see that we know more than we can say, and that this unexplained knowledge is what warrants us in making the unconditional assent of faith even though the truth of its content eludes logical proof" p. ix.

34. St. Paul asserts, "Creation awaits with eager expectation the revelation of the children [literally, sons] of God" (Rom. 8:19). Paul's terms—revelation (ἡ ἀποκάλυψις) and eager expectation (ἡ ἀποκαραδοκία) are both directly and indirectly concerned with "stretching," and thus suggest Newman's sense of expansion, enlargement, enhancement. Paul's latter term means "stretching the head higher to see farther." In this same text (Rom. 12:2), Paul also exhorts his hearers to "be transformed by the renewing of your mind."

35. St. Anselm, in his *Proslogion,* expresses the relation between an ascentive knowing and an ascentive love, with an exquisite sense of the effect of faith on understanding: "Let me seek Thee in longing, let me long for thee in seeking; let me find Thee in love, and love Thee in finding."

(Quaeram te desiderando, desiderem quaerendo. Inveniam amando, amem inveniendo: P: 100, 10–11). See Karl Barth, *Anselm: Fides Quaerens Intellectum.* Richmond, VA, John Knox, 1960. He conveys a similar sensitivity to the exchange between faith and understanding by saying, "It is not the existence of faith, but rather . . . the nature of faith, that desires knowledge. Credo ut intelligam means: It is my very faith itself that summons me to knowledge" p. 18.

36. See Karl Rahner and Herbert Vorgrimler, *Dictionary of Theology,* 2nd rev. ed., (trans.) Richard Strachan et al., New York, Crossroad, 1988, pp. 147–48, 152, 493.

37. "Christianity and Letters," in *The Idea of a University,* pp. 264–65. See also *The Letters of Gerard Manley Hopkins to Robert Bridges,* (ed.) Claude Colleer Abbott, London, Oxford University Press, 1935, Letter VI (24 September 1866), p. 5; *The Note-Books and Papers of Gerard Manley Hopkins,* (ed.) Humphrey House, London, Oxford University Press, 1937, p. 52. See also Marylou Motto, "Mind with a Motion," in *The Poetry of Gerard Manley Hopkins,* New Brunswick, NJ, Rutgers University Press, 1984. She argues, "The nature of Hopkins' response to the world touches closely on Cardinal Newman's *Grammar of Assent* . . . [which] grounds itself in the psychology of response to cognitive and sensual ways of knowing in the world" pp. 12–13.

38. "Christianity and Letters," in *The Idea of a University,* pp. 252–54.

39. Ibid., p. 255.

40. Ibid., pp. 257–58.

41. Ibid., pp. 259–62.

42. Ibid., p. 265.

43. St. Augustine, *De Civitate Dei,* 2nd rev. ed., Washington, DC, Catholic Education Press, 1956, XIV, xxviii, p. 86. See also John Figgis, *Political Aspects of St. Augustine's City of God,* London, Longmans, Green, 1921, pp. 43ff.

44. See Martin C. D'Arcy, S. J., *The Meaning and Matter of History: A Christian View,* New York, Meridian, 1961. He says, "God is bound to appear whenever we change from looking at life to being concerned with it" p. 150.

45. See, *Apologia pro vita sua: Being a History of His Religious Opinions,* New York, Longmans, Green, 1947, pp. 245ff, note F, "The Economy," pp. 310–14; see also, *A Grammar of Assent,* pp. 37ff; see also Sermon XI, "The Nature of Faith in Relation to Reason," in *Fifteen Sermons Preached Before The University of Oxford,* pp.202–21. Newman's use of the term economy (οἰκονομία), echoes St. Augustine's insight that, what concerns God cannot be fully understood, and if you understand it, it is not God. Depiction of a haloed saint, a winged angel, and flames of Hell are not literal truths, but inadequate truths; literally, they are falsehoods, but not lies. They are approximations.

46. See Leon Battista Alberti, *On Painting* (Delia pittura), (trans.) John R. Spencer, New Haven, CT, Yale University Press, 1988; *La pittura,* Bologna, A. Forni, 1988.

47. See Ruth Benedict, *Patterns of Culture,* Boston, Houghton Mifflin, 1934, p. 52. See also Richard Walzer, *Greek into Arabic,* Cambridge, Cambridge University Press, 1962, pp. 9ff.

48. An illusion is defined as a false impression from a real stimulus, as opposed to a hallucination, which is a sense perception for which there is no external stimulus. An illusion requires two orders of reference, for only against a background of non-illusion can one declare an occurrence to be an illusion. Similarly, a lie is judged against the background of truth, just as disguise (whether in theater or in espionage) conceptually requires grounding in an unconditional ontology. That is, deception becomes meaningful only when projected against a backdrop of undeception.

49. See St. Paul: "Now we are seeing a dim reflection in a mirror; but then we shall be seeing face to face. The knowledge that I have now is imperfect; but then I shall know as fully as I am known" I Cor. 13:12 (trans., *The Jerusalem Bible*).

50. See F. H. Bradley, *Appearance and Reality,* London, Oxford University Press, 1908, pp. 595ff. See esp. Chapters XVII and XXV. See also Blaise Pascal, *Pensées,* #434.

51. Sermon XI, "The Nature of Faith in Relation to Reason," in *Fifteen Sermons Preached Before the University of Oxford*, p. 203.

52. See Christopher Dawson, "Religion and the Life of Civilization," in *Enquiries into Religion and Culture,* New York, Sheed & Ward, 1933, p. 115, 25–57.

53. See T. S. Eliot, *Notes Toward the Definition of Culture,* London, Faber & Faber, 1948, pp. 29–32, 68–69. He asserts, "What is part of our culture is also part of our lived religion."

54. Josef Pieper, *Leisure: The Basis of Culture,* New York, New American Library, 1962, p. 17.

55. See "Tamworth Reading Room," p. 211.

56. *Theaetetus,* 155 D; *Metaphysica,* 982b11–17.

57. Epistle VII, 340C–342A; 343A 1–4; 344A 2–344C.

58. Josef Pieper, *Leisure: The Basis of Culture,* New York, New American Library, 1962, pp. 70–73.

59. See Ludwig Wittgenstein, *Tractatus Logico-Philosophicus,* (trans.) D. F. Pears, New York, Humanities Press, 1961, #7; see also #4. 114–15.

60. See Alfred North Whitehead, *Aims of Education*, New York, Macmillan, 1929, p. 41.

61. St. Paul (Col. 3:14) exhorts us to add love to all other virtues, because "love is the bond of perfection" (τὴν ἀγάπην ἥτις ἐστὶν σύνδεσμος τῆς τελειότητος).

62. John Henry Newman, *Discourses to Mixed Congregations,* Westminster, MD, Christian Classics, 1966, p. 151.

63. See Ernst Mayr, *The Growth of Biological Thought,* Cambridge, Belk-

nap Press, 1982; Matt Ridley, *The Red Queen: Sex and the Evolution of Human Nature,* New York, Macmillan, 1994; Gerald M. Edelman, *Bright Air, Brilliant Fire: On the Matter of the Mind,* New York, Basic Books, 1992; J. B. Rhine, *The Reach of the Mind,* London, Faber & Faber, 1956; John T. Ratey, M. D., *A User's Guide to the Brain: Perception, Attention, and the Four Theaters of the Brain,* New York, Pantheon, 2001. Compare, J. D. French, "The Reticular Formation," in *Psychobiology: The Biological Basis of Behavior,* San Francisco, W. H. Freeman, 1967, pp. 232–38; Philip N. Johnson-Laird, *Mental Models: Towards a Cognitive Science of Language, Inference, and Consciousness,* Cambridge, MA, Harvard University Press, 1983; L. Donohew, H. E. Sypher, and P. L. Cook, "Communication and Affect," in *American Behavioral Scientist* 31 (1988), 287–95.

64. John Henry Newman, "A Short Road to Perfection," in *Prayers, Verses, and Meditations,* San Francisco, Ignatius, 1989, p. 328.

65. Donald Spoto, *The Hidden Jesus: A New Life,* New York, St. Martin's Press, 1998, p. 65.

INDEX

A

abodes of knowledge, 18
abodes of wisdom, 18
academic criticism, 25
accuracy, 191, 195, 202, 225, 230
Aesthetical morality, 217-18
al-Azhar, 18-19
Almae Matres, 49, 96
an imperial intellect, 25, 33, 42, 98
ancestral documentation, 15
Anglican Church, 78, 106
anti-intellectualism, 121
anti-Newman sentiment, 119
Arabic Innovation, 21

B

beatification, 16, 149, 161
behavioral predicates, 201, 205
benevolence, 91, 100, 216-17
benevolency, 92
Bifurcating thought and action, 126
Binary Matching, 89
Binomial Institutions, 97
broad spectrum, 10-11

C

calmness, 99-100, 167-70
canonization, 11, 149
capax Dei (capable of God), 2, 68
Carolingian Renaissance, 19-20
Cathedral, 17-19, 23
Cathedral School, 18-19
Catholic Creed, 93
Catholic Conversion, 5, 12, 119
Christian Revelation, 106
Christianity, 3, 18, 45, 70, 77-78, 90, 93, 106, 117, 129, 136-37, 157-60, 213, 216, 218-19, 228-29, 233
Christendom, 17, 20, 78, 93-94, 107
Church and University, 8-9, 39-40, 49, 68-69, 77, 81, 89, 93-98, 100-01, 103, 133, 144-45
churchly tasks, 220
circle of learning, 84
clairvoyant vision, 131
cognitive-connotative definition, 209
coherence, 41, 56, 83-84, 193
collegium, 18-19, 23
complex spirit, 2
complexity, 2, 82, 124,
connectedness, 9-10, 38, 99, 143, 178

personifying, 147
philosophical exactitude, 179
philosophical habit of mind, 218
philosophical integrity, 178-80
philosophical speculation, 5
pleasantness, 202, 216
political, 8, 11, 15, 17, 21, 24, 48, 70, 85-86, 97-99, 114, 118-19, 122-24, 132, 158, 165, 172, 214, 235
political liberalism, 85
polymathic personality, 10
precision, 36, 78, 82, 184-87, 190, 193, 195-96, 225
Principia, 83
principle of connectedness, 10, 178
priviledge of intellect, 1, 2, 5, 51, 214, 223, 225, 240
prolapsed intellect, 214
Protestantism, 85, 158
psychogender, 155-56
psychological illusion, 158
publications, 196, 220

Q

Quadrivium, 193-93

R

realistic meditation, 105
reason, 9, 36, 39, 41, 47, 59, 63, 108, 112-13, 118,
127, 144, 177, 179, 182, 211, 233
refinement of mind, 92
religion, 9, 17-18, 39-41, 57-58, 86, 89-93, 99, 101-02, 109, 115, 125-28, 133, 139-40, 144-46, 158, 177, 204, 207, 210-16, 219, 229-30, 232, 234, 238-39, 242
religion of education, 1, 9, 17, 39-41, 49, 89, 133, 139, 144-45, 177, 219
religion of reason, 215-16
religious personality, 14, 65
Renaissance Effect, 22
revelation, 9, 39, 41, 96, 100, 138, 146-47, 173, 177, 230, 242
rhetorical skill, 220
rhetorical genius, 4
right reason, 6, 211, 241

S

sacramental themes, 3
Schema "A", 95
Schema "B", 168
Schema "C", 205
schola (school), 18-19
Science of Nature, 83
scriptural motivation, 144
secular, 17, 57, 72, 96, 101, 115, 119, 220, 233-34
secular and churchly tasks, 221
Seeing, 145

ABOUT THE AUTHOR

Dr. D. A. Drennen (1925–2004) was a writer and teacher whose varied career included tours as professor of philosophy, pastoral counselor, news editor of *Business Week*, associate editor of *Medical Economics*, licensed lay preacher, yachtsman, and navigator. Post-doctoral work in cultural psychology brought him to study Arabic at American University (Cairo), McGill University (Montreal), and Columbia University (New York)—and Hebrew at Hebrew Union College (New York). As U.S. Department of State scholar-diplomat, he served several assignments at the Department's Middle East Desk, The Bureau of Intelligence and Research.